Finding Out

OTHER TITLES OF RELATED INTEREST IN SOCIOLOGY

Research Methods and Statistics

Earl Babbie, THE PRACTICE OF SOCIAL RESEARCH, 5th

Earl Babbie, OBSERVING OURSELVES: ESSAYS IN SOCIAL RESEARCH

Earl Babbie, SURVEY RESEARCH METHODS

Allen Rubin/Earl Babbie, RESEARCH METHODS FOR SOCIAL WORK

William Sims Bainbridge, SURVEY RESEARCH: A COMPUTER-ASSISTED APPROACH

Margaret Jendrek, THROUGH THE MAZE: STATISTICS WITH COMPUTER APPLICATIONS

John Lofland/Lyn Lofland, ANALYZING SOCIAL SETTINGS: A GUIDE TO QUALITATIVE OBSERVATION AND ANALYSIS, 2nd

Joseph Healey, STATISTICS: A TOOL FOR SOCIAL RESEARCH

Anthony Capon, ELEMENTARY STATISTICS FOR THE SOCIAL SCIENCES

Computer Software for the Social Sciences

Rodney Stark/Cognitive Development, Inc., STUDENT SHOWCASE: INTRODUCING SOCIOLOGY THROUGH THE COMPUTER

William Sims Bainbridge, SOCIOLOGY LABORATORY: COMPUTER SIMULATIONS FOR LEARNING SOCIOLOGY

SECOND EDITION

Finding Out

CONDUCTING AND EVALUATING
SOCIAL RESEARCH

JUNE AUDREY TRUE
Trenton State College

Wadsworth Publishing Company, Belmont, California
A Division of Wadsworth, Inc.

This book is dedicated to my dearest colleagues:
Norman A. Heap, husband, linguist, semanticist
Emily G. Albert, daughter, consultant, collaborator

Sociology Editor: *Serina Beauparlant*
Editorial Assistant: *Marla Nowick*
Production Editor: *Gary Mcdonald*
Managing Designer: *James Chadwick*
Print Buyer: *Karen Hunt*
Designer: *Wendy C. Calmenson/The Book Company*
Compositor: *Thompson Type*
Cover: *John Osborne*
Signing Representative: *Jeff Wilhelms*

© 1989, 1983 by Wadsworth, Inc. All rights reserved. No part of this book may be reproduced, stored in a retrieval system, or transcribed, in any form or by any means, electronic, mechanical, photocopying, recording, or otherwise, without the prior written permission of the publisher, Wadsworth Publishing Company, Belmont, California 94002, a division of Wadsworth, Inc.

Printed in the United States of America   49

6 7 8 9 10 11 12—99 98 97 96 95 94

Library of Congress Cataloging-in-Publication Data

True, June Audrey.
    Finding out.

    Bibliography: p.
    Includes index.
    1. Social sciences—Research. I. Title.
H62.T69   1989   300′.72   88-26154
ISBN 0-534-09918-1

Contents

CHAPTER 4   **Choosing the Methods   117**

P A R T   III   **Bringing in the Sheaves   289**

C H A P T E R   9   **Analyzing the Data   291**

Preface

This book is for the student who wants to know the essentials of research methods and for the teacher who needs a clear, readable text to complement classroom lectures and discussions. It is intended as a main text in introductory methods courses.

The object of this book is to introduce research methods in practice as well as in theory, accomplished by:

> presenting theory in textual descriptions, discussions, and illustrations;
>
> using a minimum of professional jargon, accompanied by straightforward definitions of technical terms;
>
> providing exercises that enable the student to put theory into practice.

The exercises at the end of each chapter let the student wrestle with techniques and problems presented in the text. The last exercise in most chapters is a critique. These provide training in critical examination by singling out one or two aspects of a published work.

Although research methods courses have most often been designed for students who expect to enter Ph. D. programs, we now need a comprehensive introduction for those who will go directly into professional practice or business. These careers require more sophisticated knowledge of research than in the past, so students should study the principles behind scientific research, its ethical requirements, basic techniques, and potential effects. They must be prepared to do an occasional research project, for the possibility of advanced study of research, and they must also be skilled in reading and evaluating research reports relevant to their rapidly expanding fields.

Finding Out, Second Edition has an introduction and twelve chapters, organized into three parts: research design, data collection and analysis, and presentation of results. Ethical matters and political or social influence are considered as they are relevant to a discussion. Each chapter includes:

a table of contents

a summary and conclusion

main points

notes

exercises

Chapter 10, on statistics, also provides lists of test statistics and symbols. Chapter footnotes referring the student to published works are supported by a complete bibliography.

Changes in this edition of *Finding Out* include:

the inclusion of an overview of theoretical sociological perspectives with research examples in Chapter 2

the combination of the indirect and observational methods into Chapter 5

the expansion of the discussion of interviews to Chapter 6

the expansion of the discussion of questionnaires to Chapter 7

the addition of the single-case experimental method to Chapter 8

computer references and relevance throughout

This edition has five appendixes:

Random Numbers

Report Writing Mechanics (new), which includes general instructions as well as specifics on writing, punctuation, citations, illustrations, and typing, all requested by adopters

Proposal Writing (rewritten), updated and expanded to include specifics formerly in an earlier chapter

Using Research Skills for Profit (new), written by a research professional, provides an industry profile, an overview of current market research methods, types of research firms and job opportunities

Using Computers (new), explains the uses and types of computers in general, why and when the student might use one, and what to do before, during, and after doing so

These helpful complementary appendixes are followed by a glossary. Each term in the glossary is in **boldface** type where it is first used in the text. The book ends with the bibliography and a comprehensive index.

Finding Out, Second Edition is very effective when each topic is assigned for reading and then presented in class with a discussion of the exercises. As students then complete the exercises and submit them to the teacher, an enlightening postmortem can be held and experiences exchanged. Exercises can be done independently or with partners, at the teacher's discretion. My students have learned a lot from these exercises and seem to have enjoyed them as well. Some have regaled their classmates with some very funny stories during typically lively postmortems.

The Instructor's Manual provided with this text suggests modifications and assignment plans compatible with term projects and examination schedules. Any exercise may be omitted or modified to adjust the time necessary to complete it. The manual also includes examination questions, discussion topics, project ideas, and advice on using computers.

My intent was to write *Finding Out* in language clear enough to make the student comfortable with research right away. I have written simple illustrations in an easy style because I don't want the student to think of research as inscrutable, and appropriate for only a few highly trained experts in a restricted number of fields. I have related discussion topics to common experience and applied research methods to the real world.

A student completing a research methods course with the help of this text should be prepared to continue study in research methods or to go into a field that demands a basic understanding of research. *Finding Out, Second Edition* provides the practical knowledge of research methods useful to social workers, corrections personnel, agency administrators, business executives, and government employees at every level. It will be of great benefit to the student entering a training position in market or opinion survey research. All major topics of research design, data collection and analysis, and project presentation are addressed; discussions also cover the principles behind the methods, ethical dilemmas, and the emerging field of evaluation research.

I am grateful for the turn of fate that brought me under the tutelage of two dedicated and practical teachers at Rutgers University: Professors Matilda White Riley and the late Charles Herbert Stember. Much of the merit in this present work is directly traceable to their high standards and strict teaching methods.

While writing this revision and its additions I have been supported and encouraged by my husband, Dr. Norman A. Heap, and my daughter, Emily G. Albert. I am lucky enough to be able to count them as friends and as colleagues as well as beloved family members, and I am truly thankful for their advice and opinions.

Comments on and careful evaluations of my manuscript are always valuable to me and I want to thank the reviewers: Judith Balfe, College of Staten Island, Sunnyside; Loren B. Gaiters, Tennessee State University; Susan Janssen, University of Minnesota at Duluth; Egon Mayer, Brooklyn College; Robert Pegoli, University of Colorado; R. N. Singh, East Texas State University; and Gayle Wykle, University of Alabama, Birmingham. I also thank the staff at Wadsworth: Sheryl Fullerton, Serina Beauparlant, Marla Nowick, Gary Mcdonald, James Chadwick, Bob Kauser, and Jeff Wilhelms.

In addition to the inestimable help given by those already named, I thank the Trenton State College librarians, and the incomparable Carole Calu for her secretarial assistance and eagle eye.

Most of all, I would like to thank the readers who are considering this book and the students who are assigned to it; to all of you I extend a warm invitation to join me in examining the intriguing and highly rewarding business of finding out.

June Audrey True
Trenton State College

Introduction

What We Mean by Research
    The Dimensions of Research
    The Scope of Research
    The Method of Research
Why Learn Scientific Research Methods?
    Performance
    Evaluation
    Utility
    Understanding Implications
The Organization of This Book
Summary and Conclusion
Main Points
Notes

This book is about the most exciting and rewarding of the intellectual enterprises. It's about exploration and discovery, solving mysteries, confirming suspicions, and being surprised. It's about finding out. In a word, this book is about research.

What We Mean by Research

An easy definition of **research** might be "the process of studying in order to discover something." By this definition, if someone is moving in next door and you want to know about the new household, your research could consist of sitting at your window and watching as the furniture is unloaded. You might learn quite a lot that way. What you learn would depend greatly on luck—for example, your phone may ring, or you may have to go to work before the movers are finished. Our definition of research in this book is more comprehensive because we will be talking about a process that reduces the role of luck as far as possible. Therefore, our definition incorporates the three components we explore next: the dimensions, the scope, and the method of research.

The Dimensions of Research

Research has width, depth, and duration. It must be wide enough to include the relevant facts, deep enough to go beneath the superficial impression, and continued long enough to provide a reasonably complete picture. If these requirements are not met, the outcome will be as unsatisfactory as those fragments of conversation one sometimes overhears in an elevator. Our need for width, depth, and duration arises from the types of objective our research will be trying to meet, that is, the scope of research.

The Scope of Research

We include in the scope of research three main types of objective: discovery, classification, and detection. As we shall see in this section, these objectives lead to three modes of research: exploratory, descriptive, and explanatory. Let's take a look at some examples.

Suppose you wanted to find out what life is like in a society unfamiliar to you. One way you could accomplish this would be to go and live in that society until you come to understand it through direct experience. Janheinz Jahn, a student of African culture, proceeded this way. In his travels through Nigeria and Togo he insisted on living like an African and being treated like one. His objective was discovery of the African way of life.[1] His research was **exploratory**. The result is an intriguing look into the African lives of his hosts. It isn't complete, and it doesn't provide scientific explanation for anything, but it could easily serve as a starting point for research that filled in the blanks and offered possible reasons for the customs that were reported.

Another objective included in the scope of research, as we are defining it, could be to accumulate facts about something and record them for the benefit of human knowledge. John James Audubon pursued this goal when he ranged over the fields and woodlands of the nation, observing and recording the appearance of our native birds in their natural habitats.[2] His objective was **classification** of our wild birds. His research was **descriptive**. Looking at reproductions of Audubon's paintings informs one of the beauty and variety of the birds he drew and is certainly a valuable record. It is a comprehensive picture of the subject, but it is not a scientific analysis.

The last research objective with which we shall be concerned is detection. Detection is finding out the truth about something. It goes beyond discovery and classification because it searches for the reasons why something exists. Detection was the goal of Bruno Bettelheim, the world-renowned psychologist, when he studied children in the kibbutzim of Israel. The kibbutzim, or communally run farms, are organized so that children are not with their own parents except for brief visits. Nevertheless, unlike children raised in institutions in the United States, the Israeli kibbutz children do not find it difficult to adjust to life later on. Wishing to find out why this was so, Bettelheim went to Israel and studied the kibbutz way of life.[3] His objective was to learn why the child-rearing practices of the kibbutzim succeeded, counter to expectations. His research was **explanatory**. Explanatory research is the main focus of this book. It is the epitome of scientific investigation and the only type of research that can yield results on which predictions may be based.

To meet our need for width, depth, and duration and to reach our objectives, we follow an organized procedure. This is the method of research. You'll learn many research methods in this book, but they're all part of scientific research. They are subdivisions of a special approach called the **scientific method**.

The Method of Research

Scientific research means studying something carefully and thoroughly. Using a specific set of rules known since 1854 as the **scientific method**, it asks and answers questions about the world.[4] The scientific method includes ideals and procedures that guide the preparation and execution of a research design. The ideals are **objectivity**, or freedom from bias; **empirical verification**, or checking facts in the real world; contribution to knowledge, or advancing existing knowledges; and publication, or sharing the result with the scientific community.

The procedures of the scientific method are listed in the accompanying flowchart. *Specifying goals* consists of defining the object of one's project, and **reviewing the literature** means familiarizing oneself with the published work already done on the topic. **Formulating hypotheses**, or stating what one thinks is the connection between or among variable phenomena, is followed

Procedures of the scientific method

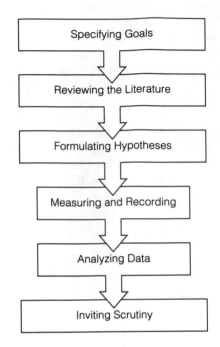

by testing the hypotheses, through *measuring and recording*, which is careful specification of what is actually observed, and *analyzing the data*, or considering the results in the light of the hypotheses. Finally, *inviting scrutiny* is submitting one's work to the judgment of others in the field of study. In Chapter 1 we consider these procedures in some detail.

The scientific method's ideals and procedures have led scientists to develop techniques and tests that may in turn be called "scientific." Throughout this book the word *research* refers to scientific research, and the use of the scientific method is assumed. There are other ways of asking and answering questions. You use some of them every day.

Competent people are all around. Hairdressers, bartenders, clergymen, friends, teachers, and family members can be consulted. You can also find things out by looking (Is the water boiling?), testing (If I stop short, will my brakes hold?), and counting (How many gallons of fuel oil did we use this month?). All of these inquiries are worthwhile. They are not scientific research, however, because they omit steps of the scientific method.

Since you already know other methods of inquiry, you may wonder why it is useful for you to study scientific research method. Let's look at four main reasons.

Why Learn Scientific Research Methods?

You have chosen to attend college and maybe you will become a professional in one of the fields of endeavor that requires training in scientific research. Modern professionals need a knowledge of research in order to perform it, evaluate it, use it, and understand its implications. Our society values research so highly that this knowledge is also needed by all levels of managers as well as by people in a wide variety of staff positions in just about every organization.

Performance

As a professional, you will be expected to be capable of performing research even if you are seldom called upon to do it. The people who hire you will take it for granted that you can conduct a piece of research if necessary. Thus a research assignment may come your way at any time, and you must be prepared for it. Moreover, the only way to gain a real understanding of research is to do it. You can, of course, acquire a superficial knowledge of research by reading books about it, just as you can acquire a superficial knowledge of how to maintain your car by reading the manual. For adequate knowledge that will carry you through in practice, however, you need hands-on experience. As you get it, you will also develop an ability to read other people's research reports and evaluate them.

Evaluation

Modern administrators and their staffs, managers and professionals, whether in the academy or in the industrial sector, need to keep up with scientific activity and progress in their own and other areas. They must be able to read intelligently, recognize superior efforts, see where a particular work fits in the collective scientific effort, and assess the importance of a contribution. They must also be able to judge the competence with which the work was carried out. Your training continues throughout your career, and your perusal of the latest developments, reported in relevant periodicals and books, is an important part of it. Your accumulation of information about your line of work is necessary because you need to use that information. Indeed, so much is published that you will need to be able to scan it quickly and evaluate it well enough to decide whether you should read a given report in full!

Utility

Our world moves very fast. Technology provides rapid international communication, and science exchanges information with business so that both can take advantage of the information. You will be expected to have the latest developments in knowledge and technique in your field at your command, insofar as is humanly possible. Your education and experience in the approach, methods, and limitations of research will help you immeasurably here. They will give you confidence and skill in incorporating new ideas into your work. One of the special skills that you will begin to acquire while studying research and will develop and refine all through your occupational life is the ability to make connections between abstract ideas and real situations. You will understand the implications of the research you do and read.

Understanding Implications

To understand the implications of research, you must be familiar with the applicable body of existing theory as well as with the related research already accomplished. Only then will you understand how the new result fits into the body of existing work and what it implies for professional practice as well as for further research. For example, theories about the social structure assume a **status set**, or number of social positions, for each person. Each status in the set has a variety of **roles** to be played, or expected behaviors. You might be a son, a truck driver, a father, a husband, and the captain of the local softball team. There is a lot of theory about the way in which people juggle their statuses to accommodate demands made on their time and energy; there is also a good deal of theory about acquiring new statuses and learning the roles and about moving through a sequence of statuses. Early research based on these theories paid little attention to the process of losing statuses, which happens gradually with age and as people experience bereavement, retirement, and infirmity.

In the late 1930s, William Foote Whyte conducted a study that at first glance has nothing to do with old age and its problems. Nonetheless, this study about unemployed young men in Boston describes an incident in which one of the study's subjects loses his status as a member of the inner circle of his group and gets sick as a result.[5] The idea that losing a status can affect one's health is an important one for medicine, social work, criminal justice, and sociology. Consider the implications for gerontological social work. A social worker who is familiar both with status and role theory and with research findings such as Whyte's will be aware of the physical problems that can be triggered by status losses, such as those occurring when a person retires.

Since Whyte's time several studies on aging have addressed the problem of losing social statuses and roles.[6] Many new research projects have been engendered by the growing awareness of the influence of social status on health. Some of the consequences have been social programs designed to deal with this problem.[7]

As this example illustrates, fledgling professionals from all fields benefit by training in basic research methods. This is the main purpose of the present book.

The Organization of This Book

To make it easier for you to learn the basics of research method, this book begins by explaining the obstacles we all face in trying to find out the truth. This is followed by a brief survey of the theory that guides sociology and then by an explanation of how to overcome the obstacles to truth by the use of the scientific method and the principles of research design.

The book continues by outlining the process of developing and putting into operation a research question. After that you will learn what considerations may lead you to choose a particular group of subjects to study. Part I concludes with an overview of the methods used to collect information and the resources needed to use them.

Part II offers a detailed discussion of the methods summarized in Part I, citing examples of how they have been used in previous research. The advantages and disadvantages of each method are explained.

The last part of the book focuses on the **analysis** and **evaluation** of the collected information and the presentation of results. We end with a discussion of the important topic of the consequences of research and the effects of social and political influences.

Throughout this book exercises are included to provide practice in basic research techniques as well as experience in grappling with typical problems. Professional terms are explained when introduced and are collected in a complete glossary at the end of the book. You will notice the appearance of many new words and some old words that have been given new meanings. The special language used in research is helpful because it adds precision to what we are saying. When we refer to information as **data**, we are saying that it is a special kind of information—for example, information collected for analysis in a research project. The key questions that should be in your mind when considering any kind of research can be expressed in very simple language: What do you know? How do you know it? How did your sources arrive at their conclusions? What's in it for them? If you remember to ask these questions, you will be able to examine reports and ideas critically, with your feet planted firmly on the ground.

Summary and Conclusion

This book is about scientific research. When we consider scientific research, we are assuming a thorough and comprehensive examination of some part of the world. This examination uses an exploratory, descriptive, or explanatory approach guided by the requirements of the scientific method. The scientific research method is important. Learn it because you will need to use and understand it in your future occupation. An agency may ask you to conduct a study to justify a new program, to support a decision about an old program, or to keep its policies current. You may be called upon to serve on a committee and contribute suggestions in light of the latest research developments in your field. This book will teach you how to cope with the difficulties of research, how to employ the basic data collection methods, and how to follow the procedures for analyzing and presenting results. We shall also examine the social context of research: its consequences and the political and social implications.

Main Points

1. The definition of research includes dimensions, scope, and method.

2. Research must be wide, deep, and lengthy enough to get a complete picture. These are its dimensions.

3. Research objectives include discovery, classification, and detection. This is its scope.

4. Discovery is the objective of exploratory research; classification is the objective of descriptive research; detection is the objective of explanatory research.

5. Scientific research is guided by a set of rules called the scientific method, requiring objectivity, empirical verification, contribution to knowledge, publication, specific goals, literature reviews, hypothesis formulation and testing (involving measurement and analysis), careful records, and scrutiny.

6. Knowledge of scientific research method is a useful part of education for everyone.

Notes

1. Janheinz Jahn, *Through African Doors*, trans. Oliver Coburn (New York: Grove Press, 1962).

2. John James Audubon, *Birds of America* (New York: Macmillan, 1985).

3. Bruno Bettelheim, *The Children of the Dream* (London: Macmillan, 1969), p. 8.

4. "Scientific research *n* (1854): principles and procedures for the systematic pursuit of knowledge involving the recognition and formulation of a problem, the collection of data through observation and experiment, and the formulation and testing

of hypotheses" *Webster's Ninth New Collegiate Dictionary* (Springfield, Massachusetts: Merriam-Webster, Inc., 1984), p. 1051.

5. William Foote Whyte, *Street Corner Society: The Social Structure of an Italian Slum*, 2nd ed. (Chicago: University of Chicago Press, 1955), pp. 45–48.

6. Matilda White Riley and Anne Foner, *Aging and Society: An Inventory of Research Findings*, Vol. 1 (New York: Russell Sage, 1968).

7. Ronald W. Toseland, James Decker, and Jim Bliesner, "A Community Outreach Program for Socially Isolated Older Persons," *Journal of Gerontological Social Work* 1, no. 3 (Spring 1979): 221–24.

PART I

Designing a Research Project

This section of the book will guide you through the essential steps in planning a research project. Chapter 1, "The Scientific Method of Research," provides a foundation for this by describing the ideals and procedures to be observed. It begins with a description of the basic handicaps to finding out the truth and the effect of each on research. The scientific method is then described in detail, followed by an outline and explanation of the procedure recommended for developing a research design.

Chapter 2, "The Research Question," explains the need to organize your thinking and relate your project to established theory. It describes the narrowing of an interest into a specific question and hypothesis and the identification and operationalization of the variables that will yield the result. It outlines the method of developing feasible indicators to achieve internal and external validity, reliability, and maximum generalizability. The chapter ends with a review of the major research modes—exploration, description, and explanation—their relation to each other, and examples of each from published research.

In Chapter 3, "The Sample and Significance," you will learn what a population and its sample are and what you need to think about when selecting them for a study. The chapter describes and illustrates ways of drawing random samples and outlines the forms of nonrandom sampling. This is followed by a description of the main types of longitudinal study and a discussion of their timing. The chapter ends with a comparison of statistical significance with social significance.

Chapter 4, "Choosing the Methods," begins with an overview of the indirect and direct methods of data collection that will be covered in detail in the separate chapters of Part II. Then, as a preparation for understanding the implications of the various methods, the chapter presents discussions of time, money, access to subjects, and ethical considerations and concludes with an explanation of the value of multifaceted research.

CHAPTER 1

The Scientific Method of Research

Does it seem to you as if there's an increase in the number of things you read and see about old people? Do you think there are more old people around than there used to be? Fewer? What's the *real* state of affairs? Studying something scientifically means you won't rely on impressions. You'll go after the facts.

Looking at Table 1.1, which gives population figures published by the United Nations, you will find that the percent of old people in the world *has* gone up recently. This could be the *start* of a scientific investigation of the growth of the senior group. You'd want to know more, however, before deciding whether this part of the population is getting larger. Was the data collection method uniform all over the world? Can you be sure people told the truth about their ages? How was the question asked? Has record keeping been consistently accurate? Has reporting been complete? You would also note the variation among the regions of the world and look into explanations for that.

Going after the facts is not simple, even when the question is straightforward. Before we begin to examine the scientific method more closely and attempt to put it into practice, let's take a look at some of the obstacles in our way. By "obstacles" we mean the basic handicaps that impede the efforts of all human beings when we try to see things objectively.

Basic Handicaps to Finding Out the Truth

Objectivity is freedom from bias. It means seeing things as they really are. Objectivity is one of the ideals of the scientific method. It is something to strive for, even though *perfect* objectivity will probably not be possible. Knowing what prevents us from being objective will enable us to find ways to get around some of these difficulties.

Let's acknowledge right now that our biggest handicap may be an unwillingness to believe that our own views and attitudes are as biased as everyone else's. We are prone to feel gratified when someone else shares our opinions and attacked when they don't. Our own perceptions and ideas seem accurate and logical to us. Even scholarly theories about the world are limiting, once accepted as likely, and scholars are often tempted to ignore evidence that contradicts their favored theory. (We'll see what the positive contribution of theory is to research later in this chapter.)

The basic handicaps to finding out the truth include six human tendencies:

selective perception and recall	culture shock
closure	distorting the response
distorting the meaning	false conclusions

TABLE 1.1 Percent of Population 65 and Over, World and More and Less Developed Regions: 1960 and 1980

Region	Percent of population aged 65 and over	
	1960	1980
World	5.2	5.8
More developed regions	8.5	11.4
North America	9.1	11.0
Europe	9.7	13.0
Oceania	7.4	7.9
U.S.S.R.	6.8	10.0
Less developed regions	3.7	3.9
Africa	3.0	3.0
Latin America	3.5	4.1
East Asia	4.8	5.9
South Asia	3.2	3.0

Source: Note 1.

Some of these have important subcategories as well. We'll examine them one at a time.

Selective Perception and Recall

Your brain is very efficient. That's an advantage. However, it's also a handicap. Your brain's goal is to ensure your survival. Your research goal is to see whatever is really there. These goals can conflict.

What is really there, or the truth, is always too much for your brain to handle. You collect information and store it in your brain, and over a lifetime it amounts to an impressive collection. Nevertheless, you can't know everyone, see and hear everything, and organize all these perceptions in your mind so that the whole makes sense. Too much information at once will confuse and distress you. Part of your brain's efficiency is its ability to screen the incoming information so that only those things that are important to you get through. **Selective perception** is the process of editing the incoming information. **Selective recall** applies this editing process to the past.

Selective perception is important to our goal of survival. It enables us to size up things quickly, and, referring to past experience, to react appropriately. We can scan a crowd and use clues to pick out the familiar person we came to meet without dwelling on the strangers. Clues can be anything, but very often appearance, including dress, is used as a classifier. Criminals as well as law enforcers take advantage of this. Thieves who dress up as movers or repairmen often get away with removing valuable items from houses or offices. Undercover investigators dress as street people, hoping not to be noticed during their observations.

Another ploy that takes advantage of selective perception is distracting people with something that is important to them so they will not notice other things going on at the same time. Magicians use bright colors, witty remarks, and attractive assistants to draw attention from their sleight of hand. Physicians use their "bedside manner" to prevent patients from concentrating on the details of the examination or treatment. As researchers we may unintentionally provide our own distractions. If we are looking for specific things, we may easily zero in on them and fail to see something we aren't seeking, possibly an item we would rather not find because it contradicts our beliefs. This is the danger of selective perception. We must be careful in research not to overlook things. Advance planning can help us to get as complete a story as possible, but we must be alert, as well, for the unexpected and the undesirable.

The second human tendency against which we must guard is almost the reverse of selective perception. It is our ability to see things that are not really there.

Closure

Can you read this?

What did your brain supply? Notice that the letter fragments can be interpreted in two ways: *How* are you? or *Who* are you? As this little example demonstrates, the less real evidence available, the more freely our imaginations may operate. Closure, or the tendency to fill in the gaps, hampers research because we supply what we think is appropriate, which may be quite far from the reality. Sometimes there are gaps in the information we collect because *nothing* was there to be collected, and our filling in obscures that fact.[2] Sometimes there are gaps because our perception is poor.

The facts may be obscured by our attachment to established meanings in our own society. For example, we may find it difficult to be objective because of preconceptions rooted in the cultural values we share with our group. When this happens, our own definitions of words and human behavior may act to distort the meaning of what we observe. We should take time to identify the ideas we have that can distort research findings.

Distorting the Meaning

Once we have an idea about what to expect, it is easier to see what we expected than to change our ideas. This is especially true if the ideas are important parts of ourselves, for example, religious beliefs, political convictions, and ethnic, racial, sexual, or family loyalties. These feelings can blind us to new information and can cause us to distort the meaning of what we are observing, seeing it as we think it should be rather than as it is. Let's examine here how our culture, our group identity, and our definitions of words and behavior operate to cause distortion.

Culture and Group Identity   When we were small, those who raised us, our **socializers**, interpreted the world as they saw it. We automatically learned our own culture's **values**: what is "good" and what is "bad." We learned how to act and how to speak our native tongue the way our socializers spoke it. Lessons of this kind are learned well. The indelible marks they leave will be colored over and supplemented by later training, but they are not erased. This is a mixed blessing for the researcher.

The researcher who knows the culture of the group being studied has an advantage in understanding, but identifying with the studied group brings a disadvantage. To identify with something means to regard it as part of one's own personality, hence worthy of zealous defense. This biased attitude hinders objectivity. Care is necessary to avoid criticizing other cultures and groups simply because they are different from your own. The anthropologist Elenore Smith Bowen gives many good examples of the value adjustments she had to make when she lived among the Tiv of Nigeria. Particularly instructive were the arguments advanced by the Tiv women to defend polygamy, which Bowen's culture had taught her was objectionable:

A co-wife is company; assistance; comfort in difficulty.

A co-wife is insurance that one's children will be cared for if one dies.

A co-wife is an ally in case of a dispute with your husband.

A co-wife shares the work so that you are not overburdened.[3]

Culture and group identity determine what we see as commonplace and what we see as exotic or strange. They also fix the meanings of words and behavior for us. Each new group that we join presents us with a new set of meanings, expressed in symbols, words, priorities, and ideals. This is as true for categories of age and sex as it is for any other. For example, if a woman visits her aged father once a week she may well describe it to someone proudly,

"I wouldn't dream of neglecting Dad. I see him faithfully every week."

while he complains to his neighbor,

> *"Kids are ungrateful for all you did for them. My daughter never manages to make it over here more than once a week!"*

The daughter and her father are experiencing the same number of visits, but for her they mean fulfillment of a value requirement and for him they mean failure to comply with expectations based on values. Values are specific to one's groups and categories. Although it is important in our society to be faithful to one's parents, people of different ages have different criteria for the obligation.

We can see that although the experienced person knows many sets of meanings, these meanings may not correspond with the meanings used by someone else. The scientific researcher, therefore, has to ascertain what meanings are being used by the people being studied.

Definitions of Words   Our statements and questions must convey the same meaning to the subjects, or people being studied, as they do to us. The necessity for shared meanings is one reason why scientific and legal language sounds "dry." Words with nuance and color are avoided in favor of words with unmistakable, universal meanings. When we are doing research, we must understand our subjects' words. One way to accomplish this is to think of the languages of all groups, subgroups, classes, or occupations other than our own as "foreign" so that we remember to acquaint ourselves with these languages before we try to carry out our research. This will not only save us from blunders but will contribute greatly to the interpretation of our work when we are trying to draw it all together and determine what it means.

Consider the following exchange between an interviewer and a respondent:

INTERVIEWER: "What do you mean when you say the Lord taught you a lesson about pride last Easter?"

RESPONDENT: "I mean . . . well . . . I looked so *fine*! And I knew I looked fine. So I went to church and the Lord *blessed* me . . . the Lord blessed me more than He ever had . . . it was more than ever before in my life . . . and I learned my lesson. About pride. He blessed me and I learned He would meet my pride. I learned my lesson. . . ."

Does the respondent's answer make sense to you? If you are not familiar with the respondent's religious group, you may have difficulty in understanding the meaning of "the Lord blessed me," and what the "lesson" was. If you know that "blessing" for this group frequently includes being seized by a spiritual fervor that results in physically demanding activity, the dialogue begins to make sense. Reread the answer. You may realize that looking "fine" means that the respondent was all dressed up. She is saying that the Lord met her pride in her appearance by causing her to become disheveled. It was a lesson in humility.

Consider the differences in meaning of the word *love* which depend on whether the speaker is a man or a woman. If she says she loves him, does that mean she feels a physical desire for him? When he says he loves her, does that mean he will faithfully follow her and subordinate his needs to hers? "I love you" may not provide enough information to go on because it doesn't mean the same thing to everyone, even in the same family, let alone within a peer group or subculture.

Just as important as understanding the meanings of words is understanding the meanings of behavior. For example, great variation exists in the significance of gestures and stance.

Definitions of Behavior   In most of the Western world evidence of honesty and sincerity includes looking directly into the eyes of persons in authority while they are asking questions or giving directions. Such behavior in West Africa, however, would be considered the ultimate in insolence and defiance. Respect in that part of the world requires looking away from the speaker's face, the very thing we regard as shifty. Similarly, it is said that Native Americans thought the Europeans did not like their children because the parents hit them. "Spare the rod and spoil the child" is a Judeo-Christian value but definitely not a Native American one.

These cultural barriers must not be overlooked in research. Many behavioral differences are hard to recognize because they are unconscious. A number of studies have been done on **territoriality**. This is the tendency for people to move, usually during a conversation, until they are at a distance from other human beings that feels comfortable. What *is* comfortable may depend on age, sex, setting, or nationality.[4]

The comfort of physical settings often depends on the meaning we ascribe to other people's behavior. To be the only member of your sex, race, or age in a crowd of others is usually to feel spotlighted. One tends to think everyone else is staring, criticizing, threatening, or evaluating, regardless of the real state of affairs. Discomfort may result in nervous movements or chatter, leading to a false impression of someone's "natural" behavior or to the belief that the nonmember of the group is lying or guilty of something.

If the values and behavior of the observer and the observed differ enough, the result may be acute distress or **culture shock**.

Culture Shock   Read the following passage describing dinner in a "great man's hall" in medieval England, and consider the questions that follow it.

> *The smoke from the hall fire escaped through a hole in the roof. . . . minstrels could play their pipes and tabors while the lord had his dinner at a table on a*

raised platform at the other end of the hall, the walls of which were covered with paintings and hung with tapestries. Below him sat the members of his household. They sat at trestle tables in the main body of the hall, the floor of which was more often of rammed earth than of stone and was so littered with scraps of food as well as with straw and rushes that it was commonly referred to as 'the marsh'. As late as the 1520s Erasmus described such floors as being 'usually of clay, strewed with rushes under which lie unmolested an ancient collection of beer, grease, fragments, bones, spittle, excrements of dogs and cats, and everything that is nasty'. . . . The procession of servants bearing food was led by the marshal of the hall, carrying a white staff, or, on the occasion of the grandest banquets, by a household officer on horseback. The procession approached the lord's table, which usually stood beneath a canopy. And, after the lord and his family had been served, dishes were carried to the table where the gentlemen of the household sat with the steward, then to those tables where the lesser servants sat, presided over by the marshal of the hall and the clerk of the kitchen. The food was served on trenchers, thick slices of bread or scooped-out crusts, which might afterwards be distributed to the poor or the family's dogs. Grace was said by the almoner and then all fell to, grabbing the spoons on the table—forks were then unknown—or using the knives which each man carried to the table with him in a case in his belt. Table manners were far from meticulous and the noise was tremendous as dogs barked under the boards; falcons sitting on perches behind the benches uttered their sharp cries; and the ushers of the hall marched up and down between the tables calling out, 'Speak softly my masters, speak softly'. Even noble pages in the fifteenth century had to be advised in books of etiquette such as The Babees Book *that wine must not be drunk when the mouth was full; that the upper part of the body must not lean forward over the table with the head hanging into the dish; that neither nose nor nails must be picked at meal times; that salt should not be flicked out of the cellar with a knife. . . . [the Duke of Gloucester added in his* Booke of Nurture] *young gentlemen must not . . . lick dishes with their tongues. Another well-known book of etiquette, the* Booke of Courtesy, *cautioned against spitting on the table, cleaning the teeth with the tablecloth. . . .[5] (Reprinted by permission of W. W. Norton & Co., Inc. and David Higham Associates, Ltd.)*

What were your emotional reactions as you read the preceding description? Do you think most Americans might enjoy such a dinner? Would they be impressed? Would they be confused? Would they be disgusted?

Imagine yourself doing research in such a setting. You are invited to partake of a feast and expected to show enjoyment of it in your hosts' style. In what ways could this affect your objectivity about the group you are studying? Once the hosts have learned that their eating behavior is unacceptable to you, will they be relaxed? Will they act "normal"? Will you?

It isn't likely that you will be invited to a feast in the authentic medieval mode, but you might well find yourself in a setting or with a subject that arouses your emotions and inspires judgmental attitudes. Censorious statements and evaluative looks are to be avoided in research. When observing an unfamiliar group, one is often exposed to behavior that violates one's own dearly held principles and challenges the comfortable ways of one's own experience. The researcher must learn to absorb this culture shock and suspend personal feelings and opinions until the research is complete. This is difficult because we are uncomfortable in the presence of what we disapprove. No matter. The feminist must repress annoyance when confronted by subjects who believe in male dominance, the smoker when surrounded by antismoking signs in someone's home or office, the poor person when observing wasteful practices. We are often reminded that others disagree with our ideas and differ in their ways.

Behavior that is unthinkable to us is the result of living conditioned by a set of meanings different from ours, often in a set of conditions different from ours. We must not only suspend judgment of the people we study, we must also refrain from interfering in their activities, consciously or unconsciously. (Ethical and legal issues surround both interference and noninterference. See Chapter 12.) Conscious interference is the easier of the two to avoid. Unconscious interference takes two distinct but related forms: interviewer effect and demand characteristics. Either will distort the subject's response.

Distorting the Response

Think of the last time you were in a group consisting solely of your own sex. Would the conversation have changed or would the people have acted differently if a member of the opposite sex had joined you? Would postures, gestures, facial expressions, or tones of voice have changed?

Max Weber, the German sociologist who has been called the father of modern social science, defined **interaction** as "behavior that takes someone else into account." When we join someone who thereupon speaks differently because of our presence, we call the change **interviewer effect**. This effect occurs frequently, because researchers are usually outsiders.

Interviewer Effect   If we want to eliminate interviewer effect from the behavior of the people we study, we have our work cut out for us. Notice what the passing of a police car does to the rate of speed of the cars around it. The other drivers recognize the police car as the symbol of authority, and they don't want to take a chance that the officers will see their driving in an unfavorable light.

Nobody wants to be seen in an unfavorable light. If we are to prevent research subjects from changing their actions because of our presence, we must get them to accept us as a nonthreatening part of their scene. Specific ways of doing this depend on the situation. We shall have more to say on the subject when we discuss specific methods of research.

Another phenomenon, very similar to interviewer effect, is an alteration in the subjects' behavior caused by their desire to cooperate with the researcher. Their impression of what it is you want of them constitutes the

demand characteristics of the situation. Whereas interviewer effect is *unconscious* change because of someone's presence, demand characteristics are the *conscious* ideas people have of what a researcher expects of them.

Demand Characteristics   We all make attempts to act "appropriately." We don't want to look or act out of place or in a way that will appear ignorant or stupid. Public figures want to appear dignified, artisans want to appear skillful, parents want to seem competent, and research subjects want to look intelligent and knowledgeable. The demand characteristics of the encounter are whatever the subject thinks you are seeking or whatever behavior or attitudes the subject thinks will impress you favorably. They are what the situation "demands" in the mind of the subject.

The net result of interviewer effect and demand characteristics is that observation changes the thing observed. The only safeguard is careful scrutiny of everything you plan to do or say, with a view to reducing these effects as much as possible. "Hard" science also has this problem, but it is most troublesome and complex for the social sciences.

The sixth handicap to finding out the truth operates mainly after the data have been collected. It is our tendency to draw false conclusions.

False Conclusions

Many things can lead us to draw false conclusions. Among them are self-consciousness, carelessness, and anxiety. We suffer needless embarrassment over imagined social slips, accidents when we thought we were safe, and groundless fears. The false conclusions to avoid in research result from still other kinds of human frailty. The three main kinds are illogical thinking, overgeneralization, and dishonesty.

Illogical Thinking   Most people think of logical thinking as *reasonable*. Logic is actually reasoning in which the conclusion follows from the premises. The **premise** is a piece of evidence that you are citing.[6] For example, your premises might be that (1) you earned an A in the first examination and (2) you earned a B in the second. A logical conclusion might be that you have a good chance of earning at least a B for the course. Notice that your information here is complete only if there are no more examinations to come. If additional examinations are scheduled—that is, if new information is added, your conclusion may change.

One type of illogical thinking is referred to as a **circular argument**. In this type the conclusion and the premise can change places without changing the argument:

PREMISE: People who commit suicide are crazy.
CONCLUSION: Only crazy people commit suicide.

Reversing these will not change anything. Let's look at a few more types of illogical reasoning.

"Rapists are male, therefore males are rapists."

The conclusion is false because the premise, while true, is not the whole story. Lots of persons other than rapists are male. The conclusion does not automatically follow. A logical statement would be "Rapists are male, therefore any male *might* be a rapist." Adding more information about the characteristics of rapists would require a change in the premise and, therefore, in the conclusion. If we know that rapists have to be at least two years old the argument becomes, "Rapists are males at least two years old, therefore any male two years old and older *might* be a rapist."

These days everyone knows that homosexual males are at high risk of getting AIDS. This leads to illogical conclusions such as:

"Homosexuals die of AIDS. X, a homosexual, has died. X must have had AIDS."

or

"X has died of AIDS. Homosexuals die of AIDS. X must have been a homosexual."

You can logically say that anyone who dies of AIDS was homosexual if the premise says that nobody else ever dies of it. You can say that a homosexual who dies had AIDS only if the premise is that homosexuals never die of anything else.

The way to avoid illogical thinking is to examine the premise on which your conclusions are based. If the premise contains the conclusion, as in the "suicides are crazy" example, reject the argument. If the conclusion does not really follow from the premises, as in the AIDS example, reject it. If the information is not complete, as in the grade prediction example, label it a *tentative* conclusion. Watch out for arguments that are perfectly logical but based on *false* premises:

"The world is flat. Flat things have edges. If I sail far enough I will come to the edge of the world and might fall off."

Insufficient investigation is the culprit responsible for the second cause of false conclusions: overgeneralization.

Overgeneralization   Overgeneralization is judging a class of people or events by one or a few examples. For instance, suppose you are on a flight during which a movie is shown. If you do not like the movie and assume all such films are the same, you might be soured on in-flight movies. You would be guilty of generalizing on the basis of one instance. This is because you did not inquire far enough to make a valid judgment. Overgeneralization is really a type of illogical thinking, but the thinking is not so much twisted as it is *hasty*.

Closing off investigation before you have enough data to make a conclusion is called **premature closure of inquiry**. This term means that overgeneralization can be remedied by reopening the inquiry. Premature closure of inquiry is the cause, and overgeneralization is the effect. (*Note:* Closure here means discontinuing, whereas the closure we talked about earlier meant completing.)

Suppose you meet an eligible prospect for dating and because you like what you see, you spend some time in casual conversation with that person. You discover that this seemingly attractive creature can't manage a simple exchange of remarks, fidgets constantly, and sports a silly smile all through the encounter. You excuse yourself and decide against pursuing the friendship because you can't imagine a whole evening with this loser, not to mention enduring your friends' probable remarks. You may be right. On the other hand, you may be wrong. You have overgeneralized from one experience. It may be that your own charm and beauty so overwhelmed the other person that normal behavior was impossible, or perhaps the person is married and had spotted an in-law standing by. Win or lose, you don't know without further investigation, and you have prematurely closed your inquiry.

The last cause of false conclusions is dishonesty. Although it is to be hoped that one would not deliberately set out to be dishonest, we must guard against even unintentional dishonesty.

Dishonesty   There are two kinds of dishonesty to guard against: plagiarism and falsification of data. **Plagiarism is using someone else's work without giving the author proper credit.** This includes ideas. Falsifying data is any distortion or misrepresentation of a project's results. Both plagiarism and falsification of data are strictly unacceptable at any time because it is both illegal and immoral.

Plagiarism includes making photocopies of published or unpublished material and using it for anything other than strictly personal convenience. For example, it is all right to copy an article so you can take it home, make notes from it at your convenience, submit it as an example (as in Exercise 1.3 at the end of this chapter), or keep it for future reference. Sometimes you need such an item and you can't remove the publication from the library or get a copy from which to clip it.

On the other hand, copying material in bulk and handing it around to members of a class or an organization without permission from the copyright holder is forbidden, unethical, and illegal, regardless of how often you see it done. Copying material and submitting it as your own work is also forbidden, unethical, and illegal. It is stealing. The author of the work is entitled to benefits from its use. If the author sells the work to a publisher, that publisher takes out a copyright on it and is entitled to the benefits from the material's use. Often all it takes to get permission to use material for academic purposes is a phone call, but that phone call must be made.

Falsification of data is an especially troubling phenomenon, because each research project builds upon the work that has already been done. If data have been invented or distorted, subsequent researchers will be thrown onto the wrong track. Research hoaxes reported in the press over the years have involved archaeology, as in the case of the bogus Piltdown Man skull, and genetics, as in the case of Sir Cyril Burt's false reports of his studies of twins. Moreover, if physicians believe conclusions based on false medical data, it may result in personal injury. It is your responsibility to be scrupulously honest in your own work.

The basic human handicaps that we have been looking at can be largely overcome, or at least controlled, by using theory to guide our research efforts and by adhering carefully to a set of rules called the scientific method. First, we'll consider the major theories used by sociologists.

Theory and Research

Philosophy, religion, mathematics, and the natural sciences are all much older than sociology. The idea that there should be a science of society meant a new academic discipline. Auguste Comte (1798–1857) wanted to develop such a science, to explain history and predict the future.[7] He called the new science **sociology** and intended it to be like the natural sciences, requiring similar research methods and also being of use to the world. Comte concentrated on **social dynamics**, meaning progress and change, and **social statics**, meaning order and stability. He thought that all human branches of knowledge passed through three stages, starting with a search for supernatural causes, moving on to a search for universal laws, and finally arriving at the study of the real world. Comte felt that sociology would be the most important science because it would express the only really universal point of view, thereby encompassing the other abstract philosophies: mathematics, astronomy, physics, chemistry, and biology.[8] He was not saying that the other sciences were unworthy, but rather that their view of the world was narrowly focused and that sociology would examine and explain the picture as a whole.

From this rather cheeky beginning, sociology grew throughout the nineteenth century, and important contributions were made by people whose main interest was economics or politics as well as sociology. For example, Herbert Spencer (1820–1903) saw society as similar to a living organism, its growth an evolutionary process. He observed that the growth of society resulted in **differentiation**, or the increasing specialization of its parts, much as the growth of an embryo from one simple cell culminates in a fully developed animal, with groups of cells assigned to carry out specific functions. Spencer thought that the natural result of such differentiation in society would be increasing interdependence of its parts. He thought that society existed for the people and that their quality would determine its quality.

Spencer felt that the natural process of evolution would result in the increasing improvement of the quality of the people, because the best would survive and rise to the top. He felt that these superior leaders should confine their activities to protection of citizens' rights and protection from enemies, but that government should not interfere in private lives. He felt that one of sociology's duties was to tell people how they could avoid governmental interference. Spencer's main contribution to sociology was his insistence that the social process can be understood as a natural, evolutionary system. This idea underlies modern **functionalism** (see below).

Karl Marx (1818–1883), Spencer's contemporary, was a major contributor to sociological ideas. He saw conflict as necessary to social progress, to stimulate growth. He thought that division of the group into classes resulted from the division of labor which exists in all societies. People do not choose the social class into which they are born, and Marx thought that humans being by nature constantly dissatisfied, sooner or later the less advantaged will rebel against those who have more than their share. Marx believed that there is always a dominant class and an oppressed class and that the lower group will develop a realization that they share a common, disadvantaged position. Once they see that they are all in the same boat, so to speak, his expectation was that they would rise up against their oppressors.

Marx saw human history accompanied by a gradually increasing *alienation* of the workers from nature because people become dominated by their own creations. He saw money as one of these alienating human inventions, and also religion; the first enslaving us and the second blinding us to our condition. He saw the means of production dominated by the upper classes, and the workers unable to enjoy the fruits of their labor. Nevertheless, he had hope for the future. He felt that the oppressed classes could and would rise up against their rulers via organization, solidarity, and development of the collective conscious. The result was to be a new, classless society in which harmony would replace conflict. The concept of alienation is important in sociological thinking. Some sociologists agree with the rest of Marx's ideas, and some do not.

Marx regarded thinking as a social activity, and felt that the thoughts of a period reflected its values. He was not the only one to hold this view, but his influence on our civilization has been, perhaps, greater than most philosophers. The idea that each era has its characteristic trains of thought that determine the type of ideas it produces has given rise to a branch of sociology called the **sociology of knowledge**.

Now that we've looked at some thinkers who attended the birth of sociology, let's examine the theoretical beginnings of its major perspectives: *functionalism*, *conflict theory*, and *symbolic interactionism*.

Functionalism

Sociology paid more attention at first to broad social patterns than to individual experience in society. Of course, social patterns are carried out by individuals, but analysts were looking at the overall scene rather than at the interaction between the individual and the group. In 1858 Emile Durkheim and Georg Simmel were born, followed by Max Weber six years later. These three were prominent contributors to the field. Durkheim, like Spencer before him, emphasized structure. He called social phenomena **social facts** and said they should be considered to be things, because they are real. For example, a social group adds up to more than the sum of the individuals, and the group force exerts pressure on the people in it. This group force is a social fact.

Durkheim's study of cohesion and integration in groups in connection with their suicide rates was a landmark in sociology around the turn of the twentieth century. Groups are not equally integrated, he pointed out, and if integration is weak, the least integrated group members are at risk of suicide. One of his study findings was that people with strong family ties were less likely to commit suicide than people without such protection. Durkheim emphasized regulation and guidance in groups. His concept **anomie** refers to the lack of group regulation due to an absence of common norms.

Durkheim developed the idea that group work at the same tasks, side by side, results in a type of unity he called **mechanical solidarity**. In a group with this type of division of labor, the workers are interchangeable, though they have a strong team spirit. When the group grows, and differentiation occurs, the unity is an interdependent kind, which Durkheim called **organic solidarity**. This is the kind of unity your body parts exemplify, since each has a different function but each needs the others, making for a strong pressure for cooperation. A tug-of-war has two mechanically solidary teams; a baseball game has two organically solidary teams.

Functionalism developed out of the ideas of Spencer and Durkheim mainly. For them, society is like a big machine; each part is useful for something (has a function) and you can find out what it is. They assumed that a part would not exist unless its advantages, or **functions**, outweighed its disadvantages, or **dysfunctions**. Because the components of the structure are interdependent, a change in any part is sure to affect all the others. However, functionalists hold that a disturbance to the social system will cause it to correct the imbalance and right itself. They consider the natural state of the system to be **equilibrium**, or balance. This idea has a counterpart in the notion of physiological **homeostasis**, the tendency of an organism to compensate for a disruption of its system. Given this parallel, functionalism has been referred to by its critics as the "big animal" theory of society.

It is true that people refer to society as if it were an organism. They mention its "heart," "brains," "guts," or "nerves," when they really mean the central idea, the decision makers, the headquarters, or the communication system. In thinking about a group, you have to be careful not to transform it into an organism in your mind. This mistake is a form of **reification**, or misplaced concreteness. While it is a strong principle of sociology that the group is more than the sum of its parts, it is going too far to suggest that a group is an organism.

The functionalists see society as an ordered system in which cooperation and consensus combine to keep things running smoothly, and equilibrium is restored after each disturbance. The next theoretical framework regards society very differently: as a scene of battle.

Conflict Theory   When analyzing a battle, it is helpful to know who is fighting, and for what reason. Karl Marx saw people drawn up according to class position, struggling for a share of society's resources. This view implies that the social conflict is a power struggle and that everyone is in competition with everyone else. It also implies continuous negotiation. This is how conflict theorists see the world. Furthermore, this approach to social analysis includes the idea that the social conflict is unequal; that is, there are said to be **dominant** and **subordinate** groups.

In the late nineteenth century a variety of conflict theory, called **social Darwinism**, likened people and groups to species of animals and plants, surviving or perishing according to the degree of their "fitness" to compete for scarce resources. This is close to Spencer's idea of the evolution and increasing improvement of society, but the emphasis here is on conflict, and scholars such as Ludwig Gumplowicz wrote gloomy books claiming the inevitability of warfare in our lives. They drew a picture of losers trying to unseat winners in an endless cycle of defeat and victory.

Conflict theory's focus is different from functionalism's, seeing conflict as not only beneficial but necessary to human society. One of the early writers who made this point was Georg Simmel, also a major contributor to symbolic interactionism, as we shall see. Simmel thought that conflict was creative because it strengthens old bonds and establishes new ones, while providing an outlet for frustrations and promoting alliances.

Functionalists see society as a whole, with needs. Conflict theorists see society as a group of parts, with needs that do not coincide. While the functionalists are identifying the parts of a social system and asking what use they have for the system as a whole, they are concentrating on **social stability** as the normal state. The conflict theorists concentrate on the tensions and negotiations between competing parts, seeing **social change** as the normal state.

A good example of the conflict approach, as applied to the analysis of communities, is James S. Coleman's *Community Conflict*, a brief **monograph** that reviews the basis for conflict analysis of communities and examines the chances for community resolution of conflict.[9] Coleman stresses the importance of people's attachments to other people and to ideas, and their need to keep these attachments consistent. If new elements are to be accepted, they must harmonize with the old. Coleman is recognizing the importance of the individual's viewpoint, or how people perceive the social definition of a situation. The sociological perspective called symbolic interactionism considers the process of establishing social definitions to be the most important business of sociology.

Symbolic Interactionism

Symbolic interactionists are concerned with the give-and-take of the individual contacts that establish common definitions of what is happening, how it should be evaluated, and what behavior is appropriate. Simmel's conception of social conflict was often centered on power shifts in small groups. His work on the effect of group size is an examination of the strategic possibilities that open up when members are added to an existing group. Simmel was interested in the number of forms interaction might take and the options open to the participants.

Max Weber, on the other hand, was primarily interested in the already internalized values that influence peoples' perception of social events and, therefore, their perception of social definitions. In his view, behavior cannot be understood without knowledge of the individual's subjective meanings. Later writers have stressed the explanatory role of past experience as well as that of present situation in conjunction with internalized values, in discussing human behavior. Recognizing that behavior is often habitual or impulsive, Weber listed four types: rational action toward a goal (e.g., working for money); value-oriented rational action (e.g., working to send one's child to college); emotional action (e.g., kissing the child goodbye); and traditional action (e.g., giving parental advice on eating habits).

Symbolic interactionists typically focus on what the subjective meaning is, rather than where it came from. To enumerate all the influences on a particular instance of human interaction would mean including the participants' definitions of the occasion, the setting, the other people and their relationships, everyone's actions, and any possible audience, present or absent. Consider a dinner party. You might come up with these possibilities:

Occasion	feast	business dinner
	family dinner	testimonial
Setting	restaurant	banquet hall
	home	backyard
Relationships	family/friends	employers/employees
	dealers/customers	neighbors
Behavior	formal/informal	jovial
	sedate	ritual
Audience	family only	neighbors
	public	newspaper readers

Such a list barely scratches the surface. What would be the effect on interaction if a guest has already eaten? Or has not eaten all day? Or has been taught to eat little at public functions? Or is unhappy? Any of these possibilities constitute prior socialization and must be considered.

Words are symbols. Symbolic interactionism includes the study of how language is used to attach specific social definitions to events and people. This branch of symbolic interactionism is called **labeling theory**. It holds that when labels are assigned to someone or something and others accept those labels, their behavior toward the labeled person or thing is no longer independent. If people are the labeled items, their own acceptance or rejection of the label will play a part, affecting their own behavior and others' reaction. For example, someone who steals may be labeled *thief*, be punished, and accept the label, stealing again when opportunity knocks. Another who steals may be labeled and punished but reject the label and not steal again. Of course, a person who steals may be labeled *kleptomaniac* and be treated by a psychiatrist instead of being punished. One thing that symbolic interactionism has in common with other sociological approaches is that the research it inspires often demonstrates that labels assigned differ according to social position, the less desirable labels going to the least advantaged people.

When we study society as a whole, we call our perspective **macrosociology**. When we study interaction in small groups, we call it **microsociology**. These terms refer to a difference in level of social analysis, not a difference of opinion about it. Functionalism and conflict theory have emphasized macrosociology, and symbolic interactionism has been mostly microsociological. Sociological researchers can use any theoretical approach at either level. Whichever they choose, their research is carried out in established ways which will be influenced by the theoretical perspective already selected. The sociological researcher studies the real world, which we call the empirical, or observable, world. We will now look at three examples of sociological research, one from each of three sociological points of view.

As we have seen, functional analysts see the social system as a unified structure of components in which people have a place. As Durkheim has shown, to be well integrated into the structure, with the rights and duties adhering to one's status, is to be secure. What light may this shed on a typical problem in our society? Pauline Bart, a contemporary sociologist, looked at depressed, middle-aged women, to see if she could uncover any reasons for their depression.[10] Bart's sample of subjects consisted of 533 hospitalized middle-aged women between the ages of 40 and 59.

A Functional Analysis of Middle-aged Depression

Since it is between the ages of 40 and 59 that a woman completes her reproductive stage in the life cycle, and since very often women of this age were observed to become depressed, many had assumed that middle-aged depression in females was due to physical (gynecological) phenomena. Bart, however, looking at the situation with a sociologist's eye, wondered if there might not be a structural reason for the problem, especially since it was well known that not all women suffered from it. (If depression were an automatic accompaniment to menopause, all women would experience it.) Bart's examination of thirty societies, and her intensive examination of monographs on six cultures, indicated that in most of these societies middle age was not considered a stressful period for women. She then studied the records of 533 depressed women in five American hospitals and went on to conduct twenty intensive interviews at two hospitals.

Bart hypothesized that depressions in middle-aged women are due to their lack of important roles and subsequent loss of self-esteem. She further expected that traditional middle-class Jewish mothers whose children had left home would have higher rates of depression than non-Jews. The sociological basis for these expectations is as follows: Since human behavior is socially determined, our statuses, with their accompanying roles, will correctly predict our typical behavior and we will be able to predict correctly others' reaction to it. This implies that a failure of a role partner to react appropriately could cause a confusion in the mind of the disappointed partner. Since the self is socially determined, feedback is crucial, and the failure of role partners to respond appropriately amounts to bad news about oneself. ("Why are they not responding? I did what I was supposed to do!") During a learning period, nonresponsiveness may be read as inadequacy due to inexperience; after years of appropriate responses from role partners, it cannot. How then will it be interpreted? As a personal loss.

Since culture determines social expectations, Bart felt that a culture that stresses the tie between mother and child would intensify the problem, and therefore, that traditional Jewish mothers would exhibit a greater tendency to middle-aged depression than others would. Once the children are grown, the role attached to mother's status is dysfunctional. The work is done, and constant attendance to the children's needs is now seen as undesirable, whereas it was praised and rewarded in the past. There is then a disruption in the norms, and, as Durkheim postulated, the condition of *anomie*. The role of *patient*, however, might be functional, if it brings the children to see the mother.

Bart found that middle-aged female depression was more likely for Jewish women than for gentiles in her sample, and that the more child-centered a woman had been, the more likely she was to be depressed, regardless of cultural background. This supports Bart's notion that it is not hormonal change that causes depression among middle-aged women, but role change, a loss of social function rather than reproductive function.

Another sociologist, Nancy M. Henley, approached the phenomenon of touching other human beings from a microsociological conflict perspective.[11]

A Conflict Analysis of Touching

Henley thought that touch is used to maintain the social hierarchy. She hypothesized that most touching is from a person of superior status to one of inferior status—for example, master touching servant, police officer touching criminal, doctor touching patient. Other researchers had described specific contexts wherein touching was acceptable only from a high-status person to a lower-status one. Historically, the touch of various people (kings, Jesus) was considered to be beneficial, and some churches still observe the "laying on of hands." Convinced of the significant character of touch, Henley conducted an assortment of research studies to investigate this matter.

Henley's first study was observational. Observers who watched people in public settings found males touching females more than the reverse, and older people touching younger people more than the reverse. Moreover, higher class people were much more likely to touch lower class people than the opposite case. These results have since been confirmed by a study done at an airport by two other researchers. Henley next attempted to test her hypothesis by distributing a questionnaire to twenty-four women and twenty-four men from the Boston area. These respondents were asked how likely they were to touch and be touched by persons in twenty-nine different relationships to them. They reported more likelihood of touching subordinates and coworkers than bosses; more likelihood of touching younger people than older. They thought superiors were more likely to touch them than inferiors were. This result was also confirmed by others. Another section of Henley's questionnaire asked about specific dominant–submissive situations, such as giving an order or asking for help, and the answers clearly showed that the person in the dominant position was more likely to touch the person in the subordinate position.

Henley also did a content analysis of touching in comics and films. She looked at nine television movies and eleven adventure comic books. In films, males touched females twice as often as females touched males. For comics, males touched females more than two and a half times as often as females touched males. Henley's analysis of one movie in detail shows that higher status males do most of the touching, regardless of the touchee. Henley concludes that touching is definitely an expression of social status relative to the person touched.

James M. Henslin looked at relative social status and perceived identity from a symbolic interactionist point of view.[12]

A Symbolic Interactionist Look at Trust

Henslin's study was of cab drivers and the things that entered into their decision to accept a passenger and trust that person to behave appropriately in the role. Henslin's definition of trust is "an actor offering a definition . . . and an audience being willing to interact with the actor on the basis of that definition." A cab driver, approaching a prospective passenger, has to size up the person quickly and decide whether the message conveyed by that person's appearance is worthy of trust.

In addition to the clues afforded by the passenger's appearance, the cabbie considers the time of day, the destination, whether the person is drunk, whether there are children along, and whether the cabbie has seen the person emerge from the place the cabbie was told to stop. Appearance clues include perceived social class, race, sex, age, and familiarity to driver.

Each piece of information adds to the driver's total picture of the person as a safe passenger or a risky one. A safe passenger is one who will not attack the driver and will pay the fare.

Some additional clues to help the driver decide are provided by the dispatcher, who will tell the driver about any suspicious circumstances associated with the order. Symbols that operate to diminish trust are lower-class status, origin or destination in deserted or slum locations, minority group status, and drunkenness. All are considered to offer potential for trouble. Henslin concludes that communication and acceptances of personal definitions are crucial in society, and it is imperative that we realize this for our own good in other areas of our endeavors, in addition to when we are trying to hail a cab.

The studies by Bart, Henley, and Henslin demonstrate the usefulness of sociological research in three areas: mental illness, power relations, and successful presentation of self. We now turn our attention to the set of rules called the scientific method.

The Scientific Method

The scientific method is a way to conduct research according to rules that specify objectivity, honesty, thoroughness, and service to the scientific world. There are other ways to conduct research. Journalists, credit bureaus, and detective squads all conduct research, but they pursue human interest stories, financial records, and evidence of criminal activity for their own purposes and with little regard for the scientific frontier. In these cases, for example, there is less analysis and interpretation of the results intended to shed light on the human condition.

The scientific method consists of ideals and procedures. The cardinal principle behind them is integrity. The ideals are objectivity, empirical verification, contribution to knowledge, and publication.

The Ideals of the Scientific Method

The first ideal, objectivity, is far easier to explain than to achieve. Because it is of paramount importance, we have already referred to it in our discussions.

Objectivity   One of the funniest of the late James Thurber's essays includes an account of his difficulty in learning to see through a microscope in biology class. Time after time he adjusted the mechanism and saw nothing. When he finally got an image, he was delighted; he immediately began to draw what he saw and triumphantly called the instructor over when he had completed his picture. Alas, his victory was short-lived. He had drawn the reflection of his own eye![13]

If we are not to be describing ourselves instead of our subjects, we must attain objectivity. We must try to see the world as it really is, uncolored by personal opinion. One of the things that will help us is our awareness of the basic handicaps discussed in the first part of this chapter. Another aid is called **intersubjectivity**. This rather unwieldy term refers to the practice of comparing your results with those of another researcher who studied the same thing. If two or more investigations come to the same conclusion, the researchers have achieved intersubjectivity, and this is taken to indicate that their results are objectively true. Moreover, each subsequent inquiry that confirms the first result increases confidence in the objective truth of that first result.

The second ideal of the scientific method contributes to objectivity and is the natural counterpoint to scientific theory. It is empirical verification.

Empirical Verification Since empirical means "derived from observation," this phrase says that we must check our scientific theories and speculations by looking at the real world. Sometimes it takes a while before this is possible. For example, Einstein's general theory of relativity could not be compared to Newtonian theory until there was a total eclipse of the sun.[14] Scientific knowledge rests on observation and interpretation.

To perform empirical verifications, you must decide what you will accept as disproving your theory. The best you will be able to do is fail to turn up evidence against your theory: You cannot ever speak of having proved it. We accept a theory as plausible only until it is disproved.

Whether a project is directed toward replication or is trying to break new ground, it must be a contribution to knowledge.

Contribution to Knowledge A research project should be useful to the scientific community. For example, students of intergroup relations have long been interested in how love and friendship develop. Two studies in 1943 found that residential propinquity is an important factor in mate selection: The closer people live to each other, the more likely they are to get married.[15] Leon Festinger, Stanley Schachter, and Kurt Back went further with the notion that residence influences choices. They examined friendship choices and distances between apartment and house entrances and found a definite relationship.[16] The first two studies provide an example of intersubjectivity and verify each other; the third carries the investigation of the social effect of spatial propinquity to a new situation. All are valuable contributions to urban sociology and hence to urban planning as well as to family theory.

In order to make a contribution, one must observe the ideal of publication to the scientific community.

Publication The researcher is expected to share the project results, including a complete report of the research experience, with the other workers in the field. Published material must include the approach, the techniques, and the consequences. Mistakes and failures must be clearly presented so that others may benefit.

An example of how research fits into the context of theory and forms a guideline for continuing research is provided by the work of Solomon Asch, a social psychologist who studied the effect of group perception on the individual. Asch made a significant contribution to the existing theories of conformity in 1951 by devising an experiment that tested the degree to which subjects would attempt to conform with the people around them by giving incorrect answers on a perceptual test.[17] Asch's study was the earliest empirical test of this issue and stimulated others in the ensuing years. The subsequent studies have varied the conditions and the scope of Asch's experiment and have expanded the implications of the investigation.[18]

Keeping the ideals of the scientific method firmly in mind, we come now to an elaboration of the procedures noted before.

The Procedures of the Scientific Method

The procedures of the scientific method are designed to enhance its ideals, to promote objectivity, to require empirical verification, and to contribute to knowledge by publication. These procedures, which are arranged to interact with each other and produce this result, are as follows: specifying goals, reviewing the literature, formulating and testing hypotheses, and inviting scrutiny. The original goals may be revised in light of what others have written; after hypotheses have been formulated and tested, the work is added to the existing literature. Scrutiny is part of the process at each step and acts as a check on logic, accuracy, and perceptual problems.

Specifying Goals The purpose of a research project should be clear. A research goal is chosen and set forth. It must be kept firmly in mind throughout the work so that the investigators' efforts remain focused on it. At the end of the project the goal is reviewed, and the results are evaluated with reference to it. A research goal is often revised in light of what has been done by others. The investigator becomes familiar with related work by reviewing the literature.

Reviewing the Literature A thorough acquaintance with the work already done is mandatory in order to learn what has been accomplished, to profit by other people's mistakes and triumphs, and to see what needs exist. The researcher reads not only the reports of research projects but also the relevant theory. The **literature review** affects the research goals and the methods chosen.

Formulating and Testing Hypotheses Before investigating a research question it is necessary to compose statement(s) setting forth clearly what one expects to find. A hypothesis is a testable statement about the relationship between two or among three or more variables. Once hypotheses are formulated, the variables can be measured and recorded and the resulting data can be analyzed.

Measuring and Recording Sometimes methods suggested by the literature review or by colleagues are chosen to measure and record things being studied; at other times new ways are developed. Whichever it is, strict attention to accuracy and devotion to detail are required. The best available techniques for measuring are to be used, and every move is to be recorded systematically. The scrutiny of other professionals provides good control.

Analyzing the Data   The recorded results of variable measurement are the collected data for the project and they are analyzed carefully, using whatever techniques are appropriate to the type and level of data collected. Techniques range from simple description and discussion of possible implications to sophisticated statistical analysis.

Inviting Scrutiny   Like the literature review, scrutiny affects both goals and methods of measuring and recording the data. At every stage of a research project the opinions and advice of colleagues should be solicited. Each worker depends on the others. Some scientists in every field work full time at improving the methods of research. Regardless of their specialized interest, all scientists can help a fellow researcher by criticizing the work, suggesting possibilities, and asking questions.

The scientific procedure, step by step, will be considered consecutively throughout this text. The practice exercises are intended to familiarize you with it. Although as students you are not held to the same standards as professional researchers, contributing to scientific knowledge and publishing the results in professional journals, you are expected to strive for the ideals and to adhere as closely as possible to the proper procedures. In fulfilling your assignments, be as objective as you can, checking for the empirical truth. You will contribute to the knowledge of the class, and sharing your results with them and with your instructor will be your "publication."

The scientific method is a code of honor. Its procedures have been developed to maintain this code. Clarification and refinement of these procedures are continuous activities. The scientific method is also the standard for the development of each **research design**. A research design serves to organize a project; it consists of a series of steps that occur in an established sequence.

Research Design

The research design has five parts or stages: establishing and defining the research question and developing its implementation; choosing the sample of subjects; selecting the methods of data collection; planning the analysis and presentation of data; and projecting the form that publication will take.

The Research Question

To establish the research question, you must identify the topic you are going to pursue and decide whether you are going to explore it, describe it, or explain something about it. Once you have a clearly defined goal, you can proceed to specify the question you hope to answer by your investigation. If your project is explanatory, you will derive one or more hypotheses from the research question. A **hypothesis** is an assertion that can be tested.

Whether exploratory, descriptive, or explanatory, your question must be operationalized. **Operationalization** is making your investigation workable by developing ways to collect the data you need to answer the question. It requires the definition of each concept used and the selection of measurement techniques. This is the topic of Chapter 2.

Once you have your research question and your plans for operationalizing it, you must decide where and from whom you will collect the data. This is called choosing the sample.

Choosing the Sample

The nature of the question you have developed and the accessibility of the facts determine the composition of your **sample, or the subjects from whom data are actually collected.** In turn, the sample chosen determines the methods of data collection you can use. For example, suppose, like Emile Durkheim, you have chosen to investigate the question: Why do people commit suicide? You need data about suicides, but obviously you can't get data by questioning people who have committed suicide. Your sample, like Durkheim's, might be official records of suicide.[19] Or, you might decide to use a sample of would-be suicides to find out why they considered ending their lives. Chapter 3 examines some of the factors to be considered when choosing a sample.

There are many possible methods of data collection. Some are direct, others indirect. Each has its advantages and disadvantages.

The Methods of Data Collection

Time, money, and access fix the range of possibilities here. Within these limits, you can choose the techniques that seem most appropriate and most likely to yield usable data. Because this is a crucial part of your research, we are going to spend a lot of time on it. Nothing else you do will matter if you collect poor data. Therefore, Chapter 4 is devoted to the considerations necessary to choosing the methods, and Chapters 5 through 8 are devoted to describing and discussing in detail the most common techniques of data collection.

Once the data have been collected, you must determine what they mean and what light they shed on the research question. Furthermore, you have to devise ways of presenting them so that the results will be clear to others.

Analysis and Presentation of Data

Data analysis requires organizing them, by hand or by computer, into tables, charts, and graphs; manipulating them statistically; and summarizing the findings with reference to the original question. Clarity is essential. A careful review of what you set out to discover and an evaluation of the project follow. Your work must be placed in the context of the literature and its contribution specified. We shall consider these matters in Chapters 9 through 11.

Deciding on the form of publication is the last requirement for a research design. You want to know in advance, insofar as possible, how it will ultimately be published so that you can foresee any special needs.

The Form of Publication

What is done with the report and what form final publication takes depend partly on who sponsored it. Official agencies have standard publication procedures. Provided the relevant decision makers accept the work, researchers who do not need to satisfy official agencies can choose to read a paper at a scholarly meeting, publish an article in a professional journal, or publish a book. Students submit papers, make oral reports, or both.

Summary and Conclusion

We are trying to find out what the world is like by asking and answering questions according to the rules of the scientific method and the principles of research design. To do so, we must remember the basic handicaps under which all humans work: selective perception, closure, distorted meanings, culture shock, distorted responses, and falsified conclusions. We must bear the responsibility for learning our subjects' point of view, their definitions, and their language. We must refrain from interfering with their responses, and we must try to be as inconspicuous as possible. We must guard against making false conclusions.

The relatively new discipline of sociology was begun with the idea of explaining history and predicting the future. Sociological theory has been focused on change and stability, social evolution, class conflict, alienation, and styles of thinking. It offers three main approaches to studying society: functionalism, conflict theory, and symbolic interactionism.

Although the rules of scientific research are difficult, they are not impossible to follow if we are loyal to the scientific method and if we learn the tested ways of finding out.

Main Points

1. Studying something scientific requires getting the facts. Because our human nature sometimes stands in the way of our discovering the facts, we must try to overcome it.

2. We tend to see what is relevant to us rather than what is really there. We also tend to provide missing information according to what we think should be there.

3. Our notions of what should be are derived from our cultural and group experience and can distort the meaning as well as the content of what we see and hear.

4. If what we see and hear departs far enough from our own ideas, we experience culture shock. We must learn to absorb this.

5. People being studied tend to respond to a researcher's interest in them by altering their normal behavior. They may also try to cooperate by doing or saying what they think the researcher wants to see or hear.

6. We must avoid the likelihood of drawing false conclusions by guarding against illogical thinking, making sure our information is complete, and being scrupulously honest. The scientific method, consisting of high ideals and strict procedures, is a way to avoid pitfalls and to make a valuable contribution to science.

7. Sociology started with macrosociology (studying broad social patterns) and then developed microsociology (studying the mutual effects of society and the individual).

8. Functionalism analyzes the parts of society and their uses. Conflict theory looks at the competition among the parts. Symbolic interactionism analyzes the communication and effect of social meanings. Any one or combination of these standpoints can inspire research.

9. The ideals of the scientific method are objectivity, empirical verification, contribution to knowledge, and publication.

10. The procedures of the scientific method are specifying goals, reviewing the literature, formulating and testing hypotheses, and inviting scrutiny.

11. The scientific method is the standard for developing a research design, which in turn consists of framing a research question, operationalizing the question, planning the data collection, analyzing and presenting the data, and deciding on the form of publication.

Notes

1. *World Population and Its Age-Sex Composition by Country, 1950–2000,* United Nations, 1980. Cited in Beth J. Soldo, "America's Elderly in the 1980s," *Population Bulletin,* Vol. 35, No. 4 (Population Reference Bureau, Inc., Washington, D.C., 1980), p. 42.

2. Julius Roth, "Hired Hand Research," in *Fist Fights in the Kitchen: Manners and Methods in Social Research,* ed. George H. Lewis (Santa Monica, Calif.: Goodyear, 1975), pp. 380–95.

3. Elenore Smith Bowen, *Return to Laughter* (New York: Doubleday, 1964), pp. 128–30.

4. E. T. Hall, *The Silent Language* (New York: Doubleday, 1959).

5. Christopher Hibbert, *The English: A Social History 1066–1945* (New York: Norton, 1987), pp. 5–7.

6. Irving M. Copi, *Introduction to Logic* (New York: Macmillan, 1953), pp. 3–6.

7. Lewis Coser, *Masters of Sociological Thought* (New York: Harcourt, Brace, Jovanovich, 1971), p. 3. This theory section owes much to Dr. Coser's comprehensive survey of sociology's major theorists.

8. George Simpson, *August Comte: Sire of Sociology* (New York: Thomas Y. Crowell, 1969), pp. 57–69.

9. James S. Coleman, *Community Conflict* (New York: Free Press, 1957), 28 pp.

10. Pauline Bart, "Depression in Middle-Aged Women," in *Women in Sexist Society*, ed. Vivian Gornick and Barbara K. Moran (New York: Basic Books, 1971), pp. 163–86.

11. Nancy M. Henley, "Tactual Politics: Touch," in *Social Interaction: Introductory Readings*, ed. Howard Robboy, Sidney L. Greenblatt, and Candace Clark (New York: St. Martin's Press, 1979), pp. 217–39.

12. James M. Henslin, "What Makes for Trust?," in Howard Robboy, Sidney L. Greenblatt, and Candace Clark, *op. cit.*, pp. 79–89.

13. James Thurber, "University Days," in *The Thurber Carnival* (New York: Harper & Brothers, 1945), pp. 221–28.

14. Copi, *Introduction to Logic*, pp. 397–98.

15. R. H. Abrams, "Residential Propinquity as a Factor in Mate Selection," *American Sociological Review* 8 (1943): 288–94. Also see R. Kennedy, "Premarital Residential Propinquity," *American Journal of Sociology* 48 (1943): 580–84.

16. Leon Festinger, Stanley Schachter, and Kurt Back, *Social Pressures in Informal Groups: A Study in Human Factors in Housing* (Stanford, Calif.: Stanford University Press, 1950), pp. 33–59.

17. Solomon Asch, *Social Psychology* (Englewood Cliffs, N.J.: Prentice-Hall, 1952), Chapters 14 and 16.

18. Harold B. Gerard, Roland A. Wilhelmy, and Edward S. Conolley, "Conformity and Group Size," in *Social Psychology: Readings and Perspective*, ed. Edgar F. Borgatta (Chicago: Rand McNally, 1969), pp. 429–33.

19. Emile Durkheim, *Suicide*, trans. John A. Spalding and George Simpson (Glencoe, Ill.: Free Press, 1951).

Exercises

Exercise 1.1 provides experience in collecting data and demonstrates the effect of selective perception and the absence of a research design. Exercise 1.2 is an empirical test of the social pressure that moves us all to conform to social expectations. Exercise 1.3 affords practice in spotting false conclusions that have resulted from illogical thinking or overgeneralization.

As you do these exercises, try to think about ways of dealing with the problems they illustrate.

Exercise 1.1

Selective perception and unfocused observation

Instructions: Wherever you are and without looking around, list the items in the room that are least visible to you. (I used the south wall of my living room, since I was facing north. See my results at the end of this exercise.)

1. List the items here.

2. Now look again. Did you miss anything? Add it here.

3. Consider your list. Are there any natural groups? Rewrite your list, grouping the items into categories. (My categories are noted at the end of the exercise.)

So far we've used only part of the scientific method: that is, writing things down and being honest. Since we didn't follow the established procedure for research, we now don't know what to do with the information collected. Framing questions about data that were collected without a purpose is time-consuming and frustrating. Having a specific goal would save time and effort and clear up the confusion. Do I want to know about the people who live in the room? Do I want to know about the condition of the room? Am I making an energy audit? Clearly, the question being asked will be the basis for the choice of the items listed and their grouping. Unfocused observation will not do. A careful plan provides for future needs and prevents disappointment. We need a research design.

In Question 1, I got

leather chair	3 pairs of curtains
3 pairs of drapes	3 window boxes with plants
radiator	table lamp
end table with cup and saucer	wall switch
end table with books	lounge chair

In Question 2, I missed: dog, no smoking sign, picture, double outlet.

In Question 3, I grouped the items into living (dog, plants) and inanimate (everything else).

Exercise 1.2   *Social pressure*

Instructions: Violate a common custom, and record other people's response to your behavior in the space provided. Do not take anyone along to
give you confidence, because this would reduce the impact of the exercise.
Write word for word what actually happened, including comments; do not
summarize. For example, don't say "people looked at me funny." Record
exactly what happened: for example, "One woman looked at me and turned
her back immediately; another frowned; a man smiled and raised his eye-
brows." If anything was said, write down exactly what it was; don't rephrase
anything. (In the past, students have ordered a meal backward—beginning
with dessert and ending with soup—used formal etiquette with their families
for a few hours, worn clothing inside out in a public place, eaten a sandwich
during a sermon, asked a clerk for an item by singing the request, taken
laundry to class and sorted it, and many other travesties.) *Do not break any
law or endanger yourself*. After writing your experience, answer the questions on the next page as thoughtfully as you can.

1. What did you learn about violating social expectations?

2. Were you uncomfortable at any time? When?

3. Was social opinion powerful enough to make you want to stop at any time? When? If not, why do you think it wasn't? Were you really out of character for that audience?

4. Considering social expectations for behavior in general, how do you think your research subjects will be affected by what *they think are your social expectations for them*?

Exercise 1.3   *False conclusions*

Instructions: Read the following excerpt from a newspaper account that illustrates overgeneralization (hasty conclusion):

"Man's lived 100 colorful years"

New Year's Eve not only will herald the arrival of 1981 but also will mark the 100th birthday of a lifelong city resident. . . .

A successful building contractor for more than 50 years, Smith has always had his headquarters and his home in Plainfield. Why? "There's no place better," he said. . . .

When asked about his secret for longevity, Smith remarked that "living close to nature" was the answer. Recalling his days building railroads, he said if he ever gets really sick, he will go back to logging camps to get well. He felt full of the most "vim" there, he explained. . . . (Used by permission.)

Argument

PREMISE 1:   Mr. Smith, who has lived longer than the average person does in our society, felt strong while at the logging camp.

IMPLIED CONCLUSION: Logging camps are good places for sick people to get well.

Premise 1 is true if we accept Mr. Smith's recollection. The conclusion, however, does not follow because it is an overgeneralization. Mr. Smith is basing his conclusion on his own experience only, and one case is not enough of a sample to justify a conclusion. If we had a large sample of formerly sick people, randomly drawn from the population, *and* most of them had got well at logging camps but not elsewhere, *then* we could conclude that logging camps were probably good places to get well. Even so, we'd have to check to make sure that our results were valid.

1.   Find an example of overgeneralization in your newspaper like the account of Mr. Smith. Attach or describe your example here. Explain the illogical thinking by writing out what you think the reported argument is: express or implied premises followed by a conclusion, then adding your criticism.

45

The Research Question

Before designing a research project, you must know its goal. What are you trying to find out? What question are you asking? This may be the hardest part of doing research. It doesn't take much equipment, but it takes a lot of determination and some creativity. Planning is important because a well-planned project is much easier to execute than an ill-planned one, and when you are finished, you have fewer regrets about things you wish you had included.

This chapter is divided into three parts: asking a question, operationalizing it, and selecting a research mode.

How to Ask the Question

Most people can think of a subject they would like to know more about, but they may panic a little when asked to name precisely what it is they want to know. This is what makes the framing of the research question such a challenge. Research requires precision; without it, data collection is unfocused, leaving the researcher with too much of some information and too little of other kinds. Fortunately, all the tools are cheap and available: writing implement, paper, quiet place, brain. What we're after is simple: a topic of interest to us.

Suppose you have to come up with an idea for a research paper. Begin by writing down your random thoughts, even if they seem of no use. Gradually try to focus on some general area. For example, you might be taking a course in marriage and the family in addition to your research course. Think about marriage. Ever wonder why people choose each other? Where they typically meet? How frequently intermarriage occurs? There are dozens of possibilities here. List as many as you can think of and have patience to write down. These are possible areas of interest. Select one of them, say "why people choose each other." In social science this topic is usually called *mate selection.*

Now write down all the things you consider important about choosing a mate. Age? Occupation? Family? Religion? Appearance? Marital status (divorced, widowed)? Parental status? Handicap? Financial status? Race? Personality? Do you think any of these are related in any way? For example, when prospective mates meet, would the influence of their families be greater for young couples than for older ones? In other words, is there a connection (relationship) between age (variable 1) and family influence (variable 2) when people are choosing their mates? Lo and behold, you have a question!

A research question is about the connection between two items that change. The items are called **variables.** You can have a variable with an infinite number of changes, like distance. You can have a variable with a specific number of changes, like marital status. You can have a variable with only two possibilities: yes or no. We'll see how some variables can be divided in more than one of these ways. Regardless, the form of the question is: "Is variable 1 connected with variable 2?" The connection between the variables can be any one of a range of strengths and types from a weak association to a strong causation. Your research project will yield data that points to the strength of the connection, if there is one.

The Need for a Question

Forcing yourself to form a question and to write it down disciplines your mind and clarifies your goal. Remember the exercise in Chapter 1 that asked you to list things without a plan? You ended up with useless data because you had made your list without knowing what would be done with the items or how they would be organized. Collecting data without specifying your question in advance is like buying a variety of wood and hardware at a sale and then trying to construct a building. You would quickly discover that you had too much material for some things, and too little for others. Crucial parts for your building would be missing, and your storage area would be cluttered with odds and ends that you couldn't use. This is inefficient and expensive and yields a poor result.

The hapless do-it-yourself carpenter who tries to build without a plan may be rescued by the easy availability of additional materials and advice. If you have the money, you can buy more lumber and hardware or call in a professional to finish the job or do it over. A research project isn't that flexible. Rarely can you go back and fill in gaps in the data. If you have failed to carry out the correct procedures, you can hardly ever find someone to come in and patch up your work; even if you could, the work would no longer be yours but theirs.[1] It is a far better practice to plan ahead carefully.

Another good reason to be specific about the purpose of your work is to clarify it for the reader. The reader who can't discover your intention has no basis for evaluating your work or for comparing it with existing work. This reduces the usefulness of the work to the scientific community.

To provide yourself with a clear question, you begin by choosing an area of study in which you are interested. You can, as in the example above, figure out a question by thinking about the topic and working it out on paper. If you are totally unfamiliar with the topic, you may have to do a little reading first. Once you have some ideas, you review the literature about the area to familiarize yourself with what has been done and what remains to be done. Then, using suggestions, theory, and experience, you are ready to specify the question. When the question is clear, you are in a position to predict what you expect to find, specify what would disprove your prediction, and decide what pieces of data you must collect. We shall examine these procedures in order. Bear in mind that we often reconsider things and change the question or even the topic. A typical change consists of narrowing the original area. This may be done more than once.

Choosing an Area

The ideal of the scientific method that is relevant to choosing an area is the desirability of making a contribution to knowledge. This is why you review the literature in the area you choose. Fortunately, no area of human activity is irrelevant to all scientific fields. You are free to choose any topic. Your professional interests and career plans may guide you, but do not omit the promptings of your own taste. Your work will be better if you are enthusiastic and curious. You should try for continuity with existing theory and research, relevance to the current concerns in that area, and timeliness for your forthcoming contribution. Avoid plagiarism, redundance, and inefficiency. You can accomplish the desirable and avoid the pitfalls by familiarizing yourself with what has already been done and by keeping up with the ongoing projects in your field. Students are not expected to do all this, but you should do your best.

Continuity, Relevance, and Contribution   Remember that the scientific method requires that everything you do in a research project be written down and shared with other researchers. Now we come to an example of the usefulness of this rule. Others have worked on your topic and have recorded their efforts and their results. These records will help to inform and direct you. By reading the reports of others, you will be guided in choosing a question that fits in with prior accomplishments. This is continuity.

While studying the theories and concerns of the best minds in your field, you can find out the subject's frontiers, the unexplored territories, the twilight zones of knowledge. You can pick something that has a bearing on topics now considered important. This is **relevance**.

Once you have become well informed, you can see the gaps in current knowledge. You can then try to fill one of them. This is a worthy contribution.

Plagiarism, Redundance, and Inefficiency   As noted in Chapter 1, plagiarism is using someone's work, written or not, and not giving them credit for it. The appearance of plagiarism is just as bad as the reality. Those who read your report assume that you are well read in the subject of the research. They expect you to give credit where credit is due and to provide footnotes when citing others' work so that those who want to consult the cited work may do so. It is not only dishonest when you fail to cite others but also illegal.

Redundance is *needless* repetition. It differs from replication, which is a necessary and useful additional test that is done to confirm a result. Perhaps the project you envision has been done many times before. You might make a greater contribution by approaching the problem from a new angle. Perhaps your sponsor wants you to do something new. You are able to avoid redundance if you are familiar with what has been done.

Inefficiency is waste of time, energy, or materials. Knowing what others have said and done saves you from some of their mistakes and gives you usable suggestions that will expedite your work. Although you may succeed at something in which another person has failed, you cannot possibly test everything personally.

The goal of scientific research is to expand human knowledge and understanding. Each academic discipline focuses on specific things and explores them as thoroughly as possible. Some areas of inquiry, or **fields**, have been studied by armies of scholars over many years. As knowledge grows, topics are subdivided again and again so that investigation of them can be handled by one or a few people in reasonable periods of time and at reasonable cost.

Whether the subject is an ancient concern or a modern "spin-off," the theoretical base for it is always changing in the light of each generation's work. Many theories compete for acceptance, and there are always disagreements and unexplored possibilities. Knowing the literature of your field supplies you with a foundation for your work and directs you to many research questions.

Reviewing the Literature

To review the literature thoroughly, you have to go to the library and look up all references to your topic. You will make many trips to the library. Your library work will begin with a general perusal of bibliographies, indexes, abstracts, and card catalogs. You might also have a conference with the research librarians, who will usually give you enthusiastic cooperation and help. If you are not familiar with the use of the library, ask the librarians to show you where to look. Do not be afraid of appearing dumb or ignorant. The librarians are there to help you, and they are well trained to do it. Your job is to make clear what you are seeking.

Before you leave for the library you'll be using pen and paper and brain again, to jot down key words and phrases to use in tracking down references. This will be the beginning of a list that you'll be able to expand as you go along.

Suppose you are interested in group homes as an alternative to institutionalizing people, and you are concerned about the attitudes of people when group homes are being established in their community. This is certainly a topic relevant to today's concerns about various types of handicapped people: the elderly, the retarded, the mentally ill, parolees, and recovering addicts of different kinds. Your first move might well be to check in the periodical room of your library and scan the most recent issues of social work, psychology, and criminal justice journals for articles on group homes or halfway houses. Take a notebook, and when you find such an article, head a notebook page with the article's title, author(s), page numbers, and the name, volume, number, and date of the journal (for later citation). As you read the article, jot down the major ideas expressed in it, and if it is the report of actual research, write down the research question and the result.

You should also carry a package of index cards and use one for each further reference you find, writing the same information on it you used to head the pages for the article summaries. Write the author's name first because that is what you will look up when you check the reference. These cards are going to come in very handy later on when you have to list your sources. You can alphabetize them before you type your list. Although photocopying everything is not recommended, photocopying can be a great convenience when more useful material is available than can be quickly handcopied, for example, when several relevant passages are scattered through a long article. (You might even find, after reading it more slowly, that more of the photocopied work is relevant to your project than you had originally thought.) Be sure to record the full journal or book citation on the top of the first page of photocopied items.

In addition to the pages for article summaries, your notebook should have a page for ideas. As you read, jot down any questions that occur to you about the subject. For example, you might wonder whether parolees are accepted more readily in communities after they have become senior citizens. Write that. You might wonder whether people in group homes are happier with rooms of their own or with roommates. Write that, too. Later on you will reread all your notes to help in deciding what question to ask. Don't try to edit anything now; put it all down, even if it seems farfetched. You never know what will give you a usable idea.

Once you have read something on a subject, you can make a list of key words and phrases to use in tracking down references. You include anything that you think might have a bearing on your topic and possible questions about it. For example, if you are thinking of a study of community acceptance of group homes, your list might read:

community acceptance	integration
group homes	halfway houses
mental patients	retardates
parolees	mental health
outpatients	handicapped
rehabilitation	attitudes
tolerance	stereotypes
senior citizens	aging
housing	gerontology

Look up every reference you can find, and be alert for additional relevant words and phrases as they suggest themselves. Get into the habit of noting things on paper. If you are interrupted, or if time runs out, your notes will make it easy for you to resume your search.

Don't expect to find studies that draw together all the things you have in mind. There may be one or more, and there may not be. Using the earlier example, you would want to look for published research on community acceptance of newcomers in general, on attitudes toward "different" people in general, on experiences of people who have tried to establish group homes, on studies of people who have lived in group homes, and on anything else you can think of that bears on the subject. At this point, because you don't yet know exactly what question you are asking, you are casting a wide net.

Once you have completed this first library survey, you should read over your notes and see if you can narrow your topic to a particular question. We'll talk about this process in the next section, but since we are now looking at the literature review requirements, let's assume that you have succeeded in formulating a question. Go back to the library at that point. Now you can eliminate all but what is relevant to your specific question.

Because you need to know as much as possible of what has been said and done about the specific components of your question, you need to peruse a limited range of items more thoroughly. Now you should have less difficulty in seeing whether a book or article is useful to you and relevant to your work. Learn to skim text to find key words and phrases. Read the prefaces, introductions, tables of contents, abstracts, and conclusions.

Your criterion for this search should be: Does this article or book discuss any of the phenomena or theories that pertain to my question? If it does, see exactly what it says. Do not use abstracts for more than the initial selection of items. Get the actual piece of literature. Take **verbatim**, or word-for-word, notes; put quotation marks around them so you do not forget that they are the author's words. Use the note card system, which is recommended by most guides for writing term papers.[2]

Go back in time as far as you can. Some think that work done before the current decade is not important, but this is a mistake. Productive theory and research have been produced for centuries. For a witty account of the errors and false claims of originality fostered by the attitude that older work is unimportant, read Pitirim Sorokin.[3]

Don't exclude material because the sources disagree. All sides of a controversy should be mentioned in your summary. Here is an example of how E. P. Hutchinson[4] summarizes conflicting opinions spanning three centuries:

> *Many writers of the Elizabethan period expressed the view that population numbers tended to grow too large,[7] and the belief that England was overpopulated is thought to have stimulated the colonizing activity of the time, including the establishment of the settlements in North America.[8] Later this position was reversed. . . . About a century later, . . . the weight of opinion as represented by Malthus and his predecessors again began to turn and to focus on the dangers of overpopulation. Movements in the prevailing views on the subject of population numbers, . . . are shown by Spengler to have occurred in France . . .*

Superscripts within the selection are in the original. These represent the author's sources, which are carefully documented in footnotes. The book is a review of the literature on population as well as a **synthesis**, or a drawing together of related parts, of population theory.

In the foregoing excerpt, E. P. Hutchinson acknowledges what has been theorized about his subject and compares the various positions that have been held. Once you have done this, you will probably side with one position and will mention that fact in your write-up, giving your reasons for the choice and predicting what you would expect to find if you are correct and what you would expect if the position is incorrect.

If you have an opinion that does not coincide with any so far published on the subject, that's perfectly all right. After you have summarized what others have said, give your reasons and make your prediction.

Guard against distorting the arguments and results that you are quoting. That is why I recommended either taking verbatim notes or photocopying. If you summarize while in the library and summarize your summaries at home, you are more likely to drift away from the original idea and inadvertently misquote people. It is better to have the authors' actual words in front of you as you write.

Now that we have outlined the requirements of a literature review in its two major stages, preliminary and specific, let's return to the process of specifying the research question. Of course you may be lucky and have a specific research question suggested to you by someone else, in person or in the literature. If you are developing a question by yourself, you do it by reasoning in one of two ways: from theory or from experience.

Specifying the Research Question

How do you know what it is you want to find out? Generally, questions arise in your mind in three ways. They may be suggested by someone else. They may be suggested by your own experience. They may be suggested by some theory you have about the world. The latter two sources are known as inductive logic and deductive logic, or reasoning, respectively.

Inductive Logic **Inductive logic** is reasoning from what you've experienced or observed to the construction of a theory, that is, from the particular instances to the general idea.

Suppose you notice that whenever you are in a particularly good mood, most of the people you meet seem also to be in a good mood. Time after time, your smiles are met with smiles, and your joking remarks are matched by similar ones. Conversely, when you are unhappy, other people also seem glum. Your sour comments are met with equally cynical observations from others. You begin to theorize from this. Going from the accumulated specific instances to a general summary, you say that people tend to reflect the mood of the person who starts an exchange of facial expressions and verbal greetings. You have generated a theory using inductive logic.

In the early 1960s Charles H. Stember, a social psychologist greatly interested in racial and cultural minorities, noticed a pattern in racial hostility: The most emotional and the strongest reactions to integration seemed to

FIGURE 2.1

Reasoning from experience to theory (i.e., from concrete to abstract) is called inductive. Deductive reasoning moves from theory to experience (i.e., from abstract to concrete)

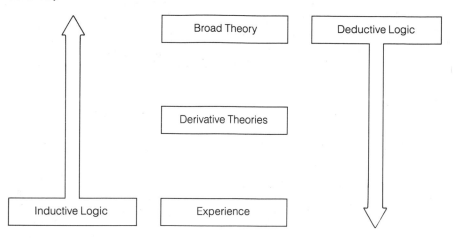

be those stimulated by any suggestion of interracial sex or marriage. This set Stember thinking about the possibility that sexual rivalry might have something to do with the matter and led ultimately to the development of his interesting and thought-provoking theory of the relationship between relative status and sexual choice.[5] This is an example of inductive logic culminating in a theory.

Stember's theory of status and sexual choice was ground-breaking in that no other writer on the subject of interracial sex had foreshadowed any of Stember's arguments; at the same time, it fit into the body of established theory on race relations as a new possible answer to an old question, Why does racial prejudice exist? It also suggested areas in which further research would be fruitful.

Deductive Logic **Deductive logic** is reasoning from theory to experience. In other words, it is reasoning from the general to the particular. For example, from the theory of behavior that says people tend to respond to the expectations of others,[6] you might deduce that people respond in kind to facial expressions and greetings regardless of whether they are cheerful or sad themselves. You might develop the question: "Will individuals reflect the mood of the person who starts an exchange of facial expressions or greetings?" This is a research question generated by deductive logic, because you reasoned from the theory to the everyday world.

When you start with experience and move toward theory, you are using inductive logic; when you start with theory and move toward experience, you are using deductive logic. Figure 2.1 illustrates this difference.

One of the ways in which Stember's race relations theory proved productive was in its suggestion that men and women might have different perspectives on interracial sex and marriage. As an undergraduate and graduate student in Stember's classes, I became familiar with his theory and reasoned from it that if sexual rivalry is the basis for racial hostility, then women, whose role in sexual competition differs from that of men, should differ markedly from men in racial hostility. In a sample of 700 people surveyed on attitudes toward racial integration in schools, housing, dating, and marriage, the attitudes of women were markedly more favorable than those of the men.[7] This is an example of an empirical investigation based on deductive logic.

Perhaps it is better to think of the interplay between the theoretical and the empirical as a continuous, somewhat circular process. Theory suggests research, which in turn suggests new theory, which in turn suggests new research. One should also remember that theory suggests new theory, and research suggests new research. Ideas come from all directions.

Whether you begin with the concrete and move toward the abstract, as in inductive logic, or begin at the abstract and move toward the concrete, as in deductive logic, you reach the hypothetical point where you have got a grip on a research question. Let's try an example. Continuing with the assumption that your area is group homes and their acceptability in the communities where they are established, let's say that you have thought of a theory.

You have noticed that people writing to newspaper editors to express their opposition to group homes in their own community frequently mention the possibility that the prospective residents would commit crimes in the neighborhood. Thinking this over, you wonder whether people might be more receptive to group homes whose residents do not have a criminal background. You are reasoning inductively. Your research question is, What effect does type of resident have on the community's acceptance of a group home?

Now you can proceed to frame a hypothesis, or prediction about the world.

Framing a Hypothesis

As mentioned in Chapter 1, a hypothesis is a testable statement about the relationship between two or more variables. A hypothesis should be brief, simple, and direct. It's a statement that says what we expect to find when we collect data in the real world. Since we are going to check it out, we speak of **testing** the hypothesis.

A hypothesis can be derived from deductive reasoning. Hypotheses derived from classical theory are of this type. For example, you can begin with Weber's theory that the two main branches of Christianity, Catholicism and Protestantism, give rise to traditional and rational approaches to human activity. Your research question might be "Do Catholics and Protestants differ in their choice of vocations?" This could give rise to hypotheses such as, "Hyp. 1. Catholics are more likely than Protestants to major in philosophy and the arts in college." "Hyp. 2. Protestants are more likely than Catholics to major in science and technology in college." A hypothesis can also be derived from inductive reasoning. Hypotheses derived from grounded theory, or theory that has been tested by research, are of this type. Later on in this book I will use a research example derived from a study I did of juvenile diabetics and their parents, based on Gerhard Lenski's work. His hypotheses were deductively derived from Weber's theory about Catholicism and Protestantism. My hypotheses were inductively derived from this grounded theory.

Included in the notion of a hypothesis is the idea of **causality**, the relationship between something that produces an effect and the effect itself. Because a hypothesis includes this concept, variables are classified into categories implying cause or effect for the duration of a project and are treated accordingly. This section of our discussion will take up these matters one by one, to illustrate the procedures involved with the successive stages of our hypothetical group home research project.

Variables A variable is a trait or dimension that varies from subject to subject. A variable appears in different ways that can be put into separate categories, or sorted. A variable's categories must be exhaustive. This means that each subject or case must fit appropriately into a category. A variable's categories must also be mutually exclusive. This means that each subject or case must fit appropriately into only one of the categories. The criteria for putting a case into a category must be definite and clear. Marital status is a variable. It can be sorted in several different ways. How you sort it depends on the concepts, or ideas, relevant to your project.

If you're interested in the legal aspects of marital status, you might use two categories:

Marital Status

single

married

If you're interested in the cohabitational aspect of marital status, you might have two different categories:

Marital Status

living with spouse or cohabiting

living alone or with platonic housemates

If you're interested in the experiential aspect of marital status, you might come up with these categories:

Marital Status

single, never married or cohabiting

single, cohabiting

single, formerly cohabiting

single, divorced

single, widowed

separated from spouse*

married, living with spouse

Note that a person could have experience in several of these categories. Clearly, the way you classify your variables depends on the research question and the hypothesis.

Considering the research question (What effect does type of resident have on the community's acceptance of a group home?), you see that there are two variables: type of resident and community acceptance. A number of hypotheses are possible, but remember that you started thinking about the possible effect of type of resident because you noticed that people were worried about criminal activity. Therefore, a hypothesis that sorts type of resident with this in mind is appropriate. One such would be:

Community acceptance is higher for group homes with senior citizens or retardates in them than for those housing parolees or addicts.

Or:

Community acceptance is lower for group homes housing residents with known criminal records than for homes housing any other type of resident.

Sometimes you list more than one hypothesis. For this study you could have

Hyp. 1.   Community acceptance of group homes varies with the type of resident served.

Hyp. 2a. Community acceptance of group homes is higher for those serving senior citizens than for those serving mental patients.

Hyp. 2b. Community acceptance of group homes is higher for those serving mental patients than for those serving parolees.

Before we attempt to classify our variables, community acceptance and type of resident, let's consider the nature of causality.

Causality   Scientists assume that observed phenomena have causes. A cause is something that makes something else happen. When we see something, we assume not only that it has a cause; we assume that the cause can be discovered. However, there are important things to remember about this. Look at Figure 2.2.

*including temporary, involuntary separation (illness, armed services, imprisonment)

FIGURE 2.2   **Some possible causal explanations for the appearance of B**

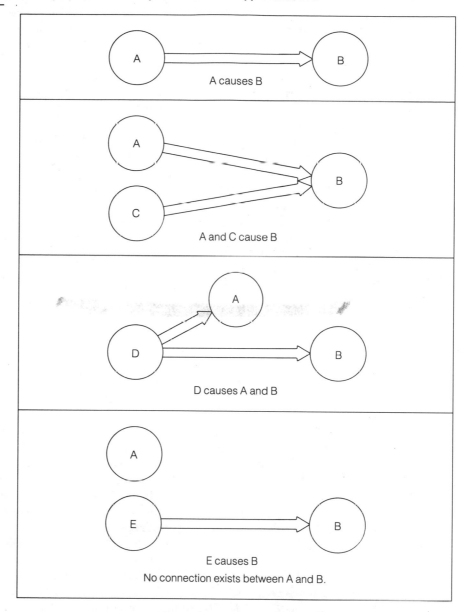

The simplest cause-effect relationship is depicted at the top of Figure 2.2: A causes B. However, we cannot assume that anything has only one cause. Therefore, we move down to the next possibility: A and C together cause B. There are several possibilities here. If B is partly the result of A and partly the result of C, we do not know whether B happens only when A and C occur simultaneously, whether A must precede C, or vice versa, or whether duration matters. It could also be that either A or C can cause B. Notice we are not saying anything about the possible connection between A and C.

Moving further down the figure, we come to another type of cause-effect pattern: D causes B, but D also causes A. We cannot assume that a cause has only one effect. Neither can we assume that we have chosen to look at the appropriate phenomenon. Look at the last pattern: E causes B. Perhaps we were examining A and haven't noticed E at all. Maybe there is a connection between A and E, but we are oblivious of it. Maybe there is no connection between A and E.

These examples do not represent all the possible cause-effect relationships. Because life is very complicated, many variables can be considered for any question. However, since the study becomes unmanageable very quickly as you add variables, we are limited to a few. If you don't focus on a few at a time, you can't figure anything out. For our example, we can stick to cause-effect possibilities of the simplest kind: A causes B, and maybe A and C cause B.

Now we come to the implications of our ideas about causality for the treatment of our variables.

Independent, Dependent, and Control Variables   The hypothesis expresses the predicted relationship of the variables to each other. Our main hypothesis is

> **Hyp. 1.** Community acceptance of group homes varies with the type of resident served.

This can be represented symbolically as follows: B varies because of variation in A.

The variable that we assume to be the cause (A) is labeled the **independent variable**, because for the duration of the study we are going to regard it as something that varies by itself, without any help. Its various categories are taken as given, and we are not going to look into their causes. Our A, or independent variable, is type of resident.

The variable that we assume to be the effect (B) is labeled the **dependent variable**, because for the duration of the study we are going to regard it as something that varies in response to A, the independent variable. Hence, when A changes, B also changes. Our B, or dependent variable, is community acceptance, which according to our hypothesis depends on type of resident.

Now we are going to open the door to another possibility: A alone does not cause B, but there is another variable, C. As already noted, there may or may not be a connection between A and C. However, if we think that C plays a role in causing B or in any way modifies the effect A has on B, then we are wise to include C in our study. Suppose we add another subhypothesis to our list:

> **Hyp. 2c.** Community acceptance of group homes for each type of resident served is higher for those with women in the populations than for those with men only.

We have introduced a new variable, sex of resident, because we think this variable may exercise some control over the cause-effect relationship of the other two. We call it, therefore, the **control variable**. We also use the word *control* when we speak of examining the A-B relationship one control variable category at a time. In our example, therefore, the variables are as follows:

Independent variable—type of resident in a group home

Dependent variable—community acceptance

Control variable—sex of resident

When we look at the community acceptance for a particular type of group home, we first consider male-only homes. Looking again, we consider mixed-sex homes. Finally, we consider female-only homes. In this process we say we are **controlling for sex**. We speak of it as controlling because we are not allowing sex to vary; we are holding it constant while we examine the A-B relationship in which we are primarily interested, that is, the relationship between type of resident (criminal, noncriminal) and community acceptance.

The control variable is also known as the **intervening variable** because it is regarded as a potential influence on the A-B relationship.

Remember, we are always going to look at the effect the independent variable has on the dependent variable. If we decide to do this one control variable category at a time, we have not shifted our focus away from A-B. We are still looking at smaller samples of A-B to eliminate the confounding effect of C. For example, you may find that senior citizens enjoy higher community acceptance than parolees. If all the senior citizens were women and all of the parolees men, however, your finding might not really confirm your hypothesis. Better look at women and men separately. In other words, control for sex.

One last point: Remember to be very conservative about claiming causality. It is safer to limit yourself to claiming association. **Association** of one variable with another means only that they vary at the same time. Bear in mind the other variables that may have an effect on the relationship you have found.

Once you have formed at least one hypothesis and have identified your variables, you must figure out how to translate the variables into observable things. You have to make plans for going out into the world and getting the data you need to test the hypothesis and answer your research question. Operationalization is the process by which we turn a hypothesis into a data collection design.

Operationalization

Operationalization is making your ideas work. You're going to try to figure out what data you need to test your hypothesis in the real world. This means you've got to define every term you use and designate pieces of information (then called data) to serve as evidence of what's out there that either supports or refutes your hypothesis. The pieces of data you actually use to test your hypothesis are referred to as **indicators**.

While operationalizing, you must pay attention to two important requirements for your research design: **reliability**, the confidence with which you can expect the same result if you replicate the study, and **feasibility**, the degree to which you can be sure that it is possible to carry out the project. Accurate measurement is essential to achieving these requirements.

Definitions

It is necessary to define each variable, and we need a special kind of definition for operationalization. It's called an **operational definition** and is a statement of what the variable includes *for the duration of your study*. For example, an operational definition of family size could be:

1. Family size = number of people living in the household

or

2. Family size = parent(s) plus children, living in the same household

or

3. Family size = number of children ever born of this mother, regardless of residence or how long each child lived

Once you've settled on an operational definition, the indicators you need are obvious. In the example above, operational definition 1 requires you to find out how many people live in each household you include in your sample. Definition 2 requires you to find out how many parents plus children there are living in each household. You wouldn't count other relatives or nonrelatives, grandparents, or children living elsewhere. You'd have to decide what to do if more than one couple and their children live together. There are lots of decisions such as this to make because the real world doesn't fit neatly into our classifications. For operational definition 3, you'd ask each woman how many children she had ever borne, and make sure the number included children born alive who died before the time of your survey.

The operational definitions are meant to be useful for testing your hypothesis. Your definitions specify what *you* mean by the labels and terms you use and you must also explain how you are arranging your variables. The variable you use as a dependent variable might be the one someone else uses as a control variable or an independent variable. Your definition of something may very well be different from anyone else's definition of it.

Theory constantly informs research. For instance, functional analysis, holding that society is a structure of interrelated parts, has generated many "theories of the middle range," or theories about the relationship between variables of different types. The idea that one's statuses influence each other and are sometimes functional alternatives to each other is one of these theoretical derivatives. For example, researchers have hypothesized that a woman's educational status is a functional alternative to motherhood. Others have thought that a woman's occupational status is another functional alternative. Someone investigating fertility trends from this perspective would choose operational definition 3 for family size because they would need to compare a woman's educational or occupational status with the number of children she bore in her lifetime. However, some population theorists feel that **density**, or the number of people occupying a given area, is an important influence on the number of children born. A researcher might well include definition 1 along with definition 3, using more specific labels, say, "household size" and "children ever born to mother." Anything that makes sense for your project is acceptable as long as it is clearly stated and used consistently for the duration of that project.

A **theoretical definition**, or the commonly accepted meaning, of type of resident would be "classification of someone living in a habitation." However, the label "type of resident" is vague enough to mean almost anything. Thus for the group home study, the operational definition of type of resident might well be "the official category to which a resident is assigned by the state." That is the information you would collect. But "type of resident" could be defined in many other ways. A worker in a group home might define the variable as "how cooperative a resident is with the staff"; another person might define it as whether a given resident is ambulatory; still another might use a diagnostic classification.

The most specific variable we are using in this example is sex of resident. Most theoretical definitions and operational definitions coincide. As long as there is no question of borderline gender or gender change, there would be little disagreement.

The dependent variable, community acceptance, presents a variety of possibilities. The choice of an operational definition is up to you. The theoretical definition of community acceptance would be something like "favorable opinion of the people residing in a community," or "absence of community protest." For your study, you may choose any plausible definition. Let's say you choose "statement of willingness to allow the group home to exist in the community."

The operational definitions suggested earlier could be easily **categorized**, or divided into subgroups. First, we'll look at the process of developing indicators.

Indicators   Indicators are the pieces of data you actually collect and sort in categories. They are what you are willing to accept as evidence to support the variable. An indicator for a variable has to conform to the operational definition and has to be subject to sorting. Therefore, if possible, you establish the sorting categories beforehand. (It is not always possible. We'll talk about types of question that result in the formation of categories later, in our discussion of interviews and questionnaires.)

Let's take a look at our variables to see what kinds of indicator might be useful. For the independent variable "type of resident," we have an operational definition, "the official category to which a resident is assigned by the state." How are we going to find this information about the homes' residents? The indicator would have to be the official category listed in the resident's file. If the group home has only one type of resident, the director's statement to the researcher is the indicator. In any case, it probably will not be necessary to do more at any home than ask the director what types of resident are there and what proportion of each type.

For the control variable, sex of resident, we can also use the director's report. So far, our data collection is easy. When we consider the dependent variable, however, we must think about how to get a "statement of willingness to allow the group home to exist in the community." One way would be to ask local residents, Are you willing to allow the group home here in your community? Then we would record their answers. We could sort the answers into categories like this:

> willing
>
> not willing
>
> conditionally willing (willing if certain conditions are met)

A category must exist for every possible answer. For respondents who cannot make up their minds, the answers need a fourth category: undecided, or don't know. Categories must also be mutually exclusive; that is, a response should clearly fit in one and only one category. Occasionally, a study may have a variable for which people can check more than one category, but multiple classification is unwieldy and is almost always avoided by grouping the categories so that only one aspect of the variable is sorted at a time.

For example, in the marital status variable, seven possible categories exist:

> single, never married or cohabiting
>
> single, cohabiting
>
> single, formerly cohabiting
>
> single, divorced
>
> single, widowed

separated from spouse for any reason

married, living with spouse

To simplify this, we could group the categories as follows:

never married

ever married*

*including cohabiting and separated couples

or

never married

formerly married

married, living with spouse

(do not count cohabiting as marriage)

or

never married

separated, divorced, or widowed

married, living with spouse

(do not count cohabiting as marriage)

The choice depends on the object of the study and the definition of marital status.

Another example comes from a recent study of American old people:[8]

Variable—marital status

Indicator—answer to a census-taker's question

Categories—never married
married, spouse present
married, spouse absent (divided into separated and others)
widowed
divorced

This sorting of the marital status variable is informative for social work and community nurse programs because it yields information about the proportions of elderly people whose family networks have been disrupted by separation, death, or divorce. Community planners might also be interested in our marital status definition 1 when they are deciding on size of dwelling units to be constructed.

All this may seem straightforward enough, even if a little complicated, but there are pitfalls for the unwary. You must be careful that your indicators truly reflect what you are after. If you want to know whether the community people are willing to have the group home, be sure not to ask some other question and report it "willing." For instance, you might ask, "Would you fight the establishment of a group home?" A person who says no is not necessarily "willing" to have the home. The response means only that the person does not intend to put up a fight.

Perhaps "willing" isn't precise enough to reflect community acceptance. You might want to ask different questions, possibly more than one. It's your job here to figure out what question will get the information you need. It's also up to you not to claim more or different information from the information you actually get.

Another important issue is whether or not your study achieves **internal validity**. Internal validity is the quality of accurate measurement of what you set out to measure. If you want to measure "acceptance" and you succeed in measuring "acceptance," you have got internal validity in your study. Internal validity is more difficult to achieve with some variables than with others. Asking people about concrete facts—such as, How many children do you have at home? or How old are you?—is quite a different matter from asking them, Are you happy? (In Chapter 7 we will discuss the problems of asking questions and getting answers when the variable presents problems of abstraction or sensitivity.) Description is enhanced and comparison made possible through accurate and precise measurement.

Kenneth Hoover presents a definition of operationalization that focuses on measurement,

> *To* operationalize *a variable means to put the variable in a form that permits some kind of measurement. . . . If it is done right, two conditions will be met: (1) the operational version fits the meaning of the original variable as closely as possible; (2) the measurement(s) indicated can be done accurately with available resources.*[9]

You can count instances of almost anything, but you cannot always assign a numerical value to things. Sometimes you can say that there is more or less of something or that it is higher or lower than something else. Most of the time you can say whether something is present or absent, always bearing in mind that you are talking about its manifestation rather than its existence, since existence cannot always be detected. (Many physical conditions, for example, exist before anyone is aware of their presence.) Occasionally, you are faced with something that can be measured exactly.

Given these variations in the describability of the world, you must pay attention to the types of data you intend to collect and decide what **levels of measurement** they are on. The four levels of measurement are nominal, ordinal, interval, and ratio.

TABLE 2.1　　　Appropriate summary operations for nominal, ordinal, interval, and ratio data

	Levels of Measurement			
Summarizing Operation	Nominal	Ordinal	Interval	Ratio
Sorting	X	X	X	X
Ranking		X	X	X
Equal spacing			X	X
Multiplying and dividing				X

S. S. Stevens defines measurement as the assignment of numbers according to rules.[10] This does not necessarily mean quantification. It always means identification as different categories. Let's look at the four levels and at Table 2.1, which illustrates our discussion.

Nominal Data　　*Nominal* means "consisting of a name," and a name is a label. **Nominal data** can be sorted into categories that are mutually exclusive. (You have already done that for your data during operationalization.) For example, the variable "political affiliation" is a nominal variable. It would be appropriate only for the first summarizing operation in Table 2.1: sorting. In our group home example, sex and type of resident are both nominal variables.

Ordinal Data　　*Ordinal* means "having a position in a numbered order." **Ordinal data** can be sorted, too, but they can also be put in order, or **ranked**. For example, "graduation honors earned" is an ordinal variable. You can not only sort, but as shown in Table 2.1, you can rank ordinal data as well:

1. Highest honors
2. High honors
3. Honors

Interval Data　　An interval is a space, and **interval data** are spaced equally. That means the distance from 1 to 2 is the same as the distance from 2 to 3, and so on. The variable intelligence quotient, or IQ, is an interval variable. It begins at some low score and ends at about 200. The lowest possible score, however, does not approach zero, because that would mean a person with such a score has no intelligence at all. Since you would have entered the range of the nonverbal people long before you got that low, you could not measure the score, if it exists. The highest level of measurement, which applies to anything that can be counted, weighed, or measured in exact amounts, beginning with zero, contains the advantage of equal spacing as well. This is the ratio level of measurement.

Ratio Data   If the categories of the variable include an absolute zero, the data are called **ratio data**. This means that you can not only add and subtract (as you can with interval) but multiply and divide. Having ratio data opens the possibility of doing statistical tests that require a ratio level. Income, years of education, height, weight, and number of people are all ratio variables.

You should be aware that you can "demote" your data from a high level of measurement to a lower one if you sort them in a way that destroys the requirements for the higher level. For example, the variable "age," which qualifies as a ratio variable, can be sorted as any of the four types:

1. Ratio—by equal periods of time, beginning with zero
2. Interval—by equal periods of time from any start other than zero
3. Ordinal—by unequal periods of time, from youngest to oldest, or the reverse
4. Nominal—by unequal periods of time, not in ascending or descending order

If you want to use age as a ratio or interval variable, watch those intervals. If you want to use it as an ordinal variable, be sure the order is there.

If you don't have fine enough distinctions when you record the data, you cannot make them later. That is one of the reasons for getting specific facts (What is your birth date?) rather than generalities (Are you old enough to vote?). One should measure as carefully and completely as possible, including everything relevant to the research hypothesis.

Another kind of validity with which you must be concerned is **external validity**. This is the representativeness and **generalizability** of your findings. For example, is what you conclude about group homes typical of group homes? Can you now speak of group homes in general as being the same as those you studied? If the answer to both these questions is yes, you have achieved external validity. Chapter 3 will deal with the matter of getting a representative group to study so that your result is generalizable.

If you succeed in achieving internal and external validity, you can be fairly confident that your project has reliability.

Reliability

If a project has reliability, it yields the same result each time the study is repeated. The more precise the definitions and indicators, the better the chance that you will achieve reliability for your project. An example of a research project with good reliability is the study of occupational prestige done by Robert W. Hodge, Paul M. Siegel, and Peter H. Rossi in 1947 and again in 1963.[11] People were asked to rank ninety occupations according to their prestige. Occupations were given scores according to the number of people ranking them in a given position, and the result was an overall ranking of occupations that reflected the consensus of opinion of the sample of people.

An important consideration in judging a project's reliability is the sample studied. If you interview leading community figures the first time and interview ordinary citizens the next time, the difference in perspective is likely to be great. This is not a fair test of the project's reliability. When we speak of reliability, we are assuming that the repeat study samples the same group.

Sometimes you may try to use variables that are not practical because you cannot get the information. This leads to a concern with feasibility.

Feasibility

Feasibility means capability of being done. Can what you want to study actually be studied? Can it be located? Is it **accessible**, or open, to your study? You have to limit yourself to things that can actually be counted or measured. Some variables are hard to supply with indicators. Many methodologists have developed tests, scales, and other strategies for getting responses for the more abstract variables such as emotions, personality traits, and attitudes. These strategies vary in difficulty and expense of implementation. They also vary in internal validity. After you have read the work of others and sought advice from more experienced hands, your judgment is your guide to the validity of these measures. You may even develop your own measures of abstract variables. If you use a measure that is commonly accepted, you probably do not have to justify its use; if you invent one, be prepared to defend it.

Feasibility depends mostly on the nature of the variable. For example, if you want to study ghosts, you can't make them appear when you want to see them and you can't measure them; therefore, you have to rely on reported appearances and other observers' descriptions. Some subjects, such as the seventeen-year locusts or Halley's comet, are available only at intervals. Feasibility also depends on your resources; the subject may be available but too expensive or too time-consuming to study.

Once you have considered all the requirements for operationalizing your hypothesis, you may decide that you are not prepared to test it yet; instead, you would like to do a study of the topic without a hypothesis. Research designs are available to you for preliminary projects. Let's look now at the major types, or modes of research, to see what they entail.

Selecting a Research Mode

The three main modes of research are exploratory, descriptive, and explanatory.[12] All are carried out according to the rules of the scientific method and the principles of research design, but they differ in requirements because their objectives are different (see Figure 2.3).

FIGURE 2.3   **Three modes of research**

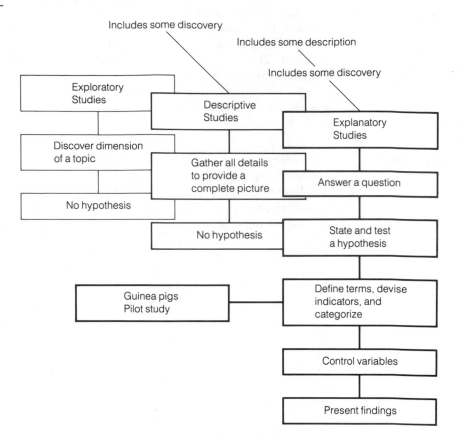

Major Research Modes

As you may recall from our discussion of the scope of research in the introduction to this book, there are three main types of research objective: discovery, classification, and detection. Perhaps, after reviewing the literature on a topic, developing a question and hypothesis, and trying to operationalize the hypothesis, you conclude that you don't really know enough about the topic to conduct an explanatory study. You may, of course, come to this conclusion earlier. You can do an exploratory study with the object of discovering the dimensions of a topic.

Exploratory Studies   Exploratory studies do not have a hypothesis because exploration of a topic itself is intended to provide enough orientation and information to enable the researcher to think of a suitable research question, which will *then* generate hypotheses. You do an exploratory study when you don't know anything about the subject but think you would like to understand it better. It is a preliminary step and implies that there will be more to follow. You do an exploratory study first when you are unsure in planning an explanatory study. Sometimes, because exploratory studies do not require rigorous sampling (and are never appropriate subjects for statistical tests), people call their projects "exploratory" to excuse the shortcomings of their sampling procedures. Do not fall into this error. Rather, follow the correct analytic procedure for the stage you are completing (see Chapter 3). The exploratory stage calls for written notes and comments to be read over and discussed; these materials are not to be subjected to statistical manipulation.

A good example of an exploratory study is "Children of Lesbians: Their Point of View" from the journal *Social Work*.[13] The investigator, Karen Gail Lewis, wondered how children might react when told that their mothers are lesbians and what impact the mother's lesbian relationship has on the children's lives. Since this subject has been written about so seldom, the researcher wisely decided to familiarize herself with it by conducting group interviews with the children. Based on her work, she or someone else can now do an explanatory study of this topic.[14] If an appropriate research question is not yet clear, one could precede the explanatory study with a descriptive one.

Descriptive Studies These differ from exploratory studies in that the researcher knows what variables are relevant to them. This type of project aims to gather all the details necessary to provide a complete picture of a specific group, activity, or situation. "Fact-finding" teams do descriptive studies. The United State Census Bureau does a descriptive study, and so do the various commercial poll-takers. No hypotheses are made here, although the researchers might well have notions about what they expect to find. Evelyn S. Newman and Susan R. Sherman's study of foster family (group home) care for the elderly is a good example of a careful descriptive study.[15] The authors reviewed the extensive literature on public attitudes toward the mentally ill and toward aging. They included 100 homes in their sample and interviewed the caretakers in depth to find out the demographic characteristics of caretakers and residents, the relationships of the homes with the sponsoring agencies, the "family nature" of the homes, and the extent of the residents' community integration. So far, their work has resulted in a number of informative articles. Their report not only contributes to the clinical practice and fieldwork in gerontology, it provides a good foundation for further research.[16]

Although we have, so far, focused mainly on the development of an explanatory study and devoted most of this chapter to this type, let's consider again the general nature of such a study and try another example. You must familiarize yourself with explanatory studies because this is what you will be doing for most of your exercises and projects.

Explanatory Studies As we have seen, an explanatory study is one that is planned to detect something about the world so as to answer a question. We do this by framing a hypothesis and testing it empirically. Because new questions are suggested, explanatory studies include exploration, and because careful specification of the people, situations, and territory studied is part of every report, explanatory studies include description. But the explanatory study also addresses the complicated and tricky issue of causation and requires procedures more elaborate than exploration or description. Hypotheses are stated and carefully tested. Statistical tests may be used if the sampling methods justify them.

The difference between explanatory research and the other types is not that more care is exercised, but that more steps are carried out. Rigor and scrupulous care should be characteristic of all research.

Let's assume you are studying **reference groups**, that is, groups that provide standards for behavior. Many professionals find this topic of interest. (Psychotherapists in an adolescent and young-adult treatment center, for example, might be focusing on the behavioral changes that accompany a young person's physical separation from the family.) You have considered reference group theory and are interested in the relative influence of reference groups such as one's family versus one's peers. You wonder whether parental influence diminishes in matters of basic importance when children grow up and leave home, and you think that since parents usually choose the child's religion, allegiance to one's childhood religion might be one of the things you could study to discover changes in parental influence.

Reasoning deductively, you decide that, if parents and peers represent competing reference groups and if we are apt to meet the expectations of those we are with, then when children grow up and leave home, they may be less loyal to their parents' wishes. They will probably be surrounded by people of different religions, who will not share the parental choice.

You could develop a number of research questions from this idea. You could ask, for example, whether religious belief diminishes when young people leave home, whether religious identification is less, or whether they go to services less often. Assume that you are going to confine yourself to the third question. Does attendance at religious services decrease when young people leave home? From this question you can easily frame a hypothesis:

Hyp. 1. Attendance at religious services decreases when young people leave home.

But wait. Whose attendance? How are you going to operationalize that? You are hypothesizing about a change in behavior. Is this feasible? Can you find out about your subjects' attendance before they left? It is much easier for a person to tell you what he or she is doing now than to recall the past.[17] Perhaps the question and hypothesis can be restated.

The revised question can be, Do young people living away from home go to services less frequently than young people still living at home? This would lead to the following hypothesis:

Hyp. 1. Young people living away from home will have lower rates of attendance at religious services than young people living at home.

Your independent variable is residence. Your dependent variable is attendance at religious services. The next thing to do is list the variables and their definitions and develop indicators for them. You also have to define your subjects. What do you mean by "young people"? For that matter, what do you mean by "home"?

Your definitions of young people and home will limit your sample and therefore the generalizability of your result. Let's look at what we have so far:

Young people—people from 18 to 25 years of age

Residence—location at which the person is living full-time, including weekends

Home—the residence at which the person's parent(s) live and where he or she lived as child of the parent(s)

Attendance at religious services—going to a place of worship or communion of the same religious group chosen by the parents for the person when he or she was a child

Leaving home—taking up residence away from home for at least 3 months

Notice that a number of decisions have been made in the preceding list: the age of "young people," the specification of weekend residence, the time period for leaving home. This may seem cumbersome, but having detailed descriptions of variables and indicators saves problems later when you are classifying and sorting responses.

To do this project, you need four pieces of data from each person: age, residence, attendance at services, and (if away from home) length of time away from home. You have to develop indicators and a simple questionnaire.

When you have decided on the indicators, you should think about the categories for sorting the responses. Some of them are self-evident. To harmonize with your hypothesis, "residence" can be sorted into two categories: at home and away. "Attendance at religious services" can be shortened to "church attendance," if you note somewhere that "church" includes any house of worship or communion so as to include establishments such as synagogues or black Muslim mosques. Next you have a problem because you don't know what the range of attendance might be. Every day? Once a week? Once a month? Easter Sunday only?

This illustrates why researchers test their variable indicators before conducting the main study. This is done in two ways: The researcher can experiment with questions and other data collection techniques on a few "guinea pigs" to expose obvious problems, or the researcher can run a small-scale

TABLE 2.2   **Church attendance by residence, 18–25-year-olds, whole sample (*N* = 575)**

| | Residence | | | | | |
| Church Attendance* | At Home | | Away | | Total | |
	No.	%	No.	%	No.	%
At least once weekly	149	60	208	64	357	62
At least once monthly	62	25	68	21	130	23
At least once yearly	39	16	49	15	88	15
Total	250	101†	325	100	575	100

* Respondents classified once each, in highest relevant attendance category.
†Rounded percentages.

version of the study, called a **pilot study**, to work out the problems in the design. Pilot studies will be discussed again in Chapter 4.

One possible categorization of church attendance is illustrated in Table 2.2: at least once weekly, at least once monthly, and at least once yearly. Constructed after the data have been collected, the table does not have any cases of "not at all" because, in this hypothetical example, there weren't any. Of course, you would include that category if there were instances of nonattendance. If you interviewed a lot of people who never went to church at all, you might sort them as "attenders" and "nonattenders" instead of indicating minimum frequency as has been done for Table 2.2.

There are rules for adding up the data and presenting them in table form (see Figure 2.4). For now, notice that the columns and rows are labeled clearly and end with totals and that the table as a whole has a title that explains what is being presented and for whom. "*N*" means number of cases. Also notice that percentages of each independent variable category are listed beside the column for the actual frequencies. A **frequency** is the number of times a thing is observed. Two things are important here. You always calculate the percentage using the total of the independent variable's category as a base. If you say that of all those in the sample living at home, 60 percent attend church at least once weekly, you are suggesting that living at home is causative. However, if you say that of all those attending church at least once weekly, 42 percent are living at home, you are implying that attending church may influence one's choice of residence. Your hypothesis didn't say that; you would have to do another study, using church attendance as the independent variable.

You are looking at one residence category at a time to see whether church attendance varies between them. You can think of the categories of the independent variable as separate boxes, which you open and inspect, one by one, recording the list of items inside in a column with the box's name at the top. One series of boxes for "at homes," another for "aways." Use any memory

FIGURE 2.4   Presenting data in tabular form

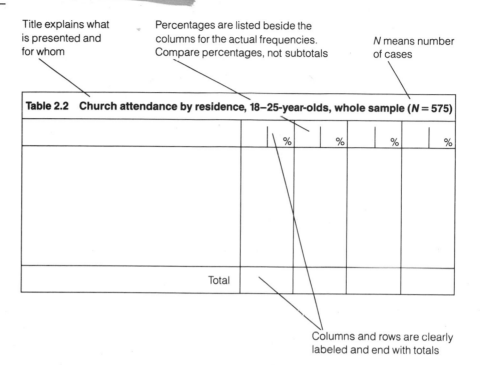

Title explains what is presented and for whom

Percentages are listed beside the columns for the actual frequencies. Compare percentages, not subtotals

N means number of cases

Table 2.2   **Church attendance by residence, 18–25-year-olds, whole sample (*N* = 575)**

Columns and rows are clearly labeled and end with totals

device that is comfortable for you, but remember to base the percentages on the categories of the independent variable.

Also remember that you can use any variable as an independent, a dependent, or a control variable in another study. Our assignments of variables to independent, dependent, and control status are for the duration of the project only. Whenever you want to use a variable in a different way, you have to begin again. If you examine the current data and formulate questions for the current study from it, you are anticipating, or setting up, the results. You have eliminated the possibility of using probability testing on your results because you have removed the possibility of negative findings. You've begun with the answer and made up a question to fit it. In research, the "Monday morning quarterbacks" have to go out and play a new game to test their ideas.

The other important point about reading a table is that you compare percentages, not the numbers or subtotals. Look at the first line (row) in Table 2.2, which represents people who attend church at least once weekly. If you compared numbers, you might conclude that people away from home are more likely to attend church weekly than people still at home. This comparison is misleading and the conclusion wrong because the total numbers are not the same. There are fewer total people in the "at home" category than in the "away" category. In fact, the percentages for the two groups in

TABLE 2.3   Church attendance by residence, 18–25-year-olds, females only (*N* = 316)

Church Attendance	At Home No.	At Home %	Away No.	Away %	Total No.	Total %
At least once weekly	81	59	143	80	224	71
At least once monthly	34	25	31	17	65	21
At least once yearly	22	16	5	3	27	9
Total	137	100	179	100	316	101*

*Rounded percentages.

the once-a-week church-attending category are about the same: 60 and 64 percent.

Since our original question about change was more difficult to operationalize, we changed the question and hypothesis to enhance internal validity and to make the study more reliable. Now we'll check for feasibility. Will people be offended by the questions we are going to ask? Given the age range of our potential subjects, there probably won't be any problem. Young people are not generally sensitive about answering any of the questions we intend to ask.

The final consideration is whether you want to introduce a control variable and if so, what it might be. If you decide to do this, you have to define the variable, decide on an indicator for it, and decide what its categories will be. For example, suppose you decide that sex might make a difference in what happens to religious practice when young people leave home. Assuming that you are thinking of gender identity, the variable will have two categories, male and female, and the indicator will be either a question for the respondent to answer on the questionnaire or one for the interviewer to check during an interview.

When testing your hypothesis and controlling for sex, you do not change the juxtaposition of the independent and dependent variables. You either divide the sample into the two sex categories and organize the data into two separate tables identical in form to the one for the whole sample, or you subdivide the categories of the independent variable into male and female (see Tables 2.3 to 2.5). When you have done this, you can say whether the hypothesis is or is not confirmed for each sex, as well as for the whole sample.

In the example given, the tables are hypothetical, but they approximate the results of a project done several years ago by one of my research students. The numbers are fictitious, but the relationship parallels what the student found. Notice how enlightening the use of a control variable can be. For females, being away from home seemed to have an effect opposite to that indicated for males. Your hypothesis is confirmed for the males but not for

TABLE 2.4   Church attendance by residence, 18–25-year-olds, males only (*N* = 259)

Church Attendance	Residence					
	At Home		Away		Total	
	No.	%	No.	%	No.	%
At least once weekly	68	60	65	45	133	51
At least once monthly	28	25	37	26	65	25
At least once yearly	17	15	44	30	61	24
Total	113	100	146	100	259	100

the females. Had you not controlled for sex, you would have missed this difference and would have concluded that young people living at home and away from home do not differ in frequency of church attendance.

Bear in mind that your finding, if you got a result like our hypothetical one, would not tell you why males and females differ. Nor could you generalize beyond your sampled group. The student who did a project similar to the one just outlined was greatly intrigued by the result and made a number of speculations about the reasons for the pattern. He did not, of course, claim to have any evidence for these speculations and clearly labeled his opinions as educated guesses. Since he got his sample from the student body of a college, his results could be generalized only to that group. It said nothing about people who do not go to college. For all we know, their patterns would be quite different. Good research typically raises questions that can be answered by the next project or two.

We have so far discussed the requirements of the three main research modes but have not gone into the issue of the choice of research design. Let's consider this briefly.

Types of Design

Regardless of the research mode appropriate to the stage of your project, you have a wide choice of research designs. You can collect data by observing behavior, asking questions, or analyzing records or **circumstantial evidence**. This is data that lead you to believe something has happened but do not offer conclusive proof of it. You can use data already collected for some other purpose, or you can reanalyze data already collected on your question. Your decision on design and techniques will be based on your general theoretical framework, your preference, your resources, and possibly the opinions of others. Part II of this book provides you with detailed instructions and advice for the various kinds of data collection currently in use.

Before you tackle those chapters, you must consider the important issues of sampling and resources, because both are going to have a decisive influence on the rest of your work. In Chapter 3 we shall look at sampling.

TABLE 2.5   Church attendance by residence and sex, 18–25-year-olds, percentages only (*N* = 575)

Church Attendance	At Home		Away		Total	
	M	**F**	**M**	**F**	**M**	**F**
At least once weekly	60	59	45	80	51	71
At least once monthly	25	25	25	17	25	21
At least once yearly	15	16	30	3	24	9
Total	100	100	100	100	100	101*

*Rounded percentages.

Summary and Conclusion

Every research project needs a specific goal. A goal is selected that will harmonize with the body of published work by contributing knowledge to advance the frontier of knowledge. Once an area has been chosen and a question asked, a hypothesis about the world is devised and plans are made to operationalize it so that the work may be completed.

To arrive at the point of decision on a research design suitable to the endeavor, the researcher must become familiar with existing work, study and formulate a logical inquiry and hypothetical prediction, and evaluate the indicators devised to collect the data. This requires attention to the level of measurement appropriate to the data one will collect. Data are classified into levels of measurement called nominal, ordinal, interval, and ratio; these levels permit manipulations of varying complexity. If your data are on the lowest level, you cannot manipulate them in ways appropriate to any of the higher levels, and so on. In order of complexity, the manipulations are sorting, ranking, spacing equally, and computing.

Care must be taken to ensure that the project has internal and external validity, reliability, and feasibility. If the project lacks these things, the researcher must decide whether it is appropriate to choose an exploratory or descriptive approach rather than an explanatory one.

Main Points

1. Every project must have a specific goal. This is usually in the form of a question to be answered.

2. Planning is essential for efficiency and clarity. The first step is to choose an area of interest, bearing in mind continuity, relevance, and contribution. Pitfalls to be avoided are plagiarism, redundancy, and inefficiency.

3. A comprehensive review of the literature is necessary and will help you narrow the topic and devise a question. Following the choice of a question, the second phase of library research consists of a review that is at once narrower in scope and deeper in purpose than the first review. The second review covers all the work on the relationships contained in the question chosen.

4. Questions result from logical reasoning, which is either inductive (from experience to theory) or deductive (from theory to experience).

5. A hypothesis is a statement about the relationship predicted between or among variables. It should be brief, simple, and direct. A hypothesis includes the idea of causality: that is, the notion that one thing is the stimulus and another thing responds.

6. The independent variable is regarded as causal for the duration of the project, the control variable is regarded as influential, and the dependent variable is regarded as the effect.

7. Each concept, including the variables, must be defined, and the variables must be categorized. Defining terms and devising indicators is called operationalization. Operationalization turns the hypothesis into a data collection plan. An indicator is a description of the actual information to be collected. You must decide what summarizing operations you can use. These will depend on the level of measurement of your data.

8. Nominal variables can only be sorted. Ordinal variables can be sorted and ranked. Interval variables can be sorted, ranked, and equally spaced. Ratio variables can be sorted, ranked, equally spaced, and arithmetically manipulated. There are no exceptions to these restrictions.

9. Definitions developed are not theoretical definitions but are called operational, which means that they are specific to the present study and its implementation.

10. The project should have reliability, the quality of being consistent when the project is repeated.

11. The project should have feasibility, the quality of being possible with reasonable cost and effort.

12. If you find that your information is insufficient to permit planning an explanatory study, you can begin with an exploratory study to discover more about your chosen area or with a descriptive study to record and classify its dimensions. Neither of these modes of research requires a hypothesis. Both are merely preliminary to a real explanatory study.

Notes

1. I have been called in to "save" two ill-planned projects. In both cases I had to explain to the disappointed researchers that much of what they had hoped to do with their data was impossible because they hadn't planned well.

2. A good source is Pauline Bart and Linda Frankel, *The Student Sociologist's Handbook*, 3rd ed. (Morristown, N.J.: General Learning Press, 1980).

3. Pitirim Sorokin, *Fads and Foibles in Modern Sociology* (Chicago: Regnery, 1956), pp. 3–16.

4. E. P. Hutchinson, *The Population Debate* (Boston: Houghton Mifflin, 1967), p. 3.

5. Charles H. Stember, *Sexual Racism* (New York: Elsevier, 1976).

6. This idea is central to labeling theory and to the methodological problems of interviewer effect and demand characteristics.

7. June True (Albert), "The Sexual Basis of White Resistance to Racial Integration." Unpublished Ph.D. dissertation, Rutgers University, 1972.

8. Beth J. Soldo, "America's Elderly in the 1980s," *Population Bulletin* 35: 1980, p. 25.

9. Kenneth Hoover, *The Elements of Social Scientific Thinking*, 2nd ed. (New York: St. Martin's Press, 1980), p. 53.

10. S. S. Stevens, "On the Theory of Scales of Measurement," *Science* 103 (7 June 1946): 677–80. See also his "Mathematics, Measurement and Psychophysics," in *Handbook of Experimental Psychology*, ed. S. S. Stevens (New York: Wiley, 1951), pp. 1–49.

11. Robert W. Hodge, Paul M. Siegel, and Peter H. Rossi, "Occupational Prestige in the United States: 1925–1963," *American Journal of Sociology* 70 (November 1964): 286–302.

12. Earl R. Babbie, *The Practice of Social Research*, 2nd ed. (Belmont, Calif.: Wadsworth, 1979), pp. 84–87.

13. Karen Gail Lewis, "Children of Lesbians: Their Point of View," *Social Work* 25, no. 3 (May 1980): 198–203.

14. Lewis found that the children had difficulty expressing their feelings about their mother's orientation and partner but that they were essentially supportive of their mother and respectful of her courage. Lewis concludes that love and security are more important to children than their parents' lifestyles.

15. Evelyn S. Newman and Susan R. Sherman, "Community Integration of the Elderly in Foster Family Care," *Journal of Gerontological Social Work* 1, no. 3 (Spring 1979): 175–86.

16. Newman and Sherman discovered that more than three-quarters of the 234 elderly subjects in foster family care had met neighbors, one-third took walks in the neighborhood, and two-fifths had visited people. The authors give a detailed description of the homes.

17. Ranjan Kumar Som, *Recall Lapse in Demographic Inquiries* (New York: Asia Publishing House, 1973), pp. 49, 60.

18. William Spinrad, "When Integration Works," in *Interracial Bonds*, ed. Rhoda G. Blumberg and Wendell Roye (New York: General Hall, 1979), p. 101.

Exercises

The following exercises give you some practice in framing a research question and hypothesis, and in operationalizing the variables you use. Exercise 2.1 begins the process by asking you to choose an area and develop a question about it and a hypothesis for the question. In Exercise 2.2 you are asked to list the pieces of data you would have to get to test the hypothesis, and then to identify the independent, dependent, and control variables and devise indicators for them. For both these exercises you can use the examples as they were worked out in the chapter.

Exercise 2.3 provides a chance for you to apply your new skills by evaluating published material.

Exercise 2.1   *Specifying a question and framing a hypothesis*

Instructions: Select an area of social organization from the following list:

intergroup relations   marriage and family
community organization   deviance and control
social class   formal organizations

1.   Enter your choice here.

2.   Think of possible problems in your chosen area and write two of them.

3.   Select one of the preceding problems and frame a research question relevant to it.

4.   Form a hypothesis from the preceding question.

EXAMPLE: Area—community organization
             Problems—changing neighborhoods (chose this one)
             —quality of schools

QUESTION: When does the "tipping point" occur in a changing neighborhood? (A tipping point is the time when most newcomers belong to the new group and the area slowly becomes their province.)[18]

HYPOTHESIS: The tipping point in a changing neighborhood occurs when the originally dominant group has been reduced to two-thirds of the population.

DATA NEEDED: Group composition of the neighborhood for several successive years.

Group membership and proportions for those moving in or out of it for the same years.

Exercise 2.2   ## *Operationalizing the variables*

Instructions: Write your question and hypothesis from Exercise 2.1 here.

Question:

Hypothesis:

Answer the following questions:

1. What pieces of data do you need before you can test the hypothesis?

2. What is your independent variable?

3. Define it.

4. What are its categories (divisions)*?

5. What indicator** will you use to collect data for it?

6. What is your dependent variable?

7. Define it.

8. What are its categories (divisions)*?

9. What indicator** will you use to collect data for it?

10. Select one control variable and write it here.

11. Define it.

12. What are its categories (divisions)*?

13. What indicator** will you use to collect data for it?

14. Using Table 2.4 as a model, design a dummy table for your variables.

---

*For example, the variable age can be divided in several ways.
**An indicator is the exact information you will collect (see the discussion of these terms in the chapter section "Indicators").

Exercise 2.3   *Critique*

Instructions: Choose a research report from any professional journal and read it. Answer the following questions as concisely as possible, giving a full citation* here:

_____

_____

1.   What is the area of interest?

2.   What is the problem chosen to investigate in that area?

3.   What is the specific research question?

4.   What is the hypothesis? (Pick one if there are more than one.)

5.   What pieces of data would test this hypothesis?

_____

*A proper citation includes the author's name (last first), title of work, source of article, publisher, date, page numbers. See a standard manual of style. Any college book store or library has them. The bibliography of this book is a list of such citations.

6. What indicators did the author(s) use?

7. Did they find the data you listed in Question 5?

8. Criticize the project you read.

CHAPTER 3

The Sample and Significance

This chapter will show you how to draw an adequate sample for your research design so that your results reflect the population you intended to study and not some other group. We'll begin by examining the concept of population so that we may understand the concept of sampling it. Next we'll look at the actual techniques of sampling, both random and nonrandom, and the number and timing of samples. Finally, we shall discuss how to choose the sampling technique appropriate to your needs.

The Sample

In Chapter 1, you learned about the danger of overgeneralization, or not looking into a matter far enough to get a complete picture and then making illogical conclusions on the basis of too little evidence. To avoid this mistake, you establish limits to the generalizability of your study by deciding in advance what population you wish to investigate and taking a sample of it in such a way that you can be confident of its typicality. As a first step in learning this procedure we'll consider the definition of a population and a sample and look at some basic factors involved in choosing samples.

Populations and Their Samples

In Chapter 2, when we talked about definitions, we were describing the process of enumerating *what* is included in the term used. Now we are going to talk about definitions that indicate *who* is included in the terms used, the two terms being **population** and **sample**.

The Definition of a Population   Most of the time the word *population* refers to the people contained in a specific geographic area such as a nation, continent, city, or other political division. Another use of the word indicates the number of people residing in an institution, as in the sentence, "Our population is up to 3000 this month." (Some officials might use the word *census* instead. Both uses of the word *population* imply that the people under consideration are all in the same area.) In this book we use "population" in one of its other senses. For us, a population doesn't have to be contained in a particular area. It might be all in the same place, but that is not what we require. For us, a population is a number of people or items all in the same category. For each study we specify the category, and our specifications draw the limits, or **parameters**, that describe our population.

When we have specified who is included in our study population, we consider how to draw a sample from it, but in no case can we generalize from our sample to any group other than the population we specified. To do so would be overgeneralization and would be invalid. As mentioned in the discussion of indicators in Chapter 2, we need to establish external validity, the representativeness and generalizability of our findings. We do this by random sampling (discussed in the second section of this chapter) and by conservative analysis, which means almost the reverse of overgeneralization. (When we take pains not to apply any result outside the boundaries of the population sampled, we have used conservative analysis.)

Suppose you set out to compare young people who leave home with young people who remain home. You define "young people" as those between the ages of 18 and 25, as we did in the study used as an example in Chapter 2. Defining your population as "young people between the ages of 18 and 25" would leave you with much too large a group to study. It would imply all persons aged 18 to 25 in the world. "*American* young people between the ages of 18 and 25" would be better, but it is still too broad, unless you have the resources of the United States Census Bureau.

You might narrow your population until you are talking about "persons aged 18 to 25 attending college in Iowa." This is fine. Your population is defined. You then obtain a sample of the population and study it. Assuming your sample is valid (see the following section), your results can be generalized only to the population of 18 to 25 year old college students in Iowa. You cannot apply your findings to anyone under 18 or over 25, anyone not a college student, or anyone not in Iowa. You have not sampled anyone outside this group.

Limiting your application to the population sampled doesn't mean that the study is useless to people interested in the general population. Your results can be compared to findings on other populations and can suggest new theories, techniques, and questions. It would be a definite contribution to behavioral science. The rule to remember is, *You can draw conclusions about the population you sampled and no other.* Since you don't want to limit the application of your results any further than you have to, you must make sure that the sample you get really represents the population sampled. First, let's consider what a sample is.

Sampling from a Population   This isn't really new to you. Sampling to form an opinion of a larger number of items is familiar. Merchants distribute samples of their product to encourage sales. Prospective employees present samples of their work to interviewers to demonstrate their skills. Contractors direct potential customers to jobs recently completed so the customer can judge the quality of the work. These are all samples, but they are **biased**, or distorted samples. They don't represent the full range of the whole population of items of which they are a sample. They have been selected to give a good impression.

Our goal is not to get a sample of the best, nor of the worst. Our goal is to get a representative sample—a sample that gives a small picture that includes some of everything in the large picture and has everything in the same proportion as in the large picture. For us, a sample is not just a part of the thing we are studying; it is an accurate *miniature* of the thing we are studying: If we don't get a typical selection with a complete range, we can't claim that our sample is sufficient to represent the whole population.

You've often encountered this challenge. Each time you see someone, your memory registers an instance of appearance and behavior. Automatically storing up these memories, you weigh and measure them so that you can reach conclusions about that person. When you reserve final judgment because you don't feel you've had enough experience or contact with someone to form a fair opinion, you're trying to get a sample of the full range of possible impressions of that person.

Some populations are easier to sample than others. This is because some populations consist of people or items that are uniform and some populations vary a lot. We refer to these two types of composition as homogeneity and heterogeneity.

Homogeneity and Heterogeneity

Homogeneity means being uniform in structure or composition. Something that is homogeneous is the same all the way through. The first glass from a bottle of homogenized milk has the same butterfat content as the last glass because the milk has been put through a process that distributes the butterfat evenly. **Heterogeneity** means being varied in structure or composition. Human populations are heterogeneous when they have a number of subcultures, several languages, many religious groups, and so on. A group might be homogeneous with respect to some things and heterogeneous with respect to others, as in the case of a biracial, multilingual, coed nursery school for diplomats' children.

If you are sampling a homogeneous population, any part of it is sufficient to represent all of it. However, you rarely find such a population because true homegeneity becomes less likely as the population gets larger. Even homogenized milk varies from bottle to bottle due to storage conditions and age. When you are studying human beings, you need to assume heterogeneity because there are so many sources of variation. Your sampling problem is how to draw a sample that reflects the typical and important variations in your population. Before we turn to the established ways of selecting a sample, however, we should think about the sources of bias that we must take care to avoid.

Sources of Bias

The sources of bias are both within ourselves and in the outside world. First, we have to watch out for the pitfalls mentioned earlier: selective perception and group identity. Second, we have to watch out for unrecognized patterns of movement and settlement that may influence our selection.

It is demonstrable that anyone who approaches strangers in a haphazard or unplanned manner will veer away from people who are frightening, dirty, apparently unreceptive, or unlike the seeker. I have sent many students out to gather interviews for practice in fieldwork. Unless they are required to do otherwise, they invariably come back with interviews of people comparable to themselves in age, sex, race, and social class. One enterprising student went to a busy terminal in a decidedly lower-class neighborhood in New York City. He returned complaining that all he had been able to find in that area were "middle-class people." The reader may recognize the operation of selective perception here. If not, read David Karp on his observations of the same neighborhood; this description will show you what my student missed. [1]

We have to be especially careful about bias if we're collecting data from written records or other historical material. History is written by the victors and they write it from their own perspective but don't add the views of the losers. Think of the history lessons about slavery presented in American schools for decades. We had to wait until recent years to learn about black people's experience, achievements, and inventions. The same is true of women's viewpoints and contributions. Recorders of events are an unrepresentative sample of their societies and their biases must be carefully considered by anyone who uses their material as a source of data.

In addition to selective perception and personal preference resulting from group identity, bias may come from patterns in the accessibility of the subjects. Consider the use of a public park. Anyone studying the park's users would be better off knowing the effects of the day, the hour, and the weather on the presence of children, mothers with babies, whole families, old people, muggers, joggers, or vendors. There may be an ethnic celebration attracting large numbers of a particular group. There may be a demonstration scheduled. There may be a free concert.

We can think of external validity as a way of making sure that our findings are valid outside the sample and all the way to the limits of our population. We do this by seeing that all variations in our chosen population have a chance to be represented in the sample. If we succeed in this, we avoid bias and are able to generalize from the sample to the population. There are a number of ways to achieve this. We'll consider them one by one.

Techniques of Sampling

The major types of sampling are random, which gives each unit an equal chance to be chosen, and nonrandom, which deliberately selects specific units. These two major types are further subdivided. The variations of random sampling are simple random sampling, stratified random sampling, systematic random sampling, and multistage (cluster or area) random sampling. Simple random sampling is designed to give each individual an equal chance

FIGURE 3.1   **Sampling techniques**

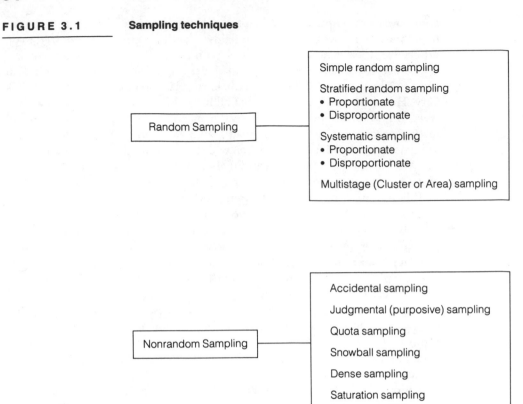

Random Sampling
- Simple random sampling
- Stratified random sampling
  - Proportionate
  - Disproportionate
- Systematic sampling
  - Proportionate
  - Disproportionate
- Multistage (Cluster or Area) sampling

Nonrandom Sampling
- Accidental sampling
- Judgmental (purposive) sampling
- Quota sampling
- Snowball sampling
- Dense sampling
- Saturation sampling

to be chosen; stratified random sampling is designed to give each relevant category an equal chance to be represented, and *within* each category individuals have an equal chance to be chosen. Systematic and multistage random sampling are variations on the mechanics of choosing subjects.

The six variations of nonrandom sampling are accidental, judgmental, quota, snowball, dense, and saturation. The first three are subjective selections for exploratory designs; the second three are selection processes aimed at covering an entire network or population (see Figure 3.1).

Random Sampling

A **random sample** of a population is one for which each unit of that population has an equal chance to be selected. This is a special use of the word *random*. In other contexts the word may mean erratic, haphazard, or unsystematic; here it means an unbiased choice of equally likely units from a larger group of such units. It is a kind of lottery, similar to a bingo game. In a bingo game, if you put all the numbers into a revolving drum and mix them up, each number theoretically has the same chance as every other number of being

TABLE 3.1   **A numbered list: Participants in a 1980 baseball game**

Chicago Cubs	Atlanta Braves
1. Dejesus	17. Royster
2. Randle	18. Ramirez
3. Kelleher	19. Matthews
4. Buckner	20. Horner
5. Kingman	21. Gomez
6. Sutter	22. Chambliss
7. Reuschel	23. Murphy
8. Tidrow	24. Hubbard
9. Johnson	25. Benedict
10. Martin	26. Boggs
11. Blackwell	27. Bradford
12. Tyson	28. Camp
13. Biitner	29. Pocoroba
14. Dillard	30. Garber
15. Lamp	31. Lum
16. Figueroa	32. Niekro

chosen. All games of chance are supposed to be run to ensure an unbiased choice of numbers.

If you select at random, you are very likely to get a sample that is typical of the whole population, and then you can generalize from it to that whole population. When you are sampling human beings, your problem is how to mix them up and pick from them. You cannot throw them into a revolving drum! Fortunately, there is a good solution to this problem. If you assign a number to each person, you can sample the numbers and create a list of numbers to use for the sample. Then you need only locate on your original list the people who were assigned the particular numbers you drew. During conscription, the government used this system to draft soldiers. Instead of assigning numbers to the men, however, they sampled birth dates for the eligible men and called up all men born on the dates selected. The original list of people in a specific population is called a **sampling frame**.

Let's try sampling randomly from a short list to clarify the technique and a few of its variations.

Simple Random Sampling   Table 3.1 lists baseball players who played in a close game between two low-ranking teams in the 1980 baseball season. The teams were the Atlanta Braves and the Chicago Cubs. The game ran eleven innings, and the score was Atlanta 5, Chicago 4. In the last inning Atlanta's manager used a relief pitcher who was 41 years old. Suppose you want to interview a random sample of the players who participated in this game to see what they thought of the Atlanta manager's decision to use such an old athlete in a tight situation.

First, you would assign a number to each player on the list. This number appears to the left of each name in Table 3.1. Next, you must decide how many men to interview. How large a sample do you need? There is no rigid rule for determining sample size. The number depends on the question and on the research design. If you want to compare players' attitudes (dependent variable) using their team membership as your independent variable, you need enough men to divide into at least four groups: Braves approving the decision; Braves disapproving; Cubs approving; Cubs disapproving. If you take a 10 percent sample, you get 3 or 4 men; 10 percent is 3.2 men, and you have to round this fraction. Having only 3 men is clearly undesirable, since one of the four theoretical outcomes could not be represented. Having 4 men in your sample avoids this problem, but most of us aren't comfortable working with so few. In general, the smaller the population, the higher the percentage that seems adequate. If you are sampling the opinions of 10 people, you would probably want about half of them, or 50 percent; if you are sampling the opinions of 10,000 people, 10 percent would certainly do. It is currently accepted that for very large populations a random sample of 1000 will suffice, even though it will be less than 10 percent.[2]

It is possible to calculate the representativeness of samples of specific sizes regardless of the size of the population from which they are drawn. (See next section, Sampling Error and Confidence Level.)

Let's say you want to choose a 25 percent sample of the baseball players, or 8 men. This many will serve to illustrate the technique. Turn to the table of random numbers (Appendix A). You are going to need eight two-digit numbers, ranging from 01 to 32. You add a zero in front of each single-digit number to make it possible to choose systematically. Begin anywhere in the table and proceed in any direction, noting down two digits at a time as you come to them, until you have eight such pairs. If you begin with the last two digits in the last column at the top of the first page of the table and proceed down the page, noting the last two digits in each line you have 00, 05, 29, 79, 13 in the first group of rows; 80, 52, 07, 41, 52 in the second group; 88, 22, 52, 68, 07 in the third; 19, 57, 51, 49, 04 in the fourth; 12, 92, 51, 10, 53 in the fifth. Examine them carefully. For your purpose, 00 is of no use, nor is any number above 32. This reduces your list immediately to 05, 29, 13, 07, 22, 07, 19, 04, 12, 10. Another look reveals that 07 appears twice, so you strike one of them out. You cannot interview the same person twice unless you're doing a special kind of study, which will be discussed later in this chapter.

You are going to use the first eight numbers you picked: 5, 29, 13, 7, 22, 19, 4, 12. If it should prove impossible to interview one of the men in your sample, the best you can do is to use the next random number you chose: 10. If more than one man in your sample is unavailable, you must take up again where you left off in the table and keep selecting numbers until you get a usable one. Now refer to Table 3.1 and see who is in your sample.

Cubs	Braves
4. Buckner	19. Matthews
5. Kingman	22. Chambliss
7. Reuschel	29. Pocoroba
12. Tyson	
13. Biitner	

You now have a random sample of players from the game in question.

You might feel that your sample is lopsided. You have a genuine random sample, but you have more players from one team than from the other. Your population consists of two teams that are equal in size, having sixteen players each. If you decide that it is desirable for the teams to be equally represented in your sample, you can arrange it by randomly sampling from each team separately, using a technique called **stratified random sampling**.

Stratified Random Sampling   You begin by renumbering the Braves from 1 to 16. Then go back to the table of random numbers and select four numbers, using the same method as before. Now you must eliminate any number that is over 16. If you begin in the same place as before, you get 5, 13, 7, and 4 for the Cubs, or Kingman, Biitner, Reuschel, and Buckner. Continuing to sample in the same area of the table (although you don't have to) gives you 12, 10, 6, and 1 for the Braves, or Camp, Boggs, Chambliss, and Royster. Note that if a number that had been selected for the Cubs also comes up for the Braves, that would be acceptable; the groups are being sampled separately, and duplication of a number on the second team does not mean an individual will be interviewed twice.

Sometimes the population you are sampling has a known minority that is so small you might not get very many representatives of it in a random sample. Our baseball player population has such a minority: Hispanic players.

If the known minority is not important to your question, you can ignore it. For example, if you sample a population of community residents that includes a small percentage of vegetarians and your question concerns attitudes toward income tax revisions, you might very well not care whether you have a representative number of vegetarians in your sample. However, if your question concerns the marketing possibilities for some new kind of foodstuff, you would want to make sure the vegetarian opinion is represented.

TABLE 3.2   **Proportions in a random sample: Baseball players by Hispanic or non-Hispanic names**

Hispanics	Non-Hispanics	
1. Dejesus	1. Randle	15. Royster
2. Figueroa	2. Kelleher	16. Matthews
3. Ramirez	3. Buckner	17. Horner
4. Gomez	4. Kingman	18. Chambliss
5. Pocoroba	5. Sutter	19. Murphy
	6. Reuschel	20. Hubbard
	7. Tidrow	21. Benedict
	8. Johnson	22. Boggs
	9. Martin	23. Bradford
	10. Blackwell	24. Camp
	11. Tyson	25. Garber
	12. Biitner	26. Lum
	13. Dillard	27. Niekro
	14. Lamp	

Proportions in the Sample   To ensure a minority a place in the sample, you have to use one of several techniques. If the limits of the minority are known and you can arrange to sample from them separately, you can use random sampling techniques to get either a proportionate or a disproportionate sample of them for your larger sample. When you don't know their exact location, you can **balloon the sample**—to do this take additional random samples of the same population until you have enough members of the minority, discarding the other subjects in the extra samples. Ballooning is cumbersome and costly.

Assume you know who the minority members are. Once you have listed the members of this minority separately, you can decide to sample a higher proportion of them than you intend to use from the majority group. For example, suppose you had a reason to be especially interested in the attitudes of the Hispanic baseball players. Using these two categories, Table 3.2 groups the players by ethnic origin. You can see that there are five apparent Hispanics[3] and twenty-seven non-Hispanics. Your first (simple random) sample included only one Hispanic, Pocoroba. Your second sample had none.

If you take a stratified random sample from these two groups, you have one or two Hispanics and six or seven non-Hispanics. This correctly reflects their actual proportions in the population and can be referred to as a **proportionate stratified random sample**. However, you may feel that you would rather have more Hispanic subjects to analyze, and you might want to use more than two of them, maybe even all of them. You can use an equal number of non-Hispanics, selected randomly, or some proportion of them that seems reasonable to you for your purposes. This will be a **disproportionate stratified random sample**.

Another way to sample from a list is called **systematic sampling**. It consists of selecting names at predetermined intervals.

Systematic Sampling   Another way to sample from a list is called **systematic sampling**. It consists of selecting names at predetermined intervals. First, you number the names, as before. Next, you decide on your sample size, also as before. Continuing with the baseball example, if you chose this method, you would want eight names out of thirty-two, or every fourth name. However, you cannot arbitrarily begin with the first player and take 1, 5, 9, 13, 17, 21, 25, 29; that would give you a biased, rather than random, sample. The other twenty-four men would not have had a chance to be chosen, and a random sample requires that every member of a population have an equal chance to be chosen. The solution is to think of the population list as a combined group of sublists. If you are choosing every fourth name, or 25 percent, there are four such sublists available:

1, 5, 9, 13, 17, 21, 25, 29
2, 6, 10, 14, 18, 22, 26, 30
3, 7, 11, 15, 19, 23, 27, 31
4, 8, 12, 16, 20, 24, 28, 32

Every player is on one of these available sublists. Using any method of random selection, you randomly choose a number from 1 to 4 and begin with that number. You automatically get the entire sublist. From the original list, using the original numbers from the table, you would have chosen 4. This automatically gives you 4, 8, (4 + 4), 12 (8 + 4), 16 (12 + 4), and so forth. Your systematic sample consists of Buckner, Tidrow, Tyson, Figueroa, Horner, Hubbard, Camp, and Niekro.

If you want a proportionate systematic sample, list the subgroups one after the other within the list. This gives you proportionate numbers of the subgroups. For example, if you list the Hispanics first, you would be numbering them 1 to 5 and you would be sure of getting one or two in the sample. You could also list them last and still be sure of getting one or two. If you want a disproportionate systematic sample, you list the subgroups separately, as before, and then you can take different proportions of them systematically.

There is some disagreement among researchers as to whether a systematic sample is random. Some methodologists classify systematic sampling as a nonrandom method. They believe that once the first number has been drawn, the rest of the choices are fixed and the names in between them do not really have a chance to be chosen.[4] I follow Selltiz and associates, who feel that a systematic sample is random as long as the first number is randomly drawn.[5]

When the population to be sampled is too large for simple random sampling because the process would be too expensive and time-consuming, there is a way to sample randomly in progressively smaller populations. It is called **multistage sampling** and sometimes **cluster**, or **area**, **sampling**.

Multistage Sampling   Suppose you want a random sample of county welfare boards in the United States. If you simply list all American welfare boards and select a sample using one of the techniques we have discussed, you might find yourself with an unwieldy sample, especially if you intend to visit each board. To solve this problem, you can design a multistage sample. First, you list the largest natural divisions of the population. For the United States, that means a list of states and territories. From this list you then select a random sample. Let's assume you chose five states: Oregon, New Hampshire, New Jersey, Louisiana, and Indiana. You have completed the first stage of your multistage sampling.

The second stage of your multistage sampling consists of a random sampling of the counties in each of your sample states. For example, New Jersey has twenty-one counties. You list them and select a random sample. This sample contains your ultimate subjects. You would take such a sample in each of the states selected.

A multistage sample can have any number of stages, but each stage consists of a random sample of units.

You must be careful to examine the nature of the population and subpopulations you use to make sure they are not arranged in some pattern that could bias your sample. If you are using lists made up by someone else, the units may be grouped according to a logical order that will result in your sample being uniform on some characteristic. For example, if you want to sample all the baseball teams playing on a particular day from the starting lineups, one after another, you would have to be careful. If you used a systematic sampling technique, you might get nothing but shortstops and pitchers. If your population is a group of tenants and you want to sample every fifth apartment, you would have to make sure that you did not get all corner apartments, all three-room apartments, and so forth.

Multistage sampling is often used to sample territories because very often there is no list that includes all inhabitants. If you use a list of voters, you miss unregistered people and those not yet old enough to vote. The only accurate method, which is outlined in the welfare board example, is to sample areas delineated on a map and proceed to subsamples. Fortunately the state, county, and local divisions in this country are well established. There are also census districts and voting districts and wards. You can sample from these and then sample dwellings in the smallest area unit. (Data are readily available. Sometimes ZIP codes are used.)

Suppose you are selecting a multistage sample of a city and have selected a sample of census tracts. You will have to discover the layout of the buildings in the tracts and devise a system of sampling them that makes sense for that

FIGURE 3.2   **Two explanations of sampling for a poll from The New York Times**

How the Poll Was Made

The latest New York Times/CBS News Poll is based on telephone interviews conducted Sept. 9 and 10 with 839 adults around the United States, excluding Alaska and Hawaii.

The sample of telephone exchanges called was selected by a computer from a complete list of exchanges in the country. The exchanges were chosen so as to insure that each region of the country was represented in proportion to its population. For each exchange, the telephone numbers were formed by random digits, thus permitting access to both listed and unlisted residential numbers. The numbers were then screened to limit calls to residences.

The results have been weighted to take account of household size and number of residential telephones and to adjust for variations in the sample relating to region, race, sex, age and education.

In theory, in 19 cases out of 20 the results based on such samples will differ by no more than 3 percentage points in either direction from what would have been obtained by interviewing all adult Americans. The error for smaller subgroups is larger. For example, for both men and women the sampling error is plus or minus 5 percentage points.

In addition to sampling error, the practical difficulties of conducting any survey of public opinion may introduce other sources of error into the poll.

How the Surveys Were Conducted

These New York Times/CBS News Polls are based on personal interviews conducted in early October. In Britain, 973 people were interviewed from Oct. 3 to Oct. 8. In West Germany, 947 people were interviewed from Oct. 4 to Oct. 12. In France, 1,070 people were interviewed from Oct. 8 to Oct. 12.

Interviews were conducted at approximately 100 randomly selected locations in each country, chosen so as to insure that each region of the country was represented in proportion to its population. Interview subjects were selected according to quotas designed to reflect each country's population in terms of sex, age, occupation and household income.

The results have been weighted to adjust for variations in the sample relating to region, sex, age and household income.

In theory, in 19 cases out of 20 the results based on samples of such a size will differ by no more than four percentage points in either direction from what would have been obtained by interviewing all adults in that country. The error for smaller subgroups is larger. For example, the margin of sampling error for men or women in each country is plus or minus five percentage points.

Barbara G. Farah, director of polling at The Times, supervised these surveys and the analysis of their findings. The interviewing was conducted by Gallup International.

Used by permission of The New York Times.

area. If it is a neighborhood of single-family homes, you might take every tenth house. If it is a block of apartment houses, you might take every fifth apartment in every second building. There is no formula that can be universally applied. You have to apply the principles of random selection to suit the case. Professional poll-takers are careful to get a representative sample. Figure 3.2 reproduces the sampling explanations for two of these polls, done by the New York Times/CBS News Poll staff.

The first, on the question of Judge Robert H. Bork's nomination to the Supreme Court, reports on a telephone survey for which a random sample of United States telephone owners was obtained via computer and explains how much confidence we may place in its results. The second, on European preferences for American presidential candidates (1984), reports on a multi-stage, stratified quota sample, interviewed by Gallup International in Great Britain, West Germany, and France. This report also includes a full explanation of the methods used.

Sampling Error and Confidence Level

The typicality of a sample, or how well it represents the population from which you drew it, rests on the size of the sample. The laws of probability say that it doesn't matter how great a proportion of the population the sample is, but that the absolute size of the sample itself is what counts. Researchers use sample size to estimate **sampling error**, or the probable variation in typicality they might get with a particular size of sample. For example, a sample size of 400 will represent the actual distribution in a population within 5 percentage points of the true distribution in either direction. So, if you have a population of 47 percent men and 53 percent women and your sample numbers 400, you can say you are likely to get 42–52 percent men and 48–58 percent women. Your sampling error is 5 percent. In this example you would expect any one of the following results:

Men (%)	Women (%)
42	58
43	57
44	56
45	55
46	54
47	53
48	52
49	51
50	50
51	49
52	48

These are only 11 of 101 possible sample distributions, but with a sample size of 400, these are the most likely. Theoretically you *could* get 0 percent of one sex and 100 percent of the other and all of the possibilities in between. When we know what the sample size is, and therefore know the sampling error, we speak of the range of likely outcomes as the **confidence interval**.

Using a standard probability formula, you can calculate the sampling error for any size sample. It is done using one variable, for example percentage of males. The formula is

$$\sqrt{\frac{P \times Q}{n}}$$

P = some percentage (e.g., male)
$Q = 1 - P$
n = sample size

The number of times you can expect the sample to meet this expectation is ninety-five out of one hundred. We call this the **confidence level** and it comes from the laws of probability concerning standard distributions of populations. One of these laws says that 95 percent of the possible outcomes in a distribution lie within two standard errors of the mean (average). Since our equation for a sample of 400 will yield an answer of 2.5, we double that to get the confidence interval, going in both directions along the continuum of possible outcomes and we have gone "two standard errors" both ways. Now we can say that we will be in that range 95 times out of 100. We will discuss standard error again in Chapter 10, in the section on inferential statistics.

You don't speak of sampling error or confidence level if your sample is 5 percent or more of the relevant population. It is used to indicate degree of confidence in results based on small samples from large populations.

A **nonrandom sample** is any selection that cannot lay a claim to randomness. Results obtained from a nonrandom sample are not generalizable beyond the sample. Nevertheless, nonrandom techniques are useful sometimes, and you should know about them.

Nonrandom Sampling

The six commonly used nonrandom sampling techniques are:

    accidental sampling
    judgmental sampling
    quota sampling
    snowball sampling
    dense sampling
    saturation sampling

We shall take these up one at a time, beginning with the least rigorous.

Accidental Sampling Typically employed by inquiring photographers, **accidental sampling** uses whatever subjects are available. This kind of sample is irretrievably biased. There is only one good reason for using such a method: to test a sample of a questionnaire on a few people to see whether the questions are usable. As mentioned at the beginning of this chapter, the researcher's own preferences and blind spots exclude whole classes of subjects from a sample unless precautions are taken.

Judgmental Sampling   A **judgmental sample** consists of subjects selected by the researcher because of their expertise on the research question or their possession of some characteristic the researcher wants to include. A judgmental sample is sometimes called a **purposive sample**. The subjects are chosen at the individual level; that is, particular individuals are included.

Quota Sampling   Midway between accidental sampling and judgmental sampling, **quota sampling** consists of choosing subjects by categories. For example, you might want a 100-person sample, composed of 50 women and 50 men. Moreover, you might want half of each sex group to be Catholic, 40 percent to be Protestant, and 10 percent to be Jews and others. You or your assistants then seek out such individuals as they may be recruited.

Snowball Sampling   Sometimes a researcher wants to examine a network rather than proportions of groups. There is a difference between surveying married people and interviewing families. **Snowball sampling** is a method of tracing the friendship, kinship, or other lines that link people together and interviewing everyone that can be discovered in a particular network. First, you select a small number of people who represent the kind of network you want to investigate. For example, you might identify community business leaders and interview a dozen of them. Each time you interview someone, you ask the respondent to identify his or her business associates, and then you interview those named. Eventually you have the entire network.

If you are doing a research project that involves difficult access, such as a deviant subculture, the snowball technique may be the only one you can use. One investigator writing a book on transvestites spent three and a half years carefully studying some fifty cases obtained in this manner.[6]

With a small population you can consider dense sampling, which includes most of a population.

Dense Sampling   **Dense sampling** covers the majority of the population. I worked on a study of colleges in the early 1970s in which questionnaires were returned from two-thirds of the four-year liberal arts colleges in the United States. This sample went far beyond the size requirements for a random sample. To make sure that the sample, even though dense, was not biased, we carefully analyzed the respondents and compared them with the nonrespondents on five factors: size, region, sponsorship, sex of student body, and scholastic rating. This was possible because this data for all colleges were listed in standard directories. No differences were found between the respondents and the nonrespondents, so we concluded that the sample was externally valid.[7]

Dense sampling is only one step away from **saturation sampling**, which *does* include the whole population.

Saturation Sampling   Saturation sampling isn't really "sampling," since no one is left out. It is used only when the population is very small or when it is essential to include everyone—as it is for the national census, which is taken for political, rather than research goals.

The world is constantly changing. Humans have a limited perspective on it. It's as if we are watching a long parade through a narrow window without having time to wait for the end, and without having been there soon enough to see the beginning. Researchers have developed a number of ways of dealing with this phenomenon. They all attempt to answer the questions, How many times should we sample and at what times?

The Number of Samples

Cross-sectional research is research for which only one sample is taken and only one examination, or data collection, is made. **Longitudinal research** is research for which more than one sample is taken or in which data are collected from a sample more than once.

Cross-sectional versus Longitudinal Samples

A cross-sectional research study is like a snapshot. It captures the research scene at a given moment. It is taken for granted that a cross-sectional study will not be the only examination of its subject. Some may already have pursued that particular research goal, and others may do so in the future. The same researcher may repeat a study. However, the cross-sectional research study makes no attempt to sample exactly the same population the second time. This is what differentiates it from a longitudinal study.

A longitudinal research study is like a filmstrip. You make successive examinations (snapshots) of the same thing to determine what changes occur. The same population is always used for the successive samplings.

There are three kinds of longitudinal study: trend studies, cohort studies, and panel studies. Trend and cohort studies take repeated samples of the same population, and panel studies take one sample and collect data from it more than once.

Trend Studies   A **trend study** takes two or more samplings of the same population, separating those samplings by an interval of time. During election years numerous trend studies are taken of the population of voters. Most parties and candidates pay careful attention to these trend studies, because such research is designed to measure the fluctuations in the candidates' popularity.

Economic trend studies measure the rise and fall of prices and sales. In another type of trend study, the public opinion poll, the population is usually a country's adult resident population, regardless of voting status. Public opinion polls are taken for dozens of reasons, political and otherwise.

Cohort Studies   A **cohort study** is a trend study that samples a special kind of population. The **cohort** is all the people who experience some event in the same time period (usually a year). For instance, a birth cohort consists of everyone born in a specific year. A marriage cohort is everyone who got married in a specific year. A graduation cohort is everyone graduated in a specific year. A person might belong to the birth cohort of 1950, the high school graduation cohort of 1968, the college graduation cohort of 1972, the marriage cohort of 1975, and the divorce cohort of 1980. Cohorts can also be grouped. The "Depression babies" are the cohorts of 1930–1939. The "baby boomers" are the cohorts of 1946–1961. Cohort studies are very important in demography, the study of population. One important series of cohorts is the birth cohort series of breeding women, showing their lifetime total of births. From it you can see the trend of decreasing family size, from the large families of colonial times to the small ones now.

Panel Studies   **Panel studies** are longitudinal studies using the same people in the successive samplings. A panel study shows individual patterns of change. Suppose you question a sample of twenty voters and find that ten intend to vote for candidate A and ten for candidate B, then you question a second sample and find the same scores. You might assume no changes were occurring between samplings. But suppose all those intending to vote for A had switched to B and all those intending to vote for B had switched to A? A tremendous amount of change would have occurred, and you wouldn't know it. You could try to find out by asking people how they intended to vote previously, but your results would then be subject to **recall lapse**, the tendency to forget the past, which increases measurably with the amount of time that has gone by.[8] A panel study reveals changes that cancel each other out at the group level and provides insight into individual changes.

The Timing of Longitudinal Studies

When you do a longitudinal study, you have to decide how many times and when you will sample. If your samples are not properly spaced, you will miss fluctuations. Look at the graph in Figure 3.3. It represents a longitudinal cohort study. The chart shows the U.S. **Total Fertility Rate** (TFR) for each year from 1930 to 1976, inclusive.[9] You can see that the TFR, or potential family size, has decreased from 2.6 children to 1.8 children in the forty-six years shown. If you had looked only at 1930 and 1976, you would have identified the long-term trend correctly, but you would have also missed a great

FIGURE 3.3   **A graph of a longitudinal cohort study**

U.S. Total Fertility Rates from 1930 to 1976
Source: U.S. Bureau of the Census, Series P-25, No. 706.

deal! The Depression years' baby bust would be out of your analysis, as well as the "baby boom" of the late 1940s and the 1950s.

Suppose you use 1945 and 1947 as your sample years. How about 1957 and 1959? Each of these pairs gives a different impression from the real long-term trend. The years 1945 and 1970, if used as the samples, would show no change at all.

Clearly, if year-to-year changes are important (as they are in birth rate studies), you cannot afford to sample at long intervals. If you are doing another kind of study, you may be interested more in the long-term than in the short-term changes and will want to avoid sampling at short intervals. Your decision hinges on the research question you are asking.

Now we come to the considerations necessary for choosing a sampling technique. Although it is relatively easy to decide on what you would prefer, it is more difficult to decide on a compromise between it and what is feasible.

Choosing a Sampling Technique

It's important to realize that you have no hope of getting a perfect random sample, although some methods will get you closer to it than others will. One problem affecting randomness is access.

Access and Feasibility

Access is the quality of being approachable. Lists go out of date quickly, and territories become inaccessible due to natural disasters, political changes, and construction. Some people selected for your sample may refuse to cooperate, some may not speak your language, and some may be missing. Taking a list of people and tracking them down require patience and perseverance.

Some populations are easy to sample because they consist of people who are registered and listed somewhere, who are not threatened by being questioned, or who can't afford to refuse. These include voters, business executives, union members, students, and welfare clients. Other populations are elusive. For example, nobody knows how many burglars there are. Burglars are understandably cautious about being interviewed. Before choosing a sampling technique, you have to consider how likely it is that you will be able to secure the sample.

There are alternatives to sampling actual people. Among the data collection methods to be presented in Part II of this book are various unobtrusive measures, including content analysis. **Unobtrusive measures** use a sample of circumstantial evidence from which to draw conclusions. **Content analysis**, a special kind of unobtrusive measure, is a method of sampling communications.

If interviewer effect, demand characteristics, or access is a problem, many researchers turn to sampling evidence instead of actual people.

Another problem might be limited resources. Novices are frequently surprised at the amount of money and time it takes to secure a sample of people and collect data from them.

Resources

The sampling technique you choose depends heavily on the resources—time, energy, and money—you have at your command. Naturally, you want to do as rigorous a study as possible, and you want to look at the applicability of your project. If you want to say something only about the actual sample you are able to get, you do not have to be concerned with generalizability and therefore random selection.

If in your analysis you want to use **statistical testing**, which is a test to see if your sample is typical of the population being studied, you will have to have as representative a sample as you can manage. There are two kinds of statistics, which are discussed in Chapter 10. One is **descriptive statistics**, numbers that describe the sample's limits. The other is **inferential statistics**, numbers that indicate how typical or how unusual the sample is in comparison to the population from which it was drawn. Descriptive statistics can be used on almost any sample. Inferential statistics require a random sample. You must remember when you decide how to sample that a nonrandom sample will prevent you from using inferential statistics on the result. Familiarizing yourself with the basic types of statistical tests will help you to realize what you want from your analysis. Chapter 10 is designed to give you this basic information.

Inferential statistics are used to determine whether a finding is rare or could easily have happened by chance. If it is rare enough to meet certain criteria, we say that the finding is statistically significant. We should be even more concerned, however, about another type of significance.

Significance

Although statistical testing enhances the aura of scientific activity for any research project, and, therefore, is sought after by many researchers, it in no way indicates whether the results demonstrate **social significance**, or importance to the community. If the accident rate goes up, you are not interested in whether it is a chance occurrence but only that it happened and how to prevent it from happening again.

Statistical tests reveal the likelihood that certain patterns found in the sample also exist in the sampled population and the probability that the result obtained via the sample could have been a chance variation. They do not test the quality of the data or the methods used and do nothing to improve either. Sometimes the use of statistical tests convinces both researcher and reader that some socially significant results have been obtained, when the results are only statistically significant. Because mathematics and the manipulation of numbers are intimidating to many people, those who are capable of handling them enjoy an immunity from criticism at times. A research report that should be considered in light of its social meaning is considered only in light of its statistical test results.

A study that is not appropriate for statistical testing may still be important socially, interesting, and useful to others. Don't expect to be perfect. Try to get a sample that includes all important categories in the population you choose, one that can later be divided in ways you deem advisable. Researchers commonly think of all kinds of things later that "we should have asked," "we might have done," "we didn't anticipate," or "we overlooked." This doesn't signify failure, however. The next person will learn from your mistakes and omissions, and you will, too. In some respects, research is like a relay race with the results as baton.

Summary and Conclusion

A researcher has to choose a population, or category of people or items, and select a representative part of it, or sample, from which to collect data. The best way to establish external validity is by drawing a random sample, which would be easy if the population were homogeneous, or uniform, in composition. Since most populations are heterogeneous, or various in composition, random sampling is harder and at the same time more desirable.

Sources of bias threaten the representativeness of the sample, and four kinds of random sampling have been developed to overcome them. Six non-random sampling techniques can be used for special cases. The researcher must decide how many samples to draw and when to draw them. Cross-sectional studies have only one data collection, but longitudinal studies have two or more, sometimes from the same sample and sometimes from different samples drawn from the same population. Timing is very important when measuring trends. Choice of sampling technique depends partly on the accessibility of the subjects, the researcher's resources, and whether statistical tests are intended for the findings.

Main Points

1. You must establish the limits of the population you are going to sample. For research purposes, a population is a number of people or items all in the same category, not necessarily all in the same place.

2. You cannot generalize beyond the population from which the sample is drawn. External validity is the generalizability and representativeness of the findings. Therefore, a sample is a small picture that if possible includes everything in the large picture.

3. Something homogeneous is the same all the way through, while something heterogeneous is varied in composition. Human populations are usually heterogeneous.

4. You have to watch out for selective perception, group identity (yours), and patterns of movement and settlement.

5. Random sampling gives each unit in a population an equal chance to be chosen. Variations of the simple random sampling technique are stratified random sampling, systematic sampling, and multistage sampling. You can estimate the probable error for a random sample. There are also six nonrandom sampling methods.

6. A cross-sectional study is one with one sample and one data collection, but it assumes that other examinations of the subject will take place.

7. A longitudinal study is one with two or more data collections, separated in time, and possibly two or more samples. Its goal is to measure change. There are three kinds of longitudinal study: trend, cohort, and panel.

8. If people are not accessible for your sample, you can use circumstantial evidence or communications.

9. Your results may be statistically significant, socially significant, or both. One type of significance does not depend on the other.

Notes

1. David A. Karp, "Observing Behavior in Public Places: Problems and Strategies," in *Fieldwork Experience: Qualitative Approaches to Social Research*, ed. William B. Shaffir, Robert A. Stebbins, and Allan Turowetz (New York: St. Martin's, 1980), pp. 82–97.

2. James A. Black and Dean J. Champion, *Methods and Issues in Social Research* (New York: Holt, Rinehart & Winston, 1981), p. 429n.

3. I have been told by a baseball fan that Pocoroba is not Hispanic, but Italian, in ethnic origin. Our college baseball coach agrees. A good example of how easily we err and of the hazards in assigning ethnic identity from a name.

4. Black and Champion, pp. 299–302.

5. Claire Selltiz, Lawrence S. Wrightsman, and Stuart W. Cook, *Selltiz, Wrightsman, and Cook's Research Methods in Social Relations*, rev. Louise H. Kidder (New York: Holt, Rinehart & Winston, 1981), p. 429n.

6. John Talamini, Scranton, Pa., personal communications.

7. Rhoda Lois Goldstein and June True Albert, "The Status of Black Studies Programs on American Campuses, 1970–71," *Journal of Behavioral and Social Sciences* 20, no. 1 (Winter 1974): 1–16.

8. Ranjan Kumar Som, *Recall Lapse in Demographic Inquiries* (New York: Asia Publishing House, 1973), p. vii.

9. The Total Fertility Rate represents the family size that would be produced if each birth cohort of women maintained for their lifetimes the same birth rate they had in the year examined. TFR averages the cohorts' rates.

Exercises

The best way to grasp the techniques of sampling and to get an idea of the amount of time the process takes is to try a small example yourself. Exercise 3.1 is designed to give you this experience. It provides you with a small population and asks you to go through the procedure given in the baseball player example in this chapter. Do this carefully, and don't rush; be sure you understand what you are doing at each step.

Once you have an idea of how sampling works, you are in a better position to evaluate a sampling job. Exercise 3.2 asks you to look at someone else's work in the light of what you have learned about sampling. (*Note:* In these critique exercises, don't feel that you have to find only good or bad things to say. A published work may be thoroughly commendable, deplorably deficient, or anything in between. Just say what you truly think. If you can't figure out what the researchers were doing, that's a minus for them; show the report to your instructor, however, so he or she has a chance to demystify it for you.)

Exercise 3.1   *Drawing samples*

Instructions: Here is a list of professionals at a community psychiatric center. Assume you are going to survey a sample of these staff members on the question of whether a judge or a psychiatrist should decide involuntary commitments to psychiatric facilities.

1. Number the staff in sequence from 01 to 40, entering the numbers on the lines preceding the names.

2. Using the table of random numbers in Appendix A, select enough two-digit numbers to provide a 25 percent sample of people listed.

3. Write all the numbers here, separated by commas, and draw a line through those you can't use:

_____

_____

___ Edward Sarafino (P)	___ Roger Chaffin (P)
___ Frances Seidman (P)	___ Joseph Gorczynski (P)
___ Daniel Phillips (P)	___ Arthur Hohmuth (P)
___ Sally Archer (P)	___ Nancy Breland (P)
___ George Saxton (P)	___ Anne Gormley (P)
___ Arthur Steinman (P)	___ Enid Campbell (P)
___ Alan Waterman (P)	___ Henry Wang (P)
___ Anthony DiGiorgio (P)	___ David Young (P)
___ Felix DelVecchio (P)	___ Carlo Racamato (P)
___ Charles Swift (P)	___ Ross Roby (P)
___ Arthur Christy (NP)	___ Bruce Mericle (NP)
___ Barbara Chapman (NP)	___ Howard Riley (NP)
___ E. John Constance (NP)	___ Regina Sanchez-Porter (NP)
___ Robert Harris (NP)	___ Andrew Hornyak (NP)
___ Pauline Jenson (NP)	___ William Jones (NP)
___ Audrey O'Brien (NP)	___ Seymour Schwartz (NP)
___ Roland Worthington (NP)	___ Diane Haines (NP)
___ James Howard (NP)	___ Aristomen Chilakos (NP)
___ Fred Oshel (NP)	___ Joseph Herzstein (NP)
___ Roger Rada (NP)	___ Kenneth Tillman (NP)

P = Psychiatrists and psychologists
NP = Other professions (nurses, special educators, counselors, recreation
        therapists, etc.)

113

4. List the ten people who constitute your sample with their assigned numbers.

_____   _____

_____   _____

_____   _____

_____   _____

_____   _____

5. Do you have equal numbers of Ps and NPs? _____
The original list has twenty of each. How many men do you have? _____
The original list is three-fourths men. Considering these two features, how representative is your sample?

6. Renumber the people. Number men 1–30 in one color and women 1–10 in another, regardless of their professional classification.

7. Take a 30 percent random sample of each list separately.

_____   _____

_____   _____

_____   _____

_____

_____

_____

_____

_____

8. Can you devise a way to get a sample that is half Ps, half NPs, and three-fourths men? Explain how you could arrange the list to take a systematic 25 percent sample with these characteristics.

9. Why might the list as originally arranged not give three-fourths men if you took a systematic sample from it?

Exercise 3.2   *Critique*

Instructions: Choose a research report from any professional journal and read it. Answer the following questions as concisely as possible after giving a full citation here:

_____

_____

1.   What was the sample used in the project?

2.   From what population was the sample drawn?

3.   Does the author generalize from the sample to a population in the conclusion?

4.   If the author does generalize, is the population the same as the one from which the sample was drawn?

5.   How was the sample drawn?

6.   What do you think of the research report's generalizability?

7.   Any other comments?

CHAPTER 4

Choosing the Methods

Now that you know the procedures for choosing a research question and making it doable and are acquainted with the various types of sample selection, it's time to look at methods of collecting data from the sample you have selected. This chapter introduces you to the approaches used today and explains the circumstances that will be most influential when you are deciding which ones to use.

Major Research Methods

It is a commonplace that our behavior varies according to whether someone is watching and who that someone is. To a sociologist, interaction is "behavior that takes someone else into account," and when that someone else is a researcher, the change in a subject's behavior is called interviewer effect. Another way to put it is that interviewer effect is the distortion of the response caused by the presence of the researcher. This distortion leads to an impression that is not so much inaccurate as it is atypical and idealized. It is similar to the impression we give of our home when an expected visitor comes. The chairs are in place, the clutter has been modified, the best cups and saucers are out, and we're wearing our "company" faces. Although it isn't a lie, it also isn't the whole truth.

Our self-appraisal operates continuously as we listen to and observe ourselves. You may recall G. H. Mead's theoretical description of the development of personality in humans. Little by little we learn the meaning of the actions we observe. Little by little we learn our own place in the pattern and imitate what we see. At last we are not only aware of what we do but can also take all the other people into account, including their reactions to us.[1] We become sensitive to the impression we are making on the others.

Our concern for making a good impression on ourselves and on others is established very early in life. We want to live up to our own notions about what we should be and generally try to put the best face on things by interpreting our own behavior as the most acceptable available alternative. (Usually, this is referred to as "my side of it.") This affects our report of past and present behavior and also our predictions of our future behavior and our stated opinions. Our forecasts are heavily influenced by what we like to think will happen, and we are not apt to predict accurately. Think back to the last time you rehearsed an impassioned speech to the bathroom mirror. When you came face to face with the person for whom the speech was intended, did you say what you had rehearsed?

The difficulty of getting an accurate account of deeds and opinions has given rise to two schools of thought about research strategy. One idea is that researchers should avoid confronting subjects with questions and should eliminate interviewer effect entirely by using indirect research methods to get the data. The other idea is that researchers should confront the subjects

FIGURE 4.1   **Research methods**

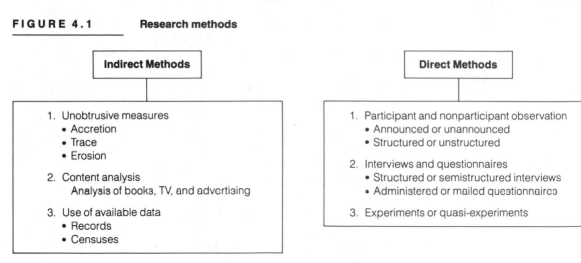

but reduce interviewer effect by refining the direct research method so as not to intimidate or influence the subjects.

**Indirect
Methods of
Data Collection**

Indirect methods of data collection are processes of gathering clues to what has happened or analyzing available data. Although the data collection methods are taken up in detail in Part II, let's look briefly at each of them now, so that the range of possibilities will be clear when we begin looking at other things that will influence your choice (see Figure 4.1).

 We begin with some ingenious ploys for collecting data called **unobtrusive measures**, which allow the researcher to keep out of ongoing interaction.

Unobtrusive Measures   The word *unobtrusive* means that a person is not part of the interaction and has no influence on it. When you're collecting data, the interaction is over. As the researcher, you come on the scene and, somewhat like a detective, collect circumstantial evidence about what has already happened. From the evidence obtained, the researcher tries to figure out what the subjects' behavior was. Unobtrusive measures are not necessarily welcomed by subjects, especially if they are well-known figures who don't have much privacy. Nonetheless, such measures have been defined as those "that do not require the cooperation of a respondent and that do not themselves contaminate the response."[2] Evidence examined might be an **accretion**, or accumulation, such as discarded trash; a **trace**, or visible mark, such as graffiti; or an **erosion**, or wearing away, such as the depletion of an item due to theft or use. Strictly speaking, unobtrusive measures also include the analysis of communication, or **content analysis**, and the use of **available data**, which refers to any data gathered for some other project. We'll talk about content analysis and available data separately.

Content Analysis   Sifting through some form of communication in order to count the **frequency** of a subject or word is called content analysis. Sometimes the researcher is just looking for the presence or absence of something in the item being examined. Some of the standard psychological tests ask people to draw a picture or tell a story, and then the psychologist examines the result. From the presence or absence of symbols of anger, for example, or distortion of familiar objects, the doctor adds to the clinical picture of the subject. Other content analyses focus on how often something appears. For example, a task force of the Central New Jersey chapter of the NOW looked at children's books to compare the treatment of girls to the treatment of boys in the stories and illustrations.[3] Examining 134 elementary school reading books then used in central New Jersey, they counted the numbers of girls and boys as central figures in the stories and made a few other comparisons. Historians employ content analysis to trace the appearance, rise, duration, or fall of a person or of a political or social idea.

Content analysis extracts data from material written for other purposes. There is also much information that has already been collected and put into statistical form, that is, counted and tabulated. All of it that can be secured for reexamination is called available data.

The Use of Available Data   "Available data" can be part of the material used for content analysis but the term usually implies material that has already been quantified by the original collector. Suppose you are interested in the censorship of mail in wartime. If you have actual censored letters available to you, as well as censor's office directives and personal testimony of various officials, and if you go through this material in order to describe patterns, from one country to another, your comparison would be referred to as a content analysis. If instead you consulted records of censorship that tabulated such things as number of pieces of mail processed and number of pieces of mail from which deletions were made, you would be using available data.

Available data need not have been, and usually have not been, collected for the same purpose the new researcher intends. Census figures, which are collected by the government for political reasons, are often analyzed to reveal social and demographic trends of interest to groups other than the government. **Demographic** studies—which examine population statistics of births, deaths, illness, migration, and so on—are themselves scrutinized by business leaders, who want to predict consumer demand.

Compared to indirect means of data collection, direct research methods, including in-person observation, interviewing, and experiment, may be more familiar to you.

**Direct
Methods of
Data Collection**
Although many research projects using **direct methods** of data collection do incorporate some features of unobtrusive measuring, the subjects are always aware that the researcher is present, is collecting data, or both. Direct methods of data collection include participant and nonparticipant observation and

all questionnaires and experiments. The student should remember that all methods of direct and indirect data collection can produce research results that can later be used in content analysis or as available data. Problems of this type of analysis are discussed in the chapters on data collection in Part II, as the techniques are presented in detail.

The word *observation* means paying attention, but we are going to use it in a stricter sense. We'll include consideration of the manner in which observation is to be carried out and of its ultimate utility to scientific research. A good research definition is the one offered by James A. Black and Dean J. Champion. "Observation . . . is . . . watching and listening to other persons' behavior over time without manipulating or controlling it, and recording findings in ways that permit some degree of analytical interpretation."[4] You can observe in an **unstructured** manner, as when you watch a sports event without taking organized notes. You can observe in a **structured** manner, as when you watch the same type of event but keep a score card. Structured observation requires careful advance planning. A good example of a research project that used both structured and unstructured observation was reported by W. F. Whyte in *Street Corner Society*. Whyte lived among poor Italian-Americans in Boston for several years. He observed a social and athletic club for several weeks and gained only "impressionistic" notions of the group. From these unstructured observations, Whyte developed a system of "positional mapmaking" and made a record of the groupings of men he observed each night at the club. From this series of structured observations he was able to develop theories about clique formation in the group. This is not only a good example of structured and unstructured observation, but it also illustrates the process of inductive logic, since Whyte reasoned from concrete experience to abstract theory.[5]

Participant and Nonparticipant Observation   Whyte was a participant observer. Participant observation means that the researcher is engaging in some activity with the group being observed. In nonparticipant observation, on the other hand, the researcher remains uninvolved in the ongoing interaction. If you sit on a park bench and watch runners practice, you are a nonparticipating observer.

There are degrees of participation. To participate fully in a group implies that the researcher is a genuine member of that group, as is sometimes the case. To abstain from participating fully in a group implies that the researcher makes no contribution to the group's activities at all. It is entirely possible that a researcher might be a participant observer at some times and a nonparticipant observer at others. The distinction is complicated by another variable: the subjects' awareness that the researcher is doing research. When the subjects are aware, the research is known as **announced observation**, and a distinction is made between announced participant observation and unannounced participant observation. Whyte's participant observation was announced. He told the other group members that he was writing a book, and they accepted him knowing that they would be described in that book.

Tearoom Trade by Laud Humphreys describes an unannounced participant observation in which Humphreys played the role of a lookout while observing homosexual encounters in public restrooms.[6] The other men accepted him in this role; they evidently believed that he was one of them and were certainly not aware that he was a researcher. Whether a participant observer is announced is important because interviewer effect is increased when subjects know they are being observed. On the other hand, unannounced participant observation is a deception and raises some ethical questions, which we discuss later in this chapter.

Nonparticipant observation can be announced or unannounced. An announced nonparticipant observer is like an audience at a performance. This type of observation is used currently in family therapy. The therapist asks an entire family to arrange themselves in a tableau, or a scene, to illustrate their self-perceived relationships to each other, usually from one member's point of view at a time. Once the scene has been set, with each person in place, the therapist asks the individuals how they feel about their positions relative to the others. Using this method, called **sculpting**, the therapist gains insight into that family's way of dealing with each other and how each person sees it.[7] Although the goal of this technique is primarily therapeutic, sculpting is definitely being used as a data collection method in what could be called an exploratory team effort by a sizable portion of social workers and psychologists. They are trying to develop and refine theories about family interaction.

The last variation in direct observation is the unannounced nonparticipant observation. Here the subjects are unaware that they are being observed and are not regarding the observer as a member of their interacting group. This kind of observation is probably done most often in public places. David A. Karp incorporated it into his study of the Times Square area. His version of unannounced nonparticipant observation was to watch the doors of pornographic bookstores and note the apparent characteristics of the men who entered them.[8]

In sum, direct observation can be either participant or nonparticipant, announced or unannounced, and structured or unstructured. Each variation has specific advantages and disadvantages, which we examine in detail in Chapters 5 and 6. The ethical questions raised by not announcing one's identity as a researcher are examined later in this chapter.

A researcher's identity is always announced when data are collected via interviews or questionnaires. Interviews and questionnaires differ from each other only in the degree of active participation of the data collector and in the degree to which they are structured. We usually refer to the cooperating subjects as *respondents*.

Interviews and Questionnaires   An interview is a conversation between an interviewer and a respondent on a specific topic. It's organized to collect particular information, and this is known to the respondent, although the specific research goal may not be. An **unstructured interview** is one in which the interviewer follows a flexible format that allows for discretion and latitude in the choice and wording of the questions asked. The interviewer is aware of the research question and the data collection goal. The interviewer usually has an outline in mind but is not restricted to specific questions. It is similar to the type of discussion that takes place between a real estate agent and a prospect. Although the agent knows the important questions there is considerable variation, from interview to interview, in which questions are asked and in the style of their asking.

If an interviewer is provided with a list of questions to be asked in a particular order and has a set of instructions about the manner of the asking, the encounter is referred to as a **semistructured interview**. Here the interviewer is expected to note down the respondent's answers as accurately as possible on the list in the spaces provided. The list of questions is called an **interview schedule**. The semistructured interview still leaves the interviewer with some discretion about the way the questions are asked and their exact wording. The **structured interview**, however, has almost no flexibility. Interviewers are expected to follow an organized procedure, ask the questions exactly as they appear on the schedule, and note the exact answers.

Semistructured and structured interviews abound in today's world, their number being exceeded only by the number of questionnaires. A questionnaire is like a structured interview schedule but is usually completed by the respondent. If the interviewer is present while it is being completed, the questionnaire is called an **administered questionnaire**. Questionnaires can be administered one at a time or to groups. An examination is a questionnaire.

Mailed questionnaires are sent out to respondents with a request that they fill them out and mail them back. The researcher encloses a self-addressed envelope for this purpose and a cover letter to explain the study and justify the request.

Chapters 6 and 7 explore the many variations in questionnaires, question types, length and number of topics, advantages and disadvantages of questionnaires, and methods for developing skill in interviewing. Before leaving this overview of methods, let's look at experiments and quasi-experiments in social research.

Experiments and Quasi-Experiments The classic **experiment** is a test in which two groups of people or items are measured concerning an attribute. Then one group, called the **experimental group**, is subjected to a treatment or intervention of some kind, while the other group, called the **control group**, is left untouched. The treatment or intervention is called the **experimental variable**. After the experimental variable has been introduced to the experimental group, both groups are measured again on the same attribute as before. For each group, the second measurement is compared with the first, and any change is recorded. A notable difference between the changes recorded for the two groups can be assumed to be due to the experimental variable.

The classic experimental design may be modified as to the number of groups used or the number and procedure of measurements. One of the important requirements of classic experimental design is that all influences on the subjects be carefully controlled. If the subjects of your experiment are rats in a laboratory or grains of wheat in a test tube, this is not an unreasonable demand. When the subjects of an experiment are people, over whose comings and goings you have no authority and who usually are bombarded by all sorts of communications, influences, and experiences every day, you cannot hope for more than an approximation of the ideal experimental conditions. Because this is universally recognized, most experiments using unconfined people as subjects are called **quasi-experiments**, or research projects that are experiments only to a degree, and lack of control over the subjects is acknowledged.

Whether we're doing experimental or quasi-experimental studies, we attempt to begin with groups that are as close to one another as possible in the relevant characteristics. There are ways to do this, which we'll examine in Chapter 8. Later in this chapter we'll see how important ethics are in any experiment with human beings. Ethical considerations are especially troublesome for medical, psychiatric, and psychological studies, but social research cannot ignore the issues either.

We have gone lightly over the major methods of research here. Keep them in mind in the following section which focuses on the means you have at your disposal. Chief among these means is time.

Time

The amount of time you have available will influence your selection of research methods. It takes much longer to do observations and write them up than it does to administer group surveys and tabulate them. Some kinds of research and some subjects require negotiations for permission to do the work. Appendix C presents these considerations in greater detail.

Time restricts research in other ways, too. In addition to the limitation of the researcher's time, you must be aware of the effects of the passage of time and of timing.

The Limitation of Time

Our time is brief. Our natural life expectancy is not enough to permit very lengthy projects unless a series of researchers work on them. The time we do have cannot be devoted entirely to one thing. We spend it on personal and domestic chores, travel and paperwork, and interruptions. Typically, as hope triumphs over experience, we underestimate the time it will take us to do things.

Those employed at research "full-time" find that administrative requirements use up many hours. Since there are comparatively few full-time research jobs, many trained professionals are found in teaching or clinical practice. Research has high prestige in our society and is considered important enough to be required in training future professionals; but, except for institutional and market research (see Appendix D), it is generally not supported as an *exclusive* pursuit.

While planning a project, you need to foresee the use of both your time and other people's. You might need help to administer questionnaires to a large group of people. You may need observers and clerical or technical help. The "other people" in your project include the subjects you use. How much time do you expect them to donate? It's unrealistic to plan as if the respondents have ample free time and are as highly motivated as you.

Typically, the novice underestimates the time it takes to do things and tends to omit important preliminaries from the time schedule. For example, even experienced researchers may need a couple of months to staff and establish project headquarters. For large projects, it may take longer. Personnel and equipment may be difficult to find and slow to be acquired. Permissions may be needed to work in particular areas; clearance may be required at several levels of authority.

An experienced researcher knows how long each operation may take. Students, of course, don't have more time than their instructor allows and will not be performing many of the "real-life" steps. Your effort will be focused on techniques of design, data collection, and analysis. As you go through this book and complete exercises, you will get an idea of how much time and effort each thing demands. The time required is often much more than you expected, but sometimes you get a pleasant surprise.

As we saw in the discussion of longitudinal studies in Chapter 3, we are aiming at a moving target. The world changes even while you are examining it. The passage of only a short time may make your findings obsolete. Many variables are **dynamic**, or constantly changing. Attributes such as age, marital status, family size, education, income, residence, and attitude do not stay the same for long. Consider the changes you have experienced in the past 5 years and see how hard it is to get a stable picture of anyone. Keep this human characteristic in mind.

The Passage of Time

In Chapter 3 we discussed recording data at intervals and developing trend, cohort, and panel studies. For cross-sectional studies the passage of time must be considered from two angles: the period of time in which the data are collected, or the **data collection period**, and the period of time between data collection and publication of the result.

The Data Collection Period   The time taken to collect the data should be kept to a minimum because you want to avoid collecting data from the last of your sample under conditions different from those existing when you started. Since you cannot control outside conditions, you can only limit yourself. For example, if you locate a sample of preschoolers and you take 2 years to get around to all the families, some of the children will have started school by the time you get to them. Or, if those you interview first discuss the interview with remaining respondents, by the time you get to the last interviews you are recording a consensus rather than individual opinions.

Publishing Promptly   Your result may be valid for only a short time. Consider the population forecasts based on steadily increasing population growth. Based on these "reasonable" forecasts, many municipalities built new school buildings throughout the 1960s and 1970s. Drastic changes became evident for many localities in the last year or two of the 1970s, when the migration to the Sun Belt accelerated. The 1980 Census confirmed these changes—often to the horror, disbelief, and outrage of municipal officials. In the same period, real estate sales underwent a radical change, dropping at least 40 percent from 1979 to 1981 and causing many lumber companies and real estate brokers to close up shop. Suppose you had surveyed realtors in 1978 about the sales picture for new and existing homes? If you waited until late 1979 or 1980 to publish, your probable conclusions would sound ludicrous. Remember that research is supposed to be of use to the society. It can become dated.

The last temporal restraint on research we need look at is the *timing* of it.

Timing

What we mean by "timing" is the political and social climate at the time the research is being attempted. The state of technology is part of this political and social climate. We need to think about the suitability, possibility, and acceptability of a project in its time and place.

Suitability   Suitability is the quality of appropriateness. If the research is suitable to its time and place, the topic fits in with the other cultural and societal features. For example, it would not be appropriate to ask: Which type of horse-drawn vehicle is preferred by most Americans? It is too late (or perhaps too soon?) for that. It would be suitable to ask about attitudes toward small cars versus large. A number of Leonardo da Vinci's blueprints for inventions were not developed in his time because the society was not technologically ready for them.

Possibility   In this country research on sex roles and the origin of behavioral differences between men and women is common, but such research could not be carried out where a traditional patriarchy holds sway, as in Iran, for example. The mere questioning of the traditional view is enough, in such situations, to call down political reprisal on the scientist. In countries with totalitarian governments or strongly entrenched established religions, the researcher is prevented from carrying out research projects contrary to the official ideology as seen by the people in power. Unless the researcher is allowed to pursue research freely, a strong political group may try to influence the published conclusions. Closely tied to the issue of possibility is the issue of acceptability.

Acceptability   Sometimes a scientist comes up with findings that not only result in reprisal by those in power but also scandalize society. This was the fate of Ignaz Phillipp Semmelweis, the "Hungarian crank," who lost his chance for advancement, his reputation, eventually his sanity, and at last his life because he devoted his entire medical career to the development of his theory that medical personnel were causing the deaths of patients, especially new mothers, by examining them with unclean hands, thereby carrying disease from other patients and from cadavers. For this theory and for his advocacy of scrupulous cleansing of the hands and bedding, Semmelweis was bitterly attacked during his entire professional life. He died at the age of 47 from an infection contracted while examining a patient. (It would be reassuring to think that we have advanced to an enlightenment that precludes our stifling of unpopular views. However, this *is* the century that has seen Bertrand Russell unable to lecture at an eastern university because of his views on marriage and also the era of Senator Joseph McCarthy's witch-hunt against Communists. William Shockley's views on genetic differences between races have gone unheard from time to time because he has been forbidden a public forum or been shouted down.)

In Europe Semmelweis shocked society by suggesting that doctors ("gentlemen") had dirty hands. At the same period and without ever hearing of Semmelweis, Oliver Wendell Holmes was coming to the same conclusions in New England.[9]

As these examples indicate, scientists do continue with their research in the face of scorn and persecution. Scientists also proceed alone with ideas in which they alone believe. You must decide for yourself whether to be innovative and whether to lead rather than follow. The scientific method requires you to be honest and objective but does not dictate your topics.

Although students' topics are less restricted in the ways just outlined than those of researchers who intend to publish their reports, you need to be aware of these limitations as you read those published results. Also, political and social climate affects more than the researcher's "freedom" to pursue an interest. It also affects project funding.

Money and Sponsorship

Most researchers are not in a position to support themselves while they carry out a project, nor can they pay for staff salaries, equipment, supplies, and facilities. They have to estimate costs, find someone who will provide the money, and make a careful budget once they know how much money they have.

Estimating Costs

Estimating your costs for a project is similar to making a vacation budget. Before going on a trip, you plan an itinerary, count the number of meals and nights' lodgings, and estimate admissions, fares, mileage, and purchases. After you have multiplied the cost of each item by the number of times you will need it, you add it all up and have the approximate cost of the trip. The estimation of a research budget is no different except for the kinds of items. You must have an outline of the proposed project in order to draw up a list of costs. You read the outline and jot down each possible expense in these general categories:

facilities and equipment	subjects
personnel	data collection
publication	analysis

There are public and private sources of funds, and you can apply to one of them for a **grant**. The grants available range from long-term funding of entire research teams using elaborate facilities to short-term mini-grants for professionals working alone part-time or during brief leaves of absence from their customary duties. It is possible to work on your own project without any leave or granted money, but it is much harder and takes much longer. Lack of funds also limits the scope of the project. Occasionally you can get free space, supplies, and/or equipment, and sometimes free consultation and volunteer assistance. Such benefits will depend on your situation, opportunities, powers of persuasion, and even luck.

Once you have selected a potential sponsor, you obtain that sponsor's standard application form and complete it. The application is usually referred to as your **proposal**, since it sets forth in the form specified by the sponsor all of the details of the proposed project. The proposal includes a budget, which you must complete by using your budget estimate as a guide.

You have to write a convincing proposal to persuade the grant committee that:

1. the question is worth asking.
2. the proposed staff has the proper **credentials** and is capable of doing the research.
3. the methods and time schedule are feasible.
4. no one will be hurt by the project.
5. no important political group will be offended.
6. the budget is realistic.
7. the project is appropriate for the agency considering it.
8. the results will be usable by somebody.

(See Appendix C for detailed instructions on these requirements.)

When you have a good estimate of the time and money you need, you are in a good position to decide where changes can be made in your plans.

Adjusting the Ideal to the Real

The best procedure is to decide what the ideal approach would be and then, considering the limits under which you will be working, modify it only as much as you absolutely must. If you need 3 years and $150,000 and you can have only one semester and free use of the Sociology Department's mimeograph machine, you have to face that. If the technical help or the facilities you need are not available, you must adjust your plans.

You might think it would be better to start with your probable time and money allowance and dream up a suitable project, but there are two advantages to outlining the ideal project first. One is that if you have the ideal in front of you, you are challenged to come up with imaginative ways to improve your resources. The other advantage is that having the ideal project in the back of your mind keeps you humble, and you are less likely to make inappropriate claims for your results.

You should not be discouraged if you have to streamline your project a lot to make it feasible. You can narrow the research question and hypothesis, or discard some hypotheses if there are several, taking care not to eliminate a solid investigation of the research question. Never compromise by sacrificing validity. A tiny valid study is better than a large invalid one.

Scarce cash is one reason people think of using available data. A lot of information lies already collected in many places, and it's cheaper and easier to use these data than to collect your own. One new source of data has emerged since the development of the modern computer. There are now many computerized files, called **data banks**, available for analysis. Computers are able to search out and find selected items for researchers to tabulate in new ways. Computers can not only find the data, but also label it and construct a variety of charts and tables for you automatically. Also, available data usually are easier to get at than real people. This brings us to the problem of access.

Access

The need for access confronts you when you start to collect data. You need a means of approaching the subjects in your sample in order to collect data, as was mentioned briefly in Chapter 3. Let's look more closely into this matter now, first paying attention to the types of group you might want to sample, both convenient and difficult to reach. Then we'll look at entry strategies and finally, the motivations that may impel subjects to cooperate (see Figure 4.2).

FIGURE 4.2   **Types of access to data**

Convenient Access

1. Captive groups: people with physical and mental illness, prisoners, infants

2. Institutional groups: students, union members

3. Occupational groups

4. Unobtrusive groups: samples of evidence

Entry Strategies

1. Informant

2. Tangible reward

3. Intangible reward

Difficult Access

1. Subcultural: national and religious groups

2. Categorically based groups: race, sex, age, physical handicap

3. Deviants: criminals, hoboes, bag ladies

Convenient Access

When people are captive members of organized groups or practicing particular occupations and professions, access to them is often convenient because they are under constraints that make it advisable or desirable for them to cooperate with you.

Captive Groups   These are people in institutions who are either not aware of being studied or not capable of resisting it. **Captive groups** include people with many forms of physical and mental illness, corpses, infants, and prisoners.[10] The researcher might be a staff member or someone with permission to enter the institution and do the study.

Very often the "permission" of the subjects or their caretakers is sought and obtained; especially with increased awareness of individuals' rights and the possibility of abuses. However, inasmuch as the subjects may easily not comprehend what is being asked of them and insofar as they might see some advantage to cooperating with anyone of higher status, they often go along with the program.

Institutional Groups   People who are not "captive" but are members of unions and clubs, students in schools, and constituencies of organizations belong to **institutional groups**. Although these subjects are aware of being studied, they are generally motivated to cooperate with the project because of their respect for the authorities in charge of their group. Here the expectation of advantage stemming from cooperation is of a different character. Whereas a prisoner or mental patient might hope for some expansion of privileges in daily life, a student or group member is thinking of making a good impression and possibly being advanced in rank. Furthermore, the expectation for the member or student is much weaker and is only a small part of a much broader attempt to "look good" in the eyes of the leaders.

Permission to study institutional groups is obtained from the leaders of the groups, and then an individual request is made of the member or a call for volunteers is issued. These requests are supported by the people in charge, often by their personal appearance, letter, or other announcement.

Occupational Groups   Members of many occupations and professions, especially those requiring higher education, feel an obligation to cooperate with researchers. College professors are an example of these occupational groups. Access to them is relatively easy, since you can appeal to your mutual membership in the community of scholars and practitioners.

Samples of evidence or available data are other kinds of data to which you may seek access.

Other Sources of Data   Sometimes you need to gain access to an observation post or to the cumulated, or gathered, data. Unless you are trying to observe something held sacred or something classified secret, such as a military installation, there is little problem. By definition available data are accessible. Some will be very easy to find, and some will require perseverance.

Data that never become "available" are usually protected by law or as part of a **privileged communication**. A confession to a priest is one type of privileged communication. The "privilege" is immunity from legal demands that the content be revealed. There are few instances of this but it has become a pressing question. Does a person have the right to withhold blood or urine samples from drug testing if those samples might reveal the presence of a stigmatized condition or its treatment? Must a physician reveal who is or is not part of a patient category?

Difficult access develops out of the researcher's identity as an outsider in the subjects' eyes and from the tendency of some groups to wander from place to place.

**Difficult
Access**

People who regard you as an outsider are called **in-groups**. They include subcultural groups (national or religious), categories (race, sex, age, for example), and deviants.

Subcultural Groups   Recognizable **subcultural groups** abound in our country. Some ethnic communities like the Amish and the Hassidic Jews keep apart from others deliberately, and others, though less exclusive, tend to form distinct clusters. Scores of cities have "little Italies" or "Chinatowns." Sometimes the people in these areas speak a foreign language, which you must know or learn before studying them. If you haven't grown up with that language, you may have a hard time understanding its subtleties, such as double meanings, nuances of words, puns, slang, or in-jokes. Their customs will not have the same import for you as they have for the group. You may mistake their meaning entirely.

Categories   The designation **category** here refers to people who have a common, identifying characteristic; they may or may not be organized into an authentic group. Race, age, sex, and physical handicap are examples of important features that affect our opportunities and experiences so much that we cannot afford to ignore them. Social class is another such category. When a researcher differs from a subject in one of these characteristics, the difference often has the same effect as if they were of different language groups. There is a language barrier here too, because the various class and age levels of any society are readily distinguishable by their speech, each with an **in-language**.

Language is limited by sex and physical handicap. You might hesitate to mention certain subjects to someone of the opposite sex; moreover, your choice of words and the degree of your self-revelation may differ when you speak to someone of the opposite sex. If some or all of the subjects of your research are deaf, you may have to communicate with them through an interpreter or learn sign language yourself. At this point you may discover that English is a foreign language to a native of this country who was born deaf. Deaf people who sign have their own language. It is called American Sign Language in this country, and it is very different in syntax from English. Signed English exists, but even skill in using it will not enable you to translate English sentences verbatim, because signs do not exist for every English word. These difficulties can be surmounted, but they must not be ignored.

The ease with which cultural and categorically based group members can recognize you as an outsider makes it easy for them to prevent you access to their private life. One danger is that they will close ranks and refuse to admit you at all, another is that they will agree to admit you and then be careful to present only "front" matter, or their public position as they want it known.[11]

Deviants   Strictly speaking, deviants are people who act in unusual ways and depart from the society's norms. Our use of the word will be restricted, however, to people who engage in criminal behavior. Access to these people presents not only all of the difficulties outlined for the other groups but also additional ones. Because they are always on their guard against discovery by the authorities, they have even more reason to regard the researcher as an interloper. They also present a risk for the researcher since they operate in dangerous settings and provide information about illegal activities. If a researcher is present at or aware of an illegal activity, this may have unpleasant consequences because everyone is supposed to report illegal acts to the police. Another unpleasant possibility is that the researcher may be seen as part of a deviant group by the authorities. [12]

Some deviants wander from place to place or are not to be found in any particular place because they have no permanent home. Hoboes, bag ladies, and street people can be hard to locate. The United States Census provides for a special "T-night" (transient night) to enumerate transients at hotels, motels, Y's and campgrounds, and a special "M-night" (mission night) to enumerate people at missions, flophouses, local jails, detention centers, and bus and railroad stations and terminals. In large cities a "casual count" is conducted of people who are to be found only on street corners and in pool halls, bars, and similar locations. [13] There are, of course, nondeviants who travel all the time: gypsies, migrant workers, and circus people.

An unusual access difficulty was reported by Michal McCall, who began her research without a definite idea of who or where her subjects might be. She wanted to study female artists but was not sure exactly what that term should include. McCall's work was exploratory and her procedure painstaking. Eventually she developed a **typology**, or classification, of female artists. [14]

For McCall to find and list types of female artists she had to devise an **entry strategy** that would not only gain her access but tell her where the female artists were. They were difficult to locate because they had no organized or official status as artists.

Entry Strategies

Michal McCall found the technique of snowball sampling useful. You will remember from our discussion in Chapter 3 that the process begins with an interview with one or more appropriate subjects, who then refer the researcher to others. As this process is repeated over and over, the researcher accumulates data from an entire network of subjects. A similar strategy involves the use of an **informant**. Whyte began his 3-year study of unemployed young men in Boston by finding an informant, with whom he was to be associated for the entire time. The trick was to find the informant. Whyte describes several false starts, including attempts to strike up casual acquaintances, all of which failed. Eventually a social worker at the settlement house recommended the man who proved to be so helpful to Whyte. [15]

An informant performs the same function as the authorities do when you are studying an institutional group: They legitimize you in the eyes of the subjects. Until you are seen as a legitimate, if temporary, addition to the scene, the subjects are not likely to cooperate. In his study of Times Square, David Karp reports that one of his strategies was to hang around the area on a regular basis so that the regular street population would get used to him and regard him as part of the scene. [16]

The importance of getting an "in" to the group you want to study is nowhere better illustrated than in Joan Eakin Hoffman's interesting report of her experience in conducting interviews with the members of hospital boards of directors. Her initial attempts to get interviews with these (upper class) people were frustrating. When she did succeed in getting interviews, the sessions were short and constantly interrupted by phone calls. Hoffman points out that busy executives direct their secretaries to intercept phone calls if they consider the conference important enough. Hoffman's interviews were not given this status, and she succeeded in getting only formal explanations, similar to the kind of information presented in a press release. (This is known as "front" information, a designation contributed by Erving Goffman.[17])

By chance a respondent discovered that Hoffman's family included one of his acquaintances. This revelation altered her entire study. As soon as the board member realized that he "knew" the researcher, he opened up and told her the inside information held back earlier. When Hoffman realized that who she was would influence the depth of her investigation, she began to capitalize on her acquaintance with some board members by getting them to refer her personally to others. This completely eased her access difficulties.[18]

Assuming that you do not want to limit your research to those populations that contain acquaintances, you have to find a way to persuade people to help you, whether they are people who will become respondents or people who will supply respondents. They will do so if their perceived cost is outweighed by their perceived rewards. Rewards can be tangible or intangible.

Tangible Rewards **Tangible rewards** may include a token payment for participation. This is sometimes used by businesses who want consumers to fill out questionnaires about their products. Often the respondent, or "tester," is given samples of that product to try out and is rewarded with other gifts after he or she submits the completed questionnaire. I have received new textbooks in the mail accompanied by this request; the publisher includes a list of free, popular titles from which the professor may choose if the questionnaire about the text already received is completed and submitted.

Intangible Rewards Some people get an **intangible reward** when they do something "for science"; that is, they feel good about themselves for doing it. Maybe the problem being studied is one they would like to see solved, for example, a chronic disease. Maybe they like the idea of participating in something that may eventually influence the course of human events. They may feel more important because their opinion has been asked. They may be bored and lonely and happy to talk to you.

The rewards mentioned for participating in research thus far have been perfectly acceptable, but at times rewards offered are questionable and also the research methods used are sometimes unacceptable because they violate the rules of good conduct that are part of society's values. These rules of good conduct are called **ethics**.

Ethics

We have ethical rules in two main areas: responsibility toward subjects of research, which involves the avoidance of any physical, mental, or social injury to the subjects, and responsibility toward colleagues and community, which involves clear and complete publication of results and care not to damage the reputation of the scientific field. There are ethical safeguards to observe.

Responsibility Toward Subjects of Research

A subject who cooperates in research can be injured in a way that is physical, mental, or social. No responsible researcher will hurt subjects in any way, including causing discomfort, unless the subjects have previously agreed to such conditions.

The Avoidance of Injury   Subjects do volunteer for studies that include sensory deprivation, dietary regimens, and many kinds of stress. It is usually possible to foresee what will be painful and to warn the research participants. The ambiguous area of mental and social injury, however, is difficult to assess and even more difficult to control. It includes the stimulation of false hopes, fear, grief, and anxiety; the use of deceit and trickery, possibly causing a loss of self-esteem; the invasion of privacy and interference in private lives; damage to the reputation of individuals and groups; and withholding beneficial treatment. Accounts of all these practices can be found in published research reports.[19]

Often respondents don't understand that there is no connection between the help they give the researcher and the subsequent policies of government or social service agencies. To many respondents, the researcher is one of "them," that is, the authorities, and "they" run things. Often a respondent will preface answers with "You can tell them for me that . . ."; he or she clearly thinks that the answer will have an effect on something. At other times a respondent may voice the hope that when the interview answers reach the sponsor of the research, some specific desired change will take place, such as fixing broken-down dwellings, increasing inadequate allowances, or passing beneficial laws. These are all false hopes.

Mental injury includes causing disturbing emotions such as fear and grief. A researcher has to consider carefully whether the proposed questions or procedures will actually stimulate these painful feelings. Questions can remind respondents of difficult periods in their lives or can raise other questions they have not considered before. A question designed to discover what someone knows about a medical condition can suggest problems that were previously unknown to the person. Another possibility is loss of self-esteem, stemming from the introduction of new ideas about "what other people think" or the subsequent impression (true or not) that one has been misled by the researcher.

When respondents cooperate with you because they are lonely and if they have any expectation that you will be a more enduring part of their life than you intend, you may be taking advantage of them. They are hoping for a friend, but you are only being friendly. When you don't follow up the initial contact(s) with further interest, they may feel rejected. They may also be embarrassed, regretful, guilty, or frightened when they consider what they have revealed to you. There is no way of knowing for sure the effect of your conversations with them.

Another negative feeling interviewing can promote is self-denigration. Not having the answers may make some people feel ignorant or stupid because they may think there are "right" answers and that they "should" know them. People often ask "Was that the right answer?" The average person seems to think there are right and wrong answers to most questions. Because the interview and survey situation resembles school testing, some people respond to it with anxiety.

Many forms of research involve the invasion of privacy, and sometimes that invasion of privacy can have serious consequences for the respondent's reputation, safety, or freedom. The publication of medical test results, referred to above, is one example. Informants may be particularly vulnerable. Consider what happens to informers and spies if the people they are reporting on discover the informant. Less drastic, but potentially just as damaging, is the effect the publication of research reports may have on individuals' standing in the community or on the attitudes of the community toward the subjects' age, sex, racial, religious, or political group.

Any research project that requires delving into people's sex lives, political opinions, intimate conversations, family interaction, or finances asks its respondents to run the risk of disrupting their social networks. This is a common outcome of newspaper publicity. Public figures often deny quotes or try to explain them away. They may have to apologize or compensate for something they are reported to have said. Very few people can afford to have their private remarks held up to public scrutiny. The possibility that a whole category or group may be criticized because of the published political and social opinions of some of its members or that those opinions may be used as justification for public policy has caused some minority group leaders to caution their constituents against cooperating with surveys.

Withholding beneficial treatment from subjects is a consideration arising mostly in experimental research when a potentially beneficial procedure or drug is given to the experimental group but not to the control group. This is especially difficult when the subjects are terminally ill. The researcher may have to discontinue the experiment because the subject needs emergency life-saving procedures or is in severe pain.[20] Behavioral research subjects may not be as immediately threatened; however, a subject may have an experimental rehabilitation treatment withheld, and no one knows what effect such a treatment might have had. Certainly, if the subject expected a benefit and it was withheld, the subject has been damaged.

Suppose you are a teacher recruiting volunteers, and you offer class credit for participation in your project. If the participation teaches the students anything relevant to the course, it is ethical. If participation is irrelevant to the course, it is not ethical because the students' opportunity to learn legitimate course material would have been sacrificed in the interest of your study.

A few rules of conduct have been developed to protect subjects of research from possible injury. We can refer to them as **ethical safeguards**.

Ethical Safeguards   It is generally agreed that ethical safeguards are desirable, though many researchers warn that following them to the letter may rule out scientific research on many subjects. The rules include:

1. Do not lie, and do not trick the subjects into cooperating with you.
2. Guarantee anonymity, or at least keep from disclosing confidential information.
3. Get the subjects' consent, if possible, and see that they understand what you are doing.
4. Do not publish information that reflects badly on individuals or groups unless you can surely conceal their identity.
5. See to it that no harm of any kind comes to subjects as a consequence of your research, unless subjects understand that they can be injured and agree to the risk in advance.

Each discipline has formulated a code of ethics. You should refer to the one that is relevant to your field of study. This is part of the researcher's responsibility toward colleagues and the scientific community. Most institutions require review of all research on human subjects by a panel on ethics.

Responsibility Toward Colleagues and Community

To avoid damaging the past, present, and future work of other people, you must not mislead those who read your work or make research look bad to the public.

Misleading Research Reports   The danger here is that your report may hinder rather than help other scientists because your analysis is incomplete, biased, or distorted in some other way. You might have neglected clarity or omitted something in describing your method and mistakes. Others need to learn from your experience whether it was good or bad.

Offensive Behavior Toward Subjects   This category incorporates all the problems involving responsibility toward subjects. It is included here because unethical conduct toward subjects is a disservice to both colleagues and community inasmuch as it tarnishes the reputation of the specific field, the academic community, and research in general. For a scathing denunciation of this kind of unethical practice, read Donald P. Warwick's "Social Scientists Ought to Stop Lying," a thought-provoking discussion of the subject.[21]

Ethical Safeguards   The rules of the scientific method, outlined in Chapter 1, are the main safeguard against unethical conduct toward colleagues and community. They specify objectivity and honest reporting. To those rules we can now add:

6. Give careful consideration to the possible consequences of your research in the community, and refrain from doing anything that might have unfortunate social or political consequences for any individual or group.

Many of the ethical issues have inspired sharp controversy. In Chapter 12, after we've examined the details of data collection, analysis, and reporting, we'll consider some ethical dilemmas and the arguments surrounding them.

One ethical safeguard requires the inclusion of other people's opinions at every stage of the research. This is important in order to overcome the limitation of one's own viewpoint and experience.

Multifaceted Research

The organizations that run our lives are very large and our nations' populations are large—all over the world. Increasingly, business and government decision makers rely on research results and experts to help them make intelligent choices. They often commission research projects to answer specific important questions. The validity of the approach and accuracy of the data are of the utmost importance because the decisions made affect us greatly.

The validity of a research project may be improved by using more than one method to collect the data. You can have more confidence in a result that has been reached by more than one route, especially if those routes are widely separated. In other words, using more than one method is most effective if the methods you choose are quite different from each other.

Diversity of Method

Each method has its own strengths and weaknesses, so the strength of one may compensate for the weakness of another. This is the value of **multifaceted research**. If, for example, a structured questionnaire provides good codable data but lacks depth and fails to provide insight, it needs to be supplemented by a few depth interviews. These may be hard to code and may not yield data that can be manipulated statistically, but they may provide background and narrative examples. If you use more than one method and get the same indications each time, you may be more confident that you have achieved internal validity in your project.

Diversity of Perspective

As mentioned earlier, other people's opinions are worth a lot to you. There are two ways in which you should seek them out. One is the normal procedure of asking colleagues and associates to read and comment on your research ideas and proposals: a professional courtesy incumbent on all. You will be asked to review other people's plans and ideas also. While you're still in school, your instructors do this for you. When you're out practicing your profession, you also practice mutual criticism and evaluation.

Always remember that your own perspective is limited. It isn't appropriate to be hurt or angry when others examine your work and suggest changes. Feeling a little disappointed is natural, but don't dwell on it. Consider each comment objectively, and take it into account in your revisions. Get several colleagues to look at your work. If you are still in school, discuss your work with your instructor and other students in the same spirit.

The other way to get more than one perspective on your research is to include other people on your research team, not as subordinates, but as partners. It's important to get the team assembled before final decisions on the methods are made so that team members are involved in those decisions from the beginning. Their enthusiasm and commitment to the project, and therefore their efficiency in working on it, are raised by their having had a voice in the plans. If you are working with professionals from different fields, a **multidisciplinary approach** to your research question is possible. If you are working with professionals from your own field, each may bring a slightly different perspective to the work. For graduate students or other trainees, the preliminary discussions and planning sessions are a valuable part of training. The clerical personnel also benefit from understanding what the project is all about, and they can contribute worthwhile suggestions. In other words, get everyone involved early. If you are working on a student team for a course, frequent meetings early in the term are a lifesaver. The early group decisions must be clearly understood by each team member if the team is to work smoothly.

Whether you are working with a group or going it alone, you begin with a scrutiny of the research question and one or more hypotheses, as well as a list of the pieces of information you must get from or about each respondent. You make estimates of time needed to complete each phase of the data collection and assemble a trial package of data collection instruments. This package may be no more than one interview schedule or as much as several data collection instruments with necessary equipment. Whatever it is, the package needs to be tested. You try out the materials and record the time taken and any problems encountered. Testing the instruments a dozen or so times enables you to establish the average time needed for the completion of one unit. Testing provides a chance for the team to practice, and it shows you where your plans should be revised. For this trial period almost anyone can be used as a respondent, but you should try to get some people on the same educational level as your ultimate sample so that you are sure your questions are understandable and are free of academic jargon. If you are not asking any questions, you may still need to test to determine such things as how long an observer can maintain an attentive attitude while standing on a street corner.

After the testing of the procedures, you must carefully analyze the results and make any indicated changes. For large and expensive studies a **pilot study**, or a trial run of the larger study, is often done. Black and Champion list four main reasons for doing this. A pilot study:

1.   Tests data collection instruments
2.   Develops better approaches to research subjects
3.   Develops categories for proposed questions
4.   Determines whether or not the larger study would be worthwhile[22]

Nearly every research project ends with the researchers recognizing ways in which they could have done better. A pilot study is a good way to find out some of these in advance. Very often a researcher will submit the results of a pilot study to a granting agency to show that the larger project is worth the agency's investment.

In Chapter 5 we shall begin to examine the methods of data collection more closely. As we go along, think carefully about ways in which the different techniques might be profitably combined in a single project.

Summary and Conclusion

Since everyone wants to make a good impression on everyone else, the researcher may have some difficulty getting an accurate account of human behavior. People being studied may try to make the "right" impression on the researcher. The researcher, therefore, may decide to use indirect research methods—that is, methods that do not require face-to-face interaction between investigator and subject. These methods include collecting circumstantial evidence and analyzing communications or available data.

Direct research methods include interviews, questionnaires, and experiments, as well as the various forms of observation. The choice among these as well as the indirect methods is strongly influenced by time available, duration, timing, money, and access. In choosing methods, the researcher must bear in mind the need for ethical conduct and must recognize responsibility to subjects and to the research community.

All the decisions in research benefit greatly if the investigator practices diversity of method and seeks diversity of perspective.

Main Points

1. Interviewer effect is likely to distort our data if we are not careful. Indirect research methods may avoid interviewer effect. They include unobtrusive measures, content analysis, and use of available data. To avoid interviewer effect, the researcher may also improve direct data collection methods or find ways to measure interviewer effect and allow for it in analysis.

2. Unobtrusive measures are ways of collecting data after the action has taken place and the people are gone.

3. Content analysis is examining some form of communication to find patterns.

4. Using available data means analyzing data that have already been collected and aggregated.

5. Observation involves paying attention with a view to recording and analyzing the things seen and heard. Observation can be done as a participant or as a nonparticipant, in a structured or an unstructured manner, and after announcing one's purpose or without doing so.

6. An interview is an organized conversation held to collect data. It can be structured or unstructured.

7. A questionnaire is a list of questions that are usually answered by the respondent on a form, with or without the researcher's help.

8. An experiment is a test in which two groups are measured; one of them is subjected to a treatment, and both are measured again. The group treated is the experimental group, the other group is the control group, and the treatment is the experimental variable. An experiment is called a quasi-experiment when the components of it cannot be rigorously controlled. This is typical of experiments with unconfined people.

9. Time is short, and parts of your research may take longer than you expect. This limits what you can do. Avoid taking so long to collect data that your first materials are out of date. Your project must be appropriate to the interest of your time, permissible according to the mores of the day, and acceptable to decision makers. Since time and money are both

scarce, sponsorship is welcome. To get sponsorship, you have to esti-mate costs, find a source of money, and convince the grantors that your project is worth funding. You must also match the scope of your research to the amount of your funding, or as the saying goes, you must learn to cut your cloth to fit your purse.

10. Some groups are more convenient to study than others because people vary in accessibility. You may have to develop an entry strategy to get cooperation from subjects. One possibility is to get the help of an inform-ant, or insider, who can introduce you to people and clue you in.

11. You have to be careful about what rewards you offer people for partici-pating in your study and make sure that you do not violate any of the rules of good conduct, which are called ethics. Responsibility toward your subjects forbids you to hurt them in any way by giving them false hopes, exposing them to criticism, or deceiving them. Responsibility toward your field requires that you do not publish any misleading in-formation or do anything that makes the field or research in general look bad.

12. You can safeguard yourself against making errors by using more than one method to collect data and by getting other people's opinions at every step. It's a good idea to get people from other disciplines to work with you if you can. A pilot study, or trial run, is a good way to test your design and to see if it works.

Notes

1. G. H. Mead, *Mind, Self and Society*, ed. Charles W. Morris (Chicago: University of Chicago Press, 1962), pp. 90–91; 139–44.

2. Eugene J. Webb, Donald J. Campbell, Richard D. Schwartz, and Lee Sechrest, *Unobtrusive Measures: Nonreactive Research in the Social Sciences* (Skokie, Ill.: Rand McNally, 1966), p. 2.

3. Women on Words and Images, *Dick and Jane as Victims: Sex Stereotyping in Children's Readers* (Princeton, N.J.: National Organization for Women, 1972).

4. James A. Black and Dean J. Champion, *Methods and Issues in Social Research* (New York: Wiley, 1976), p. 330.

5. William Foote Whyte, *Street Corner Society: The Social Structure of an Italian Slum*, 2nd ed. (Chicago: University of Chicago Press, 1955), pp. 332–35.

6. Laud Humphreys, *The Tearoom Trade: Impersonal Sex in Public Places* (Chicago: Aldine, 1970).

7. The method was invented by David Kantor. It was developed at the Boston Family Institute and the Boston State Hospital Family Training Program and is only one of the methods used in family therapy.

8. David A. Karp, "Observing Behavior in Public Places: Problems and Strategies," in *Fieldwork Experience: Qualitative Approaches to Social Research*, ed. William B. Shaffir, Robert A. Stebbins, and Allan Turowetz (New York: St. Martin's Press, 1980), pp. 82–97.

9. Harvey Graham, *Eternal Eve: The History of Gynaecology and Obstetrics* (New York: Doubleday, 1951), pp. 396–420.

10. David Sudnow, *Passing On: The Social Organization of Dying* (Englewood Cliffs, N J.: Prentice-Hall, 1967), p. 59. This provides an example of the study of corpses.

11. Joan Eakin Hoffman, "Problems of Access in the Study of Social Elites and Boards of Directors," in *Fieldwork Experience*, ed. Shaffir, Stebbins, and Turowetz, pp. 47–49.

12. W. Gordon West, "Access to Adolescent Deviants and Deviance," in *Fieldwork Experience*, ed. Shaffir, Stebbins, and Turowetz, p. 38.

13. Peter K. Francese, "The 1980 Census: The Counting of America," *Population Bulletin* 34, no. 4 (1979): 9–10.

14. Michal McCall, "Who and Where Are the Artists?" in *Fieldwork Experience*, ed. Shaffir, Stebbins, and Turowetz, pp. 145–58.

15. Whyte, *Street Corner Society*, pp. 288–91.

16. Karp, "Observing Behavior in Public Places," p. 94.

17. Erving Goffman, in *The Presentation of Self in Everyday Life* (New York: Doubleday, 1959), p. 107.

18. Hoffman, "Problems of Access," pp. 46–51.

19. Theodore C. Wagenaar, ed., *Readings for Social Research* (Belmont, Calif.: Wadsworth, 1981), pp. 30–42. The discussion here contains some hair-raising examples.

20. Judith P. Swazey and Renée C. Fox, "The Clinical Moratorium," in *Essays in Medical Sociology*, ed. Renée C. Fox (New York: Wiley, 1979), pp. 350–53.

21. Donald P. Warwick, "Social Scientists Ought to Stop Lying," in *Readings for Social Research*, ed. Wagenaar, pp. 33–37.

22. Black and Champion, *Methods and Issues in Social Research*, pp. 114–15.

Exercises

Since you are going to be instructed in detail in the methods of data collection throughout Part II of this book, you are given no exercises here that are relevant to the part of Chapter 4 that gave you an overview of this very important matter. Your exercises are intended, rather, to help you read published research with an understanding of the methods that were used. One exercise asks you to look at journal articles and find examples of some of the methods described in this chapter. The other exercise focuses your attention on examples of different kinds of subjects used by published researchers.

Exercise 4.1   *Methods of research*

Instructions: In any professional journal, find two articles that report a research project. Read the articles and answer the following questions:

Article 1:

author(s) _____

title _____

source _____

page numbers _____

1. Which of the methods included in Figure 4.1 was used in this study?

    a. Indirect or direct? _____

    b. Name of method: _____

2. What were they trying to find out?

Article 2:

author(s) _____

title _____

source _____

page numbers _____

1. Which of the methods included in Figure 4.1 was used in this study?

    a. Indirect or direct? _____

    b. Name of method: _____

2. What were they trying to find out?

Your name _____   Instructor _____

Exercise 4.2   *Finding subjects*

Instructions: Using the same articles selected for Exercise 4.1, answer the following questions about each.

Article 1:

author(s) _____

title _____

source _____

page numbers _____

1. Which of the types of groups listed in Chapter 4 did this sample of respondents represent?

    _____

2. Who were they? _____

3. Was the access convenient or difficult? _____

4. Give quotes from the article to support your answer to question 3.

    _____

    _____

5. What was the entry strategy or access method used?

    _____

6. Comments?

Article 2:

author(s) _____

title _____

source _____

page numbers _____

1. Which of the types of groups listed in Chapter 4 did this sample of respondents represent?

   _____

2. Who were they? _____

3. Was the access convenient or difficult? _____

4. Give quotes from the article to support your answer to question 3.

   _____

   _____

5. What was the entry strategy or access method used?

   _____

6. Comments?

PART II

Methods of Data Collection

The four chapters of Part II expand the overview of data collection methods presented in Chapter 4. Chapter 5, Indirect and Observational Methods of Data Collection, examines the techniques of unobtrusive measures, the use of content analysis to analyze pictures and communications, and the sources and uses of available data. The chapter ends with a review of the merits and procedures for participant and nonparticipant observation. After dealing with the issues of locating appropriate subjects and methods of recording data, the chapter presents the advantages and disadvantages of participation in the subject group's activities, of announcing one's research role, and of structuring the data collection.

Chapter 6, Interviews, covers the preparation of interview schedules, the manner of conducting interviews, and the advantages and disadvantages of each. The relationship between the researcher and the respondent is explored in detail. Chapter 7, Questionnaires and Surveys, deals with administering questionnaires in person or by telephone, and the special considerations required when mailing these instruments.

Chapter 8, Experiments and Quasi-Experiments, begins by defining and describing the classical experiment, discussing the problems it poses, and giving examples of well-known designs intended to solve some of the problems. The balance of the chapter is devoted to an examination of quasi-experiments (modifications of the classical experimental procedures made necessary by the researcher's inability to control subjects and situations typically encountered in behavioral research.) The chapter ends with a brief description of natural experiments and the single-case research method developed by clinical therapists.

CHAPTER 5

Indirect and Observational Methods of Data Collection

Unobtrusive Measures
   Evidence
   Appraisal of Data
   Advantages and Disadvantages of Unobtrusive Measures

Content Analysis
   Material
   Quantification of Data
   Advantages and Disadvantages of Content Analysis

Available Data
   Sources
   Finding Available Data
   Advantages and Disadvantages of Using Available Data

Participant and Nonparticipant Observation
   Goals and Methods
   Locating Appropriate Subjects
   Recording the Data

Modes of Observation
   Participating in the Group's Activities
   Announcing One's Purpose
   Structuring the Observations
   Alternatives

Summary and Conclusion

Main Points

Notes

Exercises
   Exercise 5.1 Content analysis
   Exercise 5.2 Participant observation
   Exercise 5.3 Nonparticipant observation
   Exercise 5.4 The sociogram
   Exercise 5.5 Critique

Now we are going to take a closer look at data collection methods outlined in the beginning of the preceding chapter. This chapter deals with the indirect methods of data collection: unobtrusive measures, content analysis, and the analysis of available data, as well as types of direct observation. Data to be collected are either **qualitative data**, which are expressed in words and give evidence of meaning and significance, or **quantitative data**, which are expressed in numbers and give a summation of frequency. **Qualitative** data include observations, conversations, anecdotes, letters, and diaries. These sources are often very rich in insights and provide a background against which a subject is greatly illuminated. **Quantitative** data consist of counted items. They can only represent the presence or absence of something that can be counted or the dimensions of something that can be measured. Sometimes this is essential. In brief, your account of how you enjoyed the show is qualitative; how much it cost you and how many times you went how far to see it are all quantitative. We sometimes criticize people who focus too much on the quantitative (cost) and neglect the qualitative (happiness). The ideal research project includes both.

Unobtrusive Measures

First we'll consider the nature of the evidence gathered for unobtrusive measures. Since this evidence has to endure from the time of the action until the researcher observes it, it can't be anything ephemeral, or short-lived, but must be something that accumulates or at least leaves something behind.

Evidence

Unobtrusive measures deal with the circumstantial evidence of research. This evidence falls into three main categories: accretions, traces, and erosions.

Accretions   Accretions are items left behind as the result of some activity, like the torn tickets and discarded candy wrappers after a show. They are additions to the scene. As these additions accumulate, you can measure and examine them and compare the results with data from other times and places.

Many scientists measure accretions. Each geological period leaves behind deposits of minerals that tell the geologist what kind of climate, vegetation, and animal life existed in each period. Each year of a tree's life results in a ring of growth around its trunk. When the tree is cut down, the rings tell its age.

Archaeologists are examining accretions when they sift through ancient garbage dumps and old ruins. They can infer a lot about the lives of societies long dead by the objects and materials they find. The Lamberg-Karlovskys at Tepe Yahya in Iran found numerous items that have shed light on the life of the ancient Elamites. The type of bronze in the items found indicates the knowledge and practice of smelting; metals not native to that area were used, indicating some type of trade route.[1]

Detectives examine accretions when they look for clues. A chef learns which dishes are popular by the amounts left on the plates. One investigator wanted to estimate liquor sales in an area that had no liquor stores. He counted the bottles in the trash.[2]

Traces A trace is not as substantial as an accretion. It may not even be tangible. Rumpled sheets tell you that someone has been in the bed. Footprints in the snow reveal a former presence. Graffiti, bloodstains, and fingerprints are all traces. You can tell something has happened when you see defacement, disturbance, damage, or decoration, as in the occasional artwork one sees on sidewalks and walls. You can even detect the influence of something. A study of paintings and sculpture has shown that the nudes of each historical era were depicted as if they wore invisible clothes. The figures were distorted to conform to the fashion of the day, deviating from the actual shape of the normal human body as the style deviated. For example, when small waists were stylish, nude women were depicted with abnormally small waists.[3] This is a subtle trace, indeed. The author's thesis is that the painted nudes of an era show evidence of the fashions of that day.

Erosions Erosion is wearing away or depletion. Wear on shoes tells you whether a child is walking straight, and wear on gloves reveals which hand is used the most. We use erosions to check on behavior patterns. Pride in one's home can be assessed by looking at its condition; damage and deterioration show less pride than neatly arranged and well-maintained furniture. The state of rented equipment after a camping trip can be used to estimate the responsibility shown by the people who used it.[4]

Appraisal of Data

When you use unobtrusive measures, you are asking whether something is present or whether it is greater in one instance than in others. You are using circumstantial evidence and can say only that the evidence "indicates" that such and such is the case. You know that something was left behind, something passed this way, or something has been worn away, but you do not know why; you can only speculate. Your sample is nonrandom, so you cannot use inferential statistics (discussed in Chapter 10). Nevertheless, these ways of finding out can be very enlightening and can certainly suggest additional questions and research strategies.

Advantages and Disadvantages of Unobtrusive Measures

The greatest advantage of unobtrusive techniques is that you avoid the problems of interviewer effect, demand characteristics, and access to a group. The two disadvantages are:

1. They are only exploratory, since you can't possibly define a population of them. A random sample of most unobtrusive measures

is impossible because it requires definition of a population from which the sample will be drawn. This is possible for some content analysis and for some available data. You must be very careful to delineate the limits of the population when designing an unobtrusive measure and devise a way to draw the sample randomly if you plan to go beyond speculation and description in the analysis of your data.

2. They may amount to invasion of privacy. People may not appreciate having their garbage analyzed. Like criminal investigators, social researchers must be careful about where and how they obtain their evidence.

The analysis of communication, or content analysis, rarely amounts to invasion of privacy because you are usually dealing with published material. Historians and biographers do a lot of this type of work.

Content Analysis

The material for content analysis ranges from things that can be measured and counted to the absence of something, which can be noted and tallied. The idea is to assess the importance of something by discovering the degree of its presence in some form of communication.

Material

Content analysis is often done on the mass media: newspapers, magazines, books, TV, radio, posters, and handbills. In analyzing content you are counting something. You might want to know how prominent a political figure is, so you count the mentions of that person's name in the daily press. Or, you might compare the amount of space given to one type of article with the space given to other types to assess the interest in a topic.

The material for content analysis can be grouped into three categories: words and mentions, pictures and appearances, and space.

Words and Mentions   Words and mentions includes single words (housing, Communist), references to a subject (Here's an energy-saving device . . .), whole discussions (Now we come to a discussion of practical investment . . .), articles ("Should I Consider a New Career After Forty?"), or books (*Practical Tips on Moving to the West*). The idea is to see how much attention is being paid to an idea or to a person. As you can see from the preceding examples, the focus of a content analysis can be almost anything: the housing crisis, a political group, alternative energy, money, midlife career changes, and the shift to the western part of the country.

The NOW task force's study of children's books described in Chapter 4 is a content analysis. Other studies have looked at the relative proportions of various groups in media productions. Many groups are interested in the lack of attention paid to certain types of people in the media. If you photograph a crowded street, or scrutinize the Census breakdowns of age, race, and sex of our population, you find a picture very different from that presented in movies and on television. You can check this out. Watch an evening of television and count the old people, the blacks, the fat people, and the handicapped. Note the gender of each character as well as the age and race. Compare the proportions shown on TV with what you see in real life. You will find distortions.

Another approach might be to examine verbal descriptions of a type ("female," "senior," "working class") to trace the changing attitude toward that type through the years.

Pictures and Appearances Current events or history can also be investigated by counting pictures in a publication or appearances on radio, TV, or the stage and screen. One of my students, temporarily disabled when she was supposed to be preparing a research report for methods class, chose to turn disadvantage to advantage and sampled TV commercials to see whether women are shown doing domestic tasks more often than men. Her report revealed that both men and women were mostly shown in recreational pursuits and that the sexes were shown in occupations roughly corresponding to their current distribution between outside work and domestic work.[5] She did notice something else. All the voice-overs were male. (A voice-over is the disembodied voice you hear during a commercial, which tells you to go right out and buy something or to remember so-and-so's product and its benefits.) Such an unexpected but informative finding is called **serendipitous**. It can stimulate further research.

As far as I know, my student never followed up on her voice-over finding, but someone else has done a research project reflecting observation of the same phenomenon. The *New York Times* of February 2, 1981, carried a report of a study, supervised by Richard M. Perloff at Cleveland State University, which was presented at the Eastern Communication Association meeting later that year. Perloff and assistants studied 1600 TV commercials and found that male announcers did 92 percent of the voice-overs in the afternoon commercials and 90 percent of those in the evening. The author of the newspaper article included quotes from subsequent interviews conducted with advertising executives, a psychologist, and some prominent women on their opinions of the Perloff findings.[6]

Space Measuring the amount of space devoted to a topic in a publication is done either by counting the number of lines or measuring square inches. You can also count the number of pages on which some particular item appears, comparing that total to the number of pages on which it does not appear, to get the proportion of space devoted to your subject.

Quantification of Data

When you quantify, you are not limited to asking whether something is present and comparing the relative amounts in different instances. If the populations sampled can be defined and estimated, a more rigorous analysis is possible. You can take a random sample of the total population of periodicals in print or in any subcategory. You can take a random sample of time slots on TV or radio, as my student did. You can compare the proportions of two newspapers' editorials devoted to a specific issue, and you can sample different decades in a longitudinal study. Whatever type of sample you take, you must calculate the percentage on the correct base. For example, to compare the proportions of cigarette ads in women's and men's magazines, you would proceed by tallying all the ads in one magazine on a tally sheet (see Figure 5.1) that provides for ads of two types: cigarette and noncigarette. A **tally sheet** is a form that provides spaces to check off each instance of an item as it appears. (*Note:* Tallies are made by indicating the first four items with vertical marks and the fifth with a crossbar for easy summing up. The total is circled so that it will not be confused with the tally marks, sometimes called **hash marks**.)

Once the ads have been tallied and summed, you can compare the percentage of cigarette ads in the two magazines. You compute the percentage of cigarette ads for each magazine by dividing the number of cigarette ads by the total number of ads for the magazine. Since the two magazines contain different numbers of ads, a comparison of percentages tells you what you want to know. In the present example, examining only the numbers would make it seem as if there are three times as many cigarette ads in the women's magazine as there are in the men's. If the percentages are calculated, we find:

Women's magazine—26.6 percent of ads are for cigarettes

Men's magazine—4 percent of ads are for cigarettes

Now we see that the women's magazine has about 6½ times as many cigarette ads as the men's. It happens that the men's magazine has twice as many pages as the women's magazine, but using percentages prevents the difference in length from distorting the results and also eliminates the need to consider space devoted to ads.

You can divide a variable into categories and count the instances of each as a measure of popularity and changing lifestyles. For example, travel advertisements could be tallied as Domestic, Other North American, South American and Caribbean, European, Asian, and African. If you compare the results for different years and note political events, you might come up with some sort of correlation. A **correlation** is a tendency of two variables to

FIGURE 5.1   **A tally sheet measuring ad frequency**

	Women's Magazine	Men's Magazine	Total
Cigarette ads	++++ ++++ // (12)	//// (4)	16
Noncigarette ads	++++ ++++ ++++ ++++ ++++ ++++ /// (33)	++++ (95)	128
Total	45	99	144

change at the same time. If they go up and down together, like the wings of a bird, the relationship is a **positive correlation**. If they go up and down alternately, like the pedals of a bicycle, the relationship is a **negative**, or **inverse**, **correlation**. Either way, a cause-and-effect relationship is not indicated by the mere fact of a strong correlation (see Figure 5.2).

Advantages and Disadvantages of Content Analysis

Using content analysis avoids interviewer effect, demand characteristics, and access problems. The technique is inexpensive and can be done by one person. It permits some imaginative analysis. For example, although current fashion in research leans toward the quantitative, some valid and valuable research projects have collected all the written material on a criminal case and reconstructed the event, thereby developing "typical roles . . . of the offender, victim, and possible bystanders . . ." and contributing an analysis of the criminal act as a social event.[7]

Court records can also yield a qualitative picture of a society's values and standards. For example, you could try to find answers to such questions as the following: Who was eligible to testify at this period? Who were considered to be responsible for their own behavior? How were types of crimes classified? What were capital crimes? You could develop further questions about treatment of mental incompetents, women, youth, the elite, slaves,

FIGURE 5.2   **Correlation of data**

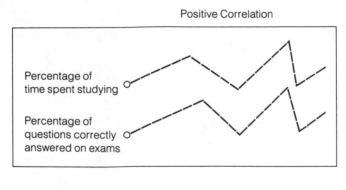

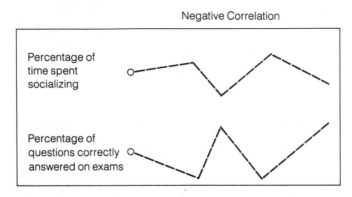

and foreigners. The body of family legislation reveals much about family lifestyles that enjoy community support as well as those that have been condemned.

When using content analysis, especially if the material examined is graphic or fictional, you must remember that depicting or mentioning something does not necessarily mean that it is or was real. Although unicorns and utopias have been drawn and described, they do not exist and never have—so far as we know. Remember, too, that you must distinguish between the incidence of something and the prevalence of it. If you find something depicted or mentioned once, this one instance tells you that the idea existed at the time of depiction but it does not tell you how widespread it was. We spend a third of our time sleeping, yet sleep is not mentioned or shown in a third of our literary or artistic productions. It is there but not in its "real" proportion.

Analyzing content calls for painstaking care and patience. It is an excellent exploratory and descriptive method and can be used alone or in combination with other methods, especially the analysis of available data, to which it is closely related.

Available Data

A lot of information has already been collected and lies waiting for someone to use. Other information, which has been gathered and used, can be used again. Data exist on almost every topic, and permanent records on individuals have data in abundance. You often have good reason to call on this evidence to provide proof of your own qualifications. Organizations want to know an individual's history so that they can tell where to begin a course of study, a diagnosis, or a training program. One's birth certificate, school records, marriage and divorce records, baptismal and other church documents, occupational credentials, social security file, and death certificate all fall into this category.

Another type of available data provides information about rates of community activity rather than about people as individuals. Building permits, sales records, crime statistics, gate receipts, welfare budgets, and figures on energy use are some examples. The possibilities are endless, but you have to know where and how to look and what types of analysis are appropriate.

Sources

We are in a record-keeping era. Organized society spends much time and money collecting and aggregating facts so that social policy may respond to the changes in population size, movement, and characteristics. Private groups use such data to describe and plan for the populations they serve. You can find data almost anywhere, but the chief sources are government, private institutions, and business. Some of the data are located in files, and some are in the form of published reports. Because the approach to published reports is different from the approach to the other forms of data, we shall consider it as a fourth category (see Figure 5.3).

Government National, state, or local governments are major sources of data. Libraries maintain a government document section that offers a gold mine of statistics on a wide variety of subjects. The federal government not only takes a decennial census but is constantly gathering information and compiling it into useful lists and charts. Not all government data are available. Many public institutions collect confidential data (usually called "classified"), such as military information and security reports. The FBI publishes crime reports but is not likely to let the public delve into its files.

Private Institutions Nonprofit institutions and social clubs maintain files on members and records of the organization's history and activities, including current and past financial records. Depending on the nature and purpose of your project, you may be able to get permission to use these files. (Using them without permission, even when you work for the group and have access to the data, is unethical.)

FIGURE 5.3　　　**Sources of available data**

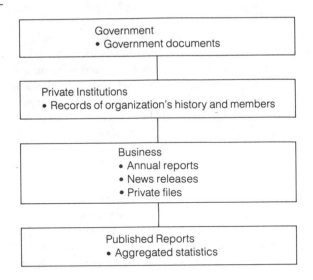

Business　Businesses are not usually willing to reveal much beyond the annual report or periodic news releases, which, in any case, are usually available at the library. If businesses do let you use their files, you can expect strict censorship of your final report. Firms cannot afford to have their private statistics published indiscriminately because it may put them at a disadvantage with competitors. Your challenge here is to convince the person to whom you apply for permission that your study will not harm the enterprise, and then you must ensure that it does not.

Published Reports　Published reports of **aggregated**, or tabulated, statistics are another useful kind of available data. Even some business data are published in aggregated form because data about an entire industry, collected by a central agency, such as the National Board of Realtors, can be freely published without singling out any particular company. Sometimes an agency collects confidential data on a subject, aggregates them, and publishes an analysis of an industry problem. Published reports include reports of research projects of all types: exploratory, descriptive, and explanatory. They are all grist for your mill.

　　A new approach to a question already investigated may reveal new patterns in the data. You can collect all the existing studies on a particular question and look for patterns among them. One behavioral scientist looked at all the opinion surveys he could find that noted both the education of the individual respondents and the respondents' attitudes toward people of other races and religions. He then analyzed the relationship between intergroup attitudes and education attained.[8]

Data Banks Since the advent of the computer and the development of large storage capacity for both personal computers and the large mainframes, we have a new type of published report as well as a new source of available data that do not exist in report form. This source is the **data bank**, or computer file of information that may be reached, or *accessed*, by using a procedure something like this:

> *The computer must be connected to a phone system. This has already been done if you are using a mainframe terminal. Instructions for this come with the disks sold for personal computers.*

1. Turn on the computer (or terminal, if using a mainframe).
2. If using a personal computer, insert the telecommunications disk (phone-dialing program is on it).
3. Type in one or more sequences of words and characters, supplied by the system you are using in its printed instructions, in the order in which the request for them appears on your screen. The instructions tell you what to expect.
4. Read the results. If you have a printer connected to your computer, type the command for a printout.

Accessing a data bank is no more difficult than typing, really. Some information is sold on disks and you can search for things in these sources without using the computer's phone (modem). For example, if you have a disk with the New Testament on it, you can use a filer program (also sold) to search for anything you want. You might want to know how many times "angel" is mentioned, for example. There are programs available to help you write and edit manuscripts; to look for, sort, and list information in an order you choose; to record and manipulate figures; and to prepare reports, including graphs, tables, and illustrations. (See Appendix E for an overview.)

Libraries are now establishing facilities to do computer searches of data banks for individuals. More and more data are accumulating as items are added to the banks daily. Think of a data bank as an enormous file on a record.

Finding Available Data

Your first point of inquiry should always be the library. Many government records are housed there, and the reference librarians can show you an amazing number of registers that contain listings for every conceivable type of publication and organization, as well as the most useful abstracts of scientific research. Pauline Bart and Linda Frankel have written a little book for student sociologists that is packed with information and much practical guidance for any field.[9] One chapter, for example, lists and describes sources of data. It is the best single guide to library research in social science.

Some data haven't been exploited or have been gathered for reasons far removed from your interest in them. For example, two demographers, Etienne van de Walle and John Knodel, studied European church registers on baptisms, marriages, and burials; provincial records of **vital statistics** (births, marriages, and deaths); and the censuses for provinces of western Europe in the eighteenth, nineteenth, and early twentieth centuries.[10] As part of a much larger study, they noted the age of each mother at the birth of her last child. Since it had already been established that in areas where no birth control is practiced the average age at which a woman has her last child is 39 or 40 years, any deviation from this biological regularity could be taken to imply some kind of family planning. The demographers were able to show that the average age at which women had their last child steadily declined in western Europe; the trend began in 1780 in some provinces and really became widespread from 1880 to 1910.

The available data provided by the United States Census have the merit of summing up characteristics of the entire population. These data proved useful to me during a study of racial intermarriage when I was examining accepted theories about motivations for such marriages. One of those theories hinges on socioeconomic differences between the partners and holds that the white partner is typically of lower social class than the minority group partner. Since education is one of the central measures of social class, the appropriate research step was to look at the census charts that specify race and education of all married couples in the country. Review of those charts showed that the census data did not support the theory. Most racial intermarriages were contracted between people of similar education, and the minority group partner was as likely to have more education as he or she was to have less than the white partner.[11]

Available data and content analysis are often combined. Many records have data that haven't been aggregated, plus accompanying commentaries. Among these are court records and testimony, lists of cargo and ships' logs, hotel and inn registers, and personal diaries of trips. Pitirim Sorokin has called our attention to the valuable record of a society's values and mores that is available in its law, music, sculpture, and paintings.[12]

All published material is a potential source of data, but you may have to aggregate them yourself. Historians, biographers, and archaeologists are familiar with this process and have used it to put a lot of fascinating information on record. Philippe Aries's *Centuries of Childhood* is a good example of an analysis that includes historical documents, courtiers' diaries, and biographies, pieced together to make a continuous chain of evidence for the educational practices and principles of the era studied.[13] A happy merging of content analysis and the use of available data, the book makes intriguing reading.

Advantages and Disadvantages of Using Available Data

Using available data has at least five substantial advantages over fieldwork. The method is cheaper, requires comparatively little travel, allows the researcher to cover a wide area and even delve into the distant past, allows the researcher to go back and fill in things that have been missed, and presents few physical hazards—with the possible exception of writer's cramp. Add to this the undeniable facts that you can work on it evenings and weekends in a safe, clean, and generally comfortable environment and you have an attractive package.

Once you get to the library or other appropriate institution, you don't have to travel far for a study of available data. So much of the material can be found in one place because of the organization of archives and records into topical sections. Comprehensive directories and reference books eliminate much fruitless searching.

If you are near a library, you are in a good position for research. I once wrote an annotated bibliography of the social aspects of dentistry and got all the material from four collections, one of them in a dental school. The completed work included 590 entries in seventeen sections.[14] In another project, I combined legal research in two libraries with letters of inquiry to all state governors, resulting in a review of American court cases concerning the free exercise of religion.[15]

Available data make it possible for you to roam the world without really leaving your hometown and to compare the past with the present. People long dead have left their thoughts, their letters, and the details of daily life on record. Another advantage of using available data is that you have repeated access to them; if you need to fill in a gap, it is possible. Compare this to the impossibility of getting data omitted from an anonymous questionnaire.

Using available data means you are not faced with trying to persuade people to cooperate or trying to find an informant. If you are shy about approaching people, you may prefer this method. You can work at your own speed, since the data will not go anywhere if you leave for a while. On the contrary, they increase. Moreover, your work is completely unobtrusive in that you cannot affect the data after the fact.

On the other hand, there is no way to improve available data because they are a *fait accompli*, or a thing already accomplished, by the time you get to them. You aren't looking at a pilot study or a pretest of a questionnaire but at a completed data collection. You can't change or improve it but must take it "as is." As you review it you may think of questions you wish the researchers had asked or details you wish they had recorded. Occasionally, the data are fragmentary. Also, the original data collector faced all of the problems mentioned in the earlier chapters of this book, and the data were subject to all those hazards at the time of collection.

Unless full explanations accompany the records, you may be in the dark about how the original events were sorted. Questions may occur to you such as: What constituted petty larceny at this time? Have these figures been adjusted for inflation? What did *they* mean by "liberal"? The number, extent, and kind of the limitations on the available data have a bearing on your analysis and conclusions. Be suspicious of summaries. They omit information. Many histories of the United States barely mention women or black people and their contributions to our society. One literary figure even managed to write his autobiography without mentioning that he was married.[16]

Those who recorded available data might have done so selectively or deceptively. It isn't hard to imagine the falsification of conditions recorded on a death certificate when survivors wish to conceal suicide, or the shading of a presentation of statistics to present a community's best side. The recorders may have been responding to their own perception of the demand characteristics of their situation. Even a national census may be completely discredited when political manipulations come to light, as happened in Nigeria in the 1960s. The 1980 United States Census came under fire because many localities felt they had been undercounted and knew they would lose out on federal funds because of this. There were court cases over whether the United States Census Bureau should be ordered to revise the figures somehow. In the end, the original figures stood.

Not everything has been recorded. Not everything that has been recorded has survived for our inspection. The further back you go, the less complete the records are, because they have had more time to disintegrate, be destroyed or misplaced. Things we now consider significant, such as birth dates, were not so considered in former times. We cannot tell how much babies weighed at birth in antiquity because this information was not recorded in lasting form. People forget many things before they get it all written down.

Regardless of the shortcomings, using available data can be rewarding, especially if you are careful to prepare yourself to understand the meanings used. If you are well informed in the area of interest of your project, you can detect major errors in the material and understand antiquated and highly specialized terminology. Careful reading on the subject of your study will alert you to possible coverage gaps and distortions and may provide you with corroboration of your results as well.

Find out who sponsored the record you are reading. It may represent an idealized, rather than a realistic, picture of the people or events. Always remember that ethnocentrism and selective perception affected the people who recorded the material just as they affect you and your reading of it. Knowing the sponsor may also clarify the reasons behind the grouping and presentation of the material.

One way to compensate for the limitations of the methods we've been talking about in this chapter is to go ahead and analyze what you have and then raise all the questions about the data in your discussion, so as not to mislead the reader. It is always a good idea to be conservative in one's research claims. Another good idea is to use a multifaceted research design.

There aren't many research projects that compare available data from different fields of study. Most people don't know what is being done in any specialty but their own. However, experts in speech communication, mass media, social psychology, and political science all study audiences. The effect of stress is studied in medicine, sociology, nursing, biology, and psychology. Demographic studies are found in business, geography, political science, sociology, and public health. The coordination of these efforts could be fruitful. Another possibility is the comparison of different eras, as in the fertility study mentioned earlier. Census records have been kept in the United States for more than 200 years, and many data collections are older than that.

As interesting and rewarding as indirect methods of observation can be, they cannot be used for every investigation because there are questions they can't answer. Too many things leave no concrete evidence. Suppose you want to study how decisions are made, who holds the power in a group, or what contributes most to group cohesion? Observing these events is essential to discovering their elements. We'll begin our examination of direct research methods next, with a look at participant and nonparticipant observation.

Participant and Nonparticipant Observation

The word *observation* is used in a special way in research. For us, the word means looking at something without influencing it and simultaneously recording it for later analysis. To carry out this process well, you have to decide what it is you want to observe, locate appropriate subjects, figure out how to record what you see, and choose among several modes of observation.

Goals and Methods

Before planning your observation, you must review your research goal and decide what data you need in order to reach it. If you're specific, you increase the chance of getting accurate information, while you reduce the chance of leaving out something important. Remember the discussion of developing indicators from a research question and hypothesis. If your observation is part of an exploratory study rather than an explanatory one, you can be more flexible than if you were testing a hypothesis. However, reviewing your general purpose is still a good idea even for these preliminary studies because it sharpens your inquiry, and you need that most in exploratory projects.

The difference between research and ordinary description lies in the existence of a scholarly field that is investigating some aspect of the scene before you. That field serves as a guide to the general nature of the phenomena you observe. You may, of course, have already narrowed down your interest to a question and hypothesis; in this case you establish indicators for your observation. You focus on what you need to know and, recording it exactly as it happened, try to get every instance of it.

Once you have your goal firmly in mind, your next decision is who and where you will observe.

Locating Appropriate Subjects

The goal itself tells you what general type of subject you need to observe. If your goal is to learn about the handicapped, you need to observe the handicapped. If you are interested in teamwork, you need to observe teams in action. If you want to know about community life, you need a community. This much is obvious. Two less apparent questions you need to answer are,

Will I use familiar people or strangers? and Will I need an interpreter or informant?

The Familiar and the Exotic   People often study their own groups. One observer, raised in a circus, has written about its decline in the United States.[17] Another, whose parents were deaf, has studied the deaf world and its interaction with the hearing world.[18] The familiar often suggests itself as an appropriate and interesting object of study. The researcher has the advantage of being able to understand the meaning of the events as the participants see them. Time is saved because the researcher doesn't have to have customs and symbols explained or words and phrases clarified. And, since the researcher knows the best way of approaching the subjects and the proper timing, access is easy.

The disadvantage of using familiar groups is that objectivity may suffer. We tend to identify with our own groups, and the society reinforces this by labeling people, in part, by the company they keep. Typically we find ourselves excusing our own people's shortcomings and magnifying their achievements, to the degree that we feel identified with them. Familiarity, in other words, may breed partisanship. Another possibility is that the researcher may fail to see things that group members take for granted. The investigator must guard against this blindness and be sure to prevent selective perception. Including research team members unfamiliar with the group helps protect against it.

In research the expression **exotic** means strange. The researcher is typically unknown to the members of the group before the project begins. It's like the first day on a new job. You can't tell the people apart, and it's easy to say or do the wrong thing. There must be a period during which the researcher learns the subjects' typical ways of interacting, including their language. Sometimes this process consists of hanging around the area until you become familiar with the patterns of movement.[19] It could mean several months of coping with totally unfamiliar and possibly alarming surroundings.[20] These are disadvantages of studying an exotic group. Another is that whatever happens may have special meanings for the subjects that you don't catch because nobody mentions them. There will be verbal nuances, double meanings, and in-jokes. It will be difficult to grasp the significance of events.

The first advantage of studying an exotic group instead of a familiar one is that the initial observations generally include details that might escape a regular viewer. Differences in this group's behavior compared to another group's behavior stand out to the unfamiliar eye. Identification and bias are at a minimum. Problems of access and orientation to strange groups may be reduced if representative members of the group to be studied are contacted ahead of time. One or more members may act as a **liaison**, or communicator, between researcher and group.

Interpreters and Informants   Many researchers begin studying an unfamiliar group by interviewing one or more of its members. This person may have been recommended by someone.[21] Or, the researcher may hang around for a while, making casual friends, and then explain the project, getting their help in reaching other people and interpreting what is happening.[22]

The advantages and disadvantages of using interpreters and informants are the same as those of using a familiar group—with some additions. First, the bias and identification as well as the intimate knowledge of the group are the intermediary's, not the researcher's, hence are beyond the researcher's control. Second, the person you choose may be part of a faction within the subject group and that will alienate others.[23] You may unwittingly contribute to some rivalry or innocently connect yourself with a social outcast, who is happy to make a friend of you, having no friends in the group. This, of course, can scuttle your study.

Despite the hazards of using interpreters and informants, there may be no other way. The best you can do is to be cautious about being too closely identified with any informant, especially when you are "new in the neighborhood." Try to get more than one informant; this will help you get different interpretations of what is happening.

There may be subgroups that you cannot reach. William Foote Whyte remarks that he did not learn anything about the women in the Boston slum, although he studied the young unemployed men there for 3 years. He couldn't study the women because local mores prevented him from being in their company, except in mixed groups.[24] Any male would have had a formidable interviewer effect on the women, anyway. One's sex, age, and race can often be barriers. Laud Humphreys studied male homosexual encounters in public restrooms. It is unlikely that he could have studied female homosexual encounters directly.

Whatever your decisions about selecting subjects and using an informant, you have to find a way to record data.

Recording the Data

The hardest part is getting it all down. Even when our selective perception is working well, there is so much to see and hear that we generally get a kind of total impression of things. When it is important to see exactly what is happening or to hear exactly what is being said and record it, we come face to face with another limitation: the difficulty of paying attention to two things at once. Observations are recorded in research in a number of ways that fall naturally into two categories: manual and mechanical.

Manual Recording of Data The simplest **manual recording** devices are pen and paper, which are used to write down everything as you see it or in notes as soon as possible afterward. These are the simplest devices but not the easiest because you can't write as fast as things happen. People speaking at a normal rate say about 250 words a minute. If they are excited, they speak more rapidly. Even those trained to take shorthand are hard-pressed to take down normal speech. Court stenographers use a special machine to record at a rapid rate.

FIGURE 5.4   **A tally sheet recording clothing choice**

BLUE JEANS			
Wearing Blue Jeans	Subjects Male	Female	Total
YES			
NO			
TOTAL			

Date: 11/18/88
Observer: J. True
Place: Entrance to Student Center
From: 8 a.m. to 9 a.m.

Hastily written notes are hard to interpret later. It's advisable to write or type a clear copy, expanding it with remembered details, as soon as you can. Remember how quickly you lose the details of a scene. If your notes were taken quickly and furtively, they may be almost illegible. Time will not improve them or your recollection.

For making structured observations, you can use a tally sheet or a sociogram. They focus on specific things and make your job easier. A tally sheet was presented earlier for the description of content analysis. This system has a number of advantages. You don't get so tired writing checkmarks instead of words. Tally sheets may be used by many different observers, and results compared. You can't do that with an unstructured observation. A tally sheet is easily summed up.

The tally sheet is ideal when you need a frequency count and distribution. A **frequency count** is a simple observation and recording of the number of times a thing happens, and a **distribution** is sorting of these happenings into categories. For example, you could tally people wearing blue jeans on

FIGURE 5.5   **Sociogram I: A four-person group**

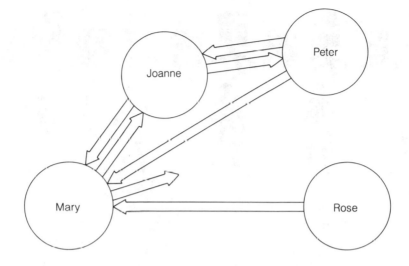

campus in November versus the number in April (job-hunting time), comparing men and women. The tally sheet can be used to record the frequency with which the separate categories of one variable occur in the separate categories of another variable. For our example, you would find out how many women wore blue jeans in November's tally; how many men wore them in November's tally; how many women wore them in April's tally; and how many men wore them in April's tally. This gives you the information you need to do a **bivariate**, or two-variable analysis, which we'll discuss in Chapter 9.

Figure 5.4, which is such a tally sheet, records whether men and women wore blue jeans when passing a checkpoint on a day in November. Note that everything is labeled and that the observer has recorded her name as well as the date and time. Notice also the hash marks grouped in fives, as before, and the circled totals in each cell. (Percentages would eventually be added.)

The tally sheet is useful as long as it is kept simple. An observer who tries to classify events into too many subcategories misses many. For more complicated observations, another method has to be used.

Another way to record interaction on paper is to draw a map of the movements. You can also do this with choices, as we shall see. The **sociogram**, a simple map of interactional direction, consists of small circles and arrows. The circles represent people, and the arrows represent either movement or communication. The basic idea of the sociogram is to show the interaction so that the underlying structure will be clear and unencumbered with the usual meaning, rationalizations, emotions, and questions. This perspective is useful if you want to know about structure. Look at Figure 5.5. In the first sociogram the observer has recorded that Mary and Joanne spoke to each

FIGURE 5.6   Sociogram II: Traffic patterns in an office

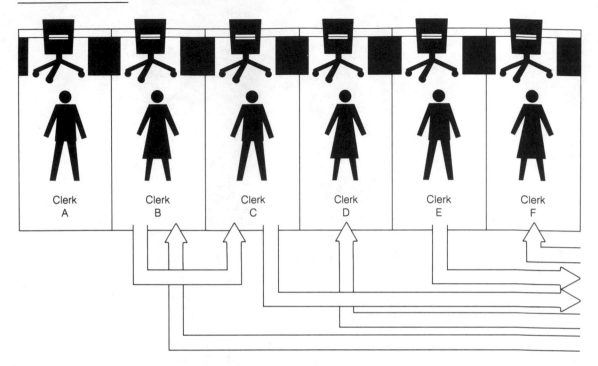

other, Joanne and Peter spoke to each other, Peter spoke to Mary, Mary
spoke to the world in general (shown as arrows that don't reach another
circle), and Rose spoke to Mary. This is a picture of the discussion. The
picture tells us that nobody spoke to Rose, who spoke to only one person,
and that Mary received the most communications. Mary is the **star**, because
she had the most comments addressed to her, and Rose is an **isolate**, because
she had the fewest. But stars might be servants, being ordered about, or
children, who are always being instructed. An isolate could be a "somebody,"
to whom few may speak directly, or a "nobody," who is ignored. To interpret
the sociogram, you would need more information.

Figure 5.6 shows another type of sociogram, depicting traffic patterns.
Clerk B has visited clerk C's cubicle and has had a visitor. Clerk C has gone
out. Here we've reduced locations to a map of their functional space and
behavior to its pattern. What does this do for us? In the present case, it tells
us at a glance that clerk A neither made nor received any visits. Four of the
other five clerks were visited, and three of them went out of their offices. We
see that clerk F can see all of the traffic passing by. If you were a clerk
choosing a cubicle and you wanted privacy, which would you choose?

Sometimes the direction in which one travels has implications for the
meaning of the interaction. The study of body language is based on this

FIGURE 5.7 **Sociogram III: A family group in a therapy session**

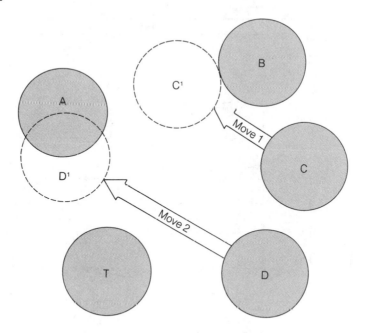

assumption. Figure 5.7 is a sociogram drawn by the writer while observing a family group through a one-way mirror.

Here is an explanation of this sociogram: T(therapist) has requested C(child) to move next to A(stepmother of C). D(natural child of A and B) waits until C is settled between B(her natural father) and A and runs across to sit on A's lap. Before this diagram was made, the training group observing this family had focused on the interaction among B, his natural daughter C, and his second wife A. Four-year-old D, the child of the present marriage, was not seen as an active participant in the complicated, difficult family life; she was simply viewed as a baby whose care had to be considered. This diagram revealed D responding immediately to her half-sister's move toward D's mother and introduced another consideration to the therapist's analysis of the family.

The sociogram is of most value when you are aware of the manifest positions of the actors in the group and want to get at the less obvious relationships, which might be expressed by the flow of remarks or the physical movement of the participants. I once asked a small class of research students to do sociograms during class, at their convenience and without telling me. They were instructed to draw a sociogram of the interactions among teacher and students for any 10 minutes during a class period. When

FIGURE 5.8 Verbal interaction in a small research class

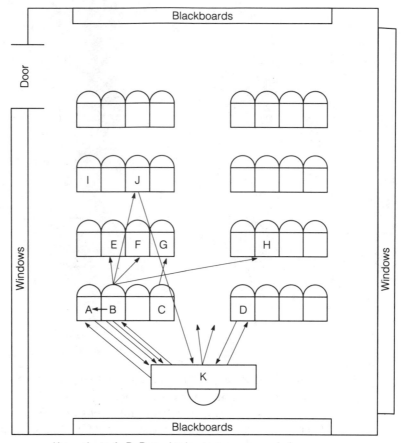

K speaks to A, B, D, and twice to group as a whole.
A speaks to K.
B speaks to A, E, F, H, J, and twice to K.
C speaks to G.
D speaks to K.
J speaks to K.
E, F, G, H, and I do not speak.

Note: Each arrow represents one communication. Order of speaking and type of communication (question, answer) are not indicated.

the due date came, I collected the sociograms and was startled to see that all but one showed strikingly similar patterns. Figure 5.8 is my sketch of the typical sociogram produced by all but one of the students.

Although *every other student's* sociogram showed communications from K (me, the teacher) to individual students and to the group at large, half a dozen or fewer communications from individual students to another student or to K, and at least half a dozen communications from B to K or to other students, B's sociogram showed only those communications from other students and from K, with two from B to K. She had not been aware of her many comments to others while the discussion was taking place and her drawn observation did not reveal that she did so much of the talking!

Sociograms can be used as illustrations of data collected in another way. For example, Leon Festinger and associates have employed sociograms to illustrate patterns of friendship choices in housing clusters.[25] Jacob Moreno, who studied group interaction, used sociograms to reveal friendship choices among small groups.[26]

Mechanical Recording of Data Modern technology makes it possible to record whole events in print or on audio or videotape. Through **mechanical recording of data**, all interactions and dialogue can be captured. Selective perception and bias are eliminated almost entirely, but the approach has certain disadvantages. For example, it's expensive; you might need special training or you might have to hire technicians. A worse disadvantage is that mechanical methods of recording data yield too many data. Huge piles of **transcript**, or typed text from recorded interviews, represent weeks of clerical work and then months of organization and analysis. Completed films must be shown repeatedly while someone extracts usable information from them. All this expense and work are hard to justify unless the data can't possibly be observed and recorded using manual techniques. Finally, recording data may have a disruptive effect on the group being observed.

Consequences of Recording the Data Taking notes or tallies by hand is likely to be noticed, and in most cases interviewer effect is inevitable. Most researchers have found it preferable to take notes in private. In his study of young men in Boston, William Foote Whyte wrote up each day's notes after getting home at night.[27] It's also possible to go into a bathroom to write or to combine note taking with a nonthreatening activity such as taking minutes or keeping score. Whatever the method, you should lose as little time as possible in getting the information down on paper.

Using mechanical devices such as a camera or tape recorder is disruptive, although subjects tend to forget about the machine if the observation goes on long enough. This is also true of people observed through a one-way mirror. (These mechanical devices are used with the knowledge of the subjects. As discussed in Chapter 4, to record people's actions and remarks without their knowledge is an unethical invasion of privacy.)

You may protest that you can't avoid interviewer effect if the subjects know you are observing them, and you are right. It's an unresolvable dilemma. You can only try to ease it. You can confine yourself to observing groups in public places because those groups have tacitly accepted being observed by others. Publishing the results is another matter. Photographers have had to defend themselves in court for photographing famous people too enthusiastically.

It's possible to get permission to observe a group secretly at a time to be known only by you; in this case the people know only that they will be observed *someday*. This is what I asked the students to do in the exercise represented by Figure 5.8. A department store does the same thing when it posts signs saying that plainclothes detectives are stationed throughout the store. After a while people forget about the sign, but they have been informed. Just remember that what is possible is not necessarily ethical and that it is wrong to lie.

Publishing study results may be disloyal. In particular, if the group being studied has done something illegal, your report can put them and you into danger from the law. Laud Humphreys found himself in this position, and he was the object of considerable pressure from the law because he had observed homosexual encounters in public places. Humphreys had traced license plates to identify, locate, and interview men he had observed in homosexual acts. He then had information about a criminal activity engaged in by people he was ethically bound to protect.[28] This dilemma is common when you do research on lawbreakers. Another danger is the possibility of revenge by the group should you do the research in secret and then publish. Some groups are dangerous to observe; in at least one case a researcher has been physically assaulted.[29]

One reason for rushing to expand and complete your notes for an observation is the need to record exactly what happened and to avoid summation.

Writing a Description   You may wish to use an event that is not altogether clear to you at the time, and if you don't record it precisely the way it happened, subsequent events may lead you to edit it as you later see it, or one of the participants may offer an interpretation that will affect your recollection. It's useful if two or more observers are there as a check on each other.

Try to get as much actual dialogue as you can, writing as if you were recording testimony, which, in a sense, you are. It may be useful to return to the scene later to remind yourself of the surroundings. To provide a clear background to the events, include a description of the scene and an identification of the characters and their relation to each other.

Once you've resolved the issues of who to observe and where and how to record the observations, you must choose among the modes of observation.

Modes of Observation

Selecting a mode of observation requires that you make three decisions about it:

1. Will you participate in the subjects' activities?

2. Will you tell the subjects that you are observing them for a research project?

3. Will you structure your observations in advance?

Participating in the Group's Activities

If you take part in your subjects' activities while you are observing them, your work is called a **participant observation**. Sanford Labovitz and Robert Hagedorn have identified five advantages and five disadvantages of this type of observation. The advantages are:

1. Natural setting
2. Access to emotions
3. Accumulation of data over time
4. Access to context
5. Development of rapport[30]

Advantages of Participating   A **natural setting** consists of the place and circumstances in which people's ordinary activities are pursued. Some theorists like to think of life as a drama, and the setting as a stage. Whatever the perspective, things do seem to go more smoothly in familiar places. Cues are so strong in accustomed settings that going back to a place where we used to live evokes the same strong feelings we had when we lived there. Researchers believe that people act with more spontaneity when surrounded by such cues. The theory is that if you want to see how people act, you must go and be among them as they live their daily lives. This move also gives you access to the subjects' emotions, since you will be right there as the emotions are expressed in behavior. Anthropologists have long relied on field studies for this reason.

Accumulating data over time by observation yields more information than you can get by questioning the subjects. People don't have to take time out from their regular life while they talk to you, and they are giving you "answers" without getting bored by doing it. Those answers are more meaningful because you have access to the context; that is, you can see the action as it happens with all the extenuating circumstances in operation, and you can judge the intensity and importance of it firsthand. You cannot see inside people's minds, but your understanding is greatly improved.

Participant observation implies getting to know people, and that means you have a chance to establish rapport, or a relationship of mutual trust. If you need to ask sensitive questions, you are in a better position to do so. Sensitive questions are those that are likely to arouse disturbing emotions: embarrassment, shame, grief, or anxiety. Asking them requires a lot of tact and considerable preparation. Rapport is indispensable.

Being there when something is happening is much more enlightening than hearing about it. George Kirkham tells how his attitude and his teaching of criminal justice changed after he served as an ordinary police officer in a tough district.[31] I vividly recall my first few weeks on the staff of a state mental hospital and my drastically changed perception of mental illness after witnessing that daily scene.

Labovitz and Hagedorn list the following disadvantages:

1. Unreliability
2. Role limitations
3. Loss of objectivity
4. Interviewer effect
5. Time consumption

Let's consider them.

Disadvantages of Participating   The first two disadvantages are two sides of the same coin. When each person sees events from the confines of his or her role, there is a low reliability from individual to individual. **Role limitations** are the restrictions that any status naturally imposes on what you can do, where you can be, and, therefore, what you can see or know about. For example, although all the members of a work crew are participating in the same event, each is experiencing a different part of it. On a road crew, one person is at the wheel of a large machine and is concentrating on getting it into place, while another is looking up the road and directing cars, and still another is looking down the same road and directing cars. A fourth is looking up *and* down the road and at the machine and is directing the driver. Although each is the "same" experience, they are not identical; one crew member sees things another misses because attention was focused elsewhere. If you were a bird in a tall tree nearby, you could view the whole scene. You would be a nonparticipant observer.

The limitations of a particular role increase the likelihood of low reliability, or unreliability. Reliability is the certainty with which you can repeatedly collect data on the same thing in the same way and get the same result. Selective perception and cultural orientation give us different views of things, and observing from within a particular role intensifies the problem. Different people see things differently, and the role they play in the activity makes it worse. In Akira Kurosawa's film *Rashomon*, for example, all that is agreed upon is that a young nobleman and his wife went on a trip in which they encountered a bandit; the young man was killed after a battle, and the young wife and the bandit, at some point, had intercourse. A priest passed by and saw the whole thing. The film presents four radically different versions of this story (the dead husband's version is presented by his spirit).

When with a group, we have a strong tendency to move from outsider to insider in our own minds. A sociologist would say we begin with a **secondary interest** in the subjects and move toward a **primary interest**. (Anybody but a sociologist would say we tend to make friends with people.) We *lose objectivity* because we begin to share the life of the group and to see things from their standpoint, although we then *understand them better*.

Whether a researcher can ever avoid distorting the data by influencing the interaction in a group is still in question. Leon Festinger and associates did an intriguing study of a group of people who anticipated the end of the world. Festinger spotted a news story about the prediction and launched a participant observation of the group by having some assistants join it as "believers." Since they had to conceal their identity to be accepted, the assistants invented plausible reasons for joining. They presented themselves as persons interested in flying saucers and extraterrestrial events, and in some instances concocted stories about supernatural communications that had led them to the prophetess. It's possible that these spurious claims reinforced the belief of the group that they *were* caught up in some supernatural event. During the course of the research, Festinger's people were often expected to participate in the group's attempts to communicate with outer space. How far this altered their own behavior Festinger could not know, although he was aware of the problem.[32]

The last disadvantage of participating in the group's activities is physical. Participation is time-consuming and sometimes uncomfortable. Long periods of waiting and watching can pass without anything of interest to the researcher taking place. Many investigators report tedious waits of this type.

The decision to announce to one's subjects that one's presence will result in a research report or a book is one that many researchers have agonized over. If you tell the subjects what you are doing, it may alter their behavior, at least until they forget about you. If you do not tell them, you are being dishonest, invading their privacy, and being disloyal; if they find out, you have to take the consequences. Festinger's study could not have been announced to the subjects and would have been destroyed had they found out about it.

Announcing One's Purpose

Typically, if you tell a few members of the group that you are "interested" in their way of life and are "writing a book," they won't be threatened, especially if you promise confidentiality and anonymity. This is very important. Although subjects may enjoy reading about themselves, they may be offended by your perceived judgment and outraged if they believe that they are recognizable. A number of researchers have reported negative reactions to their reports. Deborah Feinbloom found that her speculations about transvestites' wives were not at all well received.[33] Whyte reports criticism of his book by people he described.[34]

One controversy resulted when a researcher not only carried out his announced purpose but added an analysis of other information gathered at the same time.[35] The researcher was the field director of a research project, and he went to live in a small town, to study its organizations. After 2 years he not only reported the data requested, but also published conclusions about sources of power and distribution of decision making in the town. His book contributed to sociology and urban analysis but caused anger and resentment by the local residents. The researcher believed that he was right to report what he found. The director of the project disagreed. Although this investigator was not physically attacked by his subjects, he was roundly denounced, and the incident turned the residents sour on research projects.

Getting permission to join the group is often done and, in fact, is unavoidable if you are observing people who look markedly different from you or recognize you as a stranger. By hanging around without identifying yourself, you would leave them with no alternative but to assume a status for you. You might be taken for an investigator for the police, a process server, or a bill collector. Wary females may regard a strange male as a threat; prostitutes may regard him as a prospect. Once some explanation of your presence has been accepted, you can begin to observe. Gradually you become familiar to the group and, in principle, people forget they are being observed.

Sometimes the members of the group look to the outsider for help. Elliot Liebow, John Runcie, and many others describe such incidents.[36] If this happens, the outsider may have some hard decisions to make, and have to struggle to avoid being drawn into controversy. When you associate with a group of people for a while, you begin to care about their concerns as well as identifying with them. When they know that you have an education, money, or connections with the authorities, you may well find yourself in a quandary, in doubt as to your proper role.

One hard decision to make is whether to announce to your own group that you are going to observe them and write about it. Here you face the issue of loyalty. You might well feel that a person who "betrays" the group by reporting what goes in it is reprehensible. Sometimes people who write their memoirs are viewed in this light, especially if they report intimate details.

By definition, the more structured anything is, the less flexible it is. For preliminary exploratory work, very little structure is appropriate because the investigator wants to become familiar enough with the scene to know what questions to ask.

Structuring the Observations

For **ethnomethodological** studies the goal is "to determine the underlying rules, norms, and assumptions governing everyday life" in the group.[37] Ethnomethodologists employ a wide range of techniques: They observe what norm violation brings, take pictures, and make content analyses.

The typical approach of "small-group" research is far more structured. The observer sits behind a one-way mirror and notes the types of interaction on a tally sheet. Do the participants agree, disagree, suggest, or question? Each such event is noted on a special tally sheet in its appropriate category. There may be only two categories (yes and no), but Selltiz, Wrightsman, and Cook cite a list compiled by Bover, Simon, and Karafin that includes seventy-three such systems for observing young children. Perhaps the best-known of the small-group interaction observation systems is the one developed by Robert E. Bales. Its twelve categories of communication may be sorted into

TABLE 5.1   Tally sheet with incorrect (overlapping) categories

	Tally of Number Passing Checkpoint
Motorcycles	
Passenger cars	
Station wagons	

Trucks,
   Heavy
   Light
   Pickup	

Vans	

six pairs: for example, "4. Gives suggestion" is paired with "9. Asks for suggestion." Bales defines *communicative act* as "a communication or an indication, either verbal or nonverbal, which in its context may be understood by another member as equivalent to a single simple sentence."[38]

A structured observation is an observation organized into categories in advance. The items in such a tally, or checklist, must be clear and mutually exclusive. The observer should definitely know where to check off a particular event. No event should fit into more than one category. Look at the two examples in Tables 5.1 and 5.2. The first checklist, Table 5.1, may leave the observer confused because the categories overlap. Do station wagons get checked off only on the station wagon line, or do they also get checked off on the passenger car line? Pickup trucks and vans also qualify as light trucks. The second checklist, Table 5.2, corrects these problems.

Another requirement for a checklist is that there be a place for every kind of interaction that is going to be observed and recorded. To allow for unforeseen types, ample space should be provided for the category "other" at the bottom of the list. To sum up, there should be a place for everything and

TABLE 5.2   Tally sheet with corrected categories*

	Tally of Number Passing Checkpoint
Motorcycles	
Passenger cars	

Trucks,
   Light
   Heavy	

*Categories will depend on the research goal.

each thing should occupy one place. The instructions should make the sorting procedure perfectly clear.

Your decision about structuring your observation depends on the type of study you are doing and the specificity of your question. Sometimes, as in Whyte's study of unemployed men in Boston, you start out with some unstructured observations and develop a reasonable structure for them, which you use for subsequent observation periods.

When deciding whether to participate, to announce your purpose, or to structure your observations, you will want to consider some other possible ways to observe.

Alternatives

One way to avoid influencing the course of action is to stay out of it.

Observing Without Participating   The participant observer might wonder, What would have happened, had I not been there? "Not being there" and "observation" are almost mutually exclusive. A partial solution is to be there as an observer only and to rely on the subjects to grow accustomed to your presence and forget about you in the same way that shoppers gradually forget about the store detective. This sometimes happens. One common observation is that the presence of low-status people is often forgotten or overlooked entirely. People discuss highly intimate business in front of bartenders, waitresses, and servants as if they were not there. Ralph Ellison was moved by this phenomenon to choose the title *The Invisible Man* for his book about blacks.[39]

The danger in being a nonparticipating observer is not that you are seen as a low-status person but that you are seen as a high-status person. If *that* happens, people will not ignore you but will feel that they are being evaluated. Their behavior may be affected to a marked degree, and you won't know how much. This leads some researchers to another alternative: concealment.

Observing Without Announcing   Although any strategy that makes the subjects self-conscious distorts the data, any strategy for observing without their knowledge and consent raises ethical questions. It may also be illegal.

Donald P. Warwick identifies a number of ways in which scientists frequently practice deception. Two involve observing without announcing one's purpose: staging a false event to observe people's reaction, and playing a false role to elicit and observe the role partners' reactions.[40]

When researchers overlook the need to get permission from subjects before recording their voices or taking their pictures, they could be leaving themselves open to lawsuits. There is also the risk of getting entangled in an undesirable relationship because people don't know you are only an observer and do not intend to be a participant. David A. Karp writes of having to leave the scene of his observation because of unwelcome attention from another male.[41]

You can observe without announcing and without stooping to unethical practices if you watch only public behavior in public places. Presumably, when people are aware that what they are doing is not classified as private, they do not object to being observed.

Observing Without Structuring Notes   This approach is easier than devising a structured note-taking plan at the outset, but it makes your work harder later when you are trying to organize your data. If your project is strictly exploratory and you have no clue to the relevant questions or categories, you have no choice but to plunge in without a plan. It is better to have some plan.[42] If you're working with others, you might have two people observe, one using a tentative (draft) checklist and another without one. You can compare the results and recast your approach. If you're working alone, try it two ways yourself. The little test only requires more time.

These are the possibilities. If you join a group, you are able to watch live human behavior in its natural setting as it happens, but you may also influence that behavior greatly by your presence. If you tell people what you are doing, you are displaying integrity, but you may increase their self-consciousness and possibly may incur their displeasure. Structuring your observations helps organization but limits the data.

Despite all its difficulties and dilemmas, observation is exciting for both the researcher and for the readers. You always learn something because the material to be absorbed is endless. Although it is fun, that doesn't make it any less scientific.

Summary and Conclusion

Indirect methods of data collection include unobtrusive measures, content analysis, and the use of available data. Unobtrusive measures are examinations of evidence left behind—such as accumulations of trash or empty containers, the wearing away of an item, or the visible marks caused by an activity. Although these techniques are not appropriate for random sampling, since the population cannot be estimated or determined, they are useful as complements to other methods, and they produce research ideas. Be careful about invasion of privacy.

Content analysis and the use of available data are ways of analyzing written material, presentations, and previously collected data. Available data, which usually have been aggregated and tabulated, are mainly quantitative. Content analysis can be done with pictures and plays, books, magazines, diaries, and newspapers. You can also look at these sources to see what *isn't* there, such as mentions of something or types of people.

The biggest advantage of indirect methods is that they are totally without interviewer effect or demand characteristics. The biggest disadvantage is that you have no control over the collection of the material and no check on its internal validity or its completeness. Indirect methods can't be used for studies of process, but they can be part of a multifacted project. Scientific observation requires finding appropriate subjects and deciding how to record what you see, to get a complete picture while influencing the action as little as possible.

Be specific about what is included in your observation. You must decide whether your subjects will be people you know or strangers, whether you need a guide to help you understand what the group is doing, and whether you will record data manually or mechanically. Accurate notes are important.

Because of the disruptive effect of your presence and the twin needs to maintain objectivity and to record data, you have to make three basic decisions: whether to participate, whether to announce, and whether to structure observations. All its problems notwithstanding, observation is very rewarding.

Main Points

1. Indirect methods of collecting data include unobtrusive measures, content analysis, and using available data. Unobtrusive measures are ways of examining accretions, erosions, and traces. They are exploratory and descriptive, but not explanatory, and their abuse may be an invasion of privacy.

2. Content analysis consists of counting words and mentions, pictures and appearances, and space allotted. You can take note of the absence of these things, too. Proportions of appearances are compared to indicate trends. Content analysis can be used for explanatory research if a population can be delineated and a sample drawn.

3. Correlation is the tendency of two things to vary at the same time. Positive correlation means that the variables are going up or down together; negative, or inverse, correlation means that one goes up while the other goes down, or vice versa.

4. Content analysis can be used qualitatively, too. Not everything that is described, depicted, or mentioned is real. Much that is real is not described, depicted, mentioned, or given its real proportions in literary and graphic output. Content analysis and the use of available data are cheaper and easier than fieldwork and they can be done in libraries and institutions.

5. There are a lot of available data, varying widely in internal validity and reliability. Indirect methods are not subject to interviewer effect or

demand characteristics, but they do raise problems of internal validity. Conservative analysis and ascertaining sponsors of published material reduce the drawbacks of using this material. A multifaceted design is recommended.

6. Observation is looking at something without influencing it and recording it for later analysis. Reviewing the research goal and possible research question comes first.

7. Studying familiar groups has the advantage of built-in understanding but threatens objectivity. You reduce identification and bias by studying an unfamiliar group, and you might notice things an insider would miss; but you face access and comprehension problems. If you use an informant, remember the informant's bias and identification. The informant's position and alliances in the group must be considered. Your sex, age, and race prevent access to some people. There are other barriers of this type.

8. Manual recording of data is harder than mechanical but can be simplified by the use of shorthand, tallies, and sociograms. Mechanical recording gets all the data but leaves you with too much of it to process easily. If subjects see you taking notes, interviewer effect is greatly increased. Recording data surreptitiously can be an invasion of privacy. Publishing observations can be disloyal and can endanger you or the subjects. Write-ups must be prompt because you forget quickly.

9. Because you are part of the group and the group trusts you, participant observation gives you a truer picture and makes data collection easier. It also restricts your view to one role, makes you partial, affects what is happening, and takes time.

10. Announcing that you are an observing researcher alters the subjects' behavior. They may not like your conclusions about them when published. If your status is higher than theirs, they may want help. Not announcing may be unethical.

11. It's hard to devise a structure for observing before you go into the field; but preparing a structure makes organizing data easier. If you use one, the plan must be clear, to avoid confusion.

Notes

1. C. C. and Martha Lamberg-Karlovsky, "An Early City in Iran," in *Cities, Their Origin, Growth and Human Impact*, ed. Kingsley Davis (New York: Freeman, 1973), pp. 28–37.

2. H. G. Sawyer, "The Meaning of Numbers," American Association of Advertising Agencies, 1961, cited in *Unobtrusive Measures: Nonreactive Research in the Social Sciences*, ed. Eugene J. Webb, Donald T. Campbell, Richard D. Schwartz, and Lee Sechrest (Skokie, Ill.: Rand McNally, 1966), p. 41.

3. Anne Hollander, *Seeing Through Clothes* (New York: Viking Press, 1978).

4. Richard M. Brandt, *Studying Behavior in Natural Settings* (New York: Holt, Rinehart, & Winston, 1972), p. 201.

5. Celeste Molzen, unpublished term paper, "Analysis of Female Role Assignments in Television Advertisements," Trenton State College, May 1977.

6. Judy Klemesrud, "Voice of Authority Still Male," *New York Times*, 2 February, 1981, p. A16. No connection is implied between Ms. Molzen's project and the Perloff study.

7. David F. Luckenbill, "Criminal Homicide as a Situated Transaction," in *Readings for Social Research*, ed. Theodore C. Wagenaar (Belmont, Calif.: Wadsworth, 1981), pp. 134–43.

8. Charles H. Stember, *Education and Attitude Change* (New York: Institute of Human Relations Press, 1961).

9. Pauline Bart and Linda Frankel, *The Student Sociologist's Handbook*, 3rd ed. (Morristown, N.J.: General Learning Press, 1980).

10. Etienne van de Walle and John Knodel, "Europe's Fertility Transition: New Evidence and Lessons for Today's Developing World," *Population Bulletin* 34, no. 6 (February 1980).

11. June A. True, "Miss Anne and the Black Brother," in *Interracial Bonds*, ed. Rhoda Goldstein Blumberg and Wendell James Roye (New York: General Hall, 1979), p. 139.

12. Pitirim Sorokin, *Fads and Foibles in Modern Sociology* (Chicago: Regnery, 1956), pp. 316–17.

13. Philippe Aries, *Centuries of Childhood: A Social History of Family Life*, trans. Robert Baldick (New York: Knopf, 1962).

14. June True Albert and Edward Wellin, *Literature Review and Bibliography on Social Aspects of Dentistry* (Trenton: State of New Jersey Department of Health, Fall 1963.

15. June True Albert, "Limitations on the Free Exercise of Religion in the United States," unpublished paper, 1960.

16. Henry Adams, *The Education of Henry Adams* (New York: Book League of America, 1928).

17. Marcello Truzzi, "The Decline of the American Circus: The Shrinkage of an Institution," in *Sociology and Everyday Life*, ed. Marcello Truzzi (Englewood Cliffs, N.J.: Prentice-Hall, 1968), pp. 312–22.

18. Paul C. Higgins, *Outsiders in a Hearing World* (Beverly Hills, Calif.: Sage, 1980).

19. W. Gordon West, "Access to Adolescent Deviants and Deviance," in *Fieldwork Experience: Qualitative Approaches to Social Research*, ed. William B. Shaffir, Robert A. Stebbins, and Allan Turowetz (New York: St. Martin's Press, 1980), p. 34.

20. Elenore Smith Bowen, *Return to Laughter* (New York: Doubleday, 1964).

21. William Foote Whyte, *Street Corner Society: The Social Structure of an Italian Slum*, 2nd ed. (Chicago: University of Chicago Press, 1955), p. 290.

22. West, "Access to Adolescent Deviants," p. 34.

23. Bowen had a continual problem with this in her study of the Tiv of Nigeria. See *Return to Laughter*.

24. Whyte, *Street Corner Society*, p. 299.

25. Leon Festinger, Stanley Schachter, and Kurt Back, *Social Pressures in Informal Groups* (Stanford, Calif.: Stanford University Press, 1950), p. 134.

26. Jacob L. Moreno, *Who Shall Survive?* (New York: Beacon House, 1934), pp. 143–63.

27. Whyte, *Street Corner Society*, p. 334.

28. Laud Humphreys, *The Tearoom Trade: Impersonal Sex in Public Places* (Chicago: Aldine, 1970).

29. Hunter Thompson, *Hell's Angels* (New York: Random House, 1966), pp. 277–78.

30. Sanford Labovitz and Robert Hagedorn, *Introduction to Social Research*, 3rd ed. (New York: McGraw-Hill, 1981), p. 74.

31. George Kirkham, *Signal Zero* (Philadelphia: Lippincott, 1976), p. 9.

32. Leon Festinger, Henry W. Riecken, and Stanley Schachter, *When Prophecy Fails* (Minneapolis: University of Minnesota Press, 1956), p. 240.

33. Deborah Feinbloom, *Transvestites and Transsexualism* (New York: Delacorte Press, 1976), pp. 264–66.

34. Whyte, *Street Corner Society*, pp. 343–56.

35. Arthur Vidich and Joseph Bensman, *Small Town in Mass Society: Class, Power and Religion in a Rural Community*, rev. ed. (Princeton, N.J.: Princeton University Press, 1968).

36. Elliot Liebow, *Talley's Corner* (Boston: Little, Brown, 1967), pp. 243–45; John Runcie, *Experiencing Social Research*, rev. ed. (Homewood, Ill.: Dorsey, 1980), p. 86.

37. Theodore C. Wagenaar, ed., *Reading for Social Research* (Belmont, Calif.: Wadsworth, 1981), p. 132.

38. Claire Selltiz, Lawrence S. Wrightsman, and Stuart W. Cook, *Research Methods in Social Relations*, rev. Louise H. Kidder (New York: Holt, Rinehart, & Winston, 1981), pp. 277–99.

39. Ralph Ellison, *The Invisible Man* (New York: Random House, 1952).

40. Donald P. Warwick, "Social Scientists Ought to Stop Lying," in *Readings for Social Research*, ed. Theodore C. Wagenaar (Belmont, Calif.: Wadsworth, 1981), pp. 34–35.

41. David A. Karp, "Observing Behavior in Public Places: Problems and Strategies," in *Fieldwork Experience*, ed. Shaffer, Stebbins, and Turowetz, p. 92.

42. A good example of structured observation is found in: E. Hooper, L. Comstock, J. M. Goodwin, and J. S. Goodwin, "Patient Characteristics That Influence Physician Behaviors," *Clinical Research* 19, no. 1 (February 1981), p. 38A.

Exercises

These exercises are to give you practice in unobtrusive research and observation, but they are also fun. Exercise 5.1 continues the content analysis example given in the chapter. Exercises 5.2 and 5.3 get you started on direct observation: announced and unannounced participation and announced and unannounced nonparticipation. You will experience them firsthand. The goal of Exercise 5.4 is a sociogram, which you can complete while doing one of the observations in Exercise 5.2 or 5.3. Try out several ways of recording. No amount of reading will help you as much as actual practice. You'll be better able to tackle Exercise 5.5, the critique of published work.

Exercise 5.1 *Content analysis*

Instructions: Select a magazine—such as *Ms.*, *Playgirl*, or *Cosmopolitan*—directed toward women and a magazine—such as *Playboy*, *Sports Afield*, or *M*—directed toward men. Complete a tally sheet for the two issues (see below), and answer the questions following.

Tally sheet.

NAME OF MAGAZINE: _____ _____
                         (WOMEN)   (MEN)

ADVERTISEMENTS FOR:

Pesonal grooming, cosmetics, health items

Personal clothing, accessories

Jewelry, watches

Recreation, vacations

Liquor

Cigarettes

Household items

Children's items

Garden and yard

Automobiles, accessories

Other

TOTALS

Remember to draw a vertical line for the first four items, and then cross them with a horizontal line for the fifth item. When you numerically total each cell, circle the number to avoid confusion. See Figure 5.1, for example.

1.   How many advertisements are there altogether, counting both covers?

Mag 1 _____ Mag 2 _____

2.   Taking magazine 1, for women, figure the percentage of ads devoted to the category "Personal grooming, cosmetics, health items":

Step 1. Write the total number for this category _____.

Step 2. Divide that number by the total number of ads in the magazine:

$$\frac{\text{number of ads for personal grooming and cosmetics}}{\text{total ads}}$$

The result will be less than one: .0XXXX, for example.

Step 3. Remove the decimal and all except the first two digits, add a % sign.

[Here's a concrete example: Say there are 532 ads in a magazine and 137 of them are for personal grooming or cosmetics.

Step 1. Write the total number for this category: 137.

Step 2. Divide that number by the total number of ads in the magazine:

$$\frac{137}{532} = .25751879$$

Step 3. Remove the decimal and all except the first two digits, add a % sign:

25% (the answer)

The only other thing to note is that you can **round** the answer to be 26%, because the first unused digit (7) is more than 5.

3.   Now make a table out of your tally sheet by doing it over on the next page, replacing the hash marks and their totals with percentages.

Table of percentages.

NAME OF MAGAZINE: _____ _____
                              (WOMEN)   (MEN)

ADVERTISEMENTS FOR:

Personal grooming, cosmetics, health items

Personal clothing, accessories

Jewelry, watches

Recreation, vacations

Liquor

Cigarettes

Household items

Children's items

Garden and yard

Automobiles, accessories

Other

TOTALS

(*Note:* Remember to base your percentages on the total ads in the magazine named at the top of the column.)

4. Are there differences in advertising emphasis for the two magazines? Write your comments on them.

Exercise 5.2   *Participant observation*

Instructions: The goal of this two-part exercise is to teach you participant observation. You are to do two observations, each lasting from 15 minutes to a half-hour, if feasible. Use the same method to record the interaction both times. You may choose unstructured recording, as close to *verbatim* as you can get it; you may want to use structured recording, using a tally sheet or other instrument chosen or devised by you (keep it simple); or you can draw a sociogram. (See Exercise 5.4.)

a.   Get together with a group to which you belong. The group can be your family sitting around the living room, your friends at lunch, a meeting of any kind, or a car pool. The members should be people who are used to you. Your research question is: Who is the dominant person in this group? To answer it, you have to find out who talks, what type of remarks he or she makes, whose suggestions are followed and whose ignored, who asks questions and who answers, and any other observations you deem relevant. Figure out in advance how you are going to record the data. Do not reveal what you are doing.

When you have finished your observation and recording, review your material and write your comment. Do not summarize what the group members said, report their speech and actions as completely and accurately as you can. After you have commented, proceed to do the second observation.

b. Get together with another group or the same group, but be sure it's one to which you belong. Announce your purpose. Say you are doing homework for this course. Explain briefly that you are going to observe and record conversation in the group in order to learn the technique. (Do not lie. This is actually what you are going to do.) Proceed as before, only this time you can record openly.

Answer the following questions:

1. When you announced your purpose, was the group's behavior toward you any different from the behavior toward you when you didn't announce?

2. When you announced your purpose, was the group's behavior toward each other any different from the behavior when you didn't announce?

3. What were the differences in your feelings in the two exercises?

4. What were the differences in ease of recording?

5. Which did you prefer, and why?

Exercise 5.3   *Nonparticipant observation*

Instructions: Now go to a place where you can observe strangers.

a.   Go to a waiting room, get on a bus, eat at a cafeteria, wait in line, or
stand on a street corner. Be as inconspicuous as possible. Choose a
different recording method from the one you used in Exercises 5.2a and
5.2b. The goal of this exercise is to give you practice in nonparticipant
observation, so don't join in the group's conversation or behavior. Don't
announce your purpose. Your research question is: What are the social
expectations in this setting as revealed by regularities in the people's
behavior? For example, if you are in a waiting room, try to record what
people repeatedly do, who gets called first, who speaks to whom and
under what circumstances, and what behavior seems to be disapproved.
Write up your data as before and add your own comments. Be sure not
to summarize what actually happened. Record it as accurately and as
objectively as you can, word for word, describing every action.

b. Do another nonparticipant observation, using the same recording method as in Exercise 5.3a, but this time tell the group that you are doing your homework and have to observe and record public behavior as practice for your course. Do not lie. You can identify your school and status as a student but don't get into a prolonged discussion. Say you must write down observations without joining in. (*Hint:* People who might be cooperative include fellow students who don't know you, people playing a game, or mothers and children in the park.) Proceed with the observation and recording.

Answer the following questions:

1. How did the unannounced nonparticipant observation in Exercise 5.3a compare with the announced nonparticipant observation in Exercise 5.3b? How did they differ?

2. How did the announced nonparticipant observation in Exercise 5.3b compare with the announced participant observation in Exercise 5.2b?

3. How did the unannounced nonparticipant observation in Exercise 5.3a compare with the unannounced participant observation in Exercise 5.2a?

4. How do you now feel about the relative merits of participating and nonparticipating; announcing and not announcing?

5. Evaluate your recording procedures and compare them.

Your name _____   Instructor _____

Exercise 5.4   *The sociogram*

Instructions: Do either Exercise 5.4a or 5.4b.

a.   Observe at least two people who are interacting. (You can combine this with Exercises 5.2a and 5.2b or Exercises 5.3a and 5.3b, but not both.) Draw a sociogram as illustrated in Figure 5.5 or Figure 5.7, indicating either conversational direction or movements. (*Note:* If you use a sociogram to record data, you cannot record content except in a rudimentary fashion. For example, you can use different colored lines and arrows to indicate whether the remark was a statement, a question, or an answer; however, you cannot record the actual words.) If you use a sociogram for your participant observations, remember to include yourself. This exercise will take about 10 or 15 minutes. When you have finished, write a brief paragraph explaining who the people were and what they were doing.

b. Observe a setting, and draw a map of it similar to the one in Figure 5.6. This time your lines and arrows will indicate movement in and out of locations. You can assign a different color to each person, if that is feasible, to clarify the illustration. When you have finished, write a brief explanation as directed in 5.4a.

(*Hint:* You may find that the sociogram in Exercise 5.4a works better in participant observation and the sociogram in Exercise 5.4b works better in nonparticipant observation. You can also do Exercise 5.4 with an entirely new group.)

Exercise 5.5   *Critique*

Instructions: Referring to any journal or monograph, select a research report in which the data were collected using one or more of the methods described in this chapter: unobtrusive measures, content analysis, available data, participant or nonparticipant observation, announced or unannounced. Answer the following questions after giving a full citation here:

1.   What was the research question?

2.   How did the researcher(s) collect the data?

3.   What was the setting?

4.   What difficulties did the researcher(s) experience?

5. Compare your own experience using the same method of data collection with that of the published report.

6. Do you have any criticisms or suggested improvements with regard to the published study?

7. What cautions would you recommend in analyzing data of this type?

8. If you had read the study first, could you have done better with the type of data collection described?

CHAPTER 6

Interviews

Unobtrusive measures and direct observation will prove inadequate for some research questions. There is no way, for example, to discover a person's opinion, motivation, conclusions, or plans unless he or she has recorded them (in which case you could try content analysis). Since it is important in business, government, and science to determine people's reactions to products, programs, policies, candidates, new ideas, and subcultural groups, asking questions is very popular and has been developed to a high art. One can hardly imagine marketing without market research or an election without polls of the voters.

In modern Western society, asking one's views is not considered offensive. Most people are willing if not eager to give their opinions on a wide range of topics. Moreover, questioning has become so widespread that it is often regarded as customary, even routine. Nevertheless, there are some limits. Questions about personal background or past behavior may touch on something the respondent considers shameful. Sometimes, too, respondents suspect that the answers given will have some undesirable aftermath. Lifelong experience with the consequences of answers given to medical personnel, teachers, employers, army officers, and social workers contributes to this suspicion. The census taker sometimes finds it hard to convince people that there is no connection between questions asked by the Bureau of the Census and Internal Revenue Service tax audits. The credit bureau industry has developed an efficient system of collecting information about individuals' financial transactions, and most people are uneasily aware of this surveillance. With the emergence of employee testing, many are beginning to rethink the invasion of privacy issues and contemplate our constitutional guarantees against self-incrimination. Add to this the discomfort many people feel about computers as threats, not to mention our experience with computer goof-ups, and you have a lot of careful citizens out there!

Should you be doing research using subjects who are also inmates, students, or clients in the institution where you work, the implications to them of their participation in your project will be serious because judgments made about them may be based on their "cooperative attitude." This is a common dilemma. Often an agency or institution assigns a staff member to conduct a research project using the population at hand. It takes careful thought to devise a nonthreatening approach and all the tact you have to conduct this kind of inquiry.

Whether the setting or the issues do or do not lead to sensitivity and reluctance, the construction of an interview schedule or questionnaire requires a lot of planning and some testing. The administration of an interview or questionnaire requires planning, too, and attention must be paid to the established criteria and procedures, which have been developed from experience in hundreds of projects. This chapter focuses on face-to-face interviews, dealing first with construction and mechanics and then with the actual conduct of the encounters. The next chapter offers the same kind of analysis of questionnaires and their administration.

TABLE 6.1 | **Types of interview with examples**

Interview Type	Procedure	Example
Unstructured	Interviewer guided only by research goal	First discussion between real estate broker and customer
Semistructured	Interviewer uses schedule as guide	Job interview to determine some standard items and some unique
Structured	Interviewer asks list of exact questions	Hospital intake interview to get medical history

Types of Interview

As mentioned in Chapter 4, an interview is a conversation between two people on a specific subject. Should you decide to incorporate interviews into your research, you must decide what type to use; you must also prepare an interview schedule and choose recording methods.

Interview Structures

Interviews vary in their degree of organization or structure from having none at all (unstructured) through the semistructured to structured forms. A structured interview is almost identical to a questionnaire. The difference between an interview and a questionnaire is that an interview is flexible; the interviewer can rephrase the questions or explain them, if necessary, to adapt to each new respondent. The questionnaire is administered in a less personal manner, and the questions are exactly the same for everyone.[1] Table 6.1 outlines the types of interview and gives an example for each.

Unstructured Interviews   In the **unstructured interview** the interviewer has a goal in mind and guides the direction of the remarks, but does not limit the respondent. Since this type of interview is usually chosen for the preliminary, exploratory study and because the research goal includes the discovery of relevant issues, there is merit in allowing the respondent to suggest related topics.

An unstructured interview also may be useful if the researcher is trying to find out the answer to a delicate question, such as "Who are the people that deal drugs in this area?" You cannot come right out and ask a question like that, because the respondent will not tell you unless you have won the right to be trusted. This trust may take quite some time to establish, and you may have to conduct a number of conversations with the same person until you finally lead the respondent to give you the information you seek. If you fail, the failure can still teach you something. W. Gordon West points out that his respondents refused to introduce him to deviant contacts in certain categories, but he became aware of major social boundaries because this door was closed to him.[2]

Semistructured Interviews   If you are certain of what you want to know but still want to leave some room for exploration as the interview proceeds, the **semistructured interview** is appropriate. The interview uses a list of questions, or an interview schedule, as a guide. This schedule provides quite a bit of structure, but without requiring administration of the questions in precisely the same way every time. The instructions give a general idea of what is wanted (see Figure 6.1). The interviewer has some straightforward questions to ask, but the questions for the dependent variable, or what will eventually reveal appropriate variables, are written in a way that leaves the interviewer room to probe.

A **probe** is a word, phrase, or sentence that is uttered by the interviewer to stimulate the respondent to clarify an answer or expand it. Sometimes just looking interested and saying yes or uh-huh is enough, but often the interviewer will want to say something encouraging, such as "That's very interesting. Do you remember anything else?" or "What happened after that?" just as we do in normal conversations. In the book cited in Note 1, Stephen A. Richardson and associates refer to two kinds of probe: the **extension**, as in the examples just given, and the **echo**, which consists of a simple repetition of what the respondent has just said. For example, if the respondent has just said something about which you would like to know more:

RESPONDENT: "And then he got really violent, I mean like World War Three."
INTERVIEWER: "He got really violent." (Probe, echo type)
                or
INTERVIEWER: "What did he do?" (Probe, extension type)
                but not
INTERVIEWER: "He showed considerable hostility?"

The last example is wrong because it supplies a reason for the respondent to withhold the rest of the information about the behavior. The respondent may seize on the term "hostility" and assume that it is the approved way to describe what happened. You need to elicit exactly what the third person did, and you want to avoid a pseudopsychological summary. A correct probe elicits a description:

RESPONDENT: "Yes, and he hit me as well as two other people. One of them got a black eye."

Now notice the problem posed in the fourth question of the schedule page reproduced in Figure 6.1. The interviewer has a brief question to ask,

FIGURE 6.1 **A semistructured interview schedule**

Page 1

The Social and Emotional Aspects of Juvenile Diabetes

Mellitus—Family Survey—Part 2

(This part of the schedule is to be administered twice, once to

each parent, privately.)

1. To the best of your knowledge, M._____, does any relative of
   yours have diabetes? (If yes,) Who? What relation are
   they to you? (Just list initials and relationship; probe
   a little.)

2. Do you know any of the preceding people personally?
   (If they have mentioned close relatives such as children or
   parents, omit and just write yes.)

3. Do you have any friends or acquaintances who are
   diabetic? (As above)

4. M._____, what is diabetes? (Here we are looking for the
   salience of several possible problems: physiological, social,
   and economic as well as psychological; and knowledge of
   late complications. Probe with "Can you tell me anything
   more?" or similar. Record respondent's affective response.)

---

but the question is expected to yield a rich harvest of data. The researchers
want to know the respondent's perception of a life-threatening disease suffered by the respondent's child. The interviewer must probe carefully, waiting each time for the respondent to finish and not leading the respondent in
any way. It is especially important not to cut off the respondent's remarks
until the question is exhausted. Give the respondent 10 seconds to answer a
question and wait 10 seconds after they finish before asking the next question.
(Count to ten slowly in your mind.) You don't want ill-considered answers,

nor do you want to make the respondent uncomfortable. Note that the interviewer is also asked to note the respondent's **affective**, or emotional, response to the question. Your patience will make that response easier.

Sometimes considerable ingenuity is required of the interviewer. Linguistic investigations, in which highly specific answers are needed from the respondents, are a case in point. The researcher's goal is to develop a word list for a particular area, group, or occupation, but not all approaches are permissible. You cannot interview people by presenting them with a list of words that you think are appropriate. You are then "**leading the witnesses**" or asking the question in such a way as to indicate the desired answer. You will not find out anything—except perhaps how obliging and agreeable people can be, Once you have suggested a word, they will be aware of it, even if they formerly were not. Here is how one researcher went about finding out what a particular role player in the tobacco industry was called and whether or not the respondents knew the term:[3]

> *Four levels of response were established. The first . . . is the* spontaneous response. *. . . . The informant was given a definition and asked to supply the term to fit it. . . . ("What do you call the fellow who comes up to you while you're waiting at the scales with your truckload of tobacco, who offers to buy it right on the spot?" for example.)*
>
> *If the informant . . . was not able to supply the term, an attempt was made to elicit the desired response through* circumlocution. *. . . . ("You know, there are spectators and free-lance buyers, and the kind of person that . . ." for example.)*
>
> *If circumlocution was not successful, the response was solicited through* prompting. *("Isn't it something like 'hooking' or 'pinning'?" for example.)*
>
> *As a last resort,* direct presentation *was used. ("Have you ever heard of the term* pinhooker?" *for example.)*

In this particular study probes had to go as far as direct presentation because this kind of word list must establish the extent of the area in which a particular word is known. Ordinarily, one need not probe that much. The degree of probing depends on the research goal.

Structured Interviews   The **structured interview** differs from the other two types only in that the questions are least flexible. There is a minimum of probing, and many questions are presented to the respondent, along with a list of answers from which to choose. In structured interviews the questions must be asked of each respondent in exactly the same way and in the same order. The census taker who tracks down people who have not returned their census forms uses such an interview, reading each question aloud and noting down the reply. Figure 6.2 is an example of a structured interview schedule, from the same study as the one in Figure 6.1. Two of the eight questions on the page require a little tactful maneuvering, and the first four blanks are filled in before the interview begins.

FIGURE 6.2   **A structured interview schedule**

Page 1

The Social and Emotional Aspects of Juvenile Diabetes

Mellitus—Family Survey   Part 1

(This part of the schedule may be administered with both

parents present.)

1. Name of child:
2. Address of child:
3. Race of child (do not ask, complete from camp record):
4. Sex of child (as in #3):

Begin here:

5. (Get the religion of child and parents by asking whether or not the child is attending a church or Sunday school; if yes, which religion; if not, ask if the child is considered to be any particular religion. After getting this answer, ask if the parents are also of the _____ religion—unless they have already indicated the answer.)

     Religion: Child _____ Mother _____
     Father _____

6. Birth date of child:

7. (If parents are reluctant to give their own ages, simply mention that you will estimate; when they ask what your estimate is, guess high. They will usually correct you. If that does not work, guess realistically and write "estimate" next to your guess.)

     Age of mother _____ Age of father _____

8. Grade child is currently attending or has just finished:

Preparing the Schedule

The interviewer should be familiar with the entire research design and should know the rationale behind each question. On big projects there is usually a training period for interviewers, and the training can culminate in testing the proposed interview schedule. This step, referred to as the **pretest** of the interview, immediately reveals any flaws in the questions. As any teacher knows, a surprising number of interpretations are possible for almost any question, and changes usually have to be made. On small projects, training can consist of a simple discussion of the project. The interview testing will be the same regardless of project size.

Types of Question   Like interviews, questions range from unstructured to completely structured. The least structured kind is epitomized by Question 4 in Figure 6.1 and is called an **open-end question**. The purpose of open-end questions is to allow the respondent to volunteer descriptions, explanations, or reminiscences, which can be analyzed by the researcher. It is hoped that the response will contain more of the truth than would have been volunteered in answer to a highly structured or **closed-end question**.

There are many forms of the closed-end question. These questions ask the respondent to select an answer from a list of answers or to reply with a simple fact. The following are forms of closed-end questions:

"What is your marital status?"

_____ Single, never married

_____ Married, living with spouse

_____ Cohabiting

_____ Separated from spouse

_____ Divorced

_____ Widowed

"What is your birth date?" _____

"How long have you lived in this city?" _____

"For whom did you vote in the 1988 presidential election?"

_____ George Bush

_____ Michael Dukakis

_____ Pat Paulsen

_____ Other (please specify)

Some closed-end questions consist of a declarative sentence or two, followed by a choice of answers by which the respondent indicates an opinion or the strength of an opinion. For example:

"It is a good idea to chlorinate public water supplies in order to prevent disease, even though some people's teeth may be damaged as a result."

_____ Strongly agree

_____ Agree

_____ Disagree

_____ Strongly disagree

Some questions are arranged so that they rank responses along a particular dimension. The following is based on income:

"Which of these income categories includes your family income for last year (before taxes)?"

_____ Under $5000

_____ $5000 to $9999

_____ $10,000 to $14,999

_____ $15,000 to $19,999

_____ $20,000 to $24,999

_____ $25,000 or more

Some questions are ordered to provide a **composite score** on a particular attitude. The various kinds of ordering, ranking, and scoring questions are called **scales** and **indexes**. Since they have implications for statistical testing and other types of analysis, they are discussed in Chapter 9. There are also many tests in use that may be included with an interview schedule or incorporated in a questionnaire. A researcher desiring to investigate these possibilities can consult one of the references that compile them.[4]

Criteria for Questions   The three main criteria to be applied to see whether a question is acceptable for inclusion in your interview are **relevance**, **clarity**, and **brevity**.

As discussed previously, "relevance" means related to the matter at hand, specifically, your research question. *No question should be included that is not necessary.* Remember, it takes time, money, and effort to print, ask, answer, and analyze each question you ask; therefore, be thrifty about the asking. All you need to collect are the data that will answer the research question. A review of the discussion of **operationalization** in Chapter 2 may be useful at this point. The questions you use must be **indicators** of the independent, dependent, or intervening variables, or they must be essential to the asking of questions that are such indicators. Sometimes you have to ask more than one question because the one you are using as an indicator may be difficult for the respondent to answer; it may involve a sensitive issue, or events may have to be recalled.

Consider the following exchange.

INTERVIEWER: "How long have you lived here?"

RESPONDENT: "Twenty-five years."

INTERVIEWER: "I guess you've seen a lot of people come and go. Have many changes taken place in the neighborhood?"

RESPONDENT: "I'll say. Nothing but new people here lately."

INTERVIEWER: "What kinds of people are moving in?"

RESPONDENT: "City folks."

(Indicator)

INTERVIEWER: "How do you feel about having city folks move out here?"

In this example the first three questions are **warm-up questions**. They put the respondent at ease and make it easier for the respondent to answer the fourth question, which is what the researcher really wants to know. (We shall assume in that case that the research question was "How do the farmers feel about the urbanites moving into their area?" or some similar inquiry.)

The following example is slightly different.

INTERVIEWER: "How long have you lived here?"

RESPONDENT: "Twenty-five years."

INTERVIEWER: "It must have been quite different here when you first arrived. Can you remember what it was like?"

RESPONDENT: "Oh, yes. It was nothing but farms."

INTERVIEWER: "Was this your first farm?"

RESPONDENT: "First of my own. I was raised on a farm, but when I got married, Mary and I moved to this place."

(Indicator)

INTERVIEWER: "Mr. Jones, what were your reasons for choosing to be a farmer?"

In the second example the researcher wants to set the scene in the respondent's mind so that Mr. Jones can more easily recall how he felt 25 years ago. Bear in mind that warm-up questions are relevant to the question that is meant to elicit the desired data.

In the first example, if you want to know how the farmers feel about urbanites moving into their area, that is what you should ask. You should not ask "How do you think people out here feel about city folks moving in?" If you ask that question, you will get the respondent's opinion of what somebody else's opinion is. You want the respondent's own opinion, as accurately as possible. Newspaper stories often carry headlines such as WOMEN TIRED OF WEARING SLACKS, PROFESSOR SAYS. When you read the story under such a headline, you may find that it is not about a study of women's opinion on wearing slacks, it is an interview with a professor and presents that professor's opinion on how women feel about the matter. This is a mistake to avoid. Ask the right question.

Another type of question to avoid is the one that "leads the witness." In our second example, where we asked Mr. Jones why he chose his occupation, the question not only was preceded by warm-up questions, but was deliberately phrased so as not to give Mr. Jones any idea of our opinion of choosing farming as an occupation. Omitting the warm-up questions and getting right to the point, we could have asked, "Mr. Jones, how come you got stuck way out here farming?" or "Mr. Jones, did you really want to be a farmer when you were young?" Both questions imply that the man's occupation is undesirable. Even worse is the direct suggestion of an answer, "I assume you became a farmer because your father was one, eh, Mr. Jones?"

Clarity is clearness. Your questions must be understood by the respondents. Be very careful about the phrasing. You will most often find educational differences between the research team and the respondents because people who do research are usually people with college degrees—a minority of our population. The most tactful method is to use plain English so that anyone with elementary schooling can understand what you are asking. Don't attempt to reproduce respondents' dialect or slang because it will either amuse or insult them. Find out in advance what the language difficulties may be. Learning the language problems also helps in the analysis of your data. Avoid using professional jargon from any field unless you are interviewing its practitioners exclusively. At the end of the study you can translate the results from plain English into whatever professional or scholarly language is appropriate for your report.

The way a question is constructed also determines its clarity. Take the following question and answer.

> INTERVIEWER: "Sir, do you have the time?"
> RESPONDENT: "Yes."

This is a humorous reply, but it is also an accurate one. The exchange could have taken place as follows.

> INTERVIEWER: "Sir, will you tell me the time?"
> RESPONDENT: "Yes. It's eight o'clock."

The second question could be answered with a yes (and still be accurate), but it's not as likely to be. "Sir, please tell me the time" would be better. In constructing questions you must remember the goal of the question. If you want to know how many children the respondent has, do not ask "Do you have any children?" Ask "How many children do you have, if any?" or "How many children live in this household?" if that is what you are after.

On the other hand, you have to be careful not to ask two questions where there should be only one. The classic example of this unacceptable question form is, "Are you still beating your wife?" This is a **double-barreled question** because it ostensibly asks one question ("Are you beating your wife?"), while it not only implies another question but the answer to it: "Did you ever beat your wife? Yes." The appropriate answer to a double-barreled question is "Divide the question."

Brevity means two things: first that the questions should get right to the point and not ramble and second that the words should be short, if possible. Lengthy questions with polysyllabic words tire the respondent, tire the interviewer, and are easy to misunderstand.

Be sure that your question fulfills one or more of the following requirements.

1. The question yields essential data.
2. The question leads up to one that will yield essential data.
3. The question yields important background information.
4. The question is clear.
5. The question is as brief as it can be without losing the sense of it.

Check each question against these criteria. If it does not pass, discard or revise it. Check your schedule to make sure you have included indicators for all the variables you plan to use in the analysis. Remember, the indicators you need determine how many and what questions you must include. Now let's see how to arrange those questions in sequence.

The Sequence of Questions   The interview should begin with questions that are easy to answer and will seem routine to the respondent. This is because an interview has the character of an announced observation, and the respondent is very conscious of the interviewer's scrutiny at first. Asking matter-of-fact questions (such as "How many people live here?" "Would you list them for me, please?" "How many children do you have?" "Are they all in school?" "Where were you born?" and "What is your husband's occupation?") helps to make the respondent comfortable and confident. The questions can have a simple, correct response in each case. Opinion questions are harder, since respondents often feel that there *is* a "correct" answer that they do not know. Respondents always are aware that the interviewer has an opinion, too, and often they ask what it is or offer an apology or a justification for their own opinions, lest they differ from the interviewer's.

Your project may include sensitive questions. These are the questions that are embarrassing for the respondent or call forth emotional responses. The interview from which Figures 6.1 and 6.2 were taken was administered to the parents of chronically ill children. The respondents were led from the simplest routine background questions (see Figure 6.2), which husband and wife answered jointly, to the administration of an attitude questionnaire and the questions shown in Figure 6.1. The transition was accomplished by announcing the need to fill out the questionnaire and giving it to one parent to complete while the interview with the other parent continued. The interviewer asked the parent with the questionnaire to complete it in another room so that the interview would not cause a distraction, and then the interviewer proceeded to the very sensitive questions about the disease. As shown in Figure 6.1 the easiest questions on the disease came first, leading up to the key question, "What is diabetes?" The interview went on to even more sensitive questions about the respondent's child's experience with the disease. After the most potentially painful questions had been asked, a series of "easy" questions ended the interview. These were factual questions such as, "Does (name of child) administer (his, her) own insulin?" and questions about practical problems such as expense, transportation to the hospital and special diets. The final questions dealt with the parent's opinion of the overall adjustment of the child, allowing plenty of room for the respondents' comments. At this point the questionnaire was given to the second parent and the first answered the sensitive questions.

The unstructured interview takes longer than the others. In general, the more structure, the briefer the interview. The length of the interview is very important because a fatigued respondent may terminate the interview before you have the information you went after or may begin to say anything just to finish. A fatigued interviewer is not efficient, scribbles a hasty write-up, and takes shortcuts. The pretest tells you how long the interview will probably take and therefore whether it must be cut.

Recording the Answers

During the Interview Writing answers during the interview is similar to announced participant observation in that the respondents know you are writing everything down. Respondents often say "Be sure and put down" this or that. Occasionally, they may ask you to omit something by saying "You don't have to put this in your write-up, but between you and me . . ." Remember, if you let the respondent think you have promised not to record something, you *have* promised and that promise is binding.

Many researchers feel that writing down answers is inefficient because one cannot really get everything down. They prefer to use a tape recorder and examine the transcript later to extract the data. This technique has the merit of reducing respondents' awareness of being recorded, since they tend to forget about the recorder. However, transcription to paper is expensive, and the process results in a great volume of paper, all of which has to be scrutinized and abstracted. Time means money, because somebody is getting paid to do this work. One advantage of using a tape recorder is that the interviewer can listen to the recorded interview and take notes then, just as if notes were taken during the live interview. If you replay your interview once or twice, you may learn a lot about your own technique. Trainers use the taped interview as a teaching device, and field directors use it to see how their interviewers are doing.

Postinterview Write-up Immediately after the interview, you should write a complete summary of impressions, including the main facts about the setting and the atmosphere, if relevant. This is the time to read over your notes, transcribe any shorthand, write out any abbreviations, and fill in details before you forget them. This writer has often left an interview, driven to the nearest coffee shop, and written the summary on the spot.

A good write-up includes any explanatory material that may help in the interpretation of the responses. For example, Chapter 1 contained an exchange that would not be understood unless the reader were acquainted with the respondent's religious group and understood how that group used the word *blessed*. I was the interviewer in this case and found it necessary to explain the interview to the research director, who originally thought the respondent was "incoherent." The write-up had to include a brief explanation of the respondent's religion and terminology for the director's benefit and perhaps for the benefit of other staff members who might be processing the data. This problem can crop up in any project that includes subcultural groups.

Conducting the Interview

The best research design in the world, coupled with the most efficient interview schedule, will not succeed if the interviews are conducted poorly. Interviewers must be trained to forestall or deal with problems that may arise in connection with their relation to the respondent, the setting for the interview, sensitive questions, the exchange of information, and ethical considerations. Figure 6.3 illustrates the recommended course of an interview.

Establishing Cordial Relations   As we have already seen, interviewer effect is unavoidable, since the respondent is aware of being observed and the interviewer is asking questions and recording the answers. It remains only to try to reduce interviewer effect by making the respondent as comfortable with the interviewer as possible. One way is to see that the interviewer is presentable: clean, neat, courteous, and low-key. This is essential. The interviewer should not offend in any way. The respondent's impression begins with the telephone call that sets up the appointment. An interviewer should be prompt and unfailingly pleasant.

Another strategy to make respondents comfortable is to select an interviewer whose outward characteristics are similar to their own. If possible, interviewer and respondent should be matched as to sex, race, generation, and dress. The last item can be modified; however, in general, when interviewing rich people, the interviewer should dress well, and when interviewing poor people, the interviewer should dress plainly, but not shabbily. Avoid mimicry. It would be all right to wear casual clothes or even blue jeans to interview farmers but not all right to look like a character actor.

The characteristics on which the interviewer and respondent should be matched depend partly on the research topic. An inquiry about a political stance on the legalization of marijuana might not require sex or race matching; however, generational matching would be advisable because there is a known difference of opinion between the generations on this question. Similarly, sex matching would be advisable if your question is about women's liberation, abortion, or sexual behavior.

FIGURE 6.3   **Course of an interview**

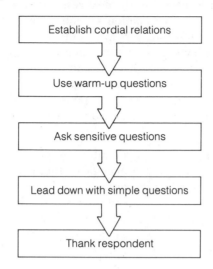

The interviewer should be pleasant and warm without being chummy. Once admitted to the respondent's confidence enough to ensure cooperation, the interviewer is wise to put the respondent at ease by making a pleasant comment or two that serves to establish some point of commonality between them. A remark of admiration or familiarity with some object usually does quite well as long as the remark is not forced or false. You might say "Oh, I see we drive the same model car. How do *you* like it?" Do not let this lead to a prolonged discussion or extensive revelation of your personal life, opinions, or tastes. Confine the pleasantries to the time it takes to settle down to the interview. Do not lose sight of the object. It is to put the respondent, not you, at ease.[5]

Occasionally a respondent may apologize for the state of the house or the behavior of the children or animals. The interviewer can reply reassuringly with some truthful remark such as "Think nothing of it, I have children myself," or "I was just thinking how much your house looks like mine!" Do not overdo it. It's not a bad idea to be prepared with a few noncommittal responses as "Children will be children, I guess!" or "My, they are active and full of energy, are they not!" Anything nonjudgmental and cordial will do.

Be careful not to say anything that can be regarded as evaluative. Respondents have a tendency to regard the interview as a test, and all respondents have been conditioned to testing situations in school. This not only leads them to think that the questions have "correct" answers, as mentioned previously, but also leads them to remember being graded. Respondents may attempt to discover whether they are giving the "right" answers. The interviewer should reassure a respondent by saying "It's your opinion we want.

There isn't any right or wrong answer." One respondent may be especially concerned about this matter, and the next respondent not at all.

The unpredictability of respondents is one of the most interesting aspects of interviewing. Now and then a respondent says "My opinions are a little oddball, you'll find. Maybe you can't use them." The appropriate response is "On the contrary! A full range of ideas and opinions is exactly what we're hoping for." In the writer's experience, a respondent who claims unique ideas often proceeds to give run-of-the-mill responses. If this happens, maintain a respectful and interested expression nevertheless.

The Setting   It is important that you interview people in privacy, unless you want a group consensus. The presence of another person, even a child, may inhibit, intimidate, or distract the respondent. In some families, asking questions of one spouse in the presence of the other results in an argument. One spouse may use the occasion to snipe at the other spouse or may try to enlist the interviewer to confirm one side of a previous argument. This can be very uncomfortable. Here is one such experience:

INTERVIEWER:	"How old is Mary?"
MOTHER:	"She was born on our second anniversary, ten years ago. We haven't had an evening out since." (Husband squirms.)
INTERVIEWER:	"Ten years old. And what grade is she in?"
MOTHER:	"Good thing you're asking me. *He'd* never know. Fifth." (Husband looks away.)
INTERVIEWER:	"What is Mary's religion?"
MOTHER:	"Well, we have a stay-away daddy. If it wasn't for Father _____ I don't know what Mary would do for moral guidance. . . ." (Husband casts pleading look at interviewer, mumbles something, and leaves room.)

This interview was a difficult one because the respondent insisted on referring to marital problems regardless of their relevance to the questions. Although not common, situations of this type occur with enough frequency to be noted. In the project from which this interview was taken, there were 100 two-hour interviews; three presented this difficulty. The best course for the interviewer to pursue is to remain pleasant, echo the part of each answer that is responsive to the question, and avoid addressing the extraneous material.

Above all, do not allow yourself to be drawn into a discussion of the respondent's personal affairs, political or religious opinions, or similar topics. There are several important reasons for this rule. First, side discussions detract from the main goal, which is to get the data for the project. Second, if you do get into an argument with a respondent, you damage the research field and your project by causing offence. Third, because you are regarded by most respondents as a source of information and will be quoted (and misquoted) by many after you leave, any comment you make about a matter unrelated to the survey adds up to interference in the personal lives of the respondents; that is unethical.

Interviews may be conducted in a respondent's home or office, in your office, or in a neutral setting. The setting should be comfortable and quiet and should offer a minimum of distraction. This is especially important if you are asking sensitive questions.

Sensitive Questions   We have already seen that sensitive questions need to be approached cautiously. The recommended procedure is to use routine questions both to lead up to sensitive questions and to conclude the interview. Death, sex, and criminal behavior are the major areas that present a challenge to the interviewer because they often involve fear, grief, and shame. Any one of these emotions is painful to the respondent, and the pain is likely to persist after the interview is over. Thus in concluding the interview, you must lead *down* from the sensitive area, asking a question that turns the respondent's thoughts to something else before you leave.

Not only may long-repressed memories come to the surface of the respondent's consciousness, but also, if you are not careful, the respondent may be encouraged to think that you can help with a problem. Should the problem be a medical or legal one, it is especially important that you not raise false hopes, suggest previously unimagined dangers, or provide advice.

For example, with many diseases a number of unfortunate outcomes are possible, though rare. Mostly these are known to the medical professions but not to the public, including those who suffer from a particular condition. Nothing is to be gained by alerting respondents to possibilities, remote or not, of which they are unaware. The interviewer, for instance, must not say "Are you aware that long-term (name of illness) sometimes results in (bad outcome)?" This also applies to good news. Telling a respondent of a new medical technique, an experimental prosthesis, a new "wonder" drug, or dietary regimen may encourage false hope in a person for whom optimism is inappropriate. It is especially hard to refrain from doing this if you feel that the respondent could use some good advice or appears singularly uninformed. Control the impulse.

As noted earlier, the interviewer is often seen as an authority and as one who has access to information about the subject of the interview. This makes all your remarks, even offhand observations, significant to the respondent. Another caution: Medical and legal recommendations from an interviewer are not only unethical and therefore unprofessional, but are also illegal because they may constitute practicing without a license.

Questioning people about sexual and criminal behavior is always hard since both the interviewer and respondent may be embarrassed about the subject. Moreover, sex and crime are both fascinating. The interviewer must guard against this fascination and make sure that no question is asked that is not necessary. Possessing knowledge about illegal activity is in itself dangerous to the interviewer and makes one vulnerable to harassment both from the authorities and from the respondents, who may regret having told what they knew or did.

Less dramatic, but just as important, are the forms of sensitivity surrounding age, income, and attitudes toward family members. Make it easy for the respondent to answer such questions. For example, asking for the respondent's birth date is more tactful than requesting his or her age. (Date of birth also has the advantage of being harder to falsify on short notice, and it provides the most precise information.) A question on income may be easier to answer if the respondent just has to check off a category that includes the right amount rather than actually saying, "I make $14,500 a year." Sometimes income categories are printed on a card that is handed to the respondent as the interviewer says, "Can you give me the number of the category in which your family income for last year is included?" The respondent replies with the appropriate number (or letter), and the interviewer checks it off on the schedule. The categories are determined by the research question and reflect current levels of income in that area.

Attitudes toward family members are sensitive because the social mores demand specific loyalties and condemn favoritism in some instances. Asking a mother which child she likes best, for example, may embarrass her. The respondent wants to please you and to give the "right" answer and she may even have a preference for one child; however, she probably has been taught that this is wrong. Similarly, attitudes toward aged parents may be ambivalent and hard to express. Added to this is the cultural pattern of family solidarity in the presence of outsiders. As interviewer, you are such an outsider. On the other hand, a respondent who is "odd man out" in the family group may be desperately looking for an ally. As noted earlier, you must carefully avoid taking sides. Even if you only serve as a sounding board for the respondent's dissatisfactions, you are getting involved.

Some strategies have been developed for dealing with sensitive questions in an interview. One strategy is to preface the question with a reassuring statement. One might say "Nowadays some people are saying that any sexual practice is all right as long as it doesn't result in injury. What is your personal reaction to this view?" (This can be followed by handing a checklist of sexual practices to the respondent.) Another way of handling sensitive questions is to use a series of statements for which the respondent is asked to indicate agreement or disagreement. Remember that respondents may be tempted to avoid sensitive questions by checking "no opinion" or "don't know." It may be better to include degrees of agreement and disagreement and omit the choice for indecision, as in the following examples:

"Premarital sex is always wrong."

_____ Strongly agree

_____ Agree

_____ Mildly agree

_____ Mildly disagree

_____ Disagree

_____ Strongly disagree

The respondent may be asked to indicate strength of agreement on a linear scale:

Strongly
agree

Strongly
disagree

1	2	3	4	5	6	7	8	9	10

Another possibility is to present a little story, or **vignette**, about a hypothetical situation and have the respondent comment on it. This type of story is prepared carefully and is designed to elicit statements about values, attitudes, and opinions. Alternatively, you can present the respondent with a hypothetical situation first, ask for an opinion, and proceed to more personal questions:

> "Some people feel that failing to report some types of income on one's tax return is not really dishonest, considering how some congressmen act. Do you disapprove of such people?"
>
> "Suppose someone in your family underreported his or her income. Would you disapprove?"
>
> "Would you consider underreporting your own income?"

What you are doing is similar to the warm-up. You are leading into a personal question from a less threatening general question.

Never allow an evaluative comment or look to escape you. If the respondent seems embarrassed or tearful, you can ease the tension by nodding to encourage the subject to proceed, looking away or at the notebook, or by adjusting something such as your briefcase or chair. Avoid condescending remarks such as "I understand. Don't feel bad."

Exchanging Information　A respondent may persist in asking questions about the interviewer's personal life, opinions, or experiences; he or she may counter the interviewer's questions by asking "What do *you* think?" After all, a normal conversation is a mutual exchange of comments, and some respondents may become increasingly uncomfortable with the one-sided nature of an interview.[6] You have to be careful to strike a balance between chummy self-revelations and inscrutable interrogation. One answer to "What do you think?" might be "Well, I guess there's quite a bit to be said on the subject." If the respondent has already expressed an opinion, you could say, "I find your remarks very interesting. Can you tell me more about. . . ."

Be vague about your personal life. You do not want the respondent interviewing you, and you do not want to turn the encounter into a social occasion. It's all right to accept a cup of tea or coffee and a cookie if you feel that will help to put the respondent at ease. Under no circumstances, however, should you drink alcoholic beverages or use drugs either before the interview or during it. This is not participant observation, and even if it were, anything that clouds your perception is to be avoided. "Thank you, but not during working hours," said with a smile, should do it.

Reminders   As in all research operations, be careful not to hurt anyone. This also means that you must not meddle in the respondent's life. It is a great temptation, especially when the respondent has deficiencies and problems that seem easily controllable or reparable to the interviewer. They may be so in the interviewer's personal experience. A random sample of citizens exhibits the full range of such problems. Some are exasperating, some pitiful, some horrifying. You might feel that you should act to help them. It is not ethical to interfere, however, because you are not in a position to follow up your actions with long-term responsibility and help. You would just be interfering and then leaving, maybe making things worse than before. You must remember that your business as a researcher is with the actual (what is), not the ideal (what should be). Do not step out of the researcher's role while you are conducting research. This may not be easy at times. I have had respondents follow me to my car, urging me to come back and visit again. Some people are very lonely. I still feel sympathy and concern for respondents interviewed as long as 20 years ago.

You may encounter difficulties because some respondents are dishonest. They may lie to you, falsify records, misrepresent past events, claim more education than they have, conceal facts, and so on. You cannot do anything about this except to be careful not to make matters worse by asking hard questions in a tactless manner. Claire Selltiz and associates cite a study by H. J. Parry and H. M. Crossley in which answers to interview questions were checked by comparing them with agency records (contributions, voting, age, library cards, driver's licenses, home ownership, auto ownership, and existence of home telephones). They found inaccuracies ranging from 2 percent (phones) to 40 percent (contributions).[7]

The interviewer must be trained, and it is helpful if the training period includes practice with fellow interviewers who deliberately try to be difficult respondents. Some possible testing behavior might include: hostility, indifference, overfamiliarity, rambling, condescension toward the questions, lack of comprehension, language difficulties, and anxiety. Although these behaviors appear in only a minority of respondents, the interviewer must be ready for them. The rest of the responses will be pleasant, easy, and interesting.

Most of the people you meet in this line of work are friendly and cooperative, and you will remember them fondly for years.

You can now see why brevity and clarity are so important. Another argument for these qualities is that complicated questions have to be explained by the interviewer, opening the way to leading the respondent in some direction the interviewer prefers (leading the witness).

Most of the topics discussed in the chapter in relation to interviews are also applicable to questionnaires. As in the health interview described above, an interview may incorporate one or more questionnaires. In fact, the structured interview differs from the individually administered questionnaire only in that the respondent fills in the answers and the researcher does not speak except to provide clarification when requested or to ask the respondent at the end of the encounter to go back and fill in some question left blank. The researcher also approaches the respondent with the request to complete the questionnaire and thanks the respondent at the end. In general, interviews are more likely in qualitatively focused research and questionnaires in quantitatively focused research, but this rule of thumb is not absolute.

There are quite a few variations in types of questionnaire and modes of administration, as well as some special considerations to review. Technological advances in communication and data processing have opened up new possibilities for procedures. Chapter 7 examines these matters.

Summary and Conclusion

Interviews and questionnaires are good ways to collect facts about people and to find out their opinions and attitudes. Most people are happy to cooperate with interviewers and questionnaire administrators, but some people have reservations about giving information because of the possibilities for its misuse. It is important, therefore, to establish a relationship of mutual trust with interviewees and to convince respondents of the harmlessness of your inquiry.

Careful planning is essential to a good interview. Interviews can range from unstructured through semistructured to completely structured. In the latter form they resemble questionnaires, which are always highly structured. The degree to which an interview is structured depends on the need to explore issues, the most exploratory interview being the least structured by necessity.

Because the answers to many questions are indicators, and other questions lead up to answers that are indicators, the researcher must refer back to the research question and hypothesis to develop the questions. In addition to relevance to the goal, the main criteria for questions are brevity and clarity.

Questioners must be careful to ask only what they want to know, and to be sure to get everything they need to know. They must neither provide an answer along with the question nor confuse respondents by using ambiguous or esoteric wording. They must not combine two questions in one or ask questions that cannot be answered easily.

Interviews should be conducted in private, unless a consensus is wanted. It is difficult to record everything manually, but if you use a tape recorder, you get an excessive amount of data to transcribe and process. However, you can play a tape over and take notes from it at your convenience. The interviewer should write up impressions and summaries immediately after the interview is concluded.

Under no circumstances should the researcher get involved in the life of the respondent or interviewee. Sensitive questions should be dealt with tactfully and approached with warm-up or transition questions that make the experience easy on the subjects. A proper interview begins and ends with simple, easy-to-answer questions. Interviewers must be careful not to reveal their own opinions.

Training periods for interviewers and pretests for questions should be scheduled to avoid problems of comprehension. Less structured questions can be used in the pretest, because structured questions can be developed from them. Interviews provide wide access to respondents' ideas and opinions but cost more than questionnaires because of the time and personal attention they require.

Main Points

1. If you want to know what people think, and they have not recorded it, you have to ask them in an interview or questionnaire. Most people are willing to answer questions unless they think bad consequences are likely. You have to approach people in as nonthreatening a manner as possible.

2. To suit your goal, interviews can be unstructured, semistructured, or structured. Unstructured interviews are guided only by the goal; semistructured interviews follow an interview schedule, or list of suggested questions; in structured interviews, the questions are exactly the same for each respondent.

3. You stimulate an interviewee to say more by saying something encouraging. That encouragement is called a probe.

4. The two main types of question are closed-end, in which the respondent is asked to choose among prepared answers, and open-end, in which the respondent is free to answer anything. There are many variations.

5. Lists of questions numerically evaluated to provide rankings and scores are called scales or indexes.

6. The main criteria for questions and schedules are relevance, clarity, and brevity.

7. Sensitive questions or questions that require recalling something may have to be preceded by warm-up questions to put respondents in the proper frame of mind.

8. You must not ask for secondhand opinions, hint at the "proper" answer, imitate respondents' speech, use language respondents do not understand, incorporate two questions in one, or ask anything but what you need to know.

9. The best way to order questions is to start with simple ones, continue with more difficult ones, and end with easy ones. Leave plenty of room for respondents' comments.

10. Writing things by hand is harder than taping, but it may be more efficient in the long run. Impressions and summaries should be written as promptly as possible.

11. It's important to establish rapport, and this is easier if interviewer and interviewee are matched on sex, age, race, and dress. An interviewer should be pleasant and friendly but not chummy or evaluative. Interviews should be conducted in private unless a consensus is desired.

12. A pretest is a trial run that tells you where the shortcomings are in your data collection instrument. You can use pretest results to develop a structured question from an unstructured one. Interviews are pretested for timing and the flow of questions. All questions should also be tested on people from the same kind of population as the eventual sample, to be sure of clarity.

Notes

1. Terminology varies. Some refer to unstructured interviews as *nonstandardized*, for example. See Stephen A. Richardson, Barbara Snell Dohrenwend, and David Klein, *Interviewing: Its Forms and Functions* (New York: Basic Books, 1965), Chapter 2.

2. W. Gordon West, "Access to Adolescent Deviants and Deviance," in *Fieldwork Experience: Qualitative Approaches to Social Research*, ed. William B. Shaffir, Robert A. Stebbins, and Allan Turowetz (New York: St. Martin's Press, 1980), p. 40.

3. Norman Arlen Heap, "A Vocabulary of Tobacco Growing in Fayette County, Kentucky," unpublished master's thesis, Louisiana State University, 1959, pp. 5, 6,

and personal interview. Material from thesis reprinted by permission of Norman A. Heap.

4. Delbert C. Miller, *Handbook of Research Design and Social Measurement*, 3rd ed. (New York: McKay, 1977), is a good example.

5. Earl R. Babbie, *The Practice of Social Research*, 2nd ed. (Belmont, Calif.: Wadsworth, 1979), p. 339.

6. Richardson, Dohrenwend, and Klein, *Interviewing*, pp. 314–32.

7. *Selltiz, Wrightsman, and Cook's Research Methods in Social Relations*, rev. Louise H. Kidder (New York: Holt, Rinehart, & Winston, 1981), p. 147 cites H. J. Parry and H. M. Crossley, "Validity of Responses to Survey Questions," *Public Opinion Quarterly* 14 (1950): 61–80.

Exercises

As you do these exercises, reread the relevant parts of the chapter. It might also be helpful to review the comments on interviewer effect in Chapters 1 and 5.

In Exercise 6.1 you are asked to conduct an unstructured interview, having a goal in mind but no schedule in hand. Exercise 6.2 asks that you develop a schedule from the information gleaned from Exercise 6.1's interview so that you can conduct a semistructured interview on the same topic. This latter exercise will give you some practice in constructing interview schedules.

Exercise 6.3 is a critique of a published interview.

Exercise 6.1   *The unstructured interview*

Instructions: Select a person, preferably from your family, who is a generation older or younger than you but at least 18 years old. Arrange to interview this person for about a half-hour in an informal manner. Your goal is to find out what his or her experience was or is now in some situation with which you are also coping: getting married, graduating, picking a career, looking for a job, moving from one home to another, or coping with financial hardship, for example. Find out how he or she felt about it, what decisions had to be made, and why they were made. When you are writing up the interview, conclude by comparing your respondent's experience with your own in the same situation. (*Example:* if you interview your father on how he felt about getting married, compare what he says with your feelings about getting married.)

Begin with general warm-up questions, and gradually get to the heart of the matter. Keep your goal in mind. Do not talk about yourself but keep the interview focused on the respondent's experience. Be careful not to lead the subject. Write as close to a verbatim account of the interview as you can and then add your conclusion. (You can add pages if you run out of space.)

Use this space to jot down your intended respondent and topic:

Respondent:

Topic:

Interview:

Respondent: _____

Date: _____

[Next page]

Conclusion:

Exercise 6.2   *The semistructured interview*

Instructions: Using the same topic you selected for Exercise 6.1, read over what you recorded in the interview and your conclusion. Using open-end questions, design a brief interview schedule. The schedule should contain instructions to the interviewer and should suggest probes where necessary so that someone could replicate the interview. Administer the interview to a respondent of about the same age as the one interviewed for Exercise 6.1. After you have filled in the blanks and written a conclusion for your interview, answer the following questions:

1.   Which type of interview did you find easier to conduct?

2.   Why?

Topic: _____ Respondent: _____

Interview: _____ Date: _____

Outline your plan here, to be filled in during interview.

Conclusion:

Exercise 6.3   *Critique*

Instructions: Select a research report from any source (including magazines) that uses interviews and includes a copy of the data collection instrument. Read it and answer the following questions after giving a full citation here:

_____

_____

1.   What was the source of the report? (Give exact name and date.)

2.   How were the interviews obtained?

3.   How many respondents were there?

4.   Did the researchers mention any refusals?

5.   What were they trying to find out?

6.   In reading the interview schedule did you see anything that you would want to change if you had to use it? What was it?

7.   If possible, list a question you found inadequate and show how you would rewrite it, as in Chapter 2.

CHAPTER 7

Questionnaires and Surveys

All questionnaires are structured, meaning that the questions are fixed in advance and are identical for everyone. Questionnaires have many purposes. Some are for collecting information to be used in processing applications; some are for collecting information to be tabulated. Any questionnaire can have more than one purpose, but if too much is included, the instrument becomes so long that it is tiresome to complete.

Questionnaires

A questionnaire with only one type of question is classified by the form of its questions: open-end, closed-end, and forced choice are familiar. For example, one might say, "Smith, using a closed-end questionnaire, surveyed attitudes toward divorcees in Iowa." However, there may well be more than one type of question in a questionnaire.

You have already had experience with questionnaires of various types or have observed something similar to them in action (see Table 7.1).

Types of Questionnaire

Questionnaires intended to get only descriptive data are easier to construct than those intended to reveal opinions, values, attitudes, and intentions. The latter can be subsumed under the title of "attitude" questionnaires (or surveys). As discussed in Chapter 6, open-end questions allow the respondent to give any response; it can be whatever the question stimulates in the respondent's mind. The researcher wants to know just that: what the respondent thinks when presented with the question.

Closed-end questions offer a choice of prepared responses. Inspired by either a theory (which predicts or requires a specific range of responses) or a pretest (which revealed what that range was most likely to be), closed-end questions allow very little leeway. Forms range from the simple listing of the options as in:

"Sex: (circle one) Male Female"

to a series of scale numbers to indicate strength of opinion:

"Please indicate your satisfaction with this class by circling the appropriate number below."

Dissatisfied   Fully satisfied
  1   2   3   4   5   6   7   8   9   10

A question is closed-end if all the choices allowed are supplied.

Two types of questionnaire have been developed as a way of getting

TABLE 7.1   **Types of questionnaire with examples**

Questionnaire Type	Procedure	Example
Open-end	Questions allow respondents to give individual answers	Essay examination
Closed-end	Questions offer choice of responses	Multiple-choice examination
Split-ballot	Questions have two parallel versions that differ in only one detail	Newlywed TV game
Forced-choice	Questions present two statements and ask respondents to choose most desirable	Voting referendum

around some characteristic response patterns, or sets. One is the split-ballot questionnaire and the other is the forced choice.

The Split Ballot   People tend to harmonize something they are saying with what they have already said in order to be consistent, although humans are not necessarily consistent in the logical sense or when viewed from a specific perspective. We often feel, say, and do things for arbitrary reasons. The answer often given, "Because," is perfectly legitimate. We may not know why we feel, say, or do something. However, when we say something out loud we hear ourselves. We are smart enough to know when something we are saying doesn't fit with something we've already said *from the perspective of whatever impression we hope to make*. This creates a problem for research. How can we find out whether people discriminate in favor or against something if such discrimination is not socially approved?

Suppose you want to know whether excessive drinking by females is viewed differently from excessive drinking by males. There are several ways to approach the issue. The most obvious would be to ask people directly whether they feel differently about men's and women's drinking. Some people may be ready to give a straightforward answer to that question, but others may be self-conscious about discrimination against women or men, and some people may have different attitudes toward the two sexes but not be aware of it.

You can ask two questions, one about males drinking excessively and one about females doing the same. If you do this, respondents who are avoiding the appearance of having sexist attitudes or are unaware of having them will tend to make their second answer harmonize with the first. One solution is to ask one version of the question early in the questionnaires and the other farther on, but the two questions would have to be separated by quite a few other questions if the respondent is to forget about the first by the time the second is reached. It makes for a lengthy questionnaire. The **split-ballot technique** was developed to circumvent this.

The split-ballot consists of one questionnaire with two parallel versions that differ only in one detail. In the case of the research question about excessive drinking, that detail would be the sex of the person mentioned in the questions. One version of the questions would ask about a female drinker, and it would be given to half of the respondents. The other version, which would ask about a male drinker, would be given to the other half. When the returns are analyzed, the researcher compares the "female" questionnaires to the "male" to see whether there are any differences in attitudes by sex of drinker. The researcher who uses this technique has to be careful about dividing the sample into halves. To avoid biasing the subsample in any way, you must either draw two random samples or draw one random sample, giving out version 1 and version 2 alternately.

Conscious structuring of replies to present one's self-perceived "best side" makes it difficult to get truly accurate data on attitudes of any kind, even when discrimination is not the issue. Some analysts feel that true attitudes will be revealed if enough choices are made and the answers examined to detect a pattern of responses.

Forced-Choice Questionnaires   The technique called **paired comparisons**, or **forced-choice questionnaires**, presents the two statements, objects, or outcomes and asks respondents to select the most desirable. Each statement, object, or outcome is paired once with every other one in the questionnaire, so that the researcher ends up with a rank order of preferences.[1] This circumvents the respondents' tendency to try for consistency of response and forces them to a choice where they might otherwise take refuge in "no opinion" or "undecided." One disadvantage is there is no allowance made for two things being really equally acceptable to the respondent, or perhaps matters of complete indifference. This type of questionnaire frustrates and annoys some people. (Me, for one.)

Although we have begun this chapter on questionnaires with an overview of types of questionnaire, one normally begins the preparation of a questionnaire without considering which type it will be. This is because the process of writing questions is a form of operationalizing the research question and hypothesis. The form of questionnaire that emerges depends on the indicators needed to provide the data. If you *need* forced-choice items, you can't plan open-end questions; if you need open-end questions, you can't plan closed-end. The best question is the one most likely to yield the data you need to test the hypotheses. Your research question and hypothesis should always be before you. It's not going too far to tack them up where you can see them often.

Preparing the Questionnaire

The order of activity in preparing a questionnaire is as follows:

1. Review research question and hypothesis.
2. List pieces of data needed from each respondent.
3. Write questions (these are your indicators), using 3 × 5 cards.
4. Assemble questions in an appropriate order and number them.
5. Write instructions for each or each group of questions.
6. Pretest sample questionnaires (be sure to time them).
7. Rewrite and rearrange if and where pretest indicates.
8. Number questionnaires to be used by respondents.

Pretesting nearly always results in revision. Once the revisions have been made, administration of the questionnaire can begin.

Writing Questions   The same need for brevity, clarity, and relevance that applies to interview questions applies to questionnaire questions. In addition, you need written instructions for questionnaires, to replace the interviewer's introductions and probes. Some common instructions are "Circle the number next to the answer you choose" and "Check each answer that applies."

For questions to be brief and clear, language must be simple and direct. No question should puzzle the respondent. The following question has three faults:

> "Can you tell me what your aggregate personal income was for the fiscal year March 18, 1987 to March 17, 1988?"

This question is unacceptable, first, because it lacks clarity. What does "aggregate personal income" mean? Does it mean "income from all sources added together"? If so, it should be called "total personal income" or "gross."

This question is unacceptable as well because it is poorly phrased. As we have seen, "Can you tell me . . . ?" is not good form for questions. A direct "What is" or "What was" is better.

Finally, this question asks something that most people probably couldn't answer. How many of us could figure out our income for some fiscal year? Many people get paid by the week or twice monthly. Those on annual salary generally know the rate ($15,000 a year, for example) but not the actual amount for a year because salary includes things such as bonuses, overtime, and midyear increases. Many people may not know the meaning of the word *fiscal*. The question could be rephrased:

> "What was your approximate personal income for 1987, before taxes?"

Quantitative questions are not the only type respondents may have trouble answering. I have known people who did not know such things as

grandparents' surnames
parents' occupations
parents' incomes
parents' ages
own or other family members' exact birth date

Don't ask for secondhand opinion. Nobody knows how someone else feels about anything. You *can* phrase a question indirectly: "Some people say that bicycles are more popular than they used to be. Do you think this is true?" This is a thinly disguised attempt to get the respondent's opinion of bicycles and is an acceptable form.

Double-barreled questions are also impossible to answer:

"Are you still wasting water?"
"Why do you think Americans are so unmannerly?"

The appropriate forms for these questions are as follows:

"Do you think you have wasted water in the past?
(If yes) "Have you changed these practices?" (If no) "Do you think you are wasting water now?"
"Do you think Americans are unmannerly?"
(If yes) "In your opinion, why are Americans unmannerly?"

You have to be careful about the phrasing because the respondent may think you want to know why he or she came to think of Americans as unmannerly. What you want to know is what he or she thinks *causes* Americans to be unmannerly. The reason for the opinion and the reason for the action are not the same thing. I may think Americans are unmannerly because I was told so or because I saw some unmannerly Americans. I may think Americans' rudeness stems from arrogance or from growing up in a heterogeneous society. What do you want to know? Be careful to ask it. (Refer to your research question and hypothesis.)

Excessively complicated questions that ask for specific information about hard-to-estimate quantities should also be avoided:

"During conversations with your spouse, at home, with nobody else present, what percentage of the time do you (1) ask questions, (2) give answers, and (3) listen?"

In this case a better form is as follows.

> "When you're talking with your spouse alone at home, sometimes you are asking questions, sometimes answering, and sometimes just listening. Can you estimate how much time you spend for each?" (Write time estimate next to each category)
>
> Approximate percentage of husband-wife conversations I spend:
>
> asking questions _____
>
> answering questions _____
>
> just listening _____

It's still not the greatest question in the world, but it's a lot better than the first version. (If a student included this question on a sample questionnaire, I would ask for a review of the research goal to see if this is what really needs to be asked.)

The rule that says to avoid the use of questions that ask for difficult quantification doesn't prevent you from asking for an estimate of frequency.

> "When you and your spouse are home alone, how much of the time would you say you spend just listening to your spouse, rather than talking?"
>
> _____ Hardly any
>
> _____ About half the time
>
> _____ Most of the time

Be sure you get what you need for later analysis. Ask yourself what you need the question for and what you are going to do with the data it yields.

Reminders Make sure you are asking what you really want to know. Using your independent, control, and dependent variables, make up **dummy tables**, or tables with no figures in them, and ask yourself what you would need to ask in order to fill in the blanks. (Use Figure 2.4 in Chapter 2 as a model.) It's a lot better to check and recheck before you ask questions than to invest hard work and time getting data that may be unsatisfactory.

Ask your questions in the form you intend to use as far as possible but do not limit yourself so much that you cannot rework the data later, if it suits you. For example, you might be trying to find out how people with children under the age of 16 feel about the elementary schools in the community. So, you ask them,

> "Do you have any children under 16 years old?"

This separates the sample into:

people with children under 16
people without children under 16

Is this enough? How about the difference between people with no children at all and people with children 16 or over? Is there a difference between people with only children over 16 and people with children in both age categories? What about people with preschoolers? You can defer categorizing the fertility variable until you see the frequency distribution. Ask the question:

"What are the ages of your children, if any?"

Then you get specific data and can combine them afterward in any way that seems useful. You could also get the sex of the child by asking for a list:

"Please list the birth dates of your children in the appropriate column."

GIRLS	**BOYS**
_____	_____
_____	_____

You would include half a dozen lines under each sex designation and enough white space around the question to allow for big families.

In the preceding example you are going to have to provide an instruction. People will not know whether they should include children who died or have left home. You can add a sentence in parentheses: "(Include all children now living, regardless of age or residence.)" You can also incorporate the instruction into the question, as long as this does not make the question cumbersome:

"Please list the birth dates of all your living children, regardless of age or residence, in the appropriate column."

Although you should be very careful to get all the information you need, in as much detail as you might want for later rearrangement, do not trouble yourself to get data you are not going to use. If you want to know whether people are or are not registered to vote, you do not need to ask how long they have been registered, whether they are married, or what their religion is. Stick to your independent, control, and dependent variables, adding only the questions that are needed for smooth transitions or warm-up.

Choosing the Type of Question When you are trying to choose between closed-end and open-end questions for your indicators, you should consider three possibilities:

1. Closed-end with a space for comments
2. Open-end followed by a closed-end on the same variable
3. Open-end pretest to develop a good closed-end question

Let's look at these possibilities more closely, beginning with the straightforward closed-end question.

"How often do you use your automobile for recreational purposes?"

_____ Never

_____ Every day

_____ Once or twice a week

_____ More than twice a week, but not every day

_____ Other (please explain)

_____

_____

There is no harm in including space for comments and explanations in almost every question. The space gives respondents a chance to clarify their answers, and the additional open space on the page makes it more readable and attractive to the eye.

The second alternative is to phrase the question as an open-end item and give respondents a list of choices.

"How often do you use your automobile for recreational purposes?"
(Leave a few lines blank here.)
"Please check the appropriate automobile use category below."

_____ Never used for recreational purposes

_____ Used for recreation once in a while

_____ Used for recreation once or twice a month

_____ Used for recreation once or twice a week

_____ Used for recreation more than twice a week

_____ Used for recreation every day

You could shorten the question by heading the list with "I use my car for recreation:" and then naming only the frequency alternatives in the checklist.

You select the third possibility (use an open-end version of a question for the pretest of the questionnaire and develop a closed-end question from it) if you do not know what the appropriate range of answers is. Here's the procedure.

1. Pretest with question open-ended.
2. Type each answer received for that question on an index card.
3. Sort the answer cards into categories that are mutually exclusive.
4. Rewrite the question in closed-end form, using the categories you got and ending with "Other (please specify)."
5. Try out the question again on half a dozen people similar to those for whom it is intended. Correct if necessary.

This process is time-consuming and tedious, but so are surgery, good cooking, and cabinetmaking. There are few shortcuts to good-quality work. When you succeed in developing a coherent questionnaire, the satisfaction makes up for the inconvenience. In any case, efficiently gathered data are much easier to work with later.

Although open-end questions are difficult to code, some researchers feel that they offer the only route to the definitions in the respondents' minds, since closed-end choices suggest alternatives and therefore lead the respondent. The practice of establishing in advance codes for open-end questions has also been criticized as a convenience that distorts the data by forcing answers into a preconceived pattern. These issues, and the decisions they require, are a bit difficult for newcomers to the art. For your student assignments and your training period, try to keep your research goal and question very straightforward and simple, so your questions can be straightforward and simple, too. It is better to get clear results on a small matter than vague ones on a large.

In closed-end questions the choices should be clear to the respondent, and there should be no overlapping of categories. There must, however, be a place for each possibility. Consider the following question.

"How long have you been working at your present job?" (Check one.)

_____ less than 6 months

_____ at least a year

_____ more than a year

What would you answer if you had been there 8 months? The question needs another category.

Aids for the Respondent In general, questionnaires require many **signposts**, or brief directions and instructions:

> "Check one."
>
> "Circle your answer."
>
> "Write your answer below."

All questions should be numbered for easy reference and to indicate to the respondents when they have finished one question and are beginning another. It must also be clear to respondents when they are to turn over the page and answer questions on the back. Because some respondents may not look on the back of pages, questions may be inadvertently omitted. You can number the pages:

> "page 1 of 3"
>
> "page 2 of 3"
>
> "page 3 of 3"

You can also number them 1, 2, 3 and write "Please turn to page 2" on the bottom of the first page. "Continued on back of page" is a good instruction if the form is printed on both sides. Do not leave anything to chance.

If you are using open-end questions, remember that you do not have the assistance of probes, so you have to be specific about how far you want the respondent to go in answering the question. You get a less spontaneous reply this way. When you want spontaneous replies, you may need to interview rather than administer questionnaires. Here's an example of an open-end question that isn't clear.

> "How do you feel about early marriages?" (Write your answer in the space below.)

Here the researcher has not said whether the question concerns the advisability of early marriage, the happiness of early marriages, or the durability of early marriages. Moreover, what is meant by "early"? The question could have been rephrased as follows:

> "Please give your opinion as to the proper age for men and women to marry."
>
> (Allow sufficient space here.)
>
> "Now please give your reasons for the answer above."

Another type of question is used whenever the answer to one question depends on the answer to the preceding question. We call this type a **contin-**

gency question because the second answer is possible because of, or contingent on, the first. The following questions are examples.

"Are you currently in school?" (Check one.)

_____ yes, full-time

_____ yes, part-time

_____ no

(If yes, full- or part-time)

"Are you enrolled in any history classes this semester?"

_____ no

_____ yes

(If yes) Please list below:

_____

_____

_____

This series constitutes a double contingency. The listing of the history courses depends on the answer to the second question, and the answering of the second question depends on the answer to the first. This type of question must be reviewed very carefully to make sure it's clear.

As you complete each question, it's a good idea to take Don Dillman's advice and ask:

> Will this question obtain the desired kind of information?
> Is it structured appropriately? (Form of question)
> Is the precise wording OK?[2]

The clarity of your questions becomes evident once you pretest the questionnaire. Almost no questionnaire emerges from a pretest without having to be changed somewhere. This does not indicate incompetence—you can't possibly foresee everything. The pretest is a learning experience that cannot be omitted.

Assembling the Questionnaire   The pretest of the questionnaire should include an appraisal of its sequence of questions. The order should be logical, and the questions should not jump around from topic to topic. They should proceed naturally from easy to difficult to easy again, as in the interview.

Some feel it is poor practice to begin the questionnaire with attitude or opinion questions, even on nonsensitive issues. One writer recommends getting the background data first, to ensure that you will have data for analyzing refusals if the respondent does not finish the questionnaire (or breaks off the interview). This writer is mainly concerned with market research surveys.[3] However, Dillman feels mailed questionnaires *must* begin with questions of social importance if your cover letter invokes social importance as a motive for cooperating with the survey. He says that asking background questions first will seem inappropriate to the respondents.[4]

The selection of the first question cannot be made in a cut-and-dried manner. You must consider your method of data collection (in-person, telephone, mail), the subject area (sensitive, commercial, attitude, knowledge, behavior), and the population sampled (education, motivation, sophistication); you must use common sense, and you must test the questionnaire. You want to give respondents a warm-up, even a brief one, so that they can get into a question-answering mood. For example, you might start with general instructions:

> "Unless otherwise indicated, please circle the number next to the answer you choose. Please answer all questions."

The first few questions can be designed to elicit standard information, but this information should be necessary to you:

1. Your date of birth _____ (month, day, year)

2. Your sex:

   Male   1

   Female   2

3. Your marital status:

   Never married   1

   Married now   2

   Formerly married   3

You can then proceed to ask attitudinal or opinion questions or sensitive questions, which are preceded by their own specific warm-up questions. You can end with more easy questions, such as additional background questions about income, education, or occupation. A final "question" can ask for additional remarks, to give respondents a chance to address matters not covered specifically. Remarks set down here may clarify some of the responses, and the question itself gives respondents a chance to air their views. They are doing you a favor, after all, and the least you can do is make it comfortable for them. People get frustrated when they have something to say and are not given a chance to say it.

In any survey, some of the respondents' extra comments are enlightening. As a researcher you can get new ideas and can be alerted to interesting side issues as you go. Do not try to include these extra topics unless they are definitely relevant to your independent, intervening, or dependent variable. Write the new ideas down. You can mention them in your conclusion and look forward to doing another project with them in it.

When the questionnaire is assembled, fill it out carefully and time yourself. Before you pretest it, ask a few colleagues or friends to complete it. Get their opinion of the clarity and flow of questions and on the length of the questionnaire. Remember that reproduction of a questionnaire costs money and filling it out takes time. Look at your draft with an eye to conserving both.

Final Considerations   Each questionnaire should be numbered, and the numbers should run consecutively. These identification or ID numbers come in handy when referring to individual questionnaires and when transferring data to data cards or code sheets for processing. They are essential for mailed questionnaires, since they enable you to keep track of the people who do not respond.

Be sure you pretest your questionnaire on a relevant population. If your sample is to be of blue-collar workers in Virginia, college students in New York would be poor subjects for pretesting the questionnaire (or interview). Pretest with people from the population you are going to sample, or as close to it as possible. Pretesting does not require random sampling, but it does require attention to similarities of pretest subjects to your ultimate sample subjects.

Modes of Questionnaire Administration

Individual Administration   This method is one step removed from the structured interview. The respondent receives the questionnaire and completes it with the researcher either present or nearby and available for clarifications if necessary. When the questionnaire has been completed and returned, the researcher scans it quickly to make sure everything has been answered. If the questionnaire is not complete, the researcher politely asks that the missing answers be supplied. If the respondent refuses, the researcher can do little more than accept this and be courteous.

Group Administration   When questionnaires are administered to groups of respondents it is a good idea to have more than one person administering them. Typically, several people finish a questionnaire simultaneously, and you must quickly scan for omissions, especially if respondents leave as they finish. Do not have completed questionnaires passed forward the way exams sometimes are collected. If the questionnaires are anonymous, you will not know who should be asked to fill in any blanks. It's discouraging to discover that important material is missing, and only vigilance will prevent it.

Do not ask people to administer questionnaires for your study because they work in a big office, teach a class, belong to a club, or supervise a group of workers. Try to be there yourself. Volunteers are notoriously unreliable, and you may lose many responses because your would-be helpers "just didn't get around to it" or "had a fire drill that day" or "forgot." You will usually find also that scanning for omissions has not been done efficiently.

Mailed Questionnaires   **Direct mail questionnaires** are sent out to a list of respondents who are asked to complete the questionnaire and mail it back. Usually the package includes a copy of the questionnaire, a stamped envelope in which to return the completed form, and a cover letter explaining the purpose of the study and requesting cooperation. If anonymity is promised, the names and addresses of the sample respondents are recorded on individual index cards along with the ID number of their questionnaires. As each questionnaire is returned, it is checked for completeness, and then the respondent's card is destroyed. All the remaining cards—identifying respondents who have failed to complete and return the questionnaire—are used to send a follow-up request with another copy of the questionnaire and another stamped return envelope. As the second batch of questionnaires arrives, the respondents' cards are destroyed. A third request can then be mailed.

In theory you can send out as many follow-up requests as you need until all the questionnaires have been returned. In practice all the questionnaires are never returned. The first mailing gets the largest number, and the returns diminish on each subsequent mailing. The reason for this pattern is that the most cooperative respondents send the questionnaire back the first time. When you send out a follow-up, your sample now has a higher proportion of uncooperative people in it. This proportion increases with each follow-up until you are mailing only to "hard-core nonresponders."

Estimates of likely return rates range from 30 to 95 percent, depending on the source of the estimate. Businessmen and women who use direct mail advertising are happy with a lower rate than scientists, because the former do not have to be concerned with the representativeness of their sample. My experience with a direct mailing to all of the four-year liberal arts colleges in the United States was that two-thirds of them replied, although it took three mailings to get that many.

Direct mail is costly, especially with the price of stamps going up constantly. It is possible to take advantage of an arrangement with the post office whereby you "prestamp" all the return envelopes but pay only for the questionnaires that are actually returned. (Instead of using ordinary stamps you use special return envelopes.)

Direct mail works better with some populations than with others. It is easier to turn down a mailed request than to refuse someone in a face-to-face encounter. On the other hand, mailed questionnaires may make it easier for some respondents to give socially undesirable answers, if appropriate, because there is no interviewer effect.[5] A large sample can be contacted by direct mail in much less time than it would take to get around to each person.

Telephone Surveys   With the arrival of computer technology it is possible to select a random sample of telephone numbers and avoid the need for a list of telephone subscribers. Since a very high percentage of Americans have a phone or have access to one, opinion researchers feel confident that they can get a representative sample using this method. They are not usually interested in the opinions of buying habits of very poor people, anyway. Telephone surveys are widely used in all types of market research, and there is an extensive literature on every conceivable decision such work entails. Dillman, Gallegas, and Frey, for example, tested various ways to reduce refusal rates for telephone surveys and found that sending a cover letter before calling got the best results.[6]

The advantage of the telephone is that it is quick and distance poses little problem. Its disadvantage is the abruptness of what may be an intrusion into respondents' lives and the ease with which the connection can be broken. Designing questions and questionnaires for telephone survey use must be done with an eye to limits on length and complexity because, unlike a mailed questionnaire, the form doesn't allow the respondent to consider questions at length or to change answers after they have been given.

Interviews Versus Questionnaires

To decide between interviews and questionnaires, you have to consider your resources and your goals, carefully weighing each aspect of the survey procedure and the constraints it dictates.

Resources

Your resources are time, money, and access to the subjects. There is no contest between interviews and questionnaires when it comes to time and money. Interviews take much longer than questionnaires and therefore are more expensive. They cost a lot more in staff time and travel as well. Since interviews generally include many more open-end questions, they also take longer to process once the data collection is over.

The choice is not quite as clear when considering access. If subjects are not fluent in English and you have no alternate questionnaires in their native language, or if their native language is English but they do not read it well, you had better plan on interviews or you will be disappointed in your data. I advised a research team for a study that used questionnaires on a sample of deaf people. People deaf from birth are "foreign" to their native language since they have never heard it spoken. They rarely read and write it well. Their native language is signs made with the hands. Filling out a questionnaire can be so challenging to them that they give up part way through it. Interviews with an interpreter or by someone who can use sign language are indicated.

Goals

If you want to gain insight into a complicated matter, don't use questionnaires because they aren't as flexible as an interview and you can't get clarification by probing. If a respondent misunderstands a question, you can't easily clear it up. You don't have time to read completed questionnaires on the spot but can only scan to see whether each is filled out completely. If respondents fail to answer what you asked, you have little chance of correcting them.

Questionnaires are often easier on the respondent if you want to ask embarrassing questions. A person who is much too self-conscious to give you a candid reply face to face will not hesitate to fill in a checklist on the same subject. Conversely, no questionnaire can give you the tone of voice, facial expression, and off-the-cuff supplementary remarks that the interview provides. An in-home interview is the only one that gives you the context as well.

To summarize:

Interviews

provide access to people who can't complete questionnaires

permit deeper questioning

allow clarification on both sides

include background and context

Questionnaires

are cheaper and easier to administer and process

are less likely to embarrass subjects

When the question of interviews versus questionnaires has been settled, the mode of administration must be chosen. There are numerous considerations here also. If you have decided on interviews, you have a choice between in-person and telephone contacts, each of which has its advantages and disadvantages. If you have decided on questionnaires, you have a choice between personally administered and mailed questionnaires. One solution is to use a variety of collection methods. The Census Bureau uses this tactic. Questionnaires are sent to everyone, but some forms are longer than others, and some people are visited by an interviewer. This is another example of multifaceted research.

Don Dillman has developed a survey planning procedure he calls the Total Design Method. It consists of listing and carefully considering all aspects of the survey process that may affect response quantity or quality, no matter how minute, and shaping each in a way that will encourage good response. Dillman is very concerned that the researcher be able to mount and carry through a precisely ordered and timed process.[7]

I think it is fair to say that professional market researchers and poll-takers have focused on refining the art of asking questions, while scholarly researchers have paid more attention to testing social theories and analyzing the data statistically in the hope of accounting for the variation in human behavior. Nonacademic researchers are selling a project, which is their product, and must consider clients' wishes and opinions. Appendix D goes into this matter in more detail.

Summary and Conclusion

Questionnaires are all structured and classified by the predominant form of the questions: open-end, closed-end, and so forth. Since respondents will be reading the questions, they must be very clear and must include signposts, or directions for answering them. Care must be taken to avoid establishing patterns of response, or mind-sets. There is also the danger of suggesting the expected answer.

Questionnaires may be administered singly or in groups, or they may be mailed. Questionnaire administrators should scan the instrument to make sure that all questions have been answered before a respondent leaves the scene. Like the interview, a questionnaire should begin and end with simple questions.

Pretests for questionnaires should be scheduled to check on problems. As before, less structured questions can be used in the pretest, and structured questions can be developed from the earlier versions. Detailed instructions are important for questionnaires. Questionnaires are cheap and easy, and they allow subject anonymity.

Main Points

1. Questionnaires are all structured. Questionnaires can be open-end or closed-end, but most are mixed.

2. Questionnaires require detailed instructions, because they are less personal than an interview and little clarification is possible. They must include written instructions, called signposts. Categories of answers must be mutually exclusive and must provide for all possible answers to the question.

3. It's important to avoid establishing response patterns and suggesting choice of answer.

4. Questionnaires can be administered in person, individually or in a group. They can also be mailed, but this costs more and returns may be low. All questionnaires should be numbered consecutively for convenience in processing data.

5. Questionnaires are cheap and can allow anonymity.

6. Pretests are necessary for questionnaires.

7. For complex questions and more insight, use interviews. For embarrassing questions and economy, use questionnaires.

Notes

1. See Delbert C. Miller, *Handbook of Research Design and Social Measurement*, 3rd ed. (New York: McKay, 1977), p. 94, for further explanation and example.

2. Don A. Dillman, *Mail and Telephone Surveys: The Total Design Method* (New York: Wiley, 1978), p. 118.

3. Patricia Labaw, *Advanced Questionnaire Design* (Cambridge, Mass.: Abt Books, 1980), p. 117.

4. Dillman, *Mail and Telephone Surveys*, p. 123.

5. Dillman, *Mail and Telephone Surveys*, pp. 62–63.

6. Don A. Dillman, Jean Gorton Gallegas, and James H. Frey, "Reducing Refusal Rates for Telephone Interviews," *Public Opinion Quarterly* 10 (1976): 66–78.

7. Dillman, *Mail and Telephone Surveys*, p. 2.

Exercises

Exercise 7.1 will provide a taste of the frustration your instructors experience when grading answers to the questions that seemed so clear when they were composed! It asks you to write questions and try them out on each other.

Exercise 7.2 gives you practice in devising a short questionnaire and pretesting it.

Exercise 7.3 is a critique of a published questionnaire.

Exercise 7.1   *Asking questions*

Instructions: You are interested in dating patterns and wish to compare men and women and different generations. Write a question each to find out:

1.   How often respondents go out on a date. (or did)

2.   How long they dated the same person. (or have)

3.   Age of respondent and age of date.

4.   Degree of involvement with date.

Take the four questions you have composed to class and take turns asking them of each other in front of the class. Everyone should criticize and suggest improvements, so that the class ends with four (or more) questions pretested for use in Exercise 7.2. Everyone should get into the spirit of this and regard it as fun, not being sensitive about their questions being unclear. (You might end up being a teacher, so it's good practice.)

Exercise 7.2   *The questionnaire*

Instructions: Using the advice contained in Chapter 7 and the four questions the class developed, construct a questionnaire in class, to collect the data necessary to test the following hypothesis:

> People date more than they used to and are less likely to be serious about their dating partner than in former generations.

Make copies of your questionnaire and administer it to five or ten people from two generations, trying to get half from one generation and half from the other. After collecting the data, answer the following questions from your experience.

1. Did you have any trouble with your questions?

2. If you were going to do a real study, would you revise your questionnaire? How?

3. What are the advantages and disadvantages of a questionnaire over an interview in your experience?

(You can use the data for exercises in Chapter 9.)

Exercise 7.3 *Critique*

Instructions: Select a research report from any source (including magazines) that uses questionnaires and that includes a copy of the data collection instrument. Read it and answer the following questions after giving a full citation here:

_____

_____

1. What was the source of the report? (Give exact name and date.)

2. How were the questionnaires administered?

3. How many respondents were there?

4. Did the researcher(s) mention any refusals?

5. What were the researcher(s) trying to find out?

6. In reading the questionnaire, did you see anything that you would want to change if you had to use the questionnaire? What was it?

7. If possible, list one or two questions you found inadequate, and rewrite them.

CHAPTER 8

Experiments and Quasi-Experiments

One of the pervasive pictures of a scientist is that of a person who conducts experiments. This white-coated figure is usually seen in a laboratory, manipulating test tubes and beakers filled with mysterious liquids. Of all the academicians who work with experiments, the chemist probably comes closest to this popular image.

Although the behavioral scientist's mode of operation is radically different from that of the chemist, we do conduct experiments for which the basic principles are the same. The main difference is in the material used and in the degree of control the scientist has over that material. Because of these differences, most of our efforts come under the heading of "quasi-experiments."

We begin this chapter with a definition and description of the classical experiment, discussing as well its procedures and main variations so that you will be able to keep this ideal in mind. The quasi-experiment, however, is more likely to be what you will encounter in the literature and what you might do in your future research practice. The remainder of the chapter treats the quasi-experiment in detail.

Experiments

An **experiment** is a test, as noted in Chapter 4. It's a test of a manipulation made by the researcher to see what difference this change will make in the subjects. To be a proper experiment, however, the exercise must include more than the test.

The Definition of an Experiment

To conduct an experiment you need an experimental group, a control group, and an experimental variable. The two groups must be identical in composition. After the groups have been measured on some attribute, which is the dependent variable of your research hypothesis, you introduce the experimental variable to the experimental group only, leaving the control group as it was. After the experimental variable has been introduced, you measure both groups on the dependent variable a second time. Although both groups may have changed, any difference between the two groups in the magnitude of that change is assumed to be the result of the experimental variable. Figure 8.1 shows the design of the classical experiment.

For example, suppose the groups are composed of babies who are similar in age, sex, race, and birth weight. They are receiving identical diets. Group 1, the experimental group, is weighed and measured, as is group 2, the control group. Both groups average 21 inches in height and 7 pounds in weight. The researcher adds a vitamin supplement to the diet of the experimental group of babies. They get the supplement for a month, while the

FIGURE 8.1   **The design of the classical experiment**

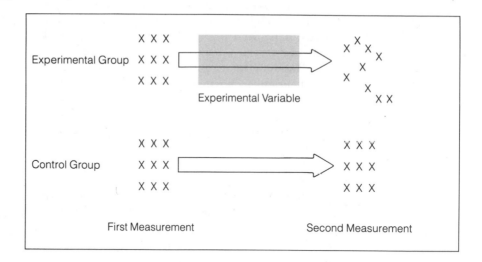

control group gets only the basic diet. At the end of the month, the babies are weighed again. The experimental group, group 1, has an average height of 21½ inches and an average weight of 10 pounds. The control group, group 2, has an average height of 21½ inches and an average weight of 9 pounds. The researcher would probably conclude that the vitamin supplement caused the additional weight gain in the experimental group.

The experimenter follows a four-step procedure in conducting a classical experiment:

1. Selecting the groups
2. Pretesting the groups
3. Introducing the experimental variable to the experimental group
4. Posttesting both groups

Experimental Procedures

The goal is to select two or more groups that are matched as closely as possible on all relevant variables.

Selecting the Groups   Traditionally, researchers have used two methods to select experimental groups: randomization and matching. Randomization consists of drawing a random sample from the population you are studying and then drawing two random samples *from that first sample*, each one amounting to half of it.

Let's examine this a bit. Say you have drawn a random sample as described in Chapter 3. Now you want to split it into two groups, but you do not want to bias your selection in any way. Selecting a random sample again within the sample, until you have half of it selected out, gives you two randomly selected groups. Now you can assume no bias. This not only saves your experiment from possible distortion but also makes the result eligible for statistical tests that assume random selection.

Matching refers to the selection of individuals for the groups by using a list of variables on which the individuals must be similar. For example, you can make sure that the people in the two groups are the same age, sex, and race, as in the earlier example of the baby diet experiment. The variables chosen depend on the research question and hypothesis. This causes some problems. The list of variables has to be short, or the researcher will find it very hard to match the groups. I was once assigned to match controls to an experimental group of children on six variables: age, sex, religion, race, grade, and IQ score. After the first three-quarters of the sample had been matched, the matching became a needle-in-the-haystack operation.

Another more serious problem must be faced if matching is to be considered for a classical experiment. There is no way of knowing whether you are omitting a crucial variable when you choose the matching characteristics. For this reason Donald T. Campbell and Julian C. Stanley reject the procedure for true experiments.[1]

For example, suppose you are matching those children and succeed in getting two groups of fifty children, matched on age, sex, religion, race, grade, and IQ score. You want to know whether their social adjustment (dependent variable) is enhanced by a rehabilitative group work (rehab) program to which one of the two matching groups is admitted.

You measure the groups on social adjustment. (In child guidance and mental health settings, this often amounts to observation and rating of a child's playtime. Such things as playmate choice and presence or absence of cooperation and conflict are noted and evaluated.)

You admit the experimental group (A) to the rehab program for 2 hours a day, one in the morning and one in the afternoon. The control group (B) continues with the regular schedule.

You measure the groups on social adjustment 4 weeks later. Group A is not doing as well as group B. You might ruefully conclude that the rehab program is detrimental rather than beneficial, but this could be too hasty a conclusion. What are the diagnostic categories and the proportions of each in the two groups? If group A has a higher percentage of children with personality disorders than group B but a lower percentage of the physically handicapped and retardates, you have not got well-matched groups in the first place. Maybe the program would have been great for group B, maybe not. All you now know is that it did not help group A (which is something learned, after all).

Since the number of variables is limitless, it's hard to know whether you have got the right ones matched. Nevertheless, if you cannot randomize for some reason, matching two groups gives you more control than not matching them.

When we used the word *pretest* earlier, we meant trying out data collection instruments to see whether they work well or need adjustment. Now we are going to use **pretest** to mean the measurement or observation of the experimental and control groups so that their initial condition with regard to the dependent variable can be established and recorded.

Pretesting the Groups   The first measurement is sometimes referred to as "time 1," and the information serves as a **benchmark**, or reference point, for each group. The second measurement, "time 2," is compared with it. As the experimenter you must measure carefully and record exactly. If you don't, you'll have trouble later trying to figure out if change has occurred.

Suppose you are doing a study of the effect of family visits on ward incidents. You have taken a random sample of state hospital wards and randomized subjects into two groups. You are going to record the number of "**incidents**" (state hospital jargon for anything from a fight to a riot) on the wards for a week or two and then increase the visiting hours for the experimental wards. You plan to keep a careful record of the number of visits for all. At the end of the experimental trial period you record the number of incidents for the same length of time as at the beginning of the project.

We shall assume that everything works well and the experimental wards receive more visitors during the experiment. Although both groups of wards have similar records of incidents at time 1, the wards in the experimental group have fewer incidents at time 2 than the wards in the control group. Great. Case closed. Or is it? What did you actually measure? Is "number of incidents" precise enough for a comparison? What justifies counting both an attack on a ward attendant and a free-for-all in the lunchroom as one incident? Do you count an argument between two patients? Some of these events may include more aggression than others. It would be better to classify the types of incident, develop a rating sheet, and distinguish between serious and mild incidents.

Anything that is measured in standard increments should be recorded as precisely as possible. This allows for greater ease in assessing change.

The experimental variable, sometimes called the **stimulus**, represents the independent variable in your study. It is assumed to be the cause of the change in the dependent variable.

Introducing the Experimental Variable   Typically, the experimental variable has two categories: presence of something and absence of something. The hypothesis is of the type: "If (experimental variable) is present, then (dependent variable) will show change." For example, "If babies are given a dietary vitamin supplement (experimental variable), they will grow faster (dependent variable) than babies not given a vitamin supplement."

The experimental variable must be as carefully operationalized as the dependent variable. Definitions and indicators for both must be established before the experiment begins. It is also essential that the experimental variable be introduced to *all* the members of the experimental group and to *none* of the members of the control group. The control group exists as a testimony to what would happen to the dependent variable if the experiment was not performed. If the control group is accidentally exposed to the experimental variable, the experiment is invalidated.

Now we come to consideration of the second measurement at time 2. It is called the posttest.

Posttesting the Groups   The **posttest** is a measurement or observation identical to the pretest. The occasion on which it is made is called time 2. If this terminology sounds familiar, it is because an experiment is a form of longitudinal study, a panel study, to be precise. You are using the same subjects at both times. In fact you are doing two parallel panel studies and comparing them. The difference between doing "just" two panel studies and doing an experiment is that you deliberately interfere with one group when you introduce the experimental variable and you don't interfere with your sample group when doing a panel study.

For both pretest and posttest, all the rules and recommendations for data collection should be observed. However, some special problems arise in achieving internal and external validity.

Problems in Achieving Internal and External Validity

Internal validity is the accuracy with which your data reflect what you set out to discover. If you are measuring weight change, do your data really tell you whether weight was gained or lost because of the stimulus, or might the change you recorded be due to some other event?

Internal Validity   Campbell and Stanley, the authorities on experimental design, list eight ways in which internal validity can be damaged.[2]

1. **History**   This effect refers to anything that happens between time 1 and time 2 in addition to the introduction of the experimental variable. You might be doing an experiment to see whether showing films increases attendance at PTA meetings. Before you finish it, there's a gas crisis that affects attendance at everything.

2. **Maturation**   This refers to the normal processes of aging that occur over time. For example, an experiment measuring growth of seventh or eighth graders is dealing with a period of life in which erratic growth spurts occur. Or, the subjects might be getting tired.

3. **Testing**   The test at time 1 may affect the scores of the test at time 2. You might weigh people at time 1, put one group on some sort of

diet, and weigh them again at time 2. How would you know whether the first weighing affected the people in the control group by making them weight-conscious and therefore careful about what *they* ate?

4. **Instrumentation**   The instruments may show wear, and the observers may experience maturation changes. Suppose your tape measure stretches imperceptibly, but the difference adds up over a large number of cases? Suppose you get tired or bored and start to measure carelessly?

5. **Statistical regression**   There is a tendency for extreme scores at one time to change to less extreme scores at another time. If something is the lowest possible amount, it has nowhere to go but up. If something is the highest possible amount, it has nowhere to go but down.

6. **Selection bias**   Distorting the subsamples by nonrandom selection of any kind is selection bias. It can happen inadvertently, as in the earlier example of the two matched groups of children that were not matched on diagnostic category.

7. **Experimental mortality**   This is the loss of cases for any reason. People die, move away, get sick of participating, or leave the group for a wide variety of other reasons. If they do leave, they are "dead" to your experiment; hence, "experimental mortality." (There is no experimental fertility, because you cannot add people once the experiment begins.)

8. **Selection-maturation interaction**   This awkward phrase combines maturation problems with selection problems. It means maturation that affects only part of your sample. Suppose you are giving a lecture (stimulus) to a group of people. Only some of them get bored because, unbeknownst to you, they have heard it before.

The classical research design is supposed to guard against these dangers. However, you must randomly select both the control group and the experimental group. You must also carefully control the conditions of the experiment, seeing to it that precise measuring is done at both time 1 and time 2 *and* that only the experimental group gets the experimental variable. In this way any validity problems are experienced by both groups. As long as validity problems affect both groups equally, the experiment is valid.

In Chapter 3 we saw that external validity, which is the accuracy with which the sample data reflect the true condition of the sampled population, depends on the representativeness of the sample.

External Validity   We assume external validity if the sample has been drawn randomly. However, now we are talking about a randomly selected sample that is subjected to special treatment that is outside the experience of the population from which the sample was drawn. Campbell and Stanley identify four problems stemming from this fact:

1. **Reactive effect of testing**   The pretest may make the sample sensitive in a way the population is not. This is the same as the third problem of internal validity, testing. Anyone who is subjected to measurement or testing is going to be more aware of whatever was measured or tested than if no test had taken place.

2. **Interaction of selection bias and experimental variable**   This simply means that there is a distorted selection in the first place, and the stimulus makes it worse. This would be the case if one group of children has too many personality disorders in it and does not match up with the other group that has a high proportion of retardates. If your experimental stimulus is a program that encourages outgoing, aggressive behavior, you have made the experimental group even more different from the control group than it originally was.

3. **Reactive effect of arrangements**   Since the setting of the experiment is often different from that of the outside world, it affects the people. Maybe your subjects are used to being outdoors and working at active tasks. You have them inside, sitting down and working with pencil and paper. They grow restive.

4. **Multiple-treatment interference**   This is the cumulative effect of pretest and posttest. Anything you repeat is not the same as it was the first time you did it. You get used to it, and your performance changes, usually for the better.

To reduce the problem of external invalidity, variations on the classical experimental design have been developed. We shall look at two variations on the classical experimental design and see what they accomplish. The first design was introduced by R. L. Solomon in 1949 and is intended to solve the problem of the reactive effect of testing, which threatens both internal and external validity.[3]

The Solomon Four-Group Design   The **Solomon four-group design** requires four matching or randomized groups composed of the individuals in the original random sample (see Figure 8.2). Two of the four groups are treated exactly as the two groups in the classical experimental design were treated. The experimental group is pretested, introduced to the experimental variable, and then posttested. The control group is pretested and posttested.

The two extra groups in the Solomon four-group design serve as a second experimental group and a second control group. Experimental group 2 is introduced to the experimental variable and posttested; it is not pretested. Control group 2 is posttested but not pretested.

FIGURE 8.2   **The Solomon four-group design: A classical experiment that adds two groups that have not been pretested so that the effect of the pretest may be assessed**

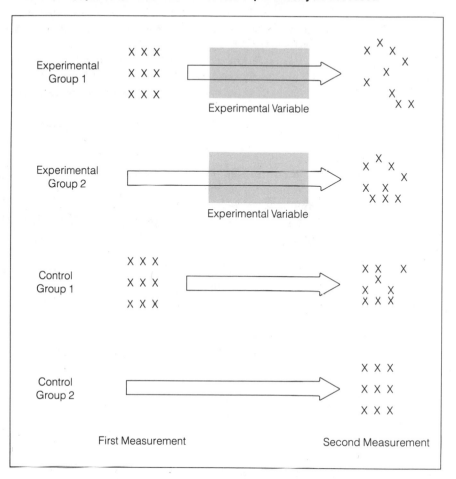

What this accomplishes is that you now have an experimental group that was not pretested to compare with the original experimental group; thus, you can see what difference the pretest made. You also have a control group that was not pretested to compare with the original control group.

Look at Figure 8.2. Let's say that it represents an experiment to see if testing schoolchildren in a noisy area affects their scores. Experimental group 1 and control group 1 are pretested in the customary room, and both produce a standard pattern of test scores, regularly spaced. Now we put experimental group 1 and experimental group 2 in a testing room with windows open on a noisy avenue. We test them again. This time we get more scattered scores, but the scores of the group that had the test before are more widely scattered than those of the group that was not pretested.

Now we test control group 1 and control group 2 in the customary testing room. They have not been exposed to noise, and the control group 2 has not been tested before. We see that the group that was pretested has slightly scattered scores, but the group that was not pretested shows the standard pattern.

Conclusion: The pretest operates to scatter the scores slightly (you would be able to measure it). The experimental variable scatters them even more, since both experimental groups had more widely scattered scores than their comparable control groups.

Another way to control the effect of the pretest is to eliminate it by using the **posttest-only control group design**.

The Posttest-Only Control Group Design   You might go back to using only two matched or randomized groups, eliminate the pretest, use the experimental variable on one group, and then posttest them both. In this way you get rid of the effect of the pretest and, since you no longer have multiple treatments, also take care of multiple-treatment interference.

Campbell and Stanley point out that some pretests are more influential than others. Students, for example, are used to being tested all the time and are less affected by any given test than people for whom the experience is a novelty. Nevertheless, the probability that measuring something does affect that something is great.

Most of the experiments behavioral scientists conduct are not classical experiments, but quasi-experiments. The reason is that we are dealing with people, the majority of whom are not under the experimenter's complete control, are very complex beings, and are conscious of what is happening to them. We now turn to an examination of the quasi-experiment.

Quasi-Experiments

Quasi is a prefix attached to words to indicate that what is being discussed is not quite the real thing. When we speak of quasi-experiments, therefore, we mean an experiment that approximates, but doesn't exactly match, the classical experiment.

Adjusting the Ideal to the Real

Quasi-experiments are not quite the same as true, or classical, experiments because they do not use randomly selected experimental and control groups. This isn't the only way in which they differ from classical experiments, but it's all the difference that is needed to classify them as *quasi*-experiments. Most behavioral research does not lend itself readily to classical experimental techniques. Once again we have to consider adjusting the ideal to the real. There are three major areas in which we have to do this:

1. Group selection
2. Measurement
3. Interviewer effect

Quasi-Experimental Procedures

Group Selection   Very often researchers do not have it in their power to assign subjects to experimental and control groups because behavioral science experiments do not always take place in a laboratory. One type of quasi-experiment is designed to test the efficacy, or effectiveness, of a treatment or an educational strategem. Such was the Highfields experiment, which sought to test the effect of a special program for juvenile first offenders. The **guided group interaction** at Highfields was intended to reduce or prevent recidivism (the tendency to relapse into criminal behavior) in delinquent boys. The researchers wanted first offenders alternately assigned to the Highfields program and to the more traditional services. In fact, judges often assigned a boy to the Highfields program when they thought he was a good candidate for rehabilitation. The sample was biased as a result, because Highfields got more than a random selection of promising rehabilitation candidates.[4] Any population under treatment, in training or in custody, may present this difficulty because the experimental variable may be seen as indicated or not indicated for a set of perfectly legitimate reasons that are very different from the experimenter's reasons for assigning it to cases.

Sometimes there has been confusion about the nature of an experimental variable compared with an intervening variable. The experimental variable is an *intervention*, a deliberate introduction of an experimental condition that is omitted for a control group. It is not simply a *variation* of an existing condition. For example, if we studied two matched groups of people, testing their reading comprehension; then exposed one group to a slide show on reading; then tested again; the experimental variable would be the slide show. This is the independent variable for the analysis, the dependent variable being the change in test results from time 1 to time 2. Any background characteristic we chose (sex, race, age, schooling) could be an intervening variable. Whether we chose one or not, and which we chose, would depend on our research goal.

Edgar F. Borgatta and George W. Bohrnstedt remark on another problem with the selection of experimental groups. This problem is chiefly found where experiments are done in labs. The most readily available subjects are college students, mostly those in their freshman or sophomore years. This fact jeopardizes the external validity of an experiment because, though lab conditions may guarantee randomness and scrupulous control over the experiment, the experimenter ends up with a finding applicable only to the lower half of a college population.[5] An example of this is the erroneous generalization of the results of small-group studies carried out by Talcott Parsons and Robert F. Bales using college students. Although they observed only small artificially composed groups of male college students for brief periods, using "instrumental" or "expressive" leaders and comparing reactions to the two types, they then applied these results to naturally established, long-term, male/female families![6]

There is another side to this argument. Morris Zelditch pointed out that the purpose of the laboratory experiment "is to create certain theoretically relevant aspects of social situations under controlled conditions."[7] He went on to say that if you are trying to construct theories, you are working with abstract material; therefore, it's all right if your explorations are abstract. Your experiment is not supposed to represent what happens in real life but is supposed to find out what would happen if extraneous influences were kept out. This position has been reiterated recently by other scholars.[8]

It all depends on your research goal. If you are trying to formulate theory and testing ideas abstractly, the selection bias of your sample does not rule out experimentation. On the other hand, one should be very cautious about testing a theory via experiment if a randomized or matched pair of groups is not available.

Many quasi-experiments are done under field conditions where what is sampled is really periods of time. Although one can make a random selection of time periods, if the object is to observe some human behavior and the subjects are whoever appears during the observation period, the experimenter cannot assume that those so appearing are a random sample of the population. If the experiment is designed to reveal some aspect of human behavior, for example, how can we say that the particular people who happened to cross our path are representative of the entire species?

So far, we have been speaking of experiments in which the pretest and posttest are identical. This condition is not always possible.

Measurement   Some measurements can be taken only once. Suppose you are going to expose the experimental group to a speech on charity to see if the group is inspired to contribute more than the control group, who won't hear the speech. Beginning with a sample of people, you first assign numbers to them and draw two random samples. Group A hears the speech on charity, but group B does not. Your pretest might be an estimate of the amount the subjects will give to the charity; the estimate is obtained by asking them. Your posttest would be the exact amount they give to the charity, recorded at the time they give it. Adding each group's estimates and dividing each total by the number of people in the appropriate group gives you the pretest average contribution. Doing the same for the actual donations gives you the posttest average contribution. You cannot ask them to contribute twice because, even were they willing, the initial contribution is bound to have an effect on the second one. Some may make a large contribution the first time and have little left for the second; some may make a small contribution the first time and compensate for it by a large contribution the second time.

Note that in the preceding example, even if you had selected randomly, you would have to pay special attention to extreme scores. If you have one or two very wealthy or very poor people in either group, it might **skew** the results, which means bias them severely. This is always a problem when you are using averages, as we shall see in Chapter 10.

For this example you would be comparing two group averages, but that in itself may pose a problem. Suppose half of a group that heard the speech give more than they had intended, and the other half give less? The group as a whole would show little or no change. Perhaps all you want to know is the overall change. Your research question determines this. If you want to know about individual changes, you have to be sure you get individual changes recorded. This might lead to an analysis of individual changes by controlling for some other variable such as income, sex, or age. For example, one possible hypothesis about the reason for change might be: People with low incomes tend to give less than they intended, while people with high incomes tend to give more than they intended. The rationale behind this hypothesis would be that poor people's generous impulses may exceed their realistic ability to give, while rich people are cautious with their money but then reconsider and raise the amount. To explore this thoroughly would take more than one investigation, since all you would have the first time would be the amounts estimated, the amounts given, and the background variables. For example, you could go back to the contributors and ask them why their contributions did not match their own estimates. This would be a quasi-experiment leading to a survey, and it is another instance of multifaceted research.

Sometimes you cannot have a pretest. Suppose you are trying to see what affects an individual's "helping" behavior? There have been a few such quasi-experiments. Like James H. Bryan and Mary A. Test, you might want to know whether people who have observed someone helping a person change a flat tire will be more apt to respond to a similar need than someone who has not observed the model helping situation. You can set up stooges to enact a model helping situation and then position someone who needs help where those who pass the model situation will then see the person "in need." For a second time period you would remove the model situation and see if the people passing by stopped to help the person staged to need help. There is no way to have a pretest in this experiment because you cannot have the people pass by twice.[9]

A complication hampering our use of experiments is our inability to produce or evaluate with certainty specific reactions in human beings. Most people will recoil from a snake or spit out a bitter substance, but more subtle reactions are hard to elicit or identify. The same behavior may indicate widely different feelings. Singing and whistling may indicate happiness (in the rain), apprehension (in the dark), or defiance (in the classroom). The same event may produce sadness at one time and joy at another. This is because our lives are complicated, and we experience life as a continuum.

When we think we have devised any measurement of emotions or attitudes, we have to be careful about our assumptions. For example, Ray Bird-whistell reminds us that there is no exact and reliable definition of a smile.[10] Another good discussion of this problem may be found in the article by

Borgatta and Bohrnstedt cited earlier. They point out that not only is there a problem with measuring the existence of an emotion in a human being, but there is also a problem with measuring the strength of that emotion.[11]

Another typical quasi-experiment that attempts to establish a mood and then test the subjects on a dependent variable might go like this: Half the subjects on their way into the testing area are subjected to what are presumed to be highly pleasurable experiences—a good-looking member of the opposite sex smiles at them, or perhaps they are told that they have been especially selected for high intelligence. All subjects are then given the opportunity to help someone "in distress" to see if those who "feel good about themselves" are more likely to help than those who did not get the pleasurable experience. The person in distress may be an actor crying for help somewhere outside the room where the subjects have been told to stay at their testing tasks. Will they go look for him? Will they help? Will they leave their appointed tasks even though they have been told their rewards depend on their staying?

In this type of experiment the researcher has assumed that people smiled at by the opposite sex will be feeling good about themselves. A similar assumption has been made about the people told that they have been selected for high intelligence. In fact, a subject might be made uneasy by attention from a good-looking person of the opposite sex, especially if the subject is committed to a fiancée or spouse but is easily tempted. A subject might perceive hypocrisy in the claim of special selection. Another assumption in this example is that the subject values the rewards offered and wants to obey the command to stay at the task assigned. In fact, the subject may be bored with the task and may welcome an excuse to leave it.

The last area of difficulty in achieving the ideal experiment is interviewer effect.

Interviewer Effect   In this context you cannot separate interviewer effect from demand characteristics. As explained in Chapter 1, interviewer effect is a change in respondents' behavior because they are taking the researcher into account; demand characteristics are what the respondents think the researcher would like them to do or say. When you are trying an experiment, you do not want the respondents to alter their behavior deliberately to please you. The very characteristic that moves people to cooperate with you and inspires them to be "good" subjects is the desire to contribute to science. It increases your chance of finding willing respondents at the same time that it increases your chance of getting biased results. One author cites a study in which people were given a very boring task to do, copying a large amount of material out of a book, and then the work was destroyed in their presence. This did not prevent the subjects from cooperating further and did not result in complaints.[12]

Not only will respondents or subjects consciously do what they think you want them to do, but subjects respond to the experimenter's expectation unconsciously as well. The most spectacular instance of this in the literature is an experiment done by Robert Rosenthal and associates.[13] When observers were told in advance that some rats were "maze bright," the rats went through the mazes faster than when the observers were told they were watching "maze dull" rats. There was really no difference in intelligence between the batches of rats. They were randomly selected from the same lot. The difference was in the observers' expectations.

Rosenthal followed this up with an experiment in which he told teachers that certain (randomly selected) pupils were likely to achieve a lot in the ensuing year on the basis of a test they had taken. Others were designated as potentially low achievers. As a result, those pupils expected to do well did so, and those expected to do poorly did so.[14]

One explanation for the Rosenthal classroom results is that the observations were somehow distorted. This is possible. (It is also just as important from a social perspective. Those of low status, of whom little is expected, would lose further from anything that adversely affects their performance *or* the observation of it.)

An incident from William F. Whyte's participant observation of Italian slum youth harmonizes with Rosenthal's conclusion that expectations affect performance. Whyte observed that there was a very close correspondence between social position and bowling performance. Men who really could bowl well did not do so when bowling with their social betters in the group. If they seemed likely to beat group leaders, they were heckled until they did poorly again.[15]

Rosenthal's work is an example of a laboratory experiment leading to a real-life quasi-experiment, the results of which are supported by a research project using a different technique. This is multifaceted research at its best, especially since different investigators did the studies.

We can sum up our discussion of interviewer effect:

People will try to cooperate with the researcher.

People are good at perceiving expectations for their behavior and will respond to them.

To this we might add that, since real-life consequences are not a factor in the lab, it is even easier for lab subjects to conform to what they think are your expectations.

One way to handle interviewer effect is to use a variation of the Solomon four-group design to assess the degree to which interviewer effect has distorted the data. In that design you incorporate an extra experimental group and an extra control to see what will happen without a pretest. To find out what the demand characteristics of an experiment are, you can add another group, which is exposed to the experimental variable and observed. You can then question them about their impressions of what you were after. This group would have to be selected in the same manner as the experimental and control groups for that experiment.

You would treat your two experimental groups and two control groups in exactly the same way as before, choosing to pretest or not according to your judgment. The fifth group would be treated the same as experimental group 2 (see Figure 8.2). You would expose them to the experimental variable, posttest them, and then interview them. The questions would be of the type, "What do you think is the purpose of the experience you have just been through?" "What do you think is the goal of this project?" "Can you tell me what we are looking for?"

There is another type of distortion caused by the experimental procedure. It is called the **Hawthorne Effect** because it was first discovered as a result of experiments conducted at the Western Electric Hawthorne Works in Chicago many years ago. Briefly, the Hawthorne Effect is the subjects' response to being singled out for study. The original experiments were designed to measure the effect of working conditions. When it was noted that productivity increased regardless of whether working conditions improved or worsened, the researchers began to suspect that something else besides the experimental variables was at work.[16]

One might also consider the effect of the experiment on control groups in quasi-experimental research when there is no way to prevent knowledge of the introduction of the experimental *variable*, even when there is little or no knowledge of the experimental *purpose*. For example, suppose you are trying to reduce or eliminate antisocial behavior by gangs of young men, and you send a detached social worker to each of several selected gangs. These workers typically spend a lot of time with the gang, trying to turn the members away from destructive acts and toward constructive behavior. Can you compare the gangs with workers and the gangs without workers to assess the efficacy of the ploy? Even if you had reliable statistics on the gangs' activities, you face a problem. The presence of the worker may well alter the experimental groups' behavior, but it may also alter the behavior of the other groups because they were left out.

Despite the difficulties and shortcomings outlined here, experiments are, as Campbell and Stanley maintain, the only test of opposing theories.[17] By this the authors mean that the most logical and carefully formulated theories must be tested in the real world before they can be accepted by the scientific community. This is another affirmation of the scientific method, which requires empirical verification.

At best, research yields only partial truths, and we should not expect clear-cut results. It is the cumulation of results that lends credence to our theories.

The unpredictability of life, which causes so many difficulties for the experimenter, also provides some delightful surprises. If you are alert and fortunate, dramatic opportunities may present themselves in the form of **natural experiments**. One such opportunity came to Hadley Cantril.

Natural Experiments

When Orson Welles's radio dramatization (1938) of *The War of the Worlds* by H. G. Wells convinced many listeners that the Martians had landed, thousands of people panicked and ran from their homes. Some ran out into the street, some hid, many said goodbye to loved ones and prepared to die. However, some did not regard the story as a real newscast, and some had not heard the program at all. Others panicked at first but then calmed down. Cantril lost no time. He interviewed people from all of these categories and was able to compare those who had not heard the broadcast, those who had heard it but not panicked, and those who had heard it and panicked. His entertaining and informative book is called *The Invasion From Mars*.[18]

Using an event over which you had no control as your experimental variable requires a combination of luck and quick response. If, like Cantril, you can interview people who were aware of the event and people who were not, before it has been hashed over by the news media, you can construct a natural experiment. It would be nice to have something important happen when you were halfway through a survey. Say you had been questioning people about their financial expectations in the first half of October 1987. The October 19th Wall Street crash would have given you a perfect opportunity to do a natural experiment, since folks questioned after that date could constitute the experimental group.

Whether or not you can get world leaders and fate to cooperate with you, and despite the multitude of things that can go wrong, experiments are fun. The satisfaction gained from completing a worthwhile experiment more than repays the trouble.

Single-Case Studies

Some social scientists who have a strong desire and a real need to experiment cannot use groups at all. Such are clinical therapists, working with one patient at a time. They cannot assemble randomly selected groups of patients and try out interventions on some of them. They must follow therapeutic indications or commit serious violations of professional ethics. On the other hand, they find it desirable to try interventions in order to change patients' unacceptable behavior and they need to know whether such interventions are effective and *to report the success or failure for the guidance of other therapists*. There is an experimental method in use, commonly referred to as the *single-case method*, which addresses these needs. It consists of specifying a behavioral goal for a patient, charting that patient's behavior, intervening by introducing the experimental condition while continuing to chart, then removing the experimental variable periodically, charting all the while. The charts will show any changes in behavior with respect to the behavioral goal as the experimental condition is introduced and removed, again and again.

The advantages of the single-case method are that it avoids the ethical dilemma of having cases who receive no treatment while others are getting it; the results are portrayed graphically and analyzed visually, so they are clear; and it provides a method of testing interventions on a highly variable population for which matching would be nearly impossible. All target behavior is clearly defined, as are the measuring procedures.[19]

The therapist who uses the single-case experimental design must be scrupulously careful not to commit methodological errors. Correct timing of the interventions, replication of the experiment, and provision of suitable graphs are all essential, and the experimenter must not be tempted to use inappropriate statistical tests to make the work look "scientific."[20] David and G. J. Frey point out that case methods have a long history in clinical work and that holistic approaches are currently in style, so the would-be single-case experimenter should think carefully about the method's appropriateness before employing it.[21]

Summary and Conclusion

Behavioral scientists conduct experiments using the same basic principles as physical scientists. However, behavioral scientists have less control over their subjects, because the subjects usually cannot be confined in a lab. Therefore, most of these experiments are quasi-experiments.

A classical experiment requires two equivalent groups; one is exposed to a treatment, and the other is not. Both groups are tested before and after the treatment to see how they compare. The groups may be selected by randomization or matching, but they must be comparable. There may be more than two groups because variation in experimental design is practiced in an effort to enhance internal and external validity.

Validity may be damaged in many ways, the most important being extraneous influences, faulty selection of subjects, and the effect of testing. There are various ways of limiting the effect of these. Some scholars feel that the results of experiments cannot be generalized to the real world if the subjects represent limited populations (for example, college students), but others point out that they are useful for developing theory, which is abstract anyway. It depends on your goal.

Sometimes it's impossible to measure things twice, and some things, such as emotions, are challenging to measure. Interviewer effect is strong for experiments because most people try to cooperate with the researcher. There are, however, ways of measuring it. Experiments are part of empirical verification and are fun to do. Now and then events occur so that you are able to utilize a natural experiment, that is, a sample of "befores" and "afters" become available to you spontaneously.

Clinical therapists, who cannot use the classical experimental method, have developed a substitute, called "single-case research." Although it is very useful and can demonstrate the efficacy of therapeutic intervention, great care must be taken not to handle it inappropriately.

Main Points

1. Most behavioral science experiments are quasi-experiments because such researchers do not have complete control over their subjects.

2. An experiment is a test to see what difference it makes if the researcher subjects one of two comparable groups to a treatment. The sequence of operations in an experiment is as follows: pretest, introduce experimental variable, posttest. The experimental group gets the treatment, the control group does not. There can be more than one of each kind of group.

3. Randomization is taking two or more random samples from a random sample of the population you are studying. Matching is finding for each of two groups people who are the same on all characteristics relevant to the experiment. Randomization is not biased but matching may be because the researcher does not know all of the possible relevant characteristics.

4. A pretest is the measurement that establishes the benchmark for each group. A posttest is the same measurement made after the experimental variable has been introduced to one or more groups. Measurement should be precise so that change can be accurately measured.

5. Internal validity can be damaged by any extraneous influence, by selection bias, or by the effect of the test itself. External validity is marred by testing effect, selection bias, and the setting in which the experiment is conducted. Variations in the classical design, such as the Solomon four-group and the posttest-only designs, have been suggested to reduce problems of validity.

6. Quasi-experiments must sometimes be carried out with groups selected by someone else or with groups that have lost members for various reasons. Sometimes the groups are periods of time, and there is little control over the segment of the population that appears for study.

7. A theoretical goal does not require external validity, but testing a theory does.

8. We often find it impossible to measure more than once, and we often need to measure abstract things such as opinions, emotions, and attitudes.

9. People are very cooperative with experimenters, and this increases interviewer effect and demand characteristic distortion. To circumvent this you can add a group and interview them to see what they thought you wanted.

10. The Hawthorne Effect is the difference in behavior people show when they are singled out for attention. Those not singled out for attention may also be affected.

11. A natural experiment is one in which the experimental variable occurs spontaneously; the researcher takes advantage of it by testing those affected and those not affected.

12. Single-case research requires the experimenter to record the behavior of a subject before, during, and after a therapeutic intervention, repeating the process several times, and constructing graphs of the results.

Notes

1. Donald T. Campbell and Julian C. Stanley, *Experimental and Quasi-experimental Designs for Research* (Skokie, Ill.: Rand McNally, 1963), p. 2.

2. Campbell and Stanley, *Experimental and Quasi-experimental Designs*, pp. 5, 6. The examples are mine.

3. R. L. Solomon, "An Extension of Control Group Design," *Psychological Bulletin* 46 (1949): 137–50.

4. H. Ashley Weeks, *Youthful Offenders at Highfields* (Ann Arbor: University of Michigan Press, 1963), pp. 25, 26.

5. Edgar F. Borgatta and George W. Bohrnstedt, "Some Limitations on Generalizability from Social Psychological Experiments," in *Readings in Social Research*, ed. Theodore C. Wagenaar (Belmont, Calif.: Wadsworth, 1981), pp. 206–210.

6. Talcott Parsons with Robert F. Bales, James Olds, Morris Zelditch, and Philip E. Slater, *Family, Socialization and Interaction Process* (New York: Free Press, 1955).

7. Morris Zelditch, Jr., "Can You Really Study an Army in the Laboratory?" in *A Sociological Reader on Complex Organizations*, rev. ed., ed. Amitai Etzioni (New York: Holt, Rinehart, & Winston, 1969), p. 530.

8. For example, Richard Henshel, "The Purposes of Laboratory Experimentation and the Virtues of Deliberate Artificiality," *Journal of Experimental Social Psychology* 16 (1980): 466–78.

9. James H. Bryan and Mary A. Test, "Models and Helping: Naturalistic Studies in Aiding Behavior," *Journal of Personality and Social Psychology* 6, no. 4 (1967): 400–407.

10. Ray Birdwhistell, "There Are Smiles . . .," in *Kinesics and Contexts: Essays on Body Motion Communication* (Philadelphia: University of Pennsylvania Press, 1970), pp. 29–39.

11. Borgatta and Bohrnstedt, "Some Limitations," pp. 208–209.

12. Martin T. Orne, "On the Social Psychology of the Psychological Experiment: With Particular Reference to Demand Characteristics and Their Implications," *American Psychologist* 17 (November 1962): 776–83.

13. Robert Rosenthal and Lenore F. Jacobson, "Teacher Expectations for the Disadvantaged," *Scientific American* 218 (April 1968): 19–23.

14. Rosenthal and Jacobson, "Teacher Expectations."

15. William Foote Whyte, *Street Corner Society: The Social Structure of an Italian Slum*, 2nd ed. (Chicago: University of Chicago Press, 1955), pp. 14–25.

16. F. J. Roethlisberger and W. J. Dickson, *Management and the Worker* (Cambridge, Mass.: Harvard University Press, 1939).

17. Campbell and Stanley, *Experimental and Quasi-experimental Designs*, p. 3.

18. Hadley Cantril, *The Invasion from Mars* (Princeton, N.J.: Princeton University Press, 1940).

19. Vincent B. Van Hasselt and Michael Hersen, "Applications of Single-Case Designs to Research with Visually Impaired Individuals," *Journal of Visual Impairment and Blindness* 75, no. 9 (1981): 359–62.

20. Steven J. Lagrow and Jane E. Prochnow-Lagrow, "Consistent Methodological Errors Observed in Single-Case Studies: Suggested Guidelines," *Journal of Visual Impairment and Blindness* 77, no. 10 (December 1983): 481–88.

21. David P. Frey and G. J. Frey, "Science and the Single Case in Counseling Research," *Personnel and Guidance Journal* 56, no. 5 (January 1978): 263–68.

Exercises

Exercise 8.1 is a field experiment completed many times by my students, usually with interesting results. It allows you to compare one set of observations (control group) with another (experimental group) for which you have introduced an experimental variable (shabby dress). Exercise 8.2 asks you to read and comment on a laboratory experiment report.

Now that we have finished the detailed discussion of data collection methods, try selecting some for hypothetical research projects. Exercise 8.3 presents you with this opportunity.

Exercise 8.1 *An experiment in the effect of dress*

Instructions: Your experiment will test the question "Is the friendliness of people who serve the public affected by the appearance of poverty in the persons served?" Follow the directions below.

1. State your hypothesis here:

2. Define *appearance of poverty* (experimental variable).

    (*Note:* Do not confuse *dirty, bizarre,* or *unkempt* with *poor.*)

3. Define *friendliness* (dependent variable).

4. Devise a simple data collection instrument to record friendly behavior.

5. Go out to one or more of the following establishments as if you were going to church or business. Wear nice clothes and be dignified in appearance. This includes hairstyle, cosmetic embellishment, and decoration. Your aim is to look like a respectable, middle-class individual. When at these establishments, approach a clerk or similar employee and ask for information about something. The object can be directions, schedules, business hours, or the location of the restrooms. It must be something that they can answer. Be pleasant and smile. Record their response exactly, including gestures and tone, so that you can evaluate it for friendliness in the light of your own definition in Question 3.

    Establishments:

bank	bus or train station	department store
library	supermarket	information desk
restaurant	service station	car dealership

6. Go to the same establishments, or others of identical type, as if you were poor. Wear clean but shabby clothes and cheap decoration. Your aim is to look as poor as possible, but respectable (no outlandish styles, nothing suggesting deviance). Ask the same question in the same manner that you did the first time. Be sure to be friendly and smile. Record the responses exactly as before.

7. Compare the responses you got when well dressed to the responses you got when poorly dressed. Was your hypothesis supported?

8. Do you think this experiment a good one? Why, or why not? Can you suggest improvements? (Glance over the limitations on quasi-experiments covered in the chapter.)

   Note: This exercise can be done as a group exercise if the whole class uses the same definitions and hypothesis and develops the data collection instrument together, or teams of students can work together.

Exercise 8.2   *Critique*

Instructions: Select a research report that describes a classical experiment and answer the following questions about it. (A good source is any psychology journal, medical journal, or journal of one of the "hard" sciences.)

1.   Give a full citation here.

_____

_____

2.   What groups were used, and how were they selected?

3.   Describe the pretest.

4.   What was the experimental variable, and how was it introduced?

5.   Describe the posttest.

6. Comment on this report in light of the first part of Chapter 8, which discusses classical experiments.

Exercise 8.3   *Choosing the methods*

Instructions: Review the summary of methods of data collection in Chapter 4. With the variety of methods that you've learned, outline a research design to test the following hypotheses:

> Prisoners who receive at least one visitor a week are less likely to be imprisoned again within 5 years of release than prisoners who do not receive at least one visitor a week.

(If you have a hypothesis that you are eager to try in place of this, use it—as long as your instructor approves.)

Follow the form below.

1.   Hypothesis:

2.   Data needed:

3.   Indicators and methods:

4. Why did you choose the method outlined above over other possibilities?

PART III

Bringing in the Sheaves

As this part's title suggests, Part III is about gathering up the harvest of data and making it available to its ultimate consumers. Chapter 9, "Analyzing the Data," reviews the goals of data analysis and illustrates the techniques presented by following an example step by step and using real data. The levels of measurement are described, and one type of ordinal measure, called a composite measure, is given special attention. The use of computers is illustrated and the process of coding data for them outlined in full.

Chapter 10, "The Significance of Tests," discusses the proper use of statistics, describing and evaluating the purposes of the major tests. Descriptive statistics are presented first, and then inferential statistics are introduced, beginning with the concepts of probability and sampling. The tests for the difference between means and the measures of association for each level of data are discussed. The chapter concludes with an examination of the use of significance tests in social science research.

Chapter 11, "Coming to Conclusions," deals with the conclusions made as a result of the successful completion of a research project. Beginning with an orientation to the original research question and hypothesis and a summary of the findings, the chapter helps the student to recognize the placement of the project in relation to what else has been done on the topic and the implications of the findings for future research. A brief section on the mechanics of putting the report together concludes this chapter.

Chapter 12, "The Consequences of Research," is a careful examination of three important topics concerned with the effect of research on society and its members. The first is ethical dilemmas that result from the conflict of scientific needs and ethical obligations. The second is the effect of research on social and political policy and, in turn, the policy's effect on research. The third is evaluation research, which is undertaken to appraise the worth of programs and recommend their continuance or discontinuance. Basic research and evaluation research are compared.

CHAPTER 9

Analyzing the Data

A good research report answers three questions: What did we attempt to find out? What result did we get? What does it all mean? In the process of making this report, the researcher also explains what has been done in the field, how the hypothesis was developed and operationalized, and how the sample was chosen and the data collected.

The Goals

This chapter is about scrutinizing the information you have collected, finding a way to summarize it efficiently, and organizing it in a way that will make it clear to the reader.

Now that you have the data, you have to figure out what to do with them. It's time to review the research question. This is especially important because, while doing your research, you have probably come across many pieces of data that have given you new ideas. Although these are worthwhile, you must guard against the temptation to add new questions and hypotheses to the present project and go off in new directions.

It's true that analyzing data has a twofold purpose: to illuminate the research question and to suggest fruitful areas for further study. All I'm saying here is: Try to keep these two areas separate. Your present data will be difficult to exploit in ways not previously anticipated and cannot provide a legitimate result. (Review the discussion in Chapter 2, under "Explanatory Studies.") Make a list headed "leads," and keep it near you for jotting down these new ideas. Once you've recorded an idea, put it out of your mind and return to the business at hand: answering the research question. This will prevent you from cluttering the body of your report with miscellaneous tidbits. You can use the "lead" sheet in your recommendations at the end of your final report.

Scrutinizing the Data

After reconsidering the research question and its hypothesis, proceed to examine the data. This may mean listening to tapes, reading the answers to open-end questions, and scanning arrays, or lists, of numbers. Another way of scanning the data is to code them, or transform them into number-labels that can be fed into a computer. The computer adds the data for you, and you can then scan the resulting **computer output**. Computer output is like a very wide cash register tape that is perforated at intervals and folded on those perforations as it emerges from the machine. Like typewriter output, it comes in two standard widths. You can have letter-size sheets or the wider ones. Most people using a mainframe computer end up with wide output and most people using a personal computer (PC) produce letter width, but no rule is hard and fast and the variation is great. The size and type of output paper and the range of printed material possible all depend on the printer being used.

We shall discuss the details of computer use later in this chapter. If the sample is a small one, or if you are doing a pilot study, you may not need to use a computer at all. You can't use a computer to look at narrative material or listen to tapes. You must examine this material yourself and decide how you want to use it and where it fits into your study.

Your job is to organize and summarize the data so that the reader can grasp the outcome of your endeavors without too much difficulty. You can't expect people who read your report to immerse themselves in the data as you have had to do.

Summarizing the Data

To be able to produce a clear report, you need to make clear to yourself the level of data you have. This would be a good time to review the discussion in Chapter 2 about level of measurement. Did you get nominal data? If you asked for marital status, the data are nominal. You can sort, count instances of each type and report the percentage of the whole:

N	Marital Status
48	Single, never married
30	Single, cohabiting
64	Married, living with spouse
16	Married, separated
22	Divorced
38	Widowed
218	

I have shown the categories and the raw numbers. It is important to translate them into percentages, unless there are so few that percentages would be ridiculous—50 percent of 6 cases, for example. Percentaging requires you to sum the cases and divide each category's number by that total:

$$48/218 = 22\% \text{ Single, never married}$$
$$30/218 = 14\% \text{ Single, cohabiting}$$
$$64/218 = 29\% \text{ Married, living with spouse}$$
$$16/218 = 7\% \text{ Married, separated}$$
$$22/218 = 10\% \text{ Divorced}$$
$$38/218 = 17\% \text{ Widowed}$$

Add up the percentages. The reason they don't add to precisely 100% is that I didn't carry them out further than two digits. One generally rounds a percentage: 1.4 or less = 1%; 1.5 or more = 2%. If your total is less than 99% or more than 101%, check your figures.

Percentages are easier to grasp because we are accustomed to using them while handling money. Each cent is 1 percent of a dollar. To say that 10 percent of our hypothetical sample are divorced is clearer than saying that 22 out of 218 are divorced.

If you asked for highest grade finished in school you have ordinal data, or data that can be ranked as well as enumerated. You can make the ranking as precise as your data allows (single grades perhaps). Or, you can combine them in broader categories such as "finished eighth grade," "some high school," "finished high school," "some college," "college degree." Your final arrangement depends on the distribution of your data, as with all levels of data. It makes no sense to include a category with nobody in it, or to divide data so that one category includes most of the respondents. If you are using a computer you can print out an array of your coded data and preliminary tables as well, allowing you to make informed decisions about the best way to show it in the final report. We'll cover coding the data later in this chapter.

As mentioned in Chapter 2, interval data categories are spaced equally along a continuum and ratio data is interval data with an absolute zero. Adding and subtracting is permissible for interval data and all basic arithmetic operations with ratio data. Inferential statistics are only appropriate if you have ratio data.

NOTE: When I say that you can't "add" nominal data, I don't mean you can't combine categories. You could, for example, change the categories in the foregoing example and have:

    78   Never married [36%]
    140   Ever married [64%]

This procedure is referred to as "collapsing categories" and is perfectly all right *as long as the categories make sense.* They have to have some feature that makes the new assortment fit your research need. In this case you would now be looking at those who have had the experience of getting married versus those who haven't.

What I do mean about not using arithmetic processes such as addition on nominal data is that you can't assign a numerical value to the category itself and do anything with it. You can't give each category a weight and each respondent a score for it. If I arbitrarily say that my six categories have weights of 1, 2, 3, 4, 5, 6, in order, then respondent A, who was once single, cohabited with three different partners, got married, then separated and finally divorced, has a score of 19. This is utter nonsense. We could call it "Marital Wear-and-Tear Score" and calculate one for each respondent, take an average score, compare people of different races, ages, and regions, run several statistical tests on it, pronounce that it has statistical significance, and publish an article. It would still be utter nonsense. If you think this isn't done all the time, look in the professional journals and consider the level of measurement used in each article and the data's treatment in the report. For that matter, consider the way college cumulative "averages" are derived. What level of measurement would you assign these categories?

A   Outstanding comprehension of subject

B   Good comprehension of subject

C   Fair comprehension of subject

D   Poor comprehension of subject

F   Unacceptable comprehension of subject

The truth is that the cumulative average, on which so much depends, is not a valid measure because the data is not ratio, but ordinal.

Once you have determined the proper measurement level for the data you have, you proceed to summarize them. The first step is to look at your variable categories once more in the light of the frequency distribution you have to see what modifications, if any, suggest themselves. For example, you might have data on years completed at school and have originally planned for these categories:

no formal education

some elementary school

completed eighth grade

some high school

completed twelfth grade

some post-high school training

When you look at the distribution, you find that nobody in the sample is in the first two categories. You drop them. Suppose you also find that you have one person in the "no formal education" category, four in the "some elementary school" category, twelve in the "completed eighth grade" category, fifty-seven in the "some high school" category, ninety-five in the "completed twelfth grade" category, twenty-two with "some post-high school training." What do you do? One possibility is:

17 eighth grade or less

57 some high school

95 completed twelfth grade

22 some post-high school training

You have combined the first three categories to make enough cases to analyze. Of course, your research question and hypotheses govern your selection of possible combinations, as already mentioned.

Notice that the modifications in categories have to be combining rather than dividing. If you did not have fine enough distinctions when you recorded the data, you cannot make them now. That is one of the reasons for getting specific facts. (What is your birth date?) rather than generalities (Are you old enough to vote?).

has two possibilities), and we have not yet decided the dependent variable categories. So far, it looks workable.

This sample consisted of forty-seven children and their parents. All the children but three had mothers, and all but seven had fathers. We had the following frequencies (number of times something is observed):

Religion

Catholics	39
Protestants	92

Sex

Males	61
Females	70

Family Role

Fathers	40
Mothers	44
Sons	21
Daughters	26

So far, the categories have posed no problem. Remember that the definitions of the variables are established before the data are collected for all the closed-end questions. We know, for example, that our definition of "religion" is religion named by the parents. We did not ask whether the religion they named was their childhood religion. We did not ask about religious practice in detail or about commitment and beliefs. Labels were what we sought and what we now have. Should we come to feel that it would be useful to know how deeply committed the subjects are to their religion, it is too late. We can add another line to our "Leads" sheet, "What difference would religious commitment make?" Then, back to our data.

The dependent variable data were obtained by an open-end question, shown in Figure 6.1. This question ("What is diabetes?") is followed by a lengthy instruction to the interviewer, which ends with the direction, "Record respondent's affective response." This means that each interviewer noted the respondent's apparent emotions as objectively as possible. There are some difficulties with categorizing these. First, you must decide what the variety, or range, of emotions was for the whole sample. Second, you must decide how to group them into as few categories as is feasible and count the number of respondents that fall into each category. But wait. You do not have interviews for the children. Since this was a large study, with several kinds of professionals on the team, the information was available for the children. It had been included in the psychiatric interviews and in the psychologist's projective material. This is an example of multifaceted research.

All professionals categorized their own material on this variable and then participated in a conference, during which final categories for it were established. Surprisingly, all three professionals devised four categories. Only minor changes in wording were necessary.

For an open-end question, it is advisable to type up each answer, word for word, on a separate file card. When this is done, the cards can be sorted until you have what you think are workable divisions. (You could do a fifty-case sample of answers if you had a large study.) For this question the cards had to be sorted several times: once for affect (emotion), once for mention of physiological problems, once for mention of social problems, and so on. In the present example only one sort would be required.

Here are examples of the four categories used and the responses classified into them:

Attitude Toward Disease

Acceptance of diabetes and willingness to adjust to it (*acceptance*)

> "It is a serious matter, a little cloud, but I must adjust to it and accept it, so that Katherine can do so."

Insistence on advantages in having diabetes (*overcompensation*)

> "Diabetics have a better diet than anybody in the world. *I'll* never have bad teeth or get too fat!"

Grief, despair, depression, over the personal misfortune of diabetes (*despair*)

> "I've cried every night since he got it. He'll never get over it. What kind of a life can he have?"

Refusal to face the seriousness and inconvenience of diabetes (*denial*)

> "How did I feel when he got it? I thought, 'Gee, that's too bad.' It isn't anything much. Life is full of little setbacks."[2]

All the variables examined so far in this example are at the nominal level of measurement. They can be sorted and nothing else. We cannot rank any of them, since we cannot measure any of them. All we can do is identify them by subdivision. If we had used a variable that could be ranked, we might have wound up with a statement such as "The higher the . . . , the more . . . we find." If we had a variable that could be spaced at equal intervals, we might have been able to say "Each increment of . . . IQ points is associated with a rise in . . . of 10 percent." If we had a variable that could be multiplied and divided, we could have said "Mary is twice as old as Joe and half as old as Agatha." Since we have only nominal variables, we are limited to comparisons.

Before moving on to examples of data presentation, let's think about labels for a minute. When reviewing your data, you ought to keep in front of you a copy of your data collection instruments and a statement of your question and hypothesis. By doing this you will not forget what it is you really asked the respondent. Since it is efficient to adopt short names for quick referral, we do it, and some of them tend to mislead when used by someone unfamiliar with the original item. For example, if your questionnaire asks "If you had to choose tea or coffee, which would you select?" those who reply "tea" will probably be referred to as "tea drinkers." In fact, we did not ask them if they were tea drinkers. We asked them which beverage they would choose if they *had* to choose. One must be careful not to refer to subjects by a misleading label in the discussion or in the tables. Often a table title can contain the original question in abbreviated form: "Table 1. Answers to questions about choosing between tea and coffee, by age and sex. Percentages only."

Another decision that you may have to make in addition to categories and labels is the disposition of cases where the respondent has left a question blank or answered "Don't know," "Undecided," and the like. Some replies are unusable because they are too vague (Interviewer: "What is your occupation?" Respondent: "Assistant."). If you simply omit these cases, you may be misleading your readers. Suppose twenty-five people say yes, fifty say no, and twenty-five are undecided. Leaving out the undecideds and transforming the data into percentages results in 33⅓ percent say yes and 66⅔ percent say no. Keeping the undecideds results in 25 percent say yes, 50 percent say no, and 25 percent are undecided. Which you do depends on your question and your goal.

A political party wants to assess its exact voting strength and the number of undecided voters it has to woo. You may be interested only in comparing those who have made a decision already. Whichever it is, you must specify what you did in your report. A footnote to the table mentioning that twenty-five people who said "undecided" were omitted from the analysis would be enough. The body of the report should include such information as the number of people in the sample who refused to participate and the number of unusable questionnaires.

Tables range from simple to complex, and all types have their place. However, it is important to remember that tables are supposed to make the data easier to comprehend. You will construct many more tables than you will ultimately use, because you will try arranging the data in as many ways as you can and will later select the most useful for your report. Sometimes the body of the report contains tables essential to the discussion, while more detailed tables are included in an appendix for those readers who would like to pursue the matter further or consider other analyses—as they might if they are using your work as available data.

Presenting the Data

Preparing the data for analysis by hand requires the construction of a **data matrix**, or chart that arranges the cases or subjects in rows and the data information in columns. Figure 9.1 is a data matrix for the families of diabetic children, with information on the variables we wish to examine.[3] Notice that the cases have been sorted by religion. The Catholics are listed first, then the

FIGURE 9.1   A data matrix on forty-seven families of juvenile diabetics showing religion, sex of child, and attitudes toward disease of parents and children—whole sample

FAMILIES OF DIABETIC CHILDREN—RELIGION, SEX OF
CHILD, ATTITUDES OF PARENTS AND CHILD TOWARD
JUVENILE DIABETES MELLITUS

Case No.	Religion	Sex of Child	Attitude Toward Disease*		
			Mother	Father	Child
08	C	M	Acc.	Acc.	Acc.
07	C	M	Acc.	Acc.	Den.
02	C	M	O/c	O/c	Desp.
37	C	M	O/c	Den.	Desp.
10	C	M	Desp.	—†	Desp.
45	C	M	Desp.	—†	Den.
13	C	M	Acc.**	—†	Desp.
09	C	M	—†	Desp.	Desp.
47	C	F	Acc.	Acc.	Acc.
52	C	F	Acc.	Acc.	Acc.
51	C	F	Acc.	Acc.	Den.
16	C	F	Den.	Den.	Desp.
46	C	F	Den.	—†	Acc.
29	C	F	Desp.	Den.	Acc.
25	C	F	Desp.	Den.	Desp.
32	P	M	Acc.	Acc.	Den.
42	P	M	Acc.	Acc.	Desp.
06	P	M	Acc.	Den.	Acc.
15	P	M	O/c	Desp.	Den.

Protestants, so the cases could be easily scanned later, since religion was the independent variable. If you have a computer available, such considerations don't matter because the computer will allow any assortment you like and show it to you on a monitor screen, print it out, or both.

Notice also that each case has an identification number. The numbers are all two-digit numbers, and the first nine have had zeros added to them to

FIGURE 9.1   **A data matrix,** *continued*

			Attitude Toward Disease*		
Case No.	Religion	Sex of Child	Mother	Father	Child
03	P	M	Den.	Den.	Den.
05	P	M	Den.	Den.	Den.
53	P	M	Den.	Den.	Den.
54	P	M	Den.	Den.	Den.
11	P	M	Den.	Den.	O/c
14	P	M	Den.	Desp.	Den.
38	P	M	Den.	Acc.	Acc.
48	P	M	Den.	—†	O/c
36	P	M	—†	Den.	Acc.
30	P	F	Acc.	Acc.	Acc.
23	P	F	Acc.	Acc.	Den.
33	P	F	Acc.	Acc.	Desp.
18	P	F	—†	Acc.	Desp.
31	P	F	Acc.	Den.	Den.
50	P	F	Acc.	Den.	O/c
17	P	F	O/c	Den.	Den.
49	P	F	Den.	Den.	Den.
55	P	F	Den.	Den.	Den.
43	P	F	Den.	Den.	Desp.
39	P	F	Den.	Den.	Desp.
21	P	F	Den.	O/c	Acc.

maintain the two-digit pattern. The reason for this will be discussed later in this chapter when we look at coding, the process of assigning number-labels to the data for computer use.

Now let's see how to use the data matrix to construct a few tables. We shall try univariate, bivariate, and multivariate tables, in that order.

FIGURE 9.1   **A data matrix,** *continued*

			Attitude Toward Disease*		
Case No.	Religion	Sex of Child	Mother	Father	Child
26	P	F	Den.	—†	Desp.
28	P	F	Den.	—†	Desp.
40	P	F	Desp.	Desp.	Desp.
19	P	F	Desp.	Den.	O/c
22	P	F	Desp.	Den.	Desp.
34	P	F	Desp.	O/c	Den.
35	P	F	Desp.	Acc.	Desp.

*Acceptance—acceptance of the fact of diabetes and a willingness to adjust to it

Overcompensation—insistence on the advantages of having diabetes

Despair—grief, despair, and depression over the personal misfortune of diabetes

Denial—refusal to face the seriousness and inconvenience of diabetes

†Parent absent, for any reason

**Mother Protestant

Univariate Table Construction   This is the simplest kind of table and illustrates the simplest level of analysis. Since our dependent variable is attitude toward diabetes, our first table illustrates the frequencies with which we found each subcategory of this variable: acceptance, overcompensation, despair, and denial. The heading of the table, or title, tells the reader what is being illustrated. For the first appearance of this variable, it is necessary to include a brief definition of the subcategory labels. This definition appears as a footnote. Later tables need not repeat this information.

Figure 9.2 presents "Table 1, Distribution of Attitudes Toward Juvenile Diabetes Mellitus in a Sampling of Families—Whole Sample." Such a title reveals three things: the variable being presented, the source of the data, and the portion of it illustrated in the table. It's a good idea to start data presentation with a distribution of the dependent variable for the whole sample to give an overall view of the results. Then you can proceed to more detailed illustrations. For this first table, since you are presenting the distribution of only one variable, it is feasible to include both the number of cases in each category of that distribution as well as the percentage of the total response each category represents. When you construct more complicated tables, you can report only the percentages, specifying the number of cases at the top of each column or in the **marginals**, that is, the total column at the extreme right and the total row at the bottom. In Table 1 in Figure 9.2, we have only a total row at the bottom, and the number of cases is the same as the total of the first column.

Percentages are calculated by dividing the total of the column into the number in the cell, or space, where the specific subcategory count appears. (Remember the example in the early part of this chapter, using the variable *marital status*. For example, there were 37 people who "accepted" diabetes, out of 131 people in the sample. Dividing 31 by 131, we get .28244274, which we shorten to 28.2 percent. We could also give the figure as 28 percent, since it was 28 plus less than 5 of the next place. Giving percentages to one decimal place, as well as rounding to whole numbers, is acceptable. As a check on your accuracy, add the percentage column.

The figures and words in the table should be separated from each other by enough white space so that the reader's eye is not taxed with a confusing jumble. It's important to line up numbers in all table columns and rows. I've always felt that tables are clearer if the totals on which the percentages are based are at the bottom, so I put my independent variable categories across the top and they are the columns. It's conventional to put N (meaning number of cases) = (the total of cases presented in the table) at the top or at the bottom of the table. Each column, or category of the independent variable, should add up to 100 percent.

Never use the total sample as a percentaging base unless you are constructing a univariate table or calculating percentages for entire rows. Percentages within columns are reached by dividing the cell number by the total for the column it is in. This rule is true of the rows too, because they are the marginal column to the right that adds up to the whole sample. (If you find this confusing, don't be discouraged. In more than two decades I have not had one class without many students who percentaged on the wrong base. Ask your instructor to spend some time on this procedure before you go further.)

FIGURE 9.2   **A table showing a univariate frequency distribution**

TABLE 1   DISTRIBUTION OF ATTITUDES TOWARD JUVENILE
DIABETES MELLITUS IN A SAMPLING OF
FAMILIES—WHOLE SAMPLE N=131

Attitude Toward Disease*	Number	Percent
Acceptance	37	28.2
Overcompensation	11	8.4
Despair	30	22.9
Denial	53	40.5
Total	131	100.0

*Acceptance—acceptance of the fact of diabetes and a
willingness to adjust to it

Overcompensation—insistence on the advantages of having
diabetes

Despair—grief, despair, depression, over the personal
misfortune of diabetes

Denial—refusal to face the seriousness and inconvenience of
diabetes

Even if you construct your tables by computer, it will still be advisable
to do rough sketches of the layout you want so you can write your commands
correctly, remembering to label everything and to end with what you want
and only what you want. It is dismaying to get output with complicated tables
of numbers and extra calculations, knowing that you have to spend precious
time figuring out what they mean.

Once a table has been constructed and you have decided that it will be useful in your report, you must summarize its message for the reader. Do not simply reproduce the table in narrative form, but point out the significant portions of it. Consider the difference between these two paragraphs about Table 1:

> *In Table 1, "Distribution of Attitudes Toward Juvenile Diabetes Mellitus in a Sampling of Families—Whole Sample," we can see that thirty-seven, or 28.2 percent, of the individuals were accepting; eleven, or 8.4 percent, of the individuals were overcompensating; thirty, or 22.9 percent, of the individuals were despairing; and fifty-three, or 40.5 percent, of the individuals were denying.*

or

> *Table 1 shows the distribution of attitudes toward diabetes in our sample. The most frequent response was* denial, *shown by over 40 percent of the sample, the next numerous being* acceptance, *shown by slightly over 28 percent.*

As we continue to explore table construction, keep two guidelines before you: First, the tables are there to organize and present the figures, and the text is there to explain them. Second, although you are immersed in your data, the reader comes to it "cold." Make your tables and your explanation as simple as possible without leaving out important items. This is not the place to impress people with your command of jargon. Be clear.

Bivariate Table Construction   Since our research question is "Do Catholics and Protestants differ in their attitude to chronic disease?" and our specific hypothesis is "Catholics will tend to accept diabetes mellitus while Protestants will tend to deny it," *all* our bivariate and multivariate tables should include these two variables as the independent, or column, variable (religion) and the dependent, or row, variable (attitude). A bivariate table is usually called a **contingency table** or a **cross-tabulation**, because the researcher is looking at the distribution of the dependent variable for each subdivision of the independent variable. The univariate table answers the question, "What were the attitudes toward diabetes of Catholics in this sample?" and "What were the attitudes toward diabetes of Protestants in this sample?"

Look at Table 2 in Figure 9.3. Notice the line just under the column headings "Catholics" and "Protestants." Here you put the *N* for each column, since the table shows only percentages. Because the reader can reconstruct the cell numbers if necessary, you do not have to clutter up the table with them. The label definitions also do not have to be repeated; the reader can be referred to Table 1.

Table 2 in Figure 9.3 can be summed up by saying that Catholics tend to accept more often than they show any other response and that Protestants tend to deny more often than they show any other response.

FIGURE 9.3 A table showing a bivariate frequency distribution

TABLE 2 DISTRIBUTION OF ATTITUDES TOWARD JUVENILE
DIABETES MELLITUS IN A SAMPLE OF FAMILIES
BY RELIGION—WHOLE SAMPLE—PERCENTAGES
(N=131)

Attitude Toward Disease*	Catholics (N=39)	Protestants (N=92)	Total
Acceptance	38.5	23.9	28.2
Overcompensation	7.7	8.7	8.4
Despair	30.8	19.6	22.9
Denial	23.1	47.8	40.5
Total	100.1	100.0	100.0

*See Table 1 for definitions.

However, you can also see that the Protestants' tendency to deny the disease is stronger than the Catholics' tendency to accept it. Also, Catholics are considerably more likely than Protestants to despair about the disease. Notice that the "Total" column on the right-hand side is the same as the "Percentage" column in Table 1. This is the distribution of the dependent variable, and it should be the same for any table that includes the whole sample.

FIGURE 9.4   **A table showing a multivariate frequency distribution**

TABLE 3   DISTRIBUTION OF ATTITUDES TOWARD
JUVENILE DIABETES MELLITUS IN A SAMPLE OF
FAMILIES BY RELIGION AND SEX—WHOLE
SAMPLE—PERCENTAGES (N=131)

Attitude Toward Disease*	Catholics		Protestants		Total†
	Male (N=19)	Female (N=20)	Male (N=42)	Female (N=50)	
Acceptance	32	45	26	22	28
Overcompensation	5	10	10	8	8
Despair	32	30	10	28	23
Denial	32	15	55	42	41
Total	101	100	101	100	100

*See Table 1 for definitions.

†Percentages rounded to whole numbers.

Multivariate Table Construction   Now we shall try a table showing three variables at once: the independent variable, religion; the dependent variable, attitude toward diabetes; and an intervening variable, sex. The intervening variable provides a subsampling of the cases. You are still examining the distribution of the dependent variable, but this time you are looking at Catholics divided by sex and at Protestants divided by sex (see Table 3 in Figure 9.4).

Some interesting differences now show up between Protestants and Catholics in their attitude toward diabetes:

1. Although Catholic females are more likely to be accepting than Catholic males, there is no difference between Protestant males and females in the frequency of this response.

2. Men are more likely to deny the disease than women in both religious groups; however, regardless of sex, the frequency of this response is greater for Protestants than it is for Catholics.

3. Despairing is more common among Catholics and Protestant females than it is among Protestant males.

We could carry this one step further and construct a table dividing the sample by the other intervening variable, family role (Table 4 in Figure 9.5). This construction makes a more complicated table, but that is not the chief difficulty. The problem that concerns us most is the division of the sample into smaller and smaller groups. Look at Figure 9.5. Two of the columns have Ns of less than 10. This makes the percentages too vulnerable to the influence of one case. We might be able to show this cross-tabulation in a better way, that is, less subject to misinterpretation. We can try to show the variation in the frequency of each type of response by drawing a bar graph for each, as pictured in Figure 9.6. All this bar graph does is give some idea of the relative frequency of a response for the eight subgroups of the two religious divisions. The width of the bars has no significance in a bar graph of a nominal variable such as this because there is no numerical measurement possible for the concept "Catholic" or the concept "Protestant."

If we had an interval or ratio variable, we could construct a bar graph called a **histogram**. In this type of bar graph the width of the bars indicates intervals, and their height indicates frequencies also.

A specialized double histogram is called a **population pyramid** (see Figure 9.7). This figure consists of two histograms laid on their sides, bottom to bottom. The intervals proceed up the figure and represent periods of years, usually 5 or 10, but they can be any interval you choose as long as it is consistent within the graph. The length of the bars indicates the number of people in the cohort represented. The left side of the population pyramid always represents males, and the right side always represents females. The figure is called a pyramid because it very often tapers at the top, where the older cohorts are.

If you have data from a longitudinal study, a line graph may be appropriate. One such is Figure 3.3. There are many types of graphic possibilities, and you can even invent your own. The important consideration is that your illustration does not confuse people but really casts light on the subject.

Another thing to remember is that interval and ratio data allow for many types of graphs and charts that you cannot use for nominal or ordinal data. Check that point carefully before choosing the form you use. A pie chart can

FIGURE 9.5   **A multivariate frequency distribution**

TABLE 4   DISTRIBUTION OF ATTITUDES TOWARD JUVENILE
DIABETES MELLITUS IN A SAMPLE OF FAMILIES
BY RELIGION AND FAMILY ROLE—WHOLE
SAMPLE—PERCENTAGES (N=131)

Attitude Toward Disease*	Catholics				Protestants				Total†
	Males		Females		Males		Females		
	Fath. N=11	Son N=8	Moth. N=13	Dtr. N=7	Fath. N=29	Son N=13	Moth. N=31	Dtr. N=19	Total†
Acceptance	46	13	39	57	28	23	29	11	28
Over-compensation	9	—	15	—	7	15	6	11	8
Despair	9	63	31	29	10	8	16	47	23
Denial	36	25	15	14	55	54	48	32	41
Total	100	101	100	100	100	100	99	101	100

*See Table 1 for definitions.

†All percentages rounded to whole numbers.

illustrate the proportions of a sample in different categories at any level, but a scattergram would not be appropriate for a variable unless it can be precisely measured and averaged—the characteristics of ratio data.

NOTE: When using a computer, you can get any kind of statistical test or chart the computer program can do, for any data you key in, because the computer does NOT have intelligence nor is it capable of discerning what your number-labels mean. For example, if you take the marital status distri-

FIGURE 9.6   The relative frequency of "acceptance" of juvenile diabetes mellitus among Catholics and Protestants by family role, depicted in a bar graph (*N* = 131)

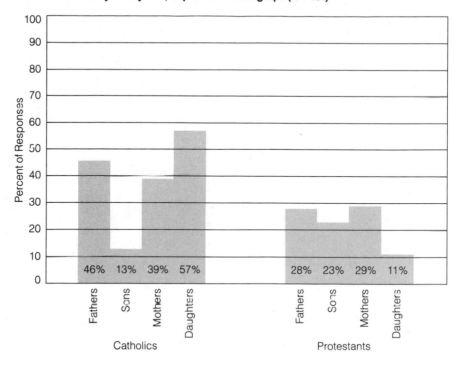

bution we have used earlier and assign a code number-label to each category you can order the machine to compute an average for codes 1 through 6. It will add the cases of each and multiply by the code. Let's see what you would get.

Code	N	Score	Category
1	48	48	Single, never married
2	30	60	Single, cohabiting
3	64	192	Married, living with spouse
4	16	64	Married, separated
5	22	110	Divorced
6	38	228	Widowed
	218	702	Marital status

The machine will divide 702 into 218 and give you an "average" or mean of 3.1 for the variable marital status. This implies that the "average" person is a little bit more than married, but not even halfway to separated. Does this make any sense at all? NO. The nominal data can only be sorted and counted. A table of percentages, a bar graph, or a pie chart will give the picture. As you read research reports, train yourself to consider the level of data collected and disregard any tables, charts, graphs and their accompanying discussion

FIGURE 9.7   **A population pyramid: age pyramid for the United States (1975). (U.S. Bureau of Census, 1975, Current Population Report, Series P-25, No. 614, Table 1.)**

A population pyramid: age pyramid for the United States (1975).

Males	Year of Birth	Females
	Before 1891	
	1891–1895	
	1896–1900	
	1901–1905	
	1906–1910	
	1911–1915	
	1916–1920	
	1921–1925	
	1926–1930	
	1931–1935	
	1936–1940	
	1941–1945	
	1946–1950	
	1951–1955	
	1956–1960	
	1961–1965	
	1966–1970	
	1971–1975	

11 10 9 8 7 6 5 4 3 2 1 0 1 2 3 4 5 6 7 8 9 10 11
Number of People (in millions)

if they are based on inappropriate numerical procedures. Chapter 10 will review the most popular statistical procedures and their proper use.

Reminders   Before we go on to the ways in which other levels of data may be treated, we shall review the following recommendations:

Keep your original question and hypothesis before you while examining and organizing your data.

Make sure your labels are (1) explained to the reader and (2) appropriate.

Be careful about reporting percentages when Ns are small.

Construct your tables in agreement with your hypothesis: Independent variable categories head the columns, and percentages go down the columns; dependent variable categories label the rows.

Use precise language in describing your results, to prevent misrepresenting them. Use as few numbers as possible in the description, pointing out the important outcomes in clear language.

All the techniques of table construction and variable division mentioned so far can be applied to any level of data, but nominal data can only be sorted and named. Ordinal data are data that can also be arranged along a continuum between two extremes.

Ordinal Data Attitudes and emotions, socioeconomic status, types of employees, grades of eggs, and quality of construction can be **ranked**, or ordered from most to least and from least to most. On the imaginary continuum for an ordinal variable one end represents the most, or highest degree, and the other end represents the least, or lowest degree of the item being ranked. It is important to remember that the intervals between each two ranks are not equal and they do not become equal because you have numbered them consecutively. Numbers can and do describe equivalent amounts of something, but they also serve as labels as in the examples already given. For nominal data, they only name; for ordinal data, they also rank. The level of measurement is inherent in the data, not in the label. Therefore, a question such as,

"Indicate on the scale below how much you liked this course (1 = not at all; 10 = very much)"

| <u>1</u> | <u>2</u> | <u>3</u> | <u>4</u> | <u>5</u> | <u>6</u> | <u>7</u> | <u>8</u> | <u>9</u> | <u>10</u> |

yields only ordinal data, not interval data. This is because there is no way of measuring "liking" except by subjective ranking. No arithmetic manipulation is possible.

When you have ordinal data, you know that any item is more or less than another item in the scale. Suppose you have some data on the preceding question and you have tabulated it with the following result:

Answers to how much students liked course

| 5 | 3 | 0 | 6 | 7 | 4 | 11 | 8 | 7 | 2 |
| <u>1</u> | <u>2</u> | <u>3</u> | <u>4</u> | <u>5</u> | <u>6</u> | <u>7</u> | <u>8</u> | <u>9</u> | <u>10</u> |

This is a typical response to evaluation questions on forms distributed to college students. What can you do with it? You may be tempted to multiply each rank position by the number of people who checked it, add the totals together, and divide by the total N to get an average. This is the same procedure as in the illustration of computer averaging, above, and is not valid because "liking" can't be measured and the intervals are not equal except in their spacing on the paper. Furthermore, you do not have any idea whether all the checks at any given position are equivalent. Maybe "not at all" means indifference to one student and hatred to another. All you can do with these data is report the rankings:

Liking for course

High (ranks 6 through 10)   32 students
Low (ranks 1 through 5)   21 students

You can combine the ranks in any way you want, but you must not change their order. Of course, you can report the whole range, as you tabulated it and you could certainly construct a pie chart or a bar graph from it.

You will note that I combined ranks into two categories: High and Low. Many times the original data have more ranks in them than are eventually used in the analysis. There are several reasons for this. The respondent is often more comfortable being able to make fine distinctions, and the opportunity should be provided for that. Sometimes it is easier to collect the exact data, such as an organization chart for a business firm, and do the ranking and combining later. (Picture yourself asking a busy personnel director to give you the number of positions at level A, level B, and so on.) An important analytic reason is that you do not know in advance what the distribution will be, and you may want to reserve the option of dividing the variable in more than one way. Suppose you are collecting data on self-perception in the high school years, and the distribution is:

Perception of Self in High School Years

Quite attractive	110
Fairly attractive	457
Fairly unattractive	124
Quite unattractive	15

If you cross-tabulate this variable with another variable, the last category, or lowest rank of attractiveness, is going to be almost unusable because there are only 15 people in it. You can combine, or **collapse**, these categories in two ways:

Quite attractive	110
Fairly attractive	457
Unattractive	139

or

Attractive	567
Unattractive	139

You couldn't combine any "attractive" category with any "unattractive" category because it wouldn't make sense for this distribution. Once you assign computer codes to categories you have to be very cautious and have the meanings in front of you lest you combine the wrong things. If you do collapse categories, you have to change the wording to indicate that and note in the report that you did both. Often a copy of the original questionnaire or schedule is included in reports as an appendix; if it is all such changes can be noted there.

So far we have discussed data that can be sorted or sorted and ranked but not arithmetically manipulated.

Interval and Ratio Data If you have data that can be sorted, ranked, and then divided into equal classes, or intervals, they are called interval data. Now you can equate any interval with any other one in the analysis: "For each 10-point rise in IQ scores at age 11, total earnings by age 21 rise by $5679." (These are hypothetical data.) IQ scores seem to be about the only interval data anyone in social science ever cites, since all data that have an absolute zero are of a higher order, that is, ratio data. You can add and subtract interval data and discuss differences in scores; with ratio data you can add, subtract, multiply, and divide. Family size is a ratio variable because it can be zero and is measured in equal intervals by the person. Anything that is measured in duration also qualifies as ratio data: school years (but not degrees), age in any time period (days, weeks, months, years, decades), working speed or output, and so on. Money is a ratio variable. (*Note:* If you use education, money, or any other variable to assign a person's socioeconomic status, you have transformed the data into ordinal data, and they are then subject to the rules for ordinal data.)

One thing you can do with interval and ratio data that you cannot do with nominal or ordinal data is to use an **arithmetic mean**, or average, to represent an interval instead of the absolute frequency. Often an interval is represented by a rate, or number per thousand cases calculated for the whole interval.

There are two major types of **composite measure** designed to refine the measurement of variables that by nature are difficult to classify. To some extent this discussion follows Earl Babbie's explanation.[4]

Composite Measures

The two types of composite measure that Babbie identifies are indexes (spelled *indices* by purists) and scales. Be prepared to find confusion about these names in the literature, and don't be dismayed if writers use them interchangeably or not at all. Both indexes and scales are ordinal measures, and it is not legitimate to manipulate their scores as if they were at a higher level of measurement. You will find it done often, however.

Indexes An index is a measure of the number of attributes an item or person possesses that can be counted as part of the same variable. For example, if you are scoring someone on the variable "marriageability," you might include the items below in a checklist:

attractive appearance	legally eligible
college degree	pleasant personality
steady job	good manners
upper-middle class family	appropriate religion

If the individual passes on all eight items, you could give him or her a score of 8; if the individual has everything but a steady job, you could score him or her a 7; if the individual lacks the appropriate religion as well, he or she would get only a 6. You might have two candidates for marriage—both with the same score, but for different reasons. You might have two candidates with the same score for the same reasons, but you might feel that one candidate is "worse" or "better" on a particular item than the other candidate. For example, if one scores a 7 because he or she has everything but a steady job and the other scores a 7 because he or she has everything but an attractive appearance, you might come to the decision that the scores should be weighted, or counted differently toward the total score. If they both scored 7 because they lack a pleasant personality but one is more surly than the other, this might suggest the need for a way to measure the intensity of an item. Thus, for example, a person could receive partial credit for a particular item.

If these weaknesses sound familiar to you, it is because you come up against similar situations when you are tested in school. An index is like an objective test in which you are presented with a number of items and scored on how many you get right. This score holds true regardless of how important the items are relative to each other, and no partial credit is given.

To construct an index, you select items on the basis of their face validity. This means that if it looks good to you, you use it. You have to try out the index and see if the items are equally weighted by large numbers of other people, preferably chosen randomly. You could ask people to rate the items on your index. If they consistently choose "steady job" over "appropriate religion," you might conclude that the items should be weighted differently.

Scales   When you feel that you ought to measure the intensity of an item, as in the example of the two marriage prospects with the same score but differing degrees of surliness, you can construct a **scale** for "pleasant personality."

Pleasant personality:

Always	Mostly	Half the time	Seldom	Never
(5)	(4)	(3)	(2)	(1)

The numbers in parentheses are the points each candidate would get for that attribute. If you scale each attribute and end up with a composite scale score for marriageability, you could then choose the man or woman with the highest score.

Now look back at the original list of attributes. One of them cannot be used in a scale because it cannot differ in intensity. The individual either is free to marry or is not. All the others can vary by degrees of commitment, prestige, acceptability, and so on. In fact, you do rate other people in this fashion all the time, but the scoring process is mostly unconscious and the criteria are highly individual.

Many indexes and scales can be found in collections, or you can devise your own.[5] However, you must remember that they cannot be more than ordinal measures regardless of what has been attempted with them. This section briefly describes some of the better known scales.

The **Thurstone scale** requires five steps. The researcher composes a large number of statements that are favorable or unfavorable to the subject of the scale—for example, "President Lincoln has done a good job and people are too critical of him." At least fifty judges (often many more) are asked to sort the statements subjectively into ordinal categories, and then the researcher rates each statement by giving it a score for the position each judge gave it and then computing its average. Seven or eleven ranks are than completed to represent each gradation of intensity of feeling toward the subject. The researcher tests the relevance of the items by computation and ends up with a scale of fifteen or twenty statements of opinion to administer to subjects.[6] This is a misuse of nominal data, which should not be subjected to such computation.

The **Likert scale** is probably familiar to you because it is so widely used. The subject is presented with a statement and asked to indicate agreement or disagreement with it in a choice of degrees. The number of choices is up to the researcher, who may also choose whether to include a neutral position such as "undecided" or "no opinion" on the statement:

___ strongly agree   ___ agree   ___ undecided

___ disagree   ___ strongly disagree

To avoid biasing the responses, the number of positive choices should be the same as the number of negative choices. You proceed by making up a scale and pretesting it on a few people. Items should not be accepted or rejected by everybody, because that would mean the item is useless for showing differences between people. People are considered "favorable" if they agree with the favorable statements and disagree with the unfavorable for the most part. People are considered "unfavorable" if they agree with the unfavorable statements and disagree with the favorable for the most part. If a statement shows up accepted among the favorables or among the unfavorables most of the time, it is probably useful as a selection tool. If it is inconsistently accepted, it should be discarded.[7] Likert scales are easy to use and to devise, and there are many variations in the literature. They can be useful and yield good nominal or ordinal data.

The **Bogardus scale** is also quite popular. Usually called the "social distance scale," it is an attempt to measure how close a person is willing to be to a member of an ethnic group. You can ask about any ethnic group, including the respondent's own. The statements range from "would admit to close kinship by marriage" to "would exclude from my country." The respondent is asked to indicate first reactions to each of the classifications for the "average" member of the groups listed.

It is logical that someone who agrees to admit a group to "employment in my occupation" would also be willing to admit those people to "citizenship" or "visiting" in the country and would not "exclude" them. The items are logically arranged in decreasing degrees of proximity. If "close kinship" is a score of 1 and "exclude from the country" a 7, you can score the answer according to the lowest number circled. If I am willing to work with French people but am not willing to live in the same neighborhood with them, I am very likely not to want them "in my club" or in my family. Therefore, I would circle the number four. Four is now the score for the French nationality on my paper. When you administer this scale to a lot of people, you can add up the scores for each nationality or race and get an average. You can then estimate the comparative acceptance or rejection position for each ethnic group you asked about in your sample.[8] Note that if you follow these instructions you will be misapplying an arithmetic procedure to ordinal data! A bar graph for each group would be better. You could even construct a table showing how each group did on each statement.

The **Guttman scale** is also called the **scalogram**. The first two steps in constructing this scale are the same as the Thurstone. A large number of statements are composed and evaluated by the researcher and submitted to a large number of judges for sorting into eleven categories. The statements are then administered to a large group of subjects, with Likert scale answer options supplied for each one. The results are analyzed in the Likert fashion, nondiscriminating statements are removed, and the scale is constructed.[9]

When the scale is used, the answers can be scored in a way that reveals whether the questions are tapping a single dimension of a variable. If they are, the patterns of people's answers are consistent, as they are in the Bogardus scale; if we know the most extreme position the answers take, we can predict the rest. If our items prove to be this consistent, with a minimum of predictive errors, we say they form a Guttman scale. However, you cannot generalize this outside the sample you used. You cannot say that the same items will form a Guttman scale next time. That remains to be seen.[10] The technique is of limited use, but it makes some researchers feel better about their questions if they "Guttman scale."

A number of objections are made in the literature to the idea that a person's attitude on something can be represented by a single score. Some theorists speak of "latitudes of acceptance and rejection," referring to the range of positions a person might find acceptable. It's hard to estimate how narrow or broad that range might be.[11]

You can see that some scaling techniques require a lot of time and complicated computations. At one point in the history of research methods, random sampling was also cumbersome and tedious. With the advent of the computer and its ability to provide endless streams of random numbers, this job was simplified. The computer's speed and accuracy make all kinds of complex manipulation possible without an army of workers and an eternity of time. As long as those manipulations are appropriate to the level of data, the technology is wonderful.

The Use of the Computer

A computer is a machine that can store information and then perform calculations and combinations at a high rate of speed. It produces long pieces of paper that are perforated at intervals and folded as they emerge to make a stack of paper, which is referred to as **output**. This paper has information printed on it in the form of words, symbols, or numbers arranged in specific patterns. The machine does the operations it has been told to do via instructions of two sorts that have been entered into it along with the data. One kind of instruction is highly technical and is written in "machine language," meaning patterns of electronic impulses that call forth predictable responses from the equipment when the power is on. These prepare the machine to take the next level of instructions, which are sets of words and characters that will trigger the machine language instructions. These prepared sets of instructions are sold as **packages** and consist of detailed sequences of commands that will be activated when the end user types in specific words as directed by the printed instructions in a handbook, usually called **documentation**.

The technical instructions that set up the machine to process your data are called names such as COBOL, FORTRAN, BASIC, PASCAL, and SPSSx (statistical package for the social sciences), and they are set up to handle data in different ways. You have to learn how to enter your data and which commands to issue to get the results you want. You have to know what each of the packages available will and will not do in order to choose wisely among them. What is available depends on what kind of data you have (social surveys, test scores, agricultural or business reports) and what you want to accomplish. The machine doesn't do your thinking for you, nor does it make your decisions. It eliminates the lengthy and tedious calculations, tabulations, and combinations you'd otherwise have to make by hand. The computer can manage in a few hours operations so time-consuming that it would take you years to do them by hand. The computer can count and sort large numbers of cases, compute means and correlations as well as more complicated statistics, construct crosstabulation tables and graphs, and display any of the work on a monitor screen or print it out on paper.

Think back to the array of data on families presented in this chapter. Producing the simple tables from it took one morning of my time. A correctly instructed computer could extract that information in a few seconds. It might not be worth the trouble to set it up if you were dealing with only a few cases and intended to do only those tables. However, if you want many comparisons and sortings made and you also want to do descriptive or inferential statistical operations (see Chapter 10), the computer is a life-saver. You have to decide whether the case of manipulating data with it is worth the time it takes to code the data and type (key) the code numbers into the computer's memory.

To use the computer, you first transform your data into number-labels because the machine can manipulate only the numbers or symbols it is programmed to "read." It will not make any decisions and has no intelligence, so mistakes in entering information or commands cause it either to reject the job or to go blindly on, responding automatically and producing nonsense results. The computer will respond only as previously instructed to respond, so you must observe rigid rules in putting the data and the instructions into the machine.

Coding the Data   When preparing data for the computer, you must be careful not to distort nominal or ordinal data into a more precise type *in your mind*. Data to be put into the computer are transformed first into numbers. These numbers imply location in a **code book**, not value. They are labels. Data are entered directly into the computer via a **terminal**, which is usually a keyboard, and TV screen (monitor) which shows you what you are typing and the machine response to it.

For example, were I using the package SPSSx, popular with social scientists, I would go to a computer lab at my college where I know I will find mainframe computer terminals. It's necessary to use the operating system commands specific to the computer installation to call up the SPSSx package, and I must be sure that the specific installation supports that package. You ask the person in charge of such matters, who usually gives you a small handbook with operating system procedures in it. Schools conduct minilabs in using these handbooks. They include matters such as how to turn the system on and off, how to edit (write and revise) a **file** (list of data and/or instructions to run it), how to name, copy, store and retrieve files, and an assortment of other procedures.

Back to me, at the lab. I tell the lab person that I want to make an SPSSx file and run it and then I follow the simple instructions for entering my name and account number (previously supplied by the school and used for billing), along with whatever else the system requires and where I want the output sent. Maybe I only want to read it on the screen. Maybe I want **hard** (printed) copy out of one of the printers. I have to specify.

I follow the instruction for "getting into" SPSSx. Once I have activated it, I want to tell the machine three things: what columns are being used for which variables, named by me; the line of codes for each case; what manipulations I want performed with the data. After that I will order the machine to save my entries in a file and to go ahead and do the work, printing it out. Before I can attempt this I must have already (1) decided what codes I want, (2) devised a coding key, and (3) transformed the data for each case into a line of codes.

Coding for the computer is like making any other code, except that each number signifies a category of a variable rather than a letter in a word. Consider the data discussed earlier in this chapter. The array we used to construct our tables included eight pieces of information about each family: case ID number, religion of child, religion of father, religion of mother, sex of child, child's attitude toward disease, mother's attitude toward disease, and father's attitude toward disease. A ninth piece of information, number of parents present, can be inferred. To code these data and prepare an array from which data can be entered, we would have to assign codes to each kind of data. Some of these variables are easy to code:

Sex of Child:

1 Male

2 Female

Others are not so easy and may require additional instructions. Look at Figure 9.8. Under the heading "Column" one or more numbers are entered for each variable. The machine "reads" the data as if they were organized in the eighty columns of a computer data card (as used to be the case). The columns are used in order. Each row represents one respondent. If a piece of data is missing, the column's space must be left blank. Think of a class of students, with some absent. If they always sit in the same places, the teacher can tell who is absent by looking at the rows. If students move into the absent ones' places, the teacher will be confused. They have to stay in their appropriate rows in order to be counted in the correct category. The ID number needs to use two columns because we have more than nine cases and so we have two-digit numbers in our ID data. We will have to tell the machine via the first instruction line that ID is in columns 1 and 2. Since the first nine ID numbers have only one digit, we will write them as "01, 02, 03," etc. to keep the number of columns used for that variable uniform and to avoid confusion between numbers such as 3 and 30. This is why the spaces called "leading blanks" are filled in with zeros in computer work. We need to keep those absent students' chairs empty because they are especially likely to tempt the adjacent folks! If we have no data at all for a variable, we can leave the column(s) blank.

The machine is consistent and cannot "read" a variable code correctly if it is entered in the wrong column location. If we tell the computer that ID is in columns 1 and 2, we can't put anything else in those columns, and we cannot put ID anywhere else unless we treat it as another variable and provide a new name for it. We can tell a person "Look in columns 1 and 2 for the ID number, and if it is not there, maybe you will find it in columns 17 and 18"; but we can't be vague with the computer because it has neither judgment nor discretion.

The line array you prepare is similar to the old IBM cards in that it has spaces for eighty columns. Most machines are set up for seventy-two to a line, however, unless you give a special instruction. You usually use one line

FIGURE 9.8   **Pages from a code book**

DIABETES RESEARCH—CODING AND PUNCHING INSTRUCTIONS (Card 01)

Column(s)	Description	Source
1-2	ID number 01-55, by ones	SIa
3	Sex of child 1 Male 2 Female	SIa
4	Religion of child 1 Catholic 2 Protestant (include Episcopalian, Christian Scientist, Quaker, and any Christian group that is not subject to the Pope) 3 Jewish 4 Other	SIa
5	Religion of mother 1 Catholic 2 Protestant (see above) 3 Jewish 4 Other 5 Mother absent	SIa
6	Religion of father 1 Catholic 2 Protestant (see above) 3 Jewish 4 Other 5 Father absent	SIa
7	Attitude toward disease—child 1 Acceptance 2 Overcompensation 3 Despair 4 Denial (See rating sheet for explanations)	Rating sheet

---

for each case and write in the code numbers. Here is the line for the first case in our array (for only nine columns, since that is as much data as we have):

081111111

We have recorded the codes for columns one through nine, according to our code book (see Figure 9.8). Others who look it up in the code book, will

FIGURE 9.8   **Pages from a code book,** *continued*

Column(s)	Description	Source
8	Attitude toward disease—mother 1 Acceptance 2 Overcompensation 3 Despair 4 Denial 5 Mother absent (See rating sheet for explanations)	Rating sheet
9	Attitude toward disease—father 1 Acceptance 2 Overcompensation 3 Despair 4 Denial 5 Father absent	Rating sheet

discover that case 08 was a male child, Catholic, with a Catholic mother and a Catholic father, and that all three of them were rated "accepting" of the child's disease.

The code book contains complete instructions, samples of data collection instruments, and rating sheets, if applicable. The object is to provide a key to the coded data so that anyone can discover what information is recorded there. Once the data have been coded and entered, and the explanation written in the code book, the original interviews or questionnaires may be destroyed.

Using the Computer   Some basic details on how to use a computer are in Appendix E. You will need to learn specific procedures for the package appropriate for your data. Packages are revised often and instructions change, so it's necessary to get current advice from the computer center staff. Nevertheless, let's proceed with our example.

I've got the machine turned on and have followed the computer center's procedure for getting into SPSSx. I have opened (started) a file, which I have named JUVENILE. I am now going to tell the machine the three things mentioned before: what columns are being used for which variables, the line of codes for each case, and what I want done with this data. Here I go:

To tell the machine what columns I am using for what, I type the first line of my new file JUVENILE:

```
DATA LIST ID 1-2  SEXCHILD 3  RELCHILD 4  RELMOTHR 5  RELFATHR 6
  ATDCHILD 7  ATDMOTHR 8  ATDFATHR 9  NUMBPARS 10
```

Notice that I typed the second line one space in from the left margin. That tells the machine that we are still on the same command line. If I start the rest of my command line in column 1 the machine will read it as a second command and not be able to do anything with it, since ATDCHILD is my label for "attitude toward disease—child" and is not a computer command. I have had to make up labels for each variable of no more than 8 characters, and they must begin with a letter, although a number can be included. I could have used something like PAR1OR2 for the last variable, which is "number of parents." Figure 9.8 doesn't show the code for that, but it is:

```
10 Number of parents in the home

1 One parent
2 Both parents
```

and it is easily coded if you have the other data, which indicate a missing parent, in columns 5, 6, 8, and 9.

Now that I have told the computer what the variable labels and columns will be, I have to give it the data, or line of code numbers for each case. I alert the machine by typing:

```
BEGIN DATA
```

so it will be able to tell commands from data. I then type in the data for my cases:

```
0811111112
0711114112
```

```
0211113222
3711113242
1011153351
4511154351
1311253151
0911513531
4721111112
5221111112
```

And I must tell the machine that we are finished with data so that it will read my commands as commands and not try to read them as data:

END DATA

Now I'll tell it I want frequencies for some of the variables:

FREQUENCIES VARIABLES = RELCHILD ATDCHILD NUMBPARS

and the machine will give me those three frequency lists when I "run" the program I just wrote. (The program is the last line. See how easy it can be?) To run the program, I must first save it, using the appropriate command:

SAVE FILE = JUVENILE

and then:

SEND JUVENILE

My output will be sent wherever I have previously specified. If the system is **time-sharing**, and mainframe computers usually are, this means that lots of people are using it and during busy times, jobs are stored in a queue and printed in turn. You may have to wait a while for your output to appear. Computer centers have alphabetic mailbox systems. The individual boxes are called bins, and you look in the one for the first letter of your surname, in my case, T. If your output isn't there yet, the assistant may be able to give you an estimate of when you can expect it. You go have coffee, or lunch, or go to class and check later.

There are a few things you should keep in mind as you are setting out to use the computer:

Know what you want to ask the computer to do for you. It is a useful servant, but you are the decision maker.

Be careful not to ask inappropriate questions. The computer will combine apples and bluebirds and will perform complicated arithmetical manipulations on them, if you so instruct it. This does not make the results valid.

Be sure you know what is programmed into the computer (the package) so you are not surprised by having your four-category variable divided into five meaningless categories because you did not know the machine was set up to handle a minimum of five. (This happened to me once, so don't scoff.)

If you think of the computer as a filing system with a clerk who operates at amazing speed and performs difficult calculations to boot, you might appreciate this marvelous invention without being intimidated by it. You deal with mechanical wonders every day. The awe-inspiring feature that a computer has, making it more impressive than other machines, is that we can see that it does MATH.

Just remember: Humans invented the machine and the math, and a human has to program the math into the machine. The computer does math in a very roundabout and crude fashion, similar to counting on your fingers and toes. It adds over and over very rapidly. It has not mastered the multiplication tables the way you have. The wonder lies in the humans who made it, not in the contraption. Anyone who remembers the old systems will bless the inventors of the computer. Think of it as a marvelously efficient servant, much like a head waiter in an expensive restaurant—a bit intimidating, but still a servant. Get used to having a servant. Learn to give it orders. If the notion of having a servant strains your imagination, think of the computer as a new foreign sportscar. (Where is the ignition on this thing? How many speeds does it have? How do you put the thing in reverse? Where is the gas cap lock? Etc., etc., etc.) It usually takes me a few weeks to learn how to regulate the fan and heat in any new car I get, not to mention moving the seat back and forth and having it flatten out behind me or suddenly hit me in the back because I did the wrong thing. I learned to drive in 1952, and I'm not stupid, but a new model is a new model. Therefore, although I learned to type, file, and use an adding machine in 1944, and got used to TV in 1957, I have to explore each new computer terminal or PC until I get accustomed to its specific characteristics. If you are desperate, write to me at the Sociology Department, Trenton State College, Trenton, New Jersey, and I promise to respond. Courage.

Summary and Conclusion

Once the data have been collected, they must be carefully examined, summarized, and organized so that they can be clearly presented to the reader. The analysis should illuminate the research question and suggest new inquiries. You can summarize by assigning number-labels and aggregating them, by computing percentages of frequencies, and by prose commentary. Entering the data into a computer makes quick manipulation possible as the computer assumes the tedious counting and sorting.

Data are classified into levels of measurement called nominal, ordinal, interval, and ratio; these levels permit manipulations of varying complexity. If your data are on the lowest level, you cannot manipulate them in ways appropriate to any of the higher levels, and so on. In order of complexity, the manipulations are sorting, ranking, spacing equally, and computing. Scrutiny of the data also includes examining the distributions to see whether categories should be combined or omitted.

Using tables, variables can be illustrated one at a time or by twos and threes; in the latter case they are referred to as cross-tabulations. Having more than three variables in a table is difficult, but not impossible. Other illustrations include charts and graphs of various kinds. The criterion for choice is clarity.

Composite measures are indexes and scales. These present subjects with items on which they are scored and the scores manipulated arithmetically to compose one score. The composite instruments are designed to measure variables with many dimensions, such as attitudes. Their computation is tedious, but the use of the computer has reduced that problem.

Computers can be programmed, or ordered, to do lengthy summarizing and complicated calculations as long as the information to be manipulated can be coded and entered into the machine. Codes are numbers that are really names and have no arithmetic meaning. A book with a key to the codes is called a code book. There is an explanation in the code book for each code number-label.

The machine can do only what you ask and only if you ask it in the language to which the machine is prepared to respond. You have to know what a specific machine is set up to do, what you want from it, and how to ask. Each computer installation has its own standard procedure, and a person on duty to answer questions. You should have your question in mind, your dummy tables set up, and your data coded before you arrive at the computer center. It's a good idea to visit there beforehand just to find out what is there and how they operate, introduce yourself, and to pick up any informative handouts available. If there is an introductory course for the equipment, take it. Don't be reluctant to ask questions, no matter how simple they seem.

Main Points

1. After you have collected the data, review the research question. Confine your analysis to what is relevant to it and record new ideas separately. After reviewing the question and hypotheses, you must decide what summarizing operations you can use. These will depend on the level of measurement of your data.

2. Nominal variables can only be sorted. Ordinal variables can be sorted and ranked. Interval variables can be sorted, ranked, and equally

spaced. Ratio variables can be sorted, ranked, equally spaced, and arithmetically manipulated. There are no exceptions to these restrictions.

3.   Care must be taken so that summarizing does not result in demoting a variable to a lower level of measurement. You can aggregate data by converting the frequencies into percentages, proportions, or rates. Sparse or vacant categories can be combined with others or omitted, as long as it does not destroy the logic of the classification. Be careful about reporting percentages when the number of cases (N) is small, for each case is then too influential on the percentage.

4.   A table presenting the tabulation of one variable is called univariate; for two variables it is called bivariate; for more it is called multivariate. The more variables presented, the more complicated the table and the harder it is to present the data clearly.

5.   If you analyze data by hand, you prepare a data matrix, which is a chart containing a number-label, or abbreviated summary of all cases.

6.   If you analyze data by machine, you prepare data by assigning number-label codes to it and entering the coded data into a computer via a terminal.

7.   Explanations should accompany presentations of aggregated data and should be stated as simply as possible. Be sure all tables are clearly labeled and include the number of cases (N). Columns should be percentaged down, with the total for 100 percent of the category at the bottom.

8.   A bivariate table is also called a contingency table or a cross-tabulation. The columns are for the independent and control variables, and the rows are for the dependent variable. Make sure the figures line up, and leave plenty of white space for clarity. One should be careful not to divide by so many variables that cells contain very few cases or none.

9.   Other illustrations you can use besides tables are charts and graphs. If you have interval or ratio data, you can use a histogram. A special kind of histogram is a population pyramid.

10.   A number-label does not indicate measurement of any kind; it indicates only sorting or ranking. You cannot add, subtract, multiply, or divide number-labels.

11.   If you have interval or ratio data, you can use an arithmetic mean to represent a frequency interval. You can also use a rate (number per 1000 per time period).

12.   Indexes and scales represent composite scores and are called composite measures. They are an attempt to measure many-sided concepts, and the results are always ordinal. An index counts attributes; a scale counts the dimensions of an attribute. Some popular scales are named after their originators: Thurstone, Likert, Bogardus, and Guttman.

13.   Complicated and time-consuming procedures such as mathematical

computations and involved sorting are handled very efficiently and quickly by a computer. The researcher must know what is permissible to ask the computer according to the level of measurement of the data, what questions are relevant to the research question and hypothesis, and how to issue the commands. Prepared commands (programs) help with some of the standard operations.

14. The preparation of data for entering into the computer involves assigning code numbers to it in a logical way. This procedure must be rigidly adhered to, and the coding key entered in a code book—along with complete instructions, samples of instruments, and rating sheets.

Notes

1. June True Albert, "Religion and the Reaction to Chronic Illness: Juvenile Diabetes Mellitus." Unpublished master's thesis, Rutgers University, 1966, pp. 5, 6. (Weber and Lenski are cited in this excerpt and referenced in Figure 11.3.)

2. Albert, "Religion and the Reaction to Chronic Illness," pp. 4, 17.

3. The original matrix had much more information not relevant to our example.

4. Earl R. Babbie, *The Practice of Social Research*, 2nd ed. (Belmont, Calif.: Wadsworth, 1979), Chapter 15.

5. Delbert C. Miller, *Handbook of Research Design and Social Measurement*, 3rd ed. (New York: McKay, 1977).

6. L. L. Thurstone, "The Measurement of Social Attitudes," *Journal of Abnormal and Social Psychology* 26 (1931): 249–69.

7. Rensis Likert, "A Technique for the Measurement of Attitudes," *Archives of Psychology* 140 (1932): 52.

8. E. S. Bogardus, "A Social Distance Scale," *Sociology and Social Research* 17 (1933): 265–71.

9. A. L. Edwards and F. P. Kirkpatrick, "A Technique for Construction of Attitude Scales," *Journal of Applied Psychology* 32 (1948): 374–84.

10. L. Guttman, "A Basis for Scaling Quantitative Data," *American Sociological Review* 9 (1944): 139–50.

11. C. Sherif, M. Sherif, and R. E. Nebergall, *Attitude and Attitude Change: The Social Judgment–Involvement Approach* (Philadelphia: Saunders, 1965).

Exercises

The exercises for this chapter are meant to give you some practice in the actual clerical work required to organize data for processing and a taste of the painstaking process of constructing a table by hand. Therefore, Exercise 9.1

asks you to prepare an array of the data in Figure 9.1 as if you were coding them for the computer, using the sample codes in Figure 9.8 and adding in one for a new variable.

Exercise 9.2 asks you to prepare a bivariate table from the array you constructed in Exercise 9.1. After you have had this practice and understand what is involved, turn to Exercise 9.3, which assigns you to focus on the labeling and coding process evident in a published report.

Exercise 9.1

Organizing the data

Instructions: Pretend you are trying to answer the research question "Does attitude toward juvenile diabetes vary by family composition?" Your hypothesis is "Individuals in families of juvenile diabetics with only one parent present will be judged 'accepting' less often than those with both parents present." Using the codes in Figure 9.8, add this code for your new variable and call it "family composition":

Column	Description	(Omit Source)
10	Number of parents	
	1 One parent	
	2 Both parents	

On the next page you will find a partially complete array of the cases in Figure 9.1, coded by the instructions in Figure 9.8. Using the codes for columns 7, 8, 9, and 10, complete this array. Total your four columns as the others have been totaled. They should all total the same. If you want to check on your subtotals for each code category, you can figure out what they ought to be from the *N*s in Table 4 in Figure 9.5. For example, array column 3 should have twenty-one 1s because there are eight Catholic sons and thirteen Protestant sons in the sample. It should have twenty-six 2s because there are seven Catholic daughters plus nineteen Protestant daughters.

COLUMNS

1	2	3	4	5	6	7	8	9	10
0	8	1	1	1	1				
0	7	1	1	1	1				
0	2	1	1	1	1				
3	7	1	1	1	1				
1	0	1	1	1	5				
4	5	1	1	1	5				
1	3	1	1	2	5				
0	9	1	1	5	1				
4	7	2	1	1	1				
5	2	2	1	1	1				
5	1	2	1	1	1				
1	6	2	1	1	1				
4	6	2	1	1	5				
2	9	2	1	1	1				
2	5	2	1	1	1				
3	2	1	2	2	2				
4	2	1	2	2	2				
0	6	1	2	2	2				
1	5	1	2	2	2				
0	3	1	2	2	2				
0	5	1	2	2	2				
5	3	1	2	2	2				
5	4	1	2	2	2				
1	1	1	2	2	2				

COLUMNS

1	2	3	4	5	6	7	8	9	10
1	4	1	2	2	2				
3	8	1	2	2	2				
4	8	1	2	2	5				
3	6	1	2	5	2				
3	0	2	2	2	2				
2	3	2	2	2	2				
3	3	2	2	2	2				
1	8	2	2	5	2				
3	1	2	2	2	2				
5	0	2	2	2	2				
1	7	2	2	2	2				
4	9	2	2	2	2				
5	5	2	2	2	2				
4	3	2	2	2	2				
3	9	2	2	2	2				
2	1	2	2	2	2				
2	6	2	2	2	5				
2	8	2	2	2	5				
4	0	2	2	2	2				
1	9	2	2	2	2				
2	2	2	2	2	2				
3	4	2	2	2	2				
3	5	2	2	2	2				

TOTALS   21 15 13 11   (1)

            26 32 31 29   (2)

            47 47

                     3   7   (5)

            47 47

Exercise 9.2   *Preparing a bivariate table*

Instructions: Using the array in Exercise 9.1, construct a table with "family composition" as your independent variable (heading the two columns with whatever labels you choose) and "attitude toward disease" as your dependent variable. Follow the form in Table 2 in Figure 9.3. Do not forget the title and the Ns.

Exercise 9.3   *Critique*

Instructions: Select a research report that presents data in a table. Read the report and answer the following questions after giving a full citation here:

_____

_____

1. What was the research question?

2. Select a table. How many variables does it present?

3. Name them.

    Independent variable:

    Intervening variable(s):

    Dependent variable:

4. Pick one of the preceding variables and list its categories.

5. Is the table clear to you? Criticize it, pointing out any improvements you can suggest.

CHAPTER 10

The Significance of Tests

A statistic is a number that reports a fact. "She went 15 and 2 on the junior varsity fencing squad this year" contains three statistics: the number of bouts (17), wins (15), and losses (2). The sentence contains other facts that are stated or implied: The person mentioned is female and attending school. She is either an underclasswoman, not having had time to make varsity, or her performance heretofore has not been good enough to make varsity. The "other facts" just mentioned are not translatable into statistics.

Statistics is a language similar to the computer command languages mentioned in Chapter 9. All these languages consist of words, numbers, and symbols used to represent something more complicated; they act like a shorthand system. The statistics that we use every day are so familiar we don't think of them as having this characteristic:

"I'm getting 42 miles to the gallon with the new buggy."

"With fringe benefits at 24 percent, how can we afford to give Cost of Living in this contract?"

"Our average discount is one-third even in these times of double-digit inflation!"

"$835 mo., util., 2 mo. sec., 3-year lease."

"The Dow-Jones hit 2000 today after a day of heavy trading."

"My cum. is 3.15 already, but I got a 93 in bio and an 89 in poly sci, so my semester average won't do it any harm if my finals are OK."

All the sentences have statistical terms and phrases to stand for things that would take longer to say in other ways.

A **sample statistic** is a number that reports a fact about a sample. Later in this chapter we shall see how sample statistics are used to estimate the same fact about the population from which the sample has been drawn. To distinguish it from the sample statistic, the population fact, or value, is known as a **parameter**. This distinction is made when discussing inferential statistics, a "dialect" of statistics that is used for generalizing beyond the sample studied and is rarely appropriate for use with social science data.

In Chapter 9 you learned that the computer is a servant, not a master. This is also true of statistical summaries, computations, and tests. You must learn how to speak and read this language competently enough to understand published material that uses it and to know what orders to give your servant, the computer, so that you can find out and report your sample statistics and, if the level of measurement of your data permits, the inferred parameters of your population. Once you have learned this language, you will be able to judge the appropriateness of the use of statistics in your own and other peoples' work. You will recognize the many instances in which claims of statistical significance should be ignored because it is irrelevant.

Many of the statistics we use are descriptive, that is, they give us a picture of something.

"The average household in the United States has 2.8 people in it, but for Mexico this figure is 3.5."

This tells us that families in Mexico have more children, or that they include more people under one roof. The number of statistics about one person can be very large, and the whole world can be summed up using one statistic[1]:

5,000,000,000

Descriptive statistics are very useful. They tell us how much to order for our shelves if we run a business:

"For the last two years, we've sold 550 a week, on the average."
or, "I'd say we sell three to five units a day, at this time of year."

They tell us where we stand in relation to everybody else:

"The median gross income for 1979 was about $12,000 a year."
or, "About half of our customers purchase the light-duty models; the others go for the heavy-duty rigs."

Descriptive statistics can tell us what is most popular:

"The big sellers are the classes held in the middle of the day; you have to twist arms to get them into the 8 A.M.'s or the Friday afternoons—only 10 percent preregister for them."
or, "Twice as many people visited the monkeys and the otters than visited any other animal in the zoo."

Other types of descriptive statistics give us the extent of something and the pattern of its distribution:

"Our folks range from 5 feet to about 6 feet, 2 inches, but you'll find two-thirds of them are between 5 feet, 6 inches and 5 feet, 11 inches."

Sometimes we want to know how typical a statistic is of the class of items we're interested in or have sampled. This is where inferential statistics are useful. They tell us whether our sample statistic reflects the parameter of the population from which the sample was taken. For example, if you look at something for a long time, you know what's usual and what's unusual. If you're planning to buy a meal ticket, you hope the excellent sample meal you ate at the cafeteria is one of the "usual" rather than the "unusual." If you had charted the twenty-one weekly meals for the previous school year and sampled them randomly, you would have more confidence in the typicality of your sample. You would infer, or conclude, what your future experience would be from the sample experience.

We often need to estimate parameters because we do not have the time or the money to examine the whole population of something. This was the focus of our discussions in Chapter 3, so you are familiar with it. Now we are going to take it one step further and see how inferential statistics are used to estimate not only parameters, but the degree of assurance we have that those estimates are correct.

We shall begin with descriptive statistics, which are of two types: the measures of central tendency, or clustering, and the measures of dispersion, or distribution. After we have gone over descriptive statistics, we shall discuss inferential statistics. The chapter concludes with an evaluation of the use of statistics in social science.[2]

Descriptive Statistics

Descriptive statistics pull together the data in your sample to draw a numerical picture, which can be represented to the reader in tables, charts, or graphs, as we have seen in earlier chapters. The measures of central tendency reveal how the cases are grouped and what is typical about them, and the measures of dispersion reveal how far they are scattered and in what proportions.

Measures of Central Tendency

The **measures of central tendency** are the mean, the median, and the mode. Respectively, they tell you what the average case is like, which is the middle one, and which is the most frequent.

The Mean   The mean, or arithmetic mean, is what is popularly called the **average**. There are other "means" and other "averages" in use, but in social science reports, you can assume that "the mean" refers to the arithmetic mean.

The mean is computed by adding all the units together and dividing by the number of units. Since you have to add and divide, you have to have at least interval level data in order to use the mean. For a small number of cases, the computation is simplicity itself:

$$\bar{X} = \Sigma N \div N, \text{ or}$$

the mean equals the sum of N divided by the number of N.

Suppose there are 10 children, and their ages are 5, 3, 4½, 7, 7, 6, 3½, 5, 6, and 4. Adding these figures together gives you 51, or ΣN (the sum of N). Since your N (number of cases) is 10, you divide 51 by 10 to get the mean: 5.1 years. Another way to put it in statistical language is:

$$\bar{X} = \frac{\Sigma(fX)}{N}$$

which says the same thing as the first equation.

Note: A formula is a mathematical statement. An equation is a statement of equality between what is on the left side of an equal sign [=] and what is on the right side of it.

In the second equation we see a new symbol (f) and a new spatial relationship, that is, one statistical "word" is above a line and another below. No matter how long you've been away from school, you once learned that the number above the line is divided by the number below it. The symbol ½ means that one is divided by two. The principle still applies. The expression

$$\frac{\Sigma(fX)}{N}$$

is $\Sigma(fX)$ divided by N. The new symbol, f, means frequency. The combination, $\Sigma(fX)$, means all of the frequencies of X added together.

When you are solving an equation, you substitute regular numbers for the symbols as you compute them and than add, subtract, multiply, or divide them to get the answer. You then have a symbol, $\bar{X}$, on one side and a number, 5.1, on the other. This example is a very simple one and can be done in the head, but in actual research practice you'll have more cases and may find it useful to compute the mean in a more formal manner. Here's an example:

X	f	fX
1	3	3
2	6	12
3	5	15
4	8	32
5	5	25
6	7	42
7	4	28
8	6	48
9	2	18
10	5	50
	$N = 51$	$\Sigma(fX) = 273$

$$\bar{X} = 273/51, \text{ or } 5.39$$

The sum of the f column is the N, or number of cases, since the column shows the frequency of each score. The sum of the fX column is the sum of all the scores for the entire sample, since the column shows the frequency of each score multiplied by its value. The X column shows these values. (When two symbols appear side by side with no intervening instruction, they are to be multiplied. Intervening instructions include Σ, which means the sum of; familiar signs such as $+$, $-$, $\times$, and $\div$; the slash, /, which also means divide and parentheses, ( ), which tell you that anything within them is to be computed before using it in another computation.)

This example has been presented in great detail to familiarize you with some of the statistical symbols you will see often. Many discussions of statistics begin with a reassuring paragraph or two telling the reader not to be afraid of the subject. Judging from this writer's experience as a student, this is usually ineffective. It may be a more useful approach to be anxious enough to review "baby" math to reassure yourself. None of the statistical material described here requires more than elementary math. Respect the complexity of the subject enough to approach it carefully and slowly; like the computer commands, statistics have to be precise and conform to rigid rules. It's another game, like football or bridge, that is mystifying to the novice, but can be learned if you give it your attention and time.

The mean is very useful in longitudinal studies because it helps you spot trends. Comparing the mean at a former time with the mean now tells you which way the trend is going: "The average family size is going down," or "the average age of college students is going up." However, the mean is greatly affected by extreme scores. Suppose that group of children we mentioned earlier has one additional person (teacher) who is 45. This would raise the mean group age to 8.7, a misleading figure, since none of the children is that old. If we want to know something about how the cases are grouped, we look at the median and the mode.

The Median   The **median** is also an "average," strictly speaking. It divides the sample in half so that you know the point at which half the cases will be higher and half will be lower.

You have to have ordinal data to use the median. You cannot find the middle unless you can arrange the cases in order, from the lowest to the highest, or vice versa. If we arrange the children in the order of their ages, we get 3, 3½, 4, 4½, 5, 5, 6, 6, 7, and 7. To divide the group in half, we count to the fifth oldest child and draw a line between the fifth and sixth:

3, 3½, 4, 4½, 5 | 5, 6, 6, 7, 7

Our median is 5 years of age. If the numbers on either side are different, the median is the point halfway between them. If the number of cases is uneven, the middle value will be the median. The median is a position average.

The median can be determined for grouped data also. Although it is not within the scope of this book to teach you these statistical methods, we can say that the general idea of finding the median for grouped data is to determine which interval the middle case is in and compute its exact position by formula.

The median is useful in two instances: You may have ordinal data and can't use the mean. You wouldn't want to use the mean if you had reason to believe your sample includes a few extreme cases, because the mean is greatly affected by extreme cases. For example, the mean income of a group of people would be greatly affected if some millionaires were in the group. The median cannot be affected by extreme scores.

The median is also used with grouped data when the last group is open-ended, as in the following example:

"Please state your annual income before taxes."

_____ $10,000 or under

_____ $10,001 to 15,000

_____ $15,001 to 20,000

_____ $20,001 to 30,000

_____ over $30,000

Although you can average the category frequencies for interval data, you can't average a category without upper and lower limits, so you would have to treat these data as ordinal.

If you have nominal data, you can't use the mean or the median, but you can use the mode.

The Mode The **mode** tells you what the most frequent finding was. It is also sometimes called the **probability average** because it is the score most likely to be encountered in any distribution. Suppose you had the following data:

Employed, full-time	48
Employed, seasonal	67
Employed, part-time	26
Unemployed	33
Unemployable	9

The mode would be "Employed, seasonal." Sometimes you have more than one mode, referred to as a _bimodal distribution_. If several candidates run for office and the top two are tied, that would be a bimodal distribution.

Although nominal data permit you to use only the mode as the measure of central tendency, ordinal permit the use of the mode and the median. Interval and ratio data permit the use of all three measures: the mode, the

FIGURE 10.1   **A bar graph showing a hypothetical distribution of dice throws**

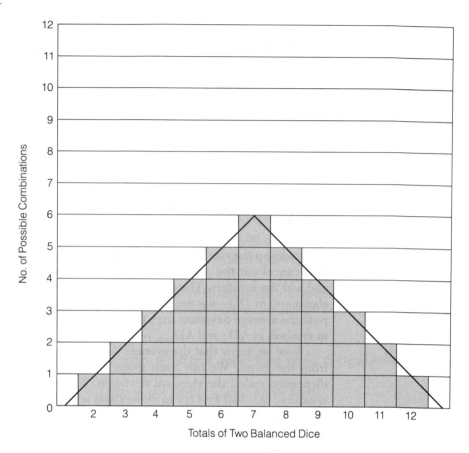

If pure chance is operating, there will be many deviations from the mean, or errors, and the scores will eventually form the bell-shaped normal curve of error. It is called the "normal curve of error" because it is formed by the deviations. The name has been shortened to the "normal curve," which is too bad, since many people think it means that everything is distributed in this pattern. Nothing could be further from the truth. Many characteristics of our world do not happen by chance. The more the social control of anything, for example, the less likely it is to show a distribution approximating the normal curve of error. This leads to an interesting paradox. The cruder our measures of social events, the more error there will be and the more likely that their distribution will be "normal."[3]

In the real world, social events show a decidedly lopsided, or skewed, distribution. For example, income is by no means distributed in the pattern of the curve. Neither is education, prestige, or family size. If you have sampled a population for which you can assume a distribution in the normal curve

FIGURE 10.2   **The normal curve of error and some frequently observed distributions**

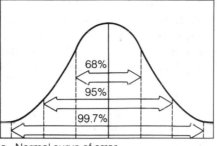

a. Normal curve of error

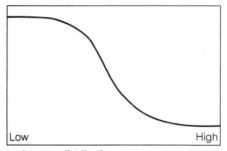

b. Income distribution

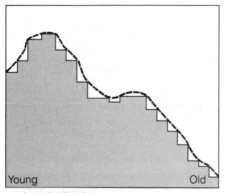

c. Age distribution

pattern, you can use a higher level of statistical tests on it to determine how likely it is that your sample could have been an average one.

Look at the picture of the normal curve of error in Figure 10.2. There is a measure of dispersion that reveals how far you have to deviate from the mean to include specific percentages of the scores. It is called the standard deviation.

The Standard Deviation   The **standard deviation** from the mean of the normal curve is based on the squared deviations from the mean. Each deviation is **squared**, or multiplied by itself, and the squares are totaled to make what is called the sum of squares. This is sometimes symbolized Σx^2 and sometimes SS. If you divide the sum of squares by the number of observations, you get the **mean square**, or average squared deviation. This is the value referred to as the **variance** and is written σ^2 or s^2. Michael A. Malec points out that there is a bit of confusion in the writing of symbols among statisticians. Usually, Greek letters are used for population values (parameters) and our familiar Roman letters for sample values. Also, N is used for the population and n for the sample. Unfortunately, although it is quite useful, this rule is not reliably followed.[4]

Once you have the average squared deviation from the mean, or variance, you can use it to get the standard deviation. All you do is find the square root of the variance. The standard deviation is written σ or s, which is simply the variance without the superscript, since it has been "unsquared."

With the standard deviation you specify the distance you have to go along the continuum in both directions from the mean in order to include 68 percent of the sample ("1 standard deviation"), 95 percent of the sample ("2 standard deviations"), and 99.7 percent of the sample ("3 standard deviations"). If you go in only one direction from the mean, you get half of each specified here.

There is a score that can be computed to express in standard deviation units how far a particular sample score lies from the mean. This descriptive score is called a **z-score** and is computed by using a table of proportions and a simple formula.

Using the measures of dispersion in your description enables you to describe your sample's distribution and to make easily apparent whether the scores were bunched together with little variance or spread out evenly to the far reaches of the range. These descriptive statistics, including those of central tendency, are used in the majority of reports when the level of measurement permits. They do not tell you anything about the external validity, or representativeness of your sample, however. For that you have to turn to inferential statistics.

Inferential Statistics

Suppose someone said "I took a sample of 500 people in River Heights, selecting randomly, and found that they had a mean income of $23,000 a year, with a standard deviation of $2,500." This tells you that a little more than two-thirds of the sample had incomes between $20,500 and $25,500 (one standard deviation in each direction from the average), and that 95 percent of them had incomes between $18,000 and $28,000 (two standard deviations).

Furthermore, 99.7 percent of them had incomes falling between $15,500 and $30,500. There were not very many poor or very many rich people in the sample, even though the lowest and the highest figures are $15,000 apart. You also know that their average income was close to the United States median for 1980. To say anything about River Heights, however, you need to know whether this sample was typical of the community. How much confidence can you place in the external validity of your finding? To determine this, we use inferential statistics.

This section will review the main bases for statistical inference, the principles of sampling, the test for the difference between sample means, and the principal measures of association now in use. Although space does not permit lengthy examinations and computational examples, a thorough understanding of the principles should leave you prepared to cope with the important decision about when and how to use inference.

Probability and Hypothesis Testing

To understand what you are doing when you use inferential statistics, commonly referred to as **testing for significance**, you need to acquaint yourself with the notion of probability and the logic followed when testing a hypothesis.

The Predictability of Chance   Look at Figure 10.1 again. If you throw those two dice a thousand times and get "snake-eyes" twenty-eight times, would you conclude that your sample is a typical one? Every time you throw those dice you can get one of thirty-six equally likely outcomes; therefore, your chance, or **probability**, of getting a single outcome is one in thirty-six, or 1/36. Since there's only one way to get "snake-eyes," you have a 1/36 probability of doing it in any one throw. You can express this as a percentage (2.7 percent) or as a proportion (.027).

Back to our example. If you get twenty-eight "snake-eyes" out of a thousand throws, your percentage is 2.8 percent, which is very close to the probability of that outcome. You would probably feel, therefore, that the dice are fair. Suppose, though, you get "snake-eyes" only once? This is only a tenth of 1 percent, or .001 expressed as a proportion. This is a very unusual result, unless the dice are loaded. If your hypothesis is that the dice are not loaded, you would not be very confident that your hypothesis is correct.

The Null Hypothesis   The hypothesis just suggested—that the dice are not loaded—is an example of a **null hypothesis**. It is a prediction that the population of events follow the normal curve of error. If your observation indicates that the events do *not* follow the normal curve of error, you have disproved the null hypothesis and can say that you have statistically significant results.

However, you must decide how far away from the typical your observation will have to be before you will call it significant. (The "typical" can be the mean, median, or mode because they are identical for the normal curve.) This brings us to the concept of the **region of rejection**, or **alpha**.

Alpha   All the varieties of outcome represented on the normal curve are possible, but some are highly improbable, or rare. You run the risk of making a mistake, therefore, if you get a rare outcome and decide it's not part of a normal curve but represents a significant departure from it. After all, it could be the least probable outcome for that curve. If it is and if you reject the null hypothesis that it's part of the curve, you are making a **Type I error**, that is, rejecting the null hypothesis when it is really true.

On the other hand, if you decide that your observation, though unusual, is part of the curve, you don't reject the null hypothesis, but maybe it isn't part of the curve. Maybe it represents something that didn't happen by chance. You've then made a **Type II error**, that is, accepting the null hypothesis when it is really false.

When you decide to reject the null hypothesis (symbolized as H_0) if the observation falls at a certain distance from the mean of the curve, you identify the point at which you regard the observation as statistically significant. This is usually the extreme 5 percent of the continuum at one or both ends, or **tails**, of the curve. Sometimes it is smaller: the extreme 1 percent, for instance. If your computations show that your observation falls far out on the tails of the curve, you say that you have significance at the .05 level or whatever it is. You are specifying the level of risk of making a Type I error. This level of risk is referred to as alpha, or α, the region of rejection of the null hypothesis.

The test that you use to determine the probability of your observation varies with the level of measurement of your data. The figure you compute that reveals the rarity of the observation is called a **test statistic**. We've already mentioned one of them: z. We shall get to others, but first we shall look again at sampling and its implications.

Sampling Distribution and Estimation

As defined in Chapter 3, a population is a number of people or things all in the same category, and a sample drawn from it is assumed to be typical of it if the sample is drawn by the rules of random selection, which give each unit an equal chance of being chosen. Now we have seen that a random distribution (the normal curve of error) has a predictable pattern and that some sample observations are more likely than others. If you think of your sample as one throw of the dice, you can understand that drawing all the possible samples from the population and plotting them on a graph would give you a normal curve, with the most common samples in the middle and the rarest ones at the ends. We can use this idea to estimate the distance from the sample mean of our sample and to compute the standard deviation of the distribution of sample means. Our estimate is called a **confidence interval** because we specify a distance along the curve within which we think our sample falls, and the new standard deviation is called the **standard error**.

You can now see why your sample has to be random. If it is not random, you cannot assume that it is part of a normal curve of samples, and therefore truly representative of the population from which it is drawn. Notice that we are now talking about a normal curve in the middle of which we would like our sample to fall, whereas earlier we were talking about a normal curve at the ends of which we wanted our observations to fall. In short, we want our sample to be typical of the population, but we also want our population's behavior to be unusual enough to reflect some influence other than chance. Therefore, we test to see if our sample is typical, and we also test to see if our observation is unusual.

One more point before we turn to the question of testing for the difference between sample means. If you increase the sample size, you cover more of the population, and, therefore, your standard error becomes smaller. You can see the logic of this if you carry it to a ridiculous extreme. Should your sample be increased to cover the whole population, your standard error would be nonexistent. This is why increasing the sample size increases the reliability of the result, as was mentioned in Chapter 3. If you use a very small sample, you have to realize that your analysis is on shakier ground than it would be if you used a large sample.

Very often in social science we want to know if two populations are different, but our only evidence is two samples, one of each population. We have to find a way to judge whether the two population means are the same by manipulating the statistics from the samples.

Testing for the Difference Between Sample Means

Testing for the difference between sample means involves understanding two approaches: the t-test and the analysis of variance.

Student's t "Student" was the pen name of W. S. Gosset, a brewer, who developed this test of means.[5] It deals with the problem of how to determine whether two samples reflect two different population means, rather than the sampling error of one population. In other words, if I find a difference between the incomes of the native-born and the incomes of the foreign-born, is it a real difference between two distinct groups, or is it a fluke? The **t-test** results in a test statistic that tells you the statistical significance of the difference between the means of the two samples. Naturally you have to calculate the means first, and then you take the difference between them and divide it by the standard error of the difference. The answer reveals the risk of a Type I error. You can compute "*t*" for small samples and for matched samples as well.

If you have more than two sample means, the use of the *t*-test runs the risk of getting statistical significance by chance, since *t*-test results occur in their own normal curve.

The Analysis of Variance The **analysis of variance** is popularly referred to as **ANOVA**, an acronym of its official title. It refers to statistical computation of the variance of each sample mean to see if the means are really different or only different samples of the same population. The variance among the samples should be great. The variance within each sample should be small. The ratio of the first variance to the second results in a test statistic called the *F*-ratio, which can be evaluated by the use of a table, and which reveals once more the risk of a Type I error.

Very often we want to know what relationship two variables have to each other. Following Robert S. Weiss, we can say that "two qualities are associated when the distribution of values of the one differs for different values of the other."[6] The issue for inferential statistics is: How do you know the strength of the association between two variables? The measures of association are used to assess this strength.

The Measures of Association

Before trying to measure association you must consider what level of measurement your data are on; that will determine what measures of association you may use. We shall consider them in order.

Measuring Association with Nominal Data   Percentages are a **measure of association**. If there is not any percentage difference between the categories of an independent variable, we conclude there is not any association between it and the dependent variable, as in the following example:

	Young People (%)	Old People (%)
Voted for A	60	60
Voted for B	36	36
Voted for C	4	4

In this example we could say that age was not associated with variation in the voting behavior of the sample. Percentages are very useful and often used. However, it would be more useful to know how much of a difference in pattern you would need in order to have a meaningful difference. The test for this is called chi-square (pronounced Kigh) and its symbol is χ^2.

The chi-square test takes the marginals from an ordinary bivariate table with any number of cells and multiplies the row and column total for each cell. For the age and voting behavior example just given, you would multiply the total number of young people by the total number of people voting for A to get the figure for the upper left-hand cell. The next step is to divide that figure by the *N* for the sample depicted. Now you have the expected frequency for that cell. The expected frequency is the number that would be in it if the proportions of the totals, or marginals, were distributed evenly throughout the table. If 50 percent of the sample approves of something, then 50 percent of each subdivision should approve of it.

In most distributions, the numbers in the cells don't come out in the frequencies indicated by the margins, but rather are distributed in a variety of ways:

	Distribution 1			Distribution 2		
	Young	Old	Total	Young	Old	Total
Yes	65	40	105	25	80	105
No	20	40	60	60	0	60
Totals	85	80	165	85	80	165

Notice that both distributions have the same marginals but not the same cell frequencies. If you multiply 105 (the "yes" row total) by 85 (the "young" column total) and divide it by 165 (the sample total), you get 54.09 as the expected frequency for that upper left-hand cell. This means that a "chance" pattern would have resulted in 54 *young* people saying *yes* for this sample.

Once you know the first figure and the marginals for a **fourfold table**, you can easily figure out the rest, because they cannot be anything other than what will add up to the totals. For that reason only the first cell in a fourfold table can vary. We say the table has one **degree of freedom**. Each column and each row you add increases the degrees of freedom by one.

When you determine the expected frequencies for all the cells in a table, you proceed to compute the formula, which requires squaring each deviation of the observed frequency from the expected frequency, cell by cell. Once you have finished multiplying and dividing according to the formula, you look up your result in a chi-square table to find out if it is statistically significant. There are some variations on this for various sized tables and some ways to compare one chi-square with another; the latter comparison can't be done without further computation unless the Ns are exactly the same for the samples being compared.

Another well-known test is lambda. For this you use the modes of the variables. It involves predicting the cell frequencies from the marginals and then judging how wrong you were. This is called a proportional reduction of error (PRE) model. Another model is Goodman and Kruskal's tau (τ), which is more sensitive in some cases and is not based on the mode.

Measuring Association with Ordinal Level Data   Once you can rank variables, you can use what is called **pairing** to see if the ranks are similar. It involves counting the number of similar pairs and the number of dissimilar pairs and computing by formula to see how closely they are associated. For this you can use measures called gamma, Kendall's tau (in three variations), and Somers's *d*.

An older and better-known ordinal measure is Spearman's rank-order correlation coefficient, rho (ρ). It uses differences between ranks to compute a statistic that is then evaluated via a table to determine significance.

Note: If you have one ordinal level variable and one nominal level variable, you can't use ordinal measures. You always use the measures appropriate to the lower level variable of the two.

Measuring Association with Interval or Ratio Data   If you have interval or ratio data, you can use the Pearson product-moment correlation coefficient (r). Now you can determine how much variation you can expect in one variable, given a specific amount of variation in the other. It's more exact than the other measures because we have more exact data to work with. The data are transformed into z-scores, and the Pearson formula is employed to get the statistic called r. If you graph the scores and draw a straight line with the smallest possible distances between it and the score locations, the slope of the line will be equivalent to the r for the relationship between the two variables you are plotting.

Pearson's r also indicates the direction of the correlation. When we say that something is positively correlated with something else, we mean they go up and down together; when we say that something is negatively, or inversely, correlated with something else, we mean that when one goes up, the other goes down.

Thus far in this discussion of measures of association we have been talking about the association between two variables. Now we turn our attention to the possible statistical tools for multivariate data sets, that is, **multivariate measures of association**.

Multivariate Measures of Association   For more than two variables, you can use **elaboration** of the tabular percentaging procedure. This was illustrated in Chapter 9 when a control variable was introduced and subdivided the independent variable in the tables. As you have seen, this can result in striking changes in the original relationship. The original pattern of association is referred to as the **zero-order association**, and after the control variable is brought in, the new patterns are called **conditional associations**.

There are formulae for partial r, partial tau (Kendall's), and partial gamma that allow you to see what the relationships look like after you remove one variable's influence. This is called **partial correlation**. Almost opposite is **multiple correlation**, which uses r, now written R, to compute the relationship between the dependent variable and two or more other variables simultaneously.

If you are going to do research and are ready to choose statistical treatments of your data, you should consult Delbert C. Miller's *Handbook of Research Design and Social Measurement*.[7] Before you do, however, be sure that you understand the purpose behind your choice.

Two Kinds of Significance

When researchers use descriptive statistics, they are trying to sum up the data. Inferential statistics are used to appraise the relationships in the data and to determine how likely it is that they occurred by chance. This is called statistical significance and association, and it can be very enlightening. It is, however, not the only kind of significance that social scientists care about and its use is invalid for most social science data.

The use of statistics has come to have a purpose other than enlightenment or clarification. Perhaps because we are in awe of math and because statistics uses numbers and symbols in formulae, the use of them lends prestige to a research report and gives credibility to its findings. Therefore, scholars who want to look scholarly are under pressure to include statistics—especially tests of significance, or tests using inferential significance to spot the unusual finding. This is a shame because it clouds the issues. A research report, which should be critically examined and called into question on the basis of its goal, question, sample, data collection methods, or consequences, is discussed only on the basis of its statistical test results. Since those who are capable of handling numbers easily enjoy a measure of immunity from criticism, much research incompetence can be obscured by the protective covering of a report bristling with as many numbers as a bus schedule.

Another issue that is clouded by the overuse of statistical tests is the difference between statistical significance and social significance. If I drive away from an automobile showroom and the transmission falls out of my new car, I really don't care if this is a typical occurrence. I care that it happened at all. A large part of social prediction and behavioral analysis is based on informed opinion, judgment, logic, experience, and observation. Although the statistical significance of a result may be great, the social significance may be minor. Pitirim Sorokin warned against the danger of dividing a meaningful system in two parts and then trying to explain part B by looking at part A. Sorokin was talking about tendencies in psychology and sociology, but his book is well worth reading regardless of your field of study.[8] The book explores the processes of thinking, understanding, and reflecting.

The social significance of a finding is not the same as its statistical significance. The test of a finding, or an idea, is whether it fits in the real world. Sorokin held that there are far too many factors to make the use of factorial analysis practical and that, in any case, no knowledge is possible without experience and intuition.

Statistical significance is commonly reported for highly questionable data. A colleague has alerted me to a 1984 Census Bureau report which cites a 12-minute-per-week difference in the self-reported study time for two racial groups, claiming statistical significance for this finding. Here you have an item that is very hard to estimate—how much time has passed—subjected to precise arithmetical summation (the mean). The difference in the amount of time estimated, less than 2 minutes a day, is trivial. It has no SOCIAL significance at all, even if we assume that the estimates were accurate, a highly dubious assumption. A closer look at the report reveals that the subjects were aged 3 to 34, casting more doubt on their "study time" estimates, and that there were 60,000 of them. Because, with a sample this large, a finding of "statistical significance" is very likely, this report is not only worthless, but misleading to the public. It implies that there is an important difference between the two groups, and the average reader will not realize the flaws in it.[9]

There are many points in the handling of data where conditions will make it impossible to use statistical inference validly. Researchers use statistical inference all the time, anyway, for reasons including those previously mentioned and through ignorance. To use descriptive or inferential statistics validly, one must choose the measure according to the level of data in hand, and that data must have been collected randomly, or the result isn't generalizable anyway. It can, in any case, only be generalized to the population from which the sample was drawn. Scales and indexes are arbitrary and cannot be precise measurements, since personality traits, attitudes, and opinions are not measurable. One can do no better than count the yeses and nos and say what percentage or proportion they are of the categories. To pretend more is to deceive. Figures can and do lie. Many statisticians are now protesting the misuse of these procedures. They are saying that this particular emperor has no clothes, and they are correct.

The issue of social significance is also very important. As in the study time example already given, a report of statistical significance implies a social significance as well. This is very often unfounded. No relationship at all between sex or race of worker and average remuneration would be highly socially significant, would it not?

To sum up, consider these five points:

1. Much of what we study cannot be measured.
2. Statistical significance bears no relation to social significance.
3. All outcomes have some probability of occurring and can be said to have happened by chance.
4. Statistics will not improve a poorly conceived and designed study.
5. Social behavior is the result of rational thought that is in response to experience and conditions and that is influenced by values. Whether a behavioral finding is likely or not isn't the issue. We need to understand and to cope.

There are reasons for using statistical methods and reasons against using them. If you take pains to ascertain *if* and *which* tests are appropriate for your project, they can be worthwhile to you and to your readers. They are not substitutes for written analysis. Sanford Labovitz and Robert Hagedorn put it very well: "Statistics . . . have appropriate uses. Not to use them when they are appropriate is silly. To use statistics when they are not appropriate is equally ridiculous."[10]

Summary and Conclusion

Statistics describe and evaluate data. They constitute a special language using symbols, numbers, and formulae. We often use statistics in daily life, sometimes to describe and sometimes to tell us where we stand in relation to everybody else.

Descriptive statistics include the measures of central tendency, or clustering, and the measures of dispersion, or distribution pattern. They provide an idea of the shape of the data sample. Inferential statistics include probability testing and measures of association. They tell you how rare your findings are, whether you are really measuring samples from different populations, and how strongly two things are related to each other.

There are a number of statistical tests and measures for each level of data. You must be careful not to use any but those appropriate for the level of the data you have. If you have two levels, use the tests for the lower one. Do not succumb to the pressure to use statistics if their use is not appropriate. Although statistical significance is important as a way of evaluating data, social significance and understanding are much more important.

Main Points

1. A statistic is a number that reports a fact; statistics is a language made up of these number-facts.

2. A sample statistic reports a fact about a sample or a parameter about a population.

3. We use statistics every day to describe the world.

4. Descriptive statistics include the measures of central tendency and the measures of dispersion.

5. Measures of central tendency are the mean, or average; the median, or middle; and the mode, or most frequent.

6. Measures of dispersion are the range, or distance from most to least; the average deviation, or typical distance of scores from the mean; and the standard deviation, or distance from the mean that will include specific proportions of the distribution.

7. The normal curve is the distribution of errors from the mean if the distribution is random.

8. Inferential statistics include testing for the difference between sample means; using the t-test and the analysis of variance; and the measures of association.

9. You can measure association in the following ways: for nominal data with chi-square or lambda; for ordinal data with various pairing measures, including Spearman's rho; for interval and ratio data with Pearson's r. Although there are other tests, these are the most common.

10. For multivariate analysis you can use elaboration, partial correlation, or multiple correlation.

11. Statistical significance is only an optional part of an analysis of data. The social significance is even more important. Statistics will not improve faulty data, nor will statistical tests add precision to measurement. Many variables cannot be quantitatively described.

Typical Test Statistics

chi-square (χ^2)	Pearson's r
F-ratio	Somers's d
gamma	Spearman's rho
Goodman and Kruskal's tau	t
Kendall's tau	z-score
lambda	

Typical Symbols

α—alpha

$AD_{\bar{x}}$—average deviation from the mean

AD_{Mdn}—average deviation from the median

χ^2—chi-square

( )—compute within before using in computation without

/—divide what is to the right into what is to the left

f—frequency

$\bar{X}$—mean

R—multiple correlation

H_0—null hypothesis

N—number of cases in population

n—number of cases in sample

r—Pearson's correlation coefficient

X, x—raw score

ρ—rho

rho—Spearman's rho—rank correlation

s—standard deviation of a sample

σ—standard deviation of a population

Σ—the sum of

ΣX^2—the sum of squares

SS—the sum of squares

τ—tau

t—t-test

s^2—variance of a sample

σ^2—variance of a population

Notes

1. *Popline* (Washington, D.C.: World Population Institute), Vol. 10, June 1988, p. 1.

2. The organization of this chapter generally follows the organization of Michael A. Malec, *Essential Statistics for Social Research* (Philadelphia: Lippincott, 1977).

3. Joseph Fashing and Ted Goertzel, "The Myth of the Normal Curve: A Theoretical Critique and Examination of Its Role in Teaching and Research," *Humanity and Society* 5, no. 1 (1981): 18–23.

4. Malec, *Essential Statistics*, p. 48n.

5. Malec, *Essential Statistics*, pp. 92, 93.

6. Robert S. Weiss, *Statistics in Social Research* (New York: Wiley, 1968), p. 158.

7. Delbert C. Miller, *Handbook of Research Design and Social Measurement*, 3rd ed. (New York: McKay, 1977), pp. 143–205.

8. Pitirim Sorokin, *Fads and Foibles in Modern Sociology* (Chicago: Regnery, 1956).

9. This example is discussed in Part 1 of a paper in preparation by Chamont W. H. Wang, "On the Scientific and Non-Scientific Practices of Statistical Inferences," Trenton State College, 1987.

10. Sanford Labovitz and Robert Hagedorn, *Introduction to Social Research*, 3rd ed. (New York: McGraw-Hill, 1981), p. 124.

Exercises

Since computation was mostly excluded from these statistical overviews, you are not going to have to use formulae for these exercises. Instead, Exercise 10.1 asks you to look at a list of variables and suggest what measures of central tendency and dispersion you think are appropriate for them. This is a small test of your comprehension of these measures.

Exercise 10.2 asks you to look at a published article and see what you think of the statistical treatment of the variables. This does not require any knowledge of formulae or computational techniques, but is rather an exercise in appraisal.

Exercise 10.1   *Descriptive statistics*

Instructions: Reread the section on descriptive statistics in this chapter. For each variable listed below, identify the level of measurement it is at and suggest what measure(s) of central tendency or dispersion might be appropriate to use.

	Level of Measurement	Appropriate Measures
1. Birth order (oldest to youngest)		
2. Weekly income (dollars)		
3. Political party membership		
4. Marital status		
5. Age (years)		
6. Occupation		
7. Hours worked per week		
8. Job satisfaction		
9. Level of education		
10. Years of schooling		

Exercise 10.2   *Critique*

Instructions: Select an article with statistics in it and read the article. Answer the following questions after giving a full citation here:

_____

_____

1. What was the research question?

2. What was one hypothesis?

3. List the independent, dependent, and intervening variables and note their levels of measurement. Look at the article again and note, for each variable, what measure of central tendency and/or dispersion the author(s) used, and whether you would have used the same one or a different one.

    Independent variable:

    Level of measurement:

    Measure(s) of central tendency or dispersion used:

    Opinion:

Independent variable:

Level of measurement:

Measure(s) of central tendency or dispersion used:

Opinion:

Intervening variable:

Level of measurement:

Measure(s) of central tendency or dispersion used:

Opinion:

4. Comment on the article's clarity and use of descriptive statistics:

CHAPTER 11

Coming To Conclusions

Front Matter
Title Page
Table of Contents
List of Illustrations
Preface
Text
The Problem
Literature Review
Research Question and the Hypotheses
Research Design
Data Collection and Results
Conclusion
Back Matter
Appendixes
The Bibliography
Reminders
Maintaining Accuracy
Mechanics
Summary and Conclusion
Main Points
Notes
Exercise
Exercise 11.1 Critique

Now we've come to the goal of every research project: drawing conclusions about the topic on the basis of the data we've collected, in the context of the entire study. Now we can write the research report, which is a lot more than simply presenting the collected data.

1. We must go back behind it and review the problem with which we began. What was it we started out to investigate? What questions did we have about the topic?

2. We must go all around it and connect it to the surrounding body of existing knowledge. Who has looked at this topic already? (We have reviewed the literature before.) What about our findings in the light of their findings and conclusions? Do our data support them or not, and in what respects?

3. We must go out in front of it and sketch its implications for the future. What are the implications of our findings? What new questions are raised?[1]

To do this coherently, you follow an established order in presenting your work. A research report should be organized into three main divisions: front matter, text, and back matter. It is similar to a published textbook in this respect. **Front matter** informs the reader of the topic and how you've arranged the report. It includes the title page (with appropriate source data), the table of contents, the list(s) of illustrations, and possibly a preface. The **text**, or body of the report, includes the statement of the problem and the research question; a careful survey of the existing literature; a description of the study design, development, and execution; a presentation of the data; and conclusions about the study's significance. **Back matter** is the reference material that supplements the pages in the text. It includes any word lists, indexes (subject or author), appendixes, and bibliography.

Because research reports differ in complexity and type, they also differ in the elements they need to have. Yours may not need a list of illustrations, preface, word list, index, or appendix; however, all the other items named earlier are mandatory. It will help if you prepare an outline, which is essentially a list of what you will include in your report, in its final order. If you also have to prepare an abstract of your study, the outline will serve as a framework for it. The outline is useful to keep you from rambling in your discussion or forgetting some vital section. Keep it tacked up in front of you as you write.

Even though the outline is in the final order of your report, you don't have to work in that order. You might find it more comfortable, for example, to start by writing up a statement of your hypothesis and method, then what your findings were, and then your analysis of their meaning. Once you have at least a first draft of that, you can read it over and write the statement of the problem and the review of the literature, which will be the opening two sections of your final report. With those done, you can reread the whole thing, in order, taking notes for your conclusion as you go past the relevant bits. Writing the conclusion will be much easier with the whole thing fresh in your mind and then you have nothing but the mechanical things to do, such as numbering and naming pages and sections, making lists of references, typing, etc. All research reports should include a title page and a table of contents. A list of illustrations and a preface are optional.

Here, the sections will be presented in their final order, so feel free to skip around as you work on your report. See Appendix B, Report Writing Mechanics, for help with technical matters.

Front Matter

The first item the reader sees when examining your report is the title page. Its clarity is crucial to the capturing of the reader's interest. It includes the title, the author's name and affiliation, the date of issue, and the place of issue.

Title Page

An accurate, understandable capsule description is what you are aiming for here. You want to tell the reader what the topic of the report is and possibly the mode of investigation. It can be catchy, but not misleading. "Card Sharks and Poor Fish: An Investigation into Gambling Abuse" would be acceptable, but "What Have You Got Up Your Sleeve, Buddy?" is a bit too flippant and fails to explain what the report contains. See Appendix C, Proposal Writing, for some special considerations that apply if you are writing an application for grant money.

The title page should include the author's name and affiliation, the date, and the place of issue. If the paper was written for a course of study, that course and the professor's name usually appear on the title page also. When the research was done in partial fulfillment of the requirements for a graduate degree, the prescribed form specified by the institution must be used. Figure 11.1 is such a title page.

Table of Contents

Each section of the report is listed in the table of contents, in order, with the number of the page on which it begins noted in a column at the extreme right. Figure 11.2 is an example of a simple table of contents that includes a list of illustrations and a bibliography in addition to the subsections of the text. Note that the front matter pages are numbered with lowercase roman

FIGURE 11.1   **A title page**

RELIGION AND THE REACTION TO CHRONIC ILLNESS:

JUVENILE DIABETES MELLITUS

A THESIS

SUBMITTED TO THE GRADUATE SCHOOL

OF

RUTGERS—THE STATE UNIVERSITY

BY

JUNE TRUE ALBERT

IN PARTIAL FULFILLMENT OF THE

REQUIREMENTS FOR THE DEGREE

OF

MASTER OF ARTS

NEW BRUNSWICK, NEW JERSEY   MAY, 1966

---

numerals and that the title page counts as "page i," even though the numeral does not appear on it.

The front matter includes a list of illustrations if there are more than four or five figures or tables in the report; otherwise, the figure captions or table titles are simply included in the appropriate places in the table of contents.

F I G U R E   1 1 . 2   **A table of contents**

ii

TABLE OF CONTENTS

**List of
Illustrations**

"Illustrations" may be tables or figures, or you might have both, depending on your topic. Each item is listed by its caption as it appears in the body of the text and with the page number at the right, as in the table of contents. If an illustration encompasses more than one page, the inclusive page numbers are indicated:

"Figure 22.9 Marital status by education   235–239"

A preface is included if you need to supply an explanation of the purpose, organization, or intended audience of the report or if you wish to acknowledge help in writing it.

Preface

The average research report does not need a preface, but you should write one if you need to explain why the report was written:

"This is number three in a series of studies . . ."

How the report is organized:

"Tables and graphs appear as an appendix rather than in the body of the text because . . ."

For whom the report is intended:

"This study was designed especially for the use of those working in minimum-security institutions . . ."

Or if you need to acknowledge assistance:

"The author is especially grateful to . . ."

The preface should be brief and include no extraneous remarks. Reaching the end of the preface, the reader should be prepared to launch into the main text and should have a good picture of what the paper includes and how it will be presented.

Text

The text begins with an introduction to the topic and the problem you chose to pursue.

The Problem

You introduce the topic by explaining what it includes and continue with reasons why you thought it important enough to investigate. You should be able to identify a problem and describe how you will attempt to contribute to a solution. The following is an abridged statement of a research problem as it appeared in a report:

Throughout recorded history people have looked to religion for the answer to life's problems. In part, religion is an explanation of . . . life . . . [A] conflict develops when a person who has been taught to trust in [a] protective God perceives . . . one of his loved ones the victim of an incurable life threat. . . .

[Religion has] placed the suffering individual in one of four categories: the martyr, the witness, the elect, or the sinner. If the victim is able to regard his handicap as a contribution to God's purpose or as a refining process, he will see himself as one of the first three types. If he thinks of his suffering as a punishment, he will consider himself a sinner. Since doctrine prescribes prayer and good behavior for the expiation of sin, he will expect, in the latter case, to be able to remove the punishment.

The object of this . . . study is to discover whether the various orientations toward suffering of the major socioreligious groups in this country result in typical reactions to an incurable and possibly fatal disease striking a family member.

. . . the juvenile diabetic is, nonetheless, normal in appearance and behavior. Society expects him to assume the roles and attempt the goals of the typical American child. Necessity demands a continuing preoccupation with his health. He is at once sick, but not allowed to be sick; well, but not allowed to be well. The child's parents, responsible for his welfare, face a corresponding dilemma. They know they must train their child to assume the management of the disease; they also know they must insure his conformity to its requirements. They must guard against the possibility of overprotecting him, through fear, and of neglecting him, through misjudgment. . . .

There appear to be four orientations that parents as well as children develop to the disease. . . .

This study will attempt to determine what differences and similarities occur in the characteristic response patterns of the major socioreligious groups in the face of the given life threat, taking into account not only group membership, but also family role.[2]

The first two paragraphs of the preceding excerpt constitute the introduction; the rest, which describes the problem to be investigated, specifies the independent variable (religious group membership), the dependent variable (attitude toward disease), and the control (family role).

After you have made the problem clear and have indicated your approach to it, you need to summarize all the relevant literature.

Literature Review

Before reading this section you might want to review the section entitled "Reviewing the Literature" in Chapter 2. During the formulation of your research question and hypotheses, you have written notes on the main issues germane to your topic and have some preliminary summaries of those. Returning to this material now, you write an overview of it as it pertains to your topic and problem, giving special attention to the components of the question you have developed.

If your topic is the relationship between attitudes toward drinking and sex of drinker, for example, you would first talk about the published work on attitudes toward drinking in general, then about the work on attitudes toward males' behavior, including drinking, and attitudes toward females' behavior, including drinking, then about the work on differences in attitudes toward males' and females' behavior in general, then about the work on differences in attitudes toward males' and females' drinking, ending with a discussion of where your work fits in with that of others.

Figure 11.3 is a review of the literature on the juvenile diabetes project cited elsewhere in this chapter and other chapters in this book. It begins with the major work that established the approach to the subject the author wishes to investigate and moves on through the works that explore this viewpoint: varying orientations to life of the major Western religious groups, namely, Catholics, Protestants, and Jews. After citing the authors who establish religion as an important independent variable, the writer goes on to the studies that use it in research on pain and suffering, physical handicap, and stress. The author points out that there are no studies on the exact question she wishes to explore, but she thoroughly examines similar work here. The review ends with an overview of the material on the control variable (family role) and its influence, and a look at some theoretical work by a prominent sociologist on the American attitude toward illness.

Your review of the literature may not be as long as this example, which was submitted as part of a master's thesis; but if you are writing a comprehensive monograph, the literature review may be considerably longer. Since previous work done on a topic may range from almost none to hundreds of items, no simple rule can be specified for the length of a review.

Once you have completed the literature review, you must show how you selected your research question and derived your hypotheses from it.

Research Question and the Hypotheses

Here again, you have already done the spadework for this step, and here you need only to summarize for the report reader what you did when you were deciding what to investigate. Use the work done by others to provide a basis for your predictions, as stated in your hypotheses, as well as for presenting any logical reasons that anticipate a particular result. Figure 11.4 shows the first three pages of such a presentation.

The hypotheses are presented after the reader has been reminded of the study goal, which was presented first, in the statement of the problem at the beginning of the main text. As shown, each hypothesis is numbered and set off from the rest of the text by indentation. Subhypotheses are numbered as indicated: 1a, 1b, and so on.

FIGURE 11.3   **A literature review**

5

II. THEORETICAL FRAMEWORK

Max Weber in his Protestant Ethic and the Spirit of
Capitalism has assumed that the manifest behavior of
the individual is largely governed by the life orientation
characteristic of his religious group.[1] Catholicism, with its
traditionalistic viewpoint, influences the individual to be
obedient to the fate God has ordained for him and to be
disinclined to action designed to change his lot. He regards
his misfortunes as analogous to the sufferings of the saints and
of the martyrs, accepting them as signs of God's favor.
Protestants, because of their commitment to the rationalistic
viewpoint, are influenced to be autonomous. They regard their
fate as the result of their own behavior either conflicting or
harmonizing with God's will. Accordingly, they seek to
change their behavior with the expectation that a change in
their fate will result.

Basing his work on Weber's theory, Gerhard Lenski
examined the life orientations and behavior patterns of a large
sample of the four major socioreligious groups in the country:
white Protestants, white Catholics, Negro Protestants, and

---

[1]Max Weber, The Protestant Ethic and the Spirit of Capitalism,
Tr. by Talcott Parsons (New York: 1958).

FIGURE 11.3   **A literature review,** *continued*

6

Jews. After completing this study, he reached the conclusion that "socioreligious group membership is a variable comparable in importance to class, both with respect to the potency and with respect to the range, or extent, of its influence."[2]   Lenski concludes that contemporary American religious groups are not only associations, but also subcommunities, the carriers of complex subcultures, relevant to nearly all aspects of human life.[3]

Lenski's study supports Weber's hypothesis that Catholics are traditionalistic while Protestants are rationalistic. The Catholic parent is convinced that learning to obey is more important to the child than learning to think for himself.   The Protestant parent is convinced that the answers to life's difficulties are to be found through rational means and that a child should be taught to think for himself, rather than to obey without question.[4]

Will Herberg presents the thesis that religious identification has become the differentiating element in our society and that the three major faiths in America have become

---

[2]Gerhard Lenski, The Religious Factor (New York: 1963), p. 326.

[3]Ibid., p. 344.

[4]Ibid., pp. 222–226.

FIGURE 11.3   **A literature review,** *continued*

7

increasingly Americanized. In brief, his claim is that the optimism and secularism of American life has penetrated the old-country religions, causing them to eliminate many of their "foreign" traits and become more like each other than like their European counterparts. This has resulted in the development of a norm of tolerance and at the same time facilitated the practice of tolerance, since difference is reduced. The American religion, in its three dominant forms, is not only optimistic and open-minded, but also practical. Religion has become a means, rather than an end. Faith is a "technique for getting results."[5]

There are few studies investigating the socioreligious variations in response to pain and suffering although some work examines cultural differences in response to pain, general response to suffering, modes of adjustment to physical handicap, and cultural differences in response to stress.

Zborowski, studying the attitudes of Italians, Jews, Irish, and Yankees to pain, found that Italians placed great emphasis on treatment designed to eliminate suffering but were not interested in understanding the nature of their physical difficulty; Jews took an intense interest in learning as much as

---

[5]Will Herberg, Protestant-Catholic-Jew (New York: 1960), pp. 23, 29, 266.

FIGURE 11.3   A literature review, *continued*

8

possible about their illness; Irishmen were stoics; Yankees were optimistic and confident.[6]

Davis, in his recent work on the adjustment of polio victims' families, found that many parents had difficulty in accepting the paralysis and tended to attribute the child's difficulty to some lapse on their own part. Many parents felt guilty about their child's illness, although one Catholic family regarded their son's misfortune as indicative of a calling to the priesthood. Davis found that the less fortunate families, i.e., those whose child did not improve after leaving the hospital, were more inclined to increase their religious activity, while those whose children improved began to return to their former churchgoing habits. He found no significant differences in disease acceptance between religious groups, but the population consisted of only 14 families.

For nine of these families, those whose children remained seriously handicapped, Davis described modes of adjustment to permanent paralysis. Normalization, urging the child to live as normal a life as possible, was more often found in those families whose life style could be described as equalitarian. Dissociation, avoiding life situations where the handicap would create a difficulty, was more often found in

[6]Mark Zborowski, "Cultural Components in Responses to Pain," Journal of Social Issues, 8, (1952), pp. 16–30.

FIGURE 11.3   **A literature review,** *continued*

9

those families whose life style could be described as traditional.
The two families in which both parents were Catholic fell into
the traditional category, as did one set of Jewish parents, one
Lutheran-Baptist couple, and one Methodist couple. All of the
other families Davis rated on this trait he called equalitarian
(one Methodist-Catholic, one Catholic-Presbyterian, one
Jewish, and one Baptist couple).[7]

Marvin Opler, in a recent publication, has discussed the
problem of variations in the concepts of health and illness as a
product of socio-cultural background.   He presents a case
study of an intermarriage between an Italian girl and an Irish
boy whose responses to stress in the marriage gave rise to
physical difficulties, which Opler describes as inextricably
linked with their differing orientations toward responsibility
and family role.[8]

Margaret Mead tells us that the American family is
"oriented towards the future, towards what the children may
become, not towards the perpetuation of the past or the
stabilization of the present."[9]   For females, motherhood

---

[7]Fred Davis, Passage Through Crisis (New York: 1963), p. 158.

[8]Marvin Opler, "Social Identity and Self-Control," in Samuel
Klauzner (ed.), The Quest for Self-Control (New York: 1965),
pp. 141–159.

[9]Margaret Mead, Male and Female (New York: 1949),
pp. 252–3.

FIGURE 11.3   **A literature review,** *continued*

10

provides a sense of solid irreversible achievement.   It is

difficult for mothers to stop wanting to provide "for the child

they have already nourished for nine months within the safe

circle of their own bodies."[10]   This natural desire is reinforced

by societal expectations that the mother will assume more

responsibility for the health and care of children than the

father will.[11]   Parsons notes,

> It is not, for instance, for nothing that pediatricians
> habitually mean the mother, not the sick child, when
> they say "my patient."   To anyone schooled in modern
> psychology the emotional significance of a child's illness
> for the mother in our society scarcely needs further
> comment.[12]

The passivity of women is, as de Beauvoir has pointed out, "a

trait that develops in her from her earliest years."[13] Women are

not expected to rebel against fate.

Men are encouraged to be doers.   Their need for

achievement surpasses that of women.   In civilized societies

the male's sense of achievement is reached, not by passive

---

[10]Ibid., p. 192.

[11]Talcott Parsons, The Social System (Glencoe, Illinois: 1963),
p. 434.

[12]Ibid., pp. 446–7.

[13]Simone de Beauvior, The Second Sex (New York: 1957),
p. 280.

FIGURE 11.3   **A literature review,** *continued*

11

acceptance of a clearly defined biologically-based role, but by active exploitation of his opportunities, so that,

> The harsh realities of a competitive world where each man's pace is determined by the pace of his rival, and the race is never ended, hit men earlier than they hit women.[14]

Parsons has noted that our culture has a strong " 'optimistic bias,' one aspect of which is the 'playing down' of death, the avoidance of too much concern with its prospect or its implications. One very possible reaction is to attempt to deny illness. . ."[15] Stanley King puts the case well,

> One might say that illness is, therefore, a kind of alienation in American society, alienation from a set of expectations that puts particular stress upon independent achievement.[16]

The sick role is one that should be vacated as soon as possible. There is every pressure on the patient and his family to "get something done," the solidarity of the family acting to push the healthy members to care for the sick one.[17]

---

[14]Mead, op. cit., p. 306.

[15]Parsons, op. cit., pp. 443–4.

[16]Stanley King, "Social Psychological Factors in Illness," in Howard Freeman, et al, Handbook of Medical Sociology (New Jersey: 1963), p. 112.

[17]Parsons, op. cit., p. 466.

FIGURE 11.4   **Presentation of research question and hypotheses**

12

III. HYPOTHESES

The main object of this exploratory study is to determine what differences and similarities there are in the reactions of the major socioreligious groups to juvenile diabetes, including general attitude toward the disease and parents' protective behavior toward the patient. The two main hypotheses are:

1. Attitudes toward juvenile diabetes mellitus will differ among the major socioreligious groups.
2. Protective behavior exhibited toward the diabetic patients by their parents will differ among the major socioreligious groups.

If Weber and Lenski are correct in considering socioreligious group membership to be a strong determinant of the individual's attitudes and behavior, significant differences will be evident. If Herberg's theory of convergence is correct, only minor differences will be evident. The general pattern of attitudes should show the influence of the American tendency to optimism and avoidance of concern with death and disease. The predominant attitude should be denial. There are no corrective measures which can remove diabetes. The only opportunity to "do" something lies in disease management, such as concentrating on the minutiae of diet and insulin requirements, frequent testing of the patient's urine for glucose

FIGURE 11.4   **Presentation of research question and hypotheses,** *continued*

13

and acetones, bombarding the physician with requests for
additional blood tests, and so forth.   The general pattern of
behavior should show the influence of American activism.
The predominant behavior should be overprotection.

The child's family must not only cope with the
inconvenience and present difficulties of diabetes, but also with
the realization that their expectations for the patient's future
have been partially destroyed.   If Catholics incline to be
obedient to fate, they should find it easier than Protestants to
accept the diagnosis of an incurable illness,

1a. Catholics will be adjudged accepting of the disease more
    often than Protestants.

If Protestants view fate as the outcome of behavior, they
should find it difficult to accept or even acknowledge a
condition which is incorrigible,

1b. Protestants will be adjudged denying more often than
    Catholics.

It is probable that women, with passivity built into their
role, will be less likely to rebel against misfortune than men,

1c. Mothers of diabetic juveniles will be adjudged accepting
    more often than fathers.

Men, oriented towards achievement, are likely to reject a

FIGURE 11.4   **Presentation of research question and hypotheses,** *continued*

14

situation which thwarts their hope of achievement by their

children,

1d. Fathers of diabetic juveniles will be adjudged denying more
   often than mothers.

The disease takes on more discouraging dimensions for the

children, who are directly affected.   They face added

dependence on parents

After you have completed this explanatory summation of the goal, relevant theory, and hypotheses, you present a concise explanation of the development of the indicators and choice of the data collection methods.

Research Design

Because the reader is unfamiliar with your project, you need to be careful to explain everything fully. Each step in the development of your work should be clearly set forth—including the definitions you established, your rationale for choosing particular indicators, and your rationale for choosing the variables themselves.

Why, for example, did you think you should control for sex, race, or age? What was your reason for asking for weekly rather than annual income? What instructions did you give your interviewers? Why did you decide to use available data? These are typical questions that you would answer in a research design description.

Don't forget that the reader may want to replicate your study and should have enough information to do so. A copy of each data collection instrument is appended to your report, unless you have only one page of such material, in which case you can include it in the research design section of the text.

Be sure to tell the reader what your sample was and what population it represented. Figure 11.5 is the first page of a report section on research design. It represents one possible way to present this material.

The fifth section of the research report is the story of how the data were collected and what results were obtained. In brief reports this section and the preceding one can be combined.

Data Collection and Results

This section answers the question, How did we go about collecting the data? Thus, you describe exactly what you did. Remember to describe blind alleys, mistakes, and false starts; these will be of great help to others coming after you.

Once you have described your experiences and the techniques used, give a broad summary of the data that you are going to present more specifically:

> "We found that while men and women were equally likely to prefer onions over radishes, men rejected artichokes overwhelmingly, while women favored them. Table 1 gives the data on vegetable preferences, by sex." Then present Table 1.

Minimize the use of actual figures in the prose description because they can hamper the understanding of relationships. It is clearer to speak of "two-thirds" rather than "66.7 percent."

Mention the comparisons that proved fruitless, but do not give numerical details: "No difference was observed in voting patterns when we controlled for length of residence, marital status, or family size." If it seems useful,

FIGURE 11.5   **Presentation of study design**

15

IV. POPULATION AND STUDY DESIGN

The population studied consists of 55 families which
include 151 individual respondents.   There are 44 fathers, 52
mothers, and 55 children. The research case is the individual.

Respondents were obtained by a thorough canvass of
four sources: a summer camp for diabetic children, in New
Jersey; practicing pediatricians in the Plainfield, New Jersey,
area; general practitioners and pediatricians in the Trenton,
New Jersey, area; and a clinic with a diabetes case load in
Burlington, New Jersey.   They were self-selected to the extent
that a few families refused to participate in the study; however,
all families located through these four sources were asked.
Forty families from the Trenton area had been studied for the
pilot study, done two years prior to this one, and none of these
were included here.

Although diabetes has long been regarded as a "Jewish"
disease,[1] only 2 Jewish diabetic juveniles were located; one of

---

[1]Van Nostrand's Scientific Encyclopedia, 3rd ed. (Princeton:
1958), p. 502, has this to say:

The time of life at which diabetes is most likely to occur is in
the 4th and 5th decades, and the disease is far more common in
women than in men. The Teutonic races are more susceptible
than the Latin. The incidence in the Jewish race is greater than
in any other; this is due in part to inbreeding, heredity, and the
tendency to obesity in middle life. Occupation can be correlated
with diabetes in that the incidence is much greater in the
professional groups, those of sedentary employment, and in

---

considering your probable readership, add an appendix for the study of tables
showing the distributions and cross-tabulations that were not included in the
report.

One caution: When reporting results, be careful with percentages and
proportions. If one category changes, the others change too. Long ago, for

example, tuberculosis (TB) was a big killer and accounted for a high percentage of deaths. Now it is less prevalent in the Western world, and cancer accounts for a high percentage of deaths. The high percentage of deaths from cancer is partly due to the drop in TB. Even if there had been no additional cancer cases, the *proportion* of cancer deaths would have to have risen because the remaining deaths after TB was deducted would have to account for the total. If all causes of death but one were to be eliminated, that one cause would account for 100 percent of the cases, regardless of the absolute number that represented.

After you have summarized the main findings you are ready to write your conclusion and recommendations for further study.

Conclusion

Begin your conclusion by writing a paragraph referring back to the original research question and hypothesis, to refresh the reader's memory. Say whether the research hypothesis was supported and what light it casts on the research question. The following excerpt is an example.

> *We set out to see if religion affects attitudes toward chronic disease and hypothesized that Catholics with juvenile diabetes mellitus in their family would be more accepting than Protestants who had it in theirs. While our results supported our hypothesis, the relationship was by no means a simple one. It was strongly affected by the intervening variables of sex and family role.*

Having made such a statement, you can go on to give the main findings in summary.

The second part of your conclusion is a careful examination of each prior theory that led to your hypothesis. You examine them in the same order in which you have discussed them in the literature review earlier in your report. You state the author's premise and then comment on it in light of your results: "Tremont's findings that lengthier lounges are preferred by those over 30 are not supported by our findings, but his claim that red upholstery is preferred over green by people under 30 is overwhelmingly confirmed." Be careful not to distort the original author's presentation.

Also remember not to use the word *prove*. It implies finality, but we can't claim that in research. Our results stand only until they are superseded by someone else's work. Be candid about your mistakes and failures. Don't be self-conscious about dead-end results. Everything you did and report will instruct and help someone. In writing the report, tell the whole story.

When you are summing up, remember that the story includes those imperfections and blots. Do not make extravagant claims. The most you should say about a really impressive result is that your hypothesis was "strongly" supported.

It's hard to prevent your enthusiasm from running away with you. The project is your "baby," and, like a doting parent, you tend to overlook its shortcomings and beam over anything that faintly resembles a virtue. Even constructing a table with fictitious data stimulates pride. Each semester, as classroom exercises are completed and discussed, this writer observes this phenomenon in herself and students. Perhaps research is such a challenge that self-congratulation is inevitable.

The last part of your text should indicate what you think the next step should be in the investigation of your topic and what the specific goals should be. Perhaps, for example, you think more descriptive work is needed. Say so. Point out gaps in the knowledge that you discovered and issues raised along the way that were tangential to your project. This is one way to use that "leads" sheet you have been compiling.

You should state the questions about the topic that now need to be asked, given the results of the present work. Also mention any methodological needs that became apparent to you. Sum up by placing your work in the context of other work on the topic so that readers can easily assess the contribution you made. Your research may have implications for the policy of an agency or of a government. (See discussion of this in Chapter 12.)

The reference material, or back matter, follows the text. In a textbook you might have a glossary or other type of word list, several appendices, one or more indexes, and a bibliography.

Back Matter

The typical research report may need one or more **appendixes**, sections containing supplementary details and added to the end of reports, and a bibliography. If highly technical language has been used and the intended readership is not educated in it, you would have to add a **glossary**, or a list of key terms and their definitions, as well.

Appendixes

Often **citations**, or footnotes, are given as an appendix of end notes, instead of appearing at the bottom of the page on which the reference occurs. The report used as an example in this chapter used the older style, as it was written in 1971. See Appendix B for some suggestions on this matter. Some reports also append maps, charts, and diagrams. You may include an overall frequency distribution of your data and possibly tables on minor findings or unfruitful comparisons not dwelt on in the text but which someone may want to check.

Every research report should have a copy of the data collection instrument, even if it is outlined in detail in the preceding discussion.

The Bibliography

A **bibliography**, a list of works consulted by the author, arranged in alphabetical order, is mandatory. Include works consulted as well as works cited. Complete instructions for this and other formal requirements can be found in Kate Turabian's *A Manual for Writers*.[3]

We end this chapter with a rundown of some mundane, but necessary, clerical matters.

Reminders

It is necessary to take the approach of a careful bookkeeper when carrying out research and arranging your report. Two things that are of paramount importance are accuracy and correct presentation.

Maintaining Accuracy

Thus far you have been cautioned against misleading anyone and distorting the data. It is perhaps easier to remember this possibility when examining someone else's work, but there is also a tendency to accept what has been printed, especially if a well-known name is attached to it. Standards do not differ when you are examining your work or that of others. What does differ is the amount of information you have and the degree of access to the details of the processes used and to the raw data. This leads to a possible problem. You cannot know what another author has failed to tell you. If you have only "labeled" data, for example, and you don't know what definitions lie behind the data, you can't compare the results to anything or accept the author's conclusions.

Be especially alert for articles that cite unsubstantiated "facts." Larry Reynolds has written of his attempt to track down a so-called fact that was referred to by a number of social scientists, *none* of whom could point to any solid verification of it.[4] Reference to findings of any kind should always have been supported with citations.

During one research project that I conducted, I came across an article in which a famous sociologist, Robert Merton, developed a logical explanation for a social phenomenon. Throughout his careful and lengthy discussion he made no reference to any empirical research of his own because the explanation was based on theory, not research.[5] Nevertheless, other researchers who referred to Merton's article mentioned his "findings" rather than his "theory," as if his discussion had been based on actual data.

If you read a claim that is important to your work, go to the original work and look up the details. Do not accept secondhand information if you can help it. The proof of this kind of pudding is not in the eating, but in what went on back in the kitchen.

Be sure your paper is neat and fulfills all the formal presentation requirements. See Appendix B.

Mechanics

Study the instructions on footnotes, paragraphing, pagination, and headings in Turabian's manual, or use a style sheet provided by your sponsor or instructor. Forms differ, but you should use one that is consistent and standard. Some organizations distribute their own style sheet so that all their in-house reports will look alike. Be careful about the appearance of your report. Incorrect citations, typographical errors, and faulty spelling or grammar debase your report and distract the reader. Check for pompous writing. One foundation administrator recently remarked that his group gives a "Garbage Award" for the application with the most meaningless jargon in it. Be careful not to win that one!

Summary and Conclusion

Writing a report requires an examination of the original proposal, a review of the question and hypotheses, and a careful organization of this material into a cogent presentation. The report text begins with an explanation of the topic chosen and a formulation of the research question. It describes how hypotheses were derived from the question and how they were operationalized. The report places the whole in the context of existing literature on the subject. After this review, the study design is presented, and the project results are described. The conclusion draws the work together, places the result in context, and lays out the implications for future research.

It is important to be conservative in one's claims, careful with one's sources, and painstaking with one's presentation.

Main Points

1. You begin a research report by examining your original proposal.

2. It's a good idea to have an outline tacked up in front of you as you write.

3. Following the outline, review the topic, justification, question, hypotheses, and the rationale behind the study design and operationalization.

4. Describe the work you did and summarize the results. Write a conclusion that refers the reader back to the original question and the literature about it.

5. Be conservative and honest, report clearly, and watch out for questionable sources.

6. Be as neat and careful with the report as possible. Organize it into front matter, text, and back matter so that the presentation is clear to the reader.

Notes

1. See Theodore C. Wagenaar, "Some Guidelines for Reading and Assessing Research Reports in the Social Sciences," in *Readings for Social Research*, ed. Theodore C. Wagenaar (Belmont, Calif.: Wadsworth, 1981), pp. 15–29.

2. June True Albert, "Religion and the Reaction to Chronic Illness: Juvenile Diabetes Mellitus." Unpublished M.A. thesis (Rutgers University, 1966), pp. 1–4. All illustrations in this chapter are taken from this study.

3. Kate Turabian, *A Manual for Writers*, rev. 3rd ed. (Chicago: University of Chicago Press, 1967). This book has appeared in several editions. Use the most recent you can find. It is frequently updated.

4. Larry Reynolds, "A Note on the Perpetuation of a 'Scientific' Fiction," *Sociometry* 29 (March 1966): 85–88.

5. Robert Merton, "Intermarriage and the Social Structure," *Psychiatry* 4 (August 1941): 363–74. See my discussion in June A. True, "Miss Anne and the Black Brother," in *Interracial Bonds*, ed. Rhoda G. Blumberg and Wendell Roye (New York: General Hall, 1979), pp. 133–52.

Exercise

The only exercise here is a critique, but it sums up the critiques you have done thus far. A complete research report is provided as a subject. As you do the exercise, try to imagine that the author will get to read your comments. This will prepare you for our discussion of evaluation research in Chapter 12.

Exercise 11.1 *Critique*

Instructions: Using the following research report, answer the exercise questions:

1. Is the problem clearly stated? What *was* the research question?

2. Is there a review of relevant work? How is it presented?

3. Is there an explanation of the study design? What does the author tell you about it?

4. How well are the data presented? Criticize.

5. What conclusion does the writer draw from the results?

6. Check the report for clerical matters. Any suggestions?

7. This report was distributed after oral presentation of the material to a professional audience. If it were to be published, what additional material would you include?

SOCIAL CONSEQUENCES

OF

JUVENILE DIABETES

by June A. True, Ph.D.
Trenton State College

Presented October 26, 1979
Assn. for Humanist Sociology
Johnstown, Pennsylvania

For the American family is oriented towards the future,
towards what the children may become, not towards the
perpetuation of the past or the stabilization of the present.

Margaret Mead. <u>Male and Female.</u>

SOCIAL CONSEQUENCES OF JUVENILE DIABETES

by June A. True

Americans view life as a competition. A handicap, including disease, is an obstacle which must be surmounted. Stanley King has called sickness an <u>alienation</u> from American society. Talcott Parsons reminds us that it is an expected part of the sick role that we try to vacate it quickly. Our family life has patterns which reinforce this expectation. Parents want children to achieve at least as much as they did themselves and willingly work to this purpose. Regardless of the logic, the economic reality or the psychological implications of this stance, it is real and it is real in its consequences.

A permanent, handicapping disease is a personal and familial disaster. "Normal" family life is hampered, social activities are diminished, the victim is stigmatized and discriminated against. Goffman identifies three phases in the socialization of such a person: learning about normals; learning what her particular disqualifications are; learning to cope with the way others treat her.

Coping may involve avoiding normals, concealing the handicap or behaving as if it did not exist in an attempt to "normalize" oneself. (See Davis.) It always requires the victim to be aware of what Goffman refers to as "unthinking routines." Nothing can be "unthinking" for the handicapped,

2

whose social life and possibly economic viability depends
entirely on the willingness of other people to overlook a flaw.
This is analogous to other types of handicap—race, sex,
age—and causes a similar psychic strain. Naturally, the
handicapped try to reduce the strain as much as possible.

Goffman remarks that one strategy stigmatized people
employ is to divide the world into "intimates" and "others,"
telling the intimates everything and the others nothing. He
claims that the intimates then serve as a protective circle
around the stigmatized person. For reasons noted below, the
juvenile diabetic cannot divide the world neatly, leaving the
"others" completely in the dark (although there is a difference
in the level of information provided to the "intimates" and the
"others"). The school staff and the other children must be told
about the disease.

Juvenile diabetes is characterized by the failure of the
pancreas to produce insulin. The child must have daily
injections of insulin and must be restricted to a diet limited in
fats and carbohydrates. The alternative is rapidly declining
health and quick death. The insulin is more important than
the diet, since its effect is immediate. Too little insulin causes
diabetic coma; too much causes insulin shock. Both
conditions result in unconsciousness and they resemble each
other. The patient must be careful to monitor her own

3

condition, having ready access to insulin and to food at all times. A mistake in diagnosis and the administration of the wrong substance is fatal.

The metabolic condition of the body alters with physical activity, emotional upset and normal growth, changing the insulin and food requirements continuously. The worst of this predicament is that even perfect control cannot prevent damage to the body. Diabetes damages the nerves (including those which control sight), reduces healing ability, and shortens one's life.

Nevertheless, the diabetic is normal in appearance. Physical activity is recommended. There is no apparent excuse for modifying the goals and achievement of the typical American child. On the other hand, the condition requires unfailing vigilance. The child is sick, but not allowed to be sick; well, but not allowed to be well. It would not be surprising if the resultant strain affects the child's peer relations or causes discouragement in either the child or her parents.

This paper is based on data from a study done some years ago at a New Jersey clinic. Diabetics 7 to 17 years old and their families were studied by a team, including the writer, which had access to medical, school, psychiatric, psychological and sociological reports for each child. The last were the

4

outcome of intensive interviews of the parents, at home. Individual ratings of the children were made and then team ratings. Disagreement was rare. For the present discussion, I am using the peer adjustment rating, parental control pattern rating, parental attitude toward disease rating and some background variables.

Table 1 illustrates the relationship we found between peer adjustment and the length of time the child had been a diabetic. ("Poor" peer adjustment, for all tables, indicated that the child did not get along with other children, did not have a close friend, was rarely included in group activities and did not exchange home visits with other children.)

TABLE 1. DURATION OF JUVENILE DIABETES X PEER ADJUSTMENT (N-40)

	Duration		
	Under 4 years	4, but under 8	8 years or more
	(N17)	(N18)	(N5)
Poor peer adjustment	11.8%	27.8%	60.0%

Since duration of the disease is unavoidably accompanied by aging, I took a look at age peer adjustment by age as well.

5

TABLE 2. AGE OF JUVENILE DIABETICS X PEER
ADJUSTMENT (N-40)

	Age		
	7–10 (N15)	11–13 (N15)	14–17 (N10)
Poor peer adjustment	13.4%	20.0%	50.0%

Within age categories, peer adjustment deteriorated the longer
the child had diabetes. Table 3 illustrates the pattern.

TABLE 3. AGE AND DURATION OF JUVENILE DIABETES X
PEER ADJUSTMENT (N-40)

	Poor peer adjustment	
7-10/under 4 years	0.0%	(N7)
7-10/4 years or more 11-13/under 8 years 14-17/under 4 years	21.8%	(N24)
11-13/8 years or more 14-17/4 years or more	55.6%	(N9)

The longer the duration and the older the child, the poorer the
peer adjustment seemed to be.

Let us now take a look at the possibilities the juvenile
diabetic has for dividing the world into "intimates" and
"others" and see if there is any effect on peer adjustment when
these variables are considered. One such possibility stems

6

from the existence of relatives with diabetes. Even though the juvenile diabetic's condition must be publicized, the presence of other diabetics in the family would raise the level of information and familiarity with the disease within the family group, sharpening the contrast between the "intimates" and the "outsiders." Table 4 presents data showing the difference in poor peer adjustment between those with diabetic relatives and those without. The presence of relatives was associated with much better peer adjustment.

TABLE 4.   PRESENCE OF DIABETIC RELATIVES X PEER ADJUSTMENT (N-40)

| | Diabetic Relatives | |
	Yes (N32)	No (N8)
Poor peer adjustment	15.6%	62.5%

Another possibility is that having brothers and sisters would enlarge the circle of "intimates." Table 5 presents this data.

TABLE 5.   FAMILY SIZE X PEER ADJUSTMENT (N-40)

| | Family Size | | |
	"Only" child (N7)	2–4 ch. (N23)	5 or more (N10)
Poor peer adjustment	42.8%	21.7%	20.0%

7

Peer adjustment for the diabetic child seemed to improve with at least one brother or sister, but there was no increment with additional children in the family. It occurred to me that the relatively poor showing of "only" children might have something to do with the parental control pattern, since team members had observed that "only" children tended to be overprotected. Table 6 presents the data for this variable. (Overprotection was restricting the child more than the doctor recommended; neglect was disregarding some or all of the recommendations.) It is clear that extremes in control were associated with problems in peer adjustment.

TABLE 6. PARENTAL CONTROL PATTERN X PEER
 ADJUSTMENT OF DIABETIC CHILDREN
 (N-71 [PARENTS])

	Parental control pattern		
	Normal (N55)	Overprotective (N13)	Neglectful (N3)
Poor peer adjustment of child	16.4%	46.2%	100%

There were four orientations that parents developed to the disease: acceptance; denial; despair; and overcompensation (insisting that the disease was an advantage). Table 7 presents the data for this variable. Realism in the parents was

8

strongly associated with better peer adjustment in the child.
When parents were considered as couples the association of
acceptance with good peer adjustment was even clearer,
children with two accepting parents never being rated poor in
peer adjustment.

TABLE 7. PARENTAL ATTITUDE TOWARD DISEASE X PEER
ADJUSTMENT OF DIABETIC CHILDREN
(N-71 [PARENTS])

	Parental attitude toward disease			
	Acceptance (N23)	Denial (N25)	Despair (N13)	Over-compensation (N10)
Poor peer adjustment of child	4.34%	24.0%	46.2%	50.0%

TABLE 8. PARENTAL ATTITUDE TOWARD DISEASE X PEER
ADJUSTMENT OF DIABETIC CHILDREN—PARENTS
IN COUPLES

	Parental attitude toward disease		
	Both Accepting (N6)	One Accepting (N11)	Neither (N23)
Poor peer adjustment	0.0%	9.1%	39.1%

For professionals who work with juvenile diabetics I
think it is important that sociological variables influencing

9

their patients' social life be understood. Some of the variables considered here are "givens." Nothing can be done about the child's age, the duration of the disease, the number of the children in the family or the presence of diabetic relatives. It <u>would</u> be beneficial if the possible influence of these things on the child's social prognosis were known. Some children might be given extra help. For example, a child with no diabetic relatives might be assisted with an educational program aimed at her non-diabetic relatives so that the information level of her "intimates" might be raised.

There is some question in my mind about the parental attitudes and control patterns. It is just possible that parents whose children have poor peer adjustment might develop extreme control patterns or depression or one of the forms of avoidance. These data show that the diabetic child's parents need help. Whether their attitudes hamper the child's adjustment or their child's social life dampens their attitudes, there is no excuse for omitting guidance and emotional support for them. If Margaret Mead is right, and parents are oriented to the future and what their children may become, then these parents will need more and more help as time goes on, the disease continues and the child ages. They will not get "used to it" and be all right on their own. Parental counseling, in conjunction with patient counseling <u>about social situations,</u>

10

should be a regular adjunct to medical supervision, and this should increase in intensity as the child grows and continue until she reaches socioeconomic independence.

WORKS CITED

Davis, Fred. Passage Through Crisis. New York, 1963.

Goffman, Erving. Stigma: Notes on the Management of Spoiled Identity. New Jersey: 1963.

King, Stanley. "Social Psychological Factors in Illness," in Freeman, Howard E., Sol Levine and Leo G. Reeder, (eds.), Handbook of Medical Sociology. Englewood Cliffs, New Jersey: 1963, pp. 99–121.

Mead, Margaret. Male and Female. New York: 1949.

Parsons, Talcott. The Social System. Illinois: 1963.

Swift, Charles R. and Frances L. Seidman. "Adjustment Problems of Juvenile Diabetes," Journal of the American Academy of Child Psychiatry, Vol. 3, No. 3, July, 1964, pp. 500–515.

CHAPTER 12

The Consequences of Research

Research is not done in a vacuum. It happens in a living, moving society of conscious people, who react to it the way they react to the other events confronting them. We have to consider the effect of research on its subjects, on its setting, and on its audience. In this chapter we look first at the balance between the researcher's obligation to science and the researcher's obligation to the subjects, as specified in the rules of professional ethics. Our second concern will be the effect of research on the social and political setting and the implications this has for freedom to do it. Finally, we'll take up the issue of **evaluation research**, the branch of research that is undertaken to appraise ongoing programs and recommend policy and that, therefore, gives rise to many ethical, social, and political questions and to many disputes.

Chapter 4 included an outline of the ethical rules we follow and their justifications. We have also already discussed the rules of the scientific method, *with which the ethical rules often conflict.*

Ethical Dilemmas

The ethical dilemmas that worry us the most are conflicts between the two main requirements of science and the two main requirements of ethics. Science requires researchers to (1) seek the objective truth and get as much of it as possible; it also requires them to (2) publish the results. Ethics requires researchers to (1) get the informed consent of the subjects before involving them in a project and to (2) protect the subjects from harm. Let's look at these cross-purposes.

Seeking Objective Truth Versus Getting Informed Consent

These two requirements conflict in two ways. One affects internal validity, and the other affects external validity.

Effect on Internal Validity   The ethical ideal is to get the subjects to agree to be part of a research project *after* informing them of its goals, methods, and possible consequences. This is similar to the reading of legal rights before questioning a suspect. There is hardly a better way imaginable to increase both interviewer effect and demand characteristics to their maximum, and thus to damage internal validity by altering the behavior of the subjects. It puts them on a stage.

Some projects are clearly impossible once the subjects have been informed. These include any research that depends on spontaneity or involves subject behavior that the subjects are not eager to have observed. Just about every unobtrusive observation as well as any kind of unannounced participant observation is eliminated in this case. You wouldn't even be able to observe the natural play of children. Try it. Tell some children you're going to watch them play and see them keep glancing in your direction, especially if you are writing. Either they'll be inhibited or they'll show off.

Effect on External Validity   If informing the subjects results in their *refusing* to be observed or questioned because they don't want their activities watched, irreparable damage is done to any kind of rigorous sampling procedure, and thus to external validity. Any research project that depends on volunteer subjects is vulnerable to criticism on this score, and many have been so criticized, Kinsey's sexual behavior studies, for example, or Shere Hite's more recent research reports on sexual behavior.

Solutions   The researcher must consider the social importance of the topic to be researched and the degree to which the subjects may be informed without damaging internal or external validity. As has been suggested earlier, it's possible to observe and *then* inform. One seemingly feasible suggestion is to take a small sample of potential research subjects and thoroughly explain the project to them. This would tell you how resistant a larger sample of that population would be and how many would be likely to refuse to participate.[1] This approach will save time and trouble.

It is not always easy to explain a project to the subjects because they may be uneducated in the language of academics and research. Furthermore, people tend to resist prophecies of harm, as you can see when health and safety experts try to convince citizens that such and such a course of action will lead to injury or ill health. However, a *sincere* attempt to inform will satisfy the ethical requirements of the situation for most people. One has to be one's own policeman here, lest the desire for the subjects' cooperation lead to hasty or vague explanations to them.

If one anticipates, using a sample or not, a high degree of resistance and altered behavior as a result of informing the subjects about the project, one must judiciously weigh the project's importance against the subjects' right to know. Claire Selltiz and associates list three kinds of benefits research brings:

1. A better understanding of human behavior, thus an advance in the behavioral sciences
2. Practical knowledge for society, resulting in better operating methods
3. Gains to the subject such as increased self-understanding, satisfaction at making a scientific contribution, money or special privileges, and increased knowledge[2]

We'll come back to these later.

Now let's look at the situations when truth-seeking conflicts with protecting subjects from harm.

Seeking Objective Truth Versus Protecting Subjects from Harm

Two issues arise here: doing *inadvertent* harm to people while finding out the truth about them and *predictable* harm resulting from the process.

Inadvertent Harm to Subjects   We have already seen how the investigation of some topics can stimulate painful memories, anxiety, or remorse. Ways to make this easier on subjects in interviews were suggested earlier. Any question can be painful for a subject, but this pain would probably be unknown to the researcher. A seemingly innocent question such as "How many years of schooling have you completed?" may make some subjects feel inadequate by their own standards, or by what they think your standards are. Observing them may cause all kinds of nervous and embarrassed reactions. People observed surreptitiously are apt to be greatly distressed when they find out about it.

Predictable Harm to Subjects   Some topics *require* that some subjects be harmed. For example, if you are doing experiments on anxiety, stress, obedience, or any kind of treatment, you are going to harm either your experimental group or your control group. You are subjecting them to something to see what happens, or treating them for something and comparing them to untreated people. A most infamous example of this is the Tuskegee study on syphilis, in which the United States Public Health Service conducted a forty-year study of syphilitics to see what would happen if the disease went untreated. This scandal broke in 1972 and has since been the subject of a book.[3]

Solutions   You must decide whether your research is important enough to society to outweigh the potential harm to the subjects. Notice the word *society*. The importance of the research to your welfare or career is not a sufficient reason to risk harm to anyone. If you are uncertain about possible damage, err on the side of protecting the subject. The subjects should be harmed as little as possible, and any temporary harm, such as anxiety or physical discomfort, should be eased quickly. Ideally, the subject should get some benefit from the research. Selltiz and associates suggest these compromises and also mention that the researcher should look at the design and consider it in the light of whether or not the participation of *researcher's own family members* would be acceptable.[4] They're saying that if you plan to expose subjects to research procedures to which you wouldn't expose your own loved ones, maybe you had better reconsider those procedures.

The subject can be exposed to harm in ways that you didn't plan on and failed to expect, which result from the publication of the research report.

Publication Versus Informed Consent

Publication of research results includes access to the files by other professionals and clerical staff as well as publication in journals and books. The conflict here centers around anonymity and confidentiality.

Anonymity   **Anonymity** literally means having an unknown name. It can be achieved in research by not asking the subjects' names. Often subjects are assured that their names, though originally known to the researcher (perhaps for sampling purposes), will not be recorded, or will remain on the sampling list only until all subjects have been contacted and will in no case be transferred to the permanent records. The need for follow-up studies or replications conflicts with this system. How are you going to get back to them if you haven't got their names?

When the data are published, the participants are sometimes recognizable to those who know them by the pattern of their responses. This is often true in case studies, which describe people and situations in detail.

Confidentiality   **Confidentiality** is even harder to achieve than anonymity because once data have been collected and recorded, they have already passed through several hands and before several pairs of eyes. Before much time passes they will be requested by other people who are variously employed in doing research projects, evaluating programs, running programs, and dealing with former subjects. Your records may be requested by a colleague, requested by a total stranger, and subpoenaed by a court, not to mention being acquired by an infamous credit bureau.

If you are using informed consent to get information, part of what you tell potential subjects may be that their responses or behavior will be strictly confidential. Unless individual records are destroyed as soon as the aggregated data have been recorded, it is highly probable that your promise of confidentiality will be impossible to carry out.[5] There are simply too many people with legitimate access to files.

A new problem stems from the computerization of so many records and the possibility of downloading information to numerous computer terminals in large organizations. The presence of the records on a computer disk or tape means that sophisticated computer users can figure out ways to get at confidential information. Many organizations with trade secrets and confidential documents have already learned this. We have a new kind of crime and a new kind of criminal, thanks to technological progress. Criminal justice and legal experts are now trying to develop some response to this phenomenon.

Solutions   If anonymity is to be preserved, data must be distorted before publication so that nobody who served as a subject can be identified. This protection has to be extended to group studies as well. (Groups are often explicitly labeled, but if they are, they can't be considered anonymous in the first place.)

If confidentiality is to be preserved, no records can be kept under any subject's name. This is clearly impossible in social agencies and institutions because, by law, they have to keep records on each client or patient. However, one can be scrupulously careful about recording potentially damaging information. One should be conservative about how much is recorded, continually asking oneself whether items are really necessary to the record. The worker's curiosity about people's private lives should be strictly curbed.

The last conflict between ethics and science that we shall discuss is the need for publication measured against the need to protect subjects.

Publication Versus Protecting Subjects from Harm

When your research report says something about your subjects' attitudes, opinions, characteristics, and behavior that could be contrary to their own or society's standards, its publication may result in personal distress or in social reactions.

Personal Distress   Few people get through life without experiencing some occasion on which they revealed things that later reflection caused them to regret. Few people are of such hardy stuff that they can read an unvarnished description of themselves without being somewhat dismayed. Publication of a research report can cause these negative feelings in its subjects if they read it. We have already seen that several researchers mentioned here received unfavorable comments on their descriptions and conclusions.[6] Criticisms ranged from mild demurral to angry denunciation.

The possible reaction your report may bring in the community can be even more devastating in its potential.

Social Reactions   If you remember that the enumeration of population was first done in ancient times in order to collect taxes and raise armies, you can see why people are suspicious of even being counted, much less questioned. Some community leaders discourage cooperation with surveys because they fear the responses may be used to control their groups. They think that the publication of the prevailing attitudes or behavior of their people may bring punitive or restrictive action. Another possibility is that publishing facts about a group may lead to the establishment, abolition, or restructuring of benefits or training programs. Arguments against the group's interest can include research citations to demonstrate that its members have the "wrong" attitudes.

Certainly the publication of facts and figures about a group creates an image of it in the public mind that may not coincide with the image the group members prefer. They may feel that these facts are damaging when unaccompanied by a description of what they see as extenuating circumstances, including past events. Indeed they may be right. The damage can be great, as stereotypes are hard to erase.

Social and political policy does respond to reports of the "latest research findings." We now turn to an examination of the influence of research on public affairs and the constraints public interests exert on the research process itself.

Social and Political Policy

If you read over the benefits of research listed in the first section of this chapter, you may decide that it might make a difference whose benefit you had in mind. Let's review these claims one by one. The first two speak of benefits to the scientific community; the third refers to advantages for the research subjects.

A Better Understanding of Human Behavior

One of the outcomes of understanding is being better able to cope with whatever it is you now understand. Since most of the people conducting research and most of the people making public policy are in the upper classes of society, *they* become the understanders who are better equipped to cope. What they are coping with is generally the human behavior of people who are not in a position to make public decisions and who often have little interest in, or knowledge of, research findings.

This is why critics of research say that social science may be making things worse for the disadvantaged by increasing the edge of the people in control. Take the famous Hawthorne Effect, a finding discussed in Chapter 8. Workers singled out for attention increased their productivity regardless of whether changes in working conditions were for the better or for the worse. Knowing this, employers might well opt to study ways to give workers the impression that they are getting special attention from management rather than studying ways to improve working conditions. The study of industrial sociology and psychology has come under considerable fire because of this potential disadvantage to labor.

Practical Knowledge Resulting in Better Methods

Research has been employed to improve the productivity of workers, the dissemination of propaganda, and the prediction of voting patterns. All these goals can easily be misused. As noted above, productivity can be enhanced at the expense of worker benefits, propaganda may conceal social disabilities, and predicting the vote may actually influence it. During the 1980 presidential election, the predicted outcome, achieved early in the evening by the use of highly sophisticated statistical computations, caused Jimmy Carter to concede the election before some people had voted. This understandably caused great resentment in the western time zones. Here, technological innovations that have revolutionized research have also revolutionized communication of developing situations and accumulating results.

Gains to the Subject

When privileged people assess gains for others, they may use a standard of worth appropriate to their own station. If the subjects are of the same station, no fault can be found. However, as has been pointed out, subjects are frequently of somewhat lower socioeconomic station than the researchers and policy makers, and this is when the "gains" have to be carefully examined. Is the self-understanding achieved according to middle-class values? Is there a scientific contribution to one group, but at some personal sacrifice for someone else? Is the research money greatly needed for something else because of maldistribution of resources? Is the increased "knowledge" really propaganda for the people in charge? These are all accusations that social activists have made in the past and will probably make in the future. They cannot be ignored.

Ideologies have clashed publicly via research. Gunnar Myrdal's contention that America would have to reconcile its treatment of blacks with its commitment to equality and Daniel Moynihan's conclusion that the black family's structural "distortion" is the root cause of black problems address themselves to radically different solutions.[7]

Studies that report mean incomes for subgroups in society sometimes result in intergroup hostility because the members of other groups may seize upon this information as "proof" that all of the members of such and such a group are "getting more than their fair share." Unfortunately, the measures of dispersion are rarely also reported in the media. A case in point is the recent spate of articles and news reports citing a "generation gap" between today's youth and the grandparental generation. The claim is that "research shows" that old folks are living high at the expense of young folks and their future. That this is bunk can be demonstrated with a careful analysis of the two categories, but such careful analyses are rarely made. Worse, talk shows pick such subjects up and cheerfully bat them around, the participants almost never getting a chance to state their own positions fully, let alone consider those of their opponents. Meanwhile, the television or radio audience is treated to an hour or so of distortions and half-truths as if they were gospel. Whatever category is under discussion is bound to suffer damage to its popular image.

Reseachers who are asked to work on a project may not be clear as to who exactly is running it. Unbeknownst to the scientists employed on it, one study of leadership patterns and norms in a foreign setting was actually a project of the Central Intelligence Agency. Many of the professionals who worked on it would not have accepted the assignment, had they known the true sponsorship. Research is also often contracted for by large companies. The sponsorship of a research project is crucial, because whoever pays the bill decides what projects are worthy of support and, therefore, what questions are going to be asked.

Sometimes a researcher may decide that a project should be abandoned because of its potential for misuse. There is little protection, however, in what popularization of a research finding may do in the general population. C. Wright Mills spoke of the "psychologizing and sociologizing" of the American public.[8] The further you get from the actual report of a research finding, the more distortion is likely to occur.

Finally, we must consider the kind of research that is designed to appraise what social policy has done and suggest what it might do in the future. This is evaluation research, possibly the top challenge a researcher can tackle.

Evaluation Research

Evaluation research is research that has implications for the programs being carried out by institutions and agencies. It is applied research, done to produce practical and immediately useful findings. The use will be to help decide whether the programs will get any more money, employ people in the future, and continue to do whatever it is they are now doing. This makes it a delicate operation.

Evaluation research is no different from any other kind in the methods used and in the requirements of the scientific method and the rules of ethical behavior. It is decidedly different, however, in the multiple nature and interaction of some of the components, namely, goals, processes, and consequences. Let's take a closer look.

Goals

Evaluation research deals not only with the research goal (question) but also with the program goal(s) and the individual goals. These three types are not only distinct, but may be at cross-purposes.

The Research Goal The research question is not arrived at by inductive or deductive logic. It is assigned by the sponsor of the research. Generally, it is "How good is this program?" and it consists of the subsidiary questions:

What is the program supposed to be doing?

What is the program actually doing?

How does the program work?

Should the program be changed, left alone, or discontinued?

Getting the answers to these questions will almost surely be highly threatening to the people who are running the program or are employed by it. Even clients of the program may not be pleased to see it evaluated. Perchance they benefit from it in unintended ways and would not like to see it discontinued. Many government programs employ people with marginal skills and provide a safe environment in which to improve them. Some of these people might not be employable elsewhere.

The Program Goal(s)   The primary program goal answers the question, What is the program supposed to be doing? and is often referred to as the program's **mandate**. A mandate is an order; thus, the goal is what the program was set up to accomplish. In addition to the primary goal, you have to bear in mind the subsidiary goals of the various program sections, such as departments or special professional services. The goal of the army is to win the war; the goal of Company B may be to take the next hill.

To know what the goal of a program is, regardless of the type, you have to distinguish between the ideals and the practical purposes. What is the goal of this school? Why, to impart knowledge, wisdom, and understanding! (Purpose: to guide the children through a curriculum gradually increasing in difficulty until they have completed it and can receive certification to that effect.)

What is the goal of this hospital? Why, to heal the sick and comfort the dying with the miracles of modern medicine! (Purpose: to accept patients of the doctors on the staff and some charity patients, following the attending doctor's orders for the first and practicing techniques on the second for the benefit of medical students.)

What is the goal of this agency? Why, to serve the people! (Purpose: to handle the administrative and clerical needs of the people in policy-making and legislative positions.)

The goals *should* be lofty and practical at the same time. For a research project, however, the definitions have to be precise and the phenomena have to be observable. You can't use the ideal goals but must focus on the practical. You need precision in definition and in measurement. You have to isolate a goal that can be recognized when it is reached, and you have to examine the work of the program to see if the program workers are reaching it. Since knowledge, wisdom, understanding, healing, comforting, and serving are abstract, you will be working with diplomas granted, number of dropouts, employment after graduation, hospital discharges, deaths, readmissions, clients served, and so on.

In addition to the performance goals of the program and the subsidiary specifics, there is the goal of continued life of the program. All organizations tend to be self-perpetuating because the people in them want them continued. To this end, one goal will be to establish and maintain a good public image. An evaluation research project threatens this goal.

Individual Goals   Every individual in the program has goals. All the staff members have career goals, and all the clients have service goals, or ideas about what they want from the program.

It is the researcher's job to specify the research goal(s) and to try to operationalize them. The researcher must also use exploratory and descriptive research methods to find out all of the program and individual goals. If this is not accomplished, it will be impossible to understand what is going on.

Once the goals are clearly understood, you can turn to an examination of the processes.

Processes   In evaluation research there are two sets of subjects: the staff and the clients. Regardless of whether you announce your research to the clients, the staff will know about it—unless you are doing covert research, which is regarded as "dirty pool" when practiced on other professionals. As an evaluator, you are going to watch people at work to see not only what effect they produce on their charges, but also what methods they use and with what degree of skill.

It is easy to understand why evaluators are not particularly welcomed by the staff. You are going to rate the staff in the course of your report, either specifically or by implication. People are not enthusiastic about criticism. I once had to evaluate social casework at a total institution. Results included a preliminary finding that certain categories of patients were never recommended for discharge regardless of how well they were doing. As soon as the supervisor heard this, all access to the patient files was cut off, and the researcher was reassigned to do a study of "the reduced length of stay since the institution of the program."

In this example the officially approved data presentation did show reduced length of stay but did not show a clear picture of the prejudice against the subgroups. My research position entitled me to demand the closed files, but the political reality inside the institution prevented it. Those in charge wanted a question asked that would produce a positive answer.

The quality of a program is indescribable in scientific terms because there are too many intangibles. The closest you can get is the number of satisfied clients, and then you have to consider what their standards might be. Some people expect more than others. We establish programs in the service of high ideals because we feel it is the right thing to do. Education, healing, and serving are all "good" and are obligatory for a "good" country. This is why the goals are stated as ideals. We are trying to keep ourselves focused on the best.

The mandates for programs have to be broad enough to allow a variety of activities because we are not sure of the best way to reach the ideals. Evaluation research is wanted so we can weigh one approach against another and choose the most effective with the least expense. This leads to a problem in getting the third kind of information: the results of the program.

What an institution or agency does to fulfill its purpose varies with the people in charge; therefore, when you evaluate the method and implementation, you are also evaluating their ideas and competence. Although everyone is familiar with false starts, trial-and-error methods, failures, and disappointments on their own job, we view other professions in a different light because most of us are able to keep our shortcomings from each other most of the time. It is important, no matter how lowly an occupation you have, to be able to present your best work in public. Everyone resents scrutiny while working and most people get nervous about it.

Consequences

You have to consider consequences to three groups: scientists, program staff, and clients. In addition there is the usual consequence to research knowledge and practice.

Consequences to the scientists, both in and out of the particular project, have to do with credibility and future opportunities for research of this type. Many studies emerge with findings that conflict with existing evaluation research findings. Consider the lively controversies over the effects of school integration, busing, and the role of education in lifetime achievement. Many studies emerge with findings that disappoint the implementers of programs. Each time such a report appears, no matter how justified, the zeal with which program staff welcome and cooperate with an evaluator is lessened.

Consequences to the program are, or can be, immediate and decisive. Sponsors contract for evaluative research so that they may decide how to allocate funds for future time periods. A program may be discontinued or curtailed on the strength of a report, and new programs may commence if recommended by a report. There is often a battle royal between the supporters of a program, waving favorable research reports, and the detractors of it, waving unfavorable research reports. This has been the history of the Head Start programs for preschoolers.

Consequences to individuals depend on their connection with the evaluated program. Staff, of course, can lose jobs or be promoted, demoted, or reassigned. The clients' situation is not so clear-cut. Studies of client satisfaction have come up with strikingly similar results: Most of the time the clients feel that a program is beneficial, regardless of what evaluations of that program show and regardless of its objective result. Surprisingly, when people are asked about their satisfaction with something, including marriage, high percentages of them report satisfaction.[9] This is such a pervasive pattern that some researchers feel you cannot place any reliance on inquiries about client satisfaction with service or benefits. If qualitative data can be quantified or regularized in some way, the patterns they show offer more reassurance to the evaluators.

One innovative approach in this direction is that of Robert Collins, who designed a computer simulation model for assessing the benefit of individual retirement accounts (IRA) so that this program could be evaluated in advance, for the guidance of the taxpayers.[10] It is much easier to do something like that if you have quantitative data, such as money. A word of warning about simulations: They are great for illustrating simple relationships among a small number of variables, but the simulation can show only the results of those; it cannot react to the enormous variety of influences we deal with every day in the real world. Simulations provide illustrations and suggestions, not answers.

Evaluation research, while essentially the same as other research, is conducted under conditions that alter the nature of the problems facing the researcher.

Differences Between Evaluation Research and Basic Research

Theodore C. Wagenaar cites several studies and draws together the following list of important differences between the two kinds of research:

1. Basic research is concerned with cumulative theoretical knowledge, and evaluation is concerned with application.
2. Basic research answers self-generated questions, while evaluation research questions are client-provided.
3. Basic research focuses on "what is" and evaluation research focuses on "what ought to be."
4. Basic research is less likely than evaluation research to be subjected to overt political pressure.
5. Basic research emphasizes generalizability, while evaluation research emphasizes specific policy answers.[11]

Summary and Conclusion

We must consider the context of research and the consequences it brings. First among our concerns is the existence of ethical dilemmas stemming from the conflicting demands of science and moral standards. We must try to seek the truth and publish it; at the same time, we are hoping for the informed consent of subjects whom we are pledged to protect from harm. These goals are often incompatible, and we must try to find an acceptable compromise or abandon the research.

Social and political policy is made by people more highly placed in society than most of the subjects of research, and, therefore, the "benefits" of research to the subjects have to be examined with care. The misuse of research is an ever-present danger. We should always ask who is getting the benefit of it.

Evaluation research exists to appraise the operation and consequences of programs and to make recommendations as to their continuance, modification, or elimination. An evaluation researcher has to identify several sets of goals, processes, and results to be able to make a judgment. The researcher must also be alert to the consequences for science, for the staff, and for the clients. Evaluation research differs from basic research in its motives, questions, and expectations.

Main Points

1. The consequences of research include the conflict between science and ethics, the effect on social and political events, and the fate of evaluated programs.
2. Ethical dilemmas arise because science requires the whole truth and publication of it, and ethics requires informed and consenting subjects, who are protected from harm.
3. Ethical dilemmas cannot be resolved, but compromises may be made. Each project must be carefully examined to decide whether its benefits to humanity will outweigh potential harm to subjects.
4. Social and political policy is affected by research findings and, in turn, affects the scope of research.
5. The credibility of research is damaged by conflicting findings.
6. The researcher has little control over the misuse of research findings.
7. Evaluation research is applied research with multiple goals, multiple processes, and two sets of subjects to examine.
8. The consequences of applied research are more immediate than those of basic research, and, therefore, the researcher is under more pressure from both clients and program staff.
9. The goal of applied research is to find answers that can be implemented.

Notes

1. E. Berscheid, R. S. Baron, M. Dermer, and M. Libman, "Anticipating Informed Consent: An Empirical Approach," *American Psychologist* 28 (1973): 913–25.
2. Claire Selltiz, Lawrence Wrightsman, and Stuart W. Cook, *Selltiz, Wrightsman and Cook's Research Methods in Social Relations*, rev. ed. Louise H. Kidder (New York: Holt, Rinehart, & Winston, 1981), p. 369.
3. James H. Jones, *Bad Blood: The Tuskegee Syphilis Experiment* (New York: Free Press, 1981).
4. Selltiz, Wrightsman, and Cook, *Research Methods*, p. 373.
5. Suanna J. Wilson, *Confidentiality in Social Work* (New York: Free Press, 1978).

6. See William F. Whyte, *Street Corner Society*, 2nd ed. (Chicago: University of Chicago Press, 1955); Arthur Vidich and Joseph Bensman, *Small Town in Mass Society* (Princeton, N.J.: Princeton University Press, 1968); Deborah Feinbloom, *Transvestites and Transsexuals* (New York: Delacorte Press, 1976).

7. Gunnar Myrdal, *An American Dilemma* (New York: Harper & Row, 1944); Daniel Moynihan, *The Negro Family: The Case for National Action* (Washington, D.C.: Office of Planning and Research, United States Department of Labor, March 1965).

8. C. Wright Mills, *The Sociological Imagination* (New York: Oxford University Press, 1959).

9. Selltiz, Wrightsman, and Cook, *Research Methods*, pp. 98–100.

10. Robert A. Collins, "Estimating the Benefits of Individual Retirement Accounts: A Simulation Approach," *Journal of Consumer Affairs* 14, no. 1 (Summer 1980): 124–41.

11. Theodore C. Wagenaar, *Readings for Social Research* (Belmont, Calif.: Wadsworth, 1981), p. 212.

Epilogue

Research is very enjoyable. Nonetheless, there are hazards, tedium, and plenty of hard work. Sometimes what you can discover in one research project seems small in relation to what you wanted to know. You may be disappointed at not reaching some momentous conclusion. Remember that your work may be just what someone else needed to help them on their way to an answer. In that sense we all work together.

It's the challenge of research that makes the end of it all the sweeter. When you have got the findings, constructed the tables and charts, and have something to show for all your trouble, it's a proud occasion.

My favorite moment in the school year comes when my student research teams arrive in class with their final reports. Team by team, serious and a little nervous, they assemble in front of the room. They begin by telling their classmates what they set out to do, how they planned and carried it out, and what went wrong along the way.

And then the speaker's manner changes. The whole team acquires a slightly self-satisfied look, and there is a triumphant note to the rest of the presentation. . . .

"Now, here is what we found. . . ."

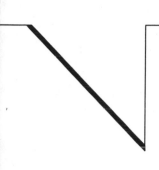

Appendixes

Random Numbers

10480	15011	01536	02011	81647	91646	69179	14194	62590	36207	20969	99570	91291	90700
22368	46573	25595	85393	30995	89198	27982	53402	93965	34095	52666	19174	39615	99505
24130	48360	22527	97265	76393	64809	15179	24830	49340	32081	30680	19655	63348	58629
42167	93093	06243	61680	07856	16376	39440	53537	71341	57004	00849	74917	97758	16379
37570	39975	81837	16656	06121	91782	60468	81305	49684	60672	14110	06927	01263	54613
77921	06907	11008	42751	27756	53498	18602	70659	90655	15053	21916	81825	44394	42880
99562	72905	56420	69994	98872	31016	71194	18738	44013	48840	63213	21069	10634	12952
96301	91977	05463	07972	18876	20922	94595	56869	69014	60045	18425	84903	42508	32307
89579	14342	63661	10281	17453	18103	57740	84378	25331	12566	58678	44947	05585	56941
85475	36857	53342	53988	53060	59533	38867	62300	08158	17983	16439	11458	18593	64952
28918	69578	88231	33276	70997	79936	56865	05859	90106	31595	01547	85590	91610	78188
63553	40961	48235	03427	49626	69445	18663	72695	52180	20847	12234	90511	33703	90322
09429	93969	52636	92737	88974	33488	36320	17617	30015	08272	84115	27156	30613	74952
10365	61129	87529	85689	48237	52267	67689	93394	01511	26358	85104	20285	29975	89868
07119	97336	71048	08178	77233	13916	47564	81056	97735	85977	29372	74461	28551	90707
51085	12765	51821	51259	77452	16308	60756	92144	49442	53900	70960	63990	75601	40719
02368	21382	52404	60268	89368	19885	55322	44819	01188	65255	64835	44919	05944	55157
01011	54092	33362	94904	31273	04146	18594	29852	71585	85030	51132	01915	92747	64951
52162	53916	46369	58586	23216	14513	83149	98736	23495	64350	94738	17752	35156	35749
07056	97628	33787	09998	42698	06691	76988	13602	51851	46104	88916	19509	25625	58104
48663	91245	85828	14346	09172	30168	90229	04734	59193	22178	30421	61666	99904	32812
54164	58492	22421	74103	47070	25306	76468	26384	58151	06646	21524	15227	96909	44592
32639	32363	05597	24200	13363	38005	94342	28728	35806	06912	17012	64161	18296	22851
29334	27001	87637	87308	58731	00256	45834	15398	46557	41135	10367	07684	36188	18510
02488	33062	28834	07351	19731	92420	60952	61280	50001	67658	32586	86679	50720	94953
81525	72295	04839	96423	24878	82651	66566	14778	76797	14780	13300	87074	79666	95725
29676	20591	68086	26432	46901	20849	89768	81536	86645	12659	92259	57102	80428	25280
00742	57392	39064	66432	84673	40027	32832	61362	98947	96067	64760	64584	96096	98253
05366	04213	25669	26422	44407	44048	37937	63904	45766	66134	75470	66520	34693	90449
91921	26418	64117	94305	26766	25940	39972	22209	71500	64568	91402	42416	07844	69618
00582	04711	87917	77341	42206	35126	74087	99547	81817	42607	43808	76655	62028	76630
00725	69884	62797	56170	86324	88072	76222	36086	84637	93161	76038	65855	77919	88006
69011	65795	95876	55293	18988	27354	26575	08625	40801	59920	29841	80150	12777	48501
25976	57948	29888	88604	67917	48708	18912	82271	65424	69774	33611	54262	85963	03547
09763	83473	73577	12908	30883	18317	28290	35797	05998	41688	34952	37888	38917	88050
91567	42595	27958	30134	04024	86385	29880	99730	55536	84855	29080	09250	79656	73211
17955	56349	90999	49127	20044	59931	06115	20542	18059	02008	73708	83517	36103	42791
46503	18584	18845	49618	02304	51038	20655	58727	28168	15475	56942	53389	20562	87338
92157	89634	94824	78171	84610	82834	09922	25417	44137	48413	25555	21246	35509	20468
14577	62765	35605	81263	39667	47358	56873	56307	61607	49518	89656	20103	77490	18062
98427	07523	33362	64270	01638	92477	66969	98420	04880	45585	46565	04102	46880	45709
34914	63976	88720	82765	34476	17032	87589	40836	32427	70002	70663	88863	77775	69348
70060	28277	39475	46473	23219	53416	94970	25832	69975	94884	19661	72828	00102	66794
53976	54914	06990	67245	68350	82948	11398	42878	80287	88267	47363	46634	06541	97809
76072	29515	40980	07391	58745	25774	22987	80059	39911	96189	41151	14222	60697	59583
90725	52210	83974	29992	65831	38857	50490	83765	55657	14361	31720	57375	56228	41546
64364	67412	33339	31926	14883	24413	59744	92351	97473	89286	35931	04110	23726	51900
08962	00358	31662	25388	61642	34072	81249	35648	56891	69352	48373	45578	78547	81788
95012	68379	93526	70765	10592	04542	76463	54328	02349	17247	28865	14777	62730	92277
15664	10493	20492	38391	91132	21999	59516	81652	27195	48223	46751	22923	32261	85653

Reprinted with permission from *Handbook of Tables for Probability and Statistics*, Second Edition, edited by William H. Beyer, 1968. Copyright The Chemical Rubber Company, CRC Press, Inc.

16408	81899	04153	53381	79401	21438	83035	92350	36693	31238	59649	91754	72772	02338
18629	81953	05520	91962	04739	13092	97662	24822	94730	06496	35090	04822	86774	98289
73115	35101	47498	87637	99016	71060	88824	71013	18735	20286	23153	72924	35165	43040
57491	16703	23167	49323	45021	33132	12544	41035	80780	45393	44812	12515	98931	91202
30405	83946	23792	14422	15059	45799	22716	19792	09983	74353	68668	30429	70735	25499
16631	35006	85900	98275	32388	52390	16815	69298	82732	38480	73817	32523	41961	44437
96773	20206	42559	78985	05300	22164	24369	54224	35083	19687	11052	91491	60383	19746
38935	64202	14349	82674	66523	44133	00697	35552	35970	19124	63318	29686	03387	59846
31624	76384	17403	53363	44167	64486	64758	75366	76554	31601	12614	33072	60332	92325
78919	19474	23632	27889	47914	02584	37680	20801	72152	39339	34806	08930	85001	87820
03931	33309	57047	74211	63445	17361	62825	39908	05607	91284	68833	25570	38818	46920
74426	33278	43972	10119	89917	15665	52872	73823	73144	88662	88970	74492	51805	99378
09066	00903	20795	95452	92648	45454	09552	88815	16553	51125	79375	97596	16296	66092
42238	12426	87025	14267	20979	04508	64535	31355	86064	29472	47689	05974	52468	16834
16153	08002	26504	41744	81959	65642	74240	56302	00033	67107	77510	70625	28725	34191
21457	40742	29820	96783	29400	21840	15035	34537	33310	06116	95240	15957	16572	06004
21581	57802	02050	89728	17937	37621	47075	42080	97403	48626	68995	43805	33386	21597
55612	78095	83197	33732	05810	24813	86902	60397	16489	03264	88525	42786	05269	92532
44657	66999	99324	51281	84463	60563	79312	93454	68876	25471	93911	25650	12682	73572
91340	84979	46949	81973	37949	61023	43997	15263	80644	43942	89203	71795	99533	50501
91227	21199	31935	27022	84067	05462	35216	14486	29891	68607	41867	14951	91696	85065
50001	38140	66321	19924	72163	09538	12151	06878	91903	18749	34405	56087	82790	70925
65390	05224	72958	28609	81406	39147	25549	48542	42627	45233	57202	94617	23772	07896
27504	96131	83944	41575	10573	08619	64442	73923	36152	05184	94142	25299	84387	34925
37169	94851	39117	89632	00959	16487	65536	49071	39782	17095	02330	74301	00275	48280
11508	70225	51111	38351	19444	66499	71945	05422	13442	78675	84081	66938	93654	59894
37449	30362	06694	54690	04052	53115	62757	95348	78662	11163	81651	50245	34971	52924
46515	70331	85922	38320	57015	15765	97161	17869	45349	61796	66345	81073	49106	79860
30986	81223	42416	58353	21532	30502	32305	86482	05174	07901	54339	58861	74818	46942
63798	64995	46583	09785	44160	78128	83991	42865	92520	83531	80377	35909	81250	54238
82486	84846	99254	67632	43218	50076	21361	64816	51202	00124	41870	52689	51275	83556
21885	32906	92431	09060	64297	51674	64126	62570	26123	05155	59194	52799	28225	85762
60336	98782	07408	53458	13564	59089	26445	29789	85205	41001	12535	12133	14645	23541
43937	46891	24010	25560	86355	33941	25786	54990	71899	15475	95434	98227	21824	19585
97656	63175	89303	16275	07100	92063	21942	18611	47348	20203	18534	03862	78095	50136
03299	01221	05418	38982	55758	92237	26759	86367	21216	98442	08303	56613	91511	75928
79626	06486	03574	17668	07785	76020	79924	25651	83325	88428	85076	72811	22717	50585
85636	68335	47539	03129	65651	11977	02510	26113	99447	68645	34327	15152	55230	93448
18039	14367	61337	06177	12143	46609	32989	74014	64708	00533	35398	58408	13261	47908
08362	15656	60627	36478	65648	16764	53412	09013	07832	41574	17639	82163	60859	75567
79556	29068	04142	16268	15387	12856	66227	38358	22478	73373	88732	09443	82558	05250
92608	82674	27072	32534	17075	27698	98204	63863	11951	34648	88022	66148	34925	57031
23982	25835	40055	07000	12293	02753	14827	23235	35071	99704	37543	11601	35503	85171
09915	96306	05908	97901	28395	14186	00821	80703	70426	75647	76310	88717	37890	40129
59037	33300	26695	62247	69927	76123	50842	43834	86654	70959	79725	93872	28117	19233
42488	78077	69882	61657	34136	79180	97526	43092	04098	73571	80799	76536	71255	64239
46764	86273	63003	93017	31204	36692	40202	35275	57306	55543	53203	18098	47625	88684
03237	45430	55417	63282	90816	17349	88298	90183	36600	78406	06216	95787	42579	90730
86591	81482	52667	61582	14972	90053	89534	76036	49199	43716	97548	04379	46370	28672
38534	01715	94964	87288	65680	43772	39560	12918	86537	62738	19636	51132	25739	56947

Report Writing Mechanics

General Instructions

When you prepare your work for presentation to your instructor, your first task is to organize the material in the divisions of the final paper: front matter, text, and back matter. For the typical student paper these will include:

Front matter:

*title page

*table of contents

  list of illustrations, if any

  preface, if any

Text:

*introduction to the problem and research question

*survey of literature

*description of study design, development, and execution

*data presentation

*analysis and conclusion

Back matter:

*endnotes

  appendices, if any

  word list, if any

*bibliography

All the starred items are necessary. This list can be used as the framework for your outline—simply substitute your own section titles and add subsection divisions as appropriate. You don't have to work on the sections in any particular order as long as they are assembled in proper order for presenting to your instructor.

Generations of college students have used two standard books to help them write papers. These are W. S. Strunk and E. B. White's *Elements of Style* and Kate Turabian's *A Manual for Writers.* Any college bookstore has them; Strunk and White will help you to write clearly, and Turabian will guide you through the technicalities of preparing the finished paper. If these are not available, or if you already have a book on writing a paper, that's OK, but consult something. Be sure your work is correctly written and organized.

Plan to type your paper on good stock. If you can't type, learn. While you're learning, get someone to type your paper for you. This will cost money, which will motivate you to learn. Typing is a more important skill than ever because you need to type in order to use most computers, and many jobs now require you to use one. The "hunt and peck" system is too slow.

Writing the Paper

If you are writing anything, from a short note to a three-volume work, you should use words appropriately and spell them correctly. As a student, you will know you have a writing problem when your instructors comment on your written work. If you have such a problem, DO SOMETHING about it. Read Strunk and White and other books on writing. Get a tutor. Take a course in English composition or remedial writing. If your school has a writing lab, go to it. Don't just let it go while trying to avoid writing assignments. An inability to write (or read) is a serious handicap in our society and may well prevent you from earning a decent living, let alone doing satisfying work.

Your *first* draft can be written freely, without much regard for mistakes in usage or spelling, or the flow of words. However, this is not the finished product by a long shot. Read your first draft aloud to yourself, making corrections and notes in the margins as you go. Rewrite the draft and then take a break and do something else. Don't pick up the work again for at least a few hours, preferably overnight. This will enable you to look at the copy with fresh eyes and brain, and you will be more objective in judging it.

Read your second draft aloud to yourself just as you did the first draft, making corrections and notes. You should have fewer this time. If you aren't happy with the paper, repeat the "break and return" process. If you think it's shaping up, it's time to let someone else read it. (Don't ask the instructor unless the whole class has been invited to presubmit their papers. Some instructors may offer this service, but most haven't the time.) You and another student can switch papers and read them, making comments and asking questions about meanings. If you read someone's paper, make sure you understand every word. If not, ask questions, so that the other person will know where the ambiguities are in their work. If you have a tutor or a reading lab, you can get your paper read that way. You can ask a co-worker, a neighbor, or a relative. You must find out whether your work is understandable. Don't be sensitive about criticisms. They teach you something.

When you have your first or second draft, it's time to write a concise title, which will reveal the topic of your paper. Your object is to inform and interest the reader. Don't try to make it (or anything else) sound academic or intellectual. You will only make your work stuffy, and you may destroy its clarity.

Punctuation

After you've got the paper in good shape for sense and progression of ideas, and someone has had a chance to react to it, read each sentence aloud to yourself with an eye to editing the punctuation. Most people put too many commas, dashes, and exclamation points in their sentences and are timid about using colons and semicolons. Few people know how to punctuate sentences with quotations in them. Let's go over these points.

COMMAS are used to signal a pause, and to prevent ambiguity by indicating logical division of thought, or ends of clauses. Consider the difference between these two sentences:

> I was mad enough to kill, Mike!
>
> I was mad enough to kill Mike!

There'd be a big difference to poor Mike.

SEMICOLONS divide a sentence into logical pauses more definitely than commas do and create an expectation of something coming that will complement what has been said:

> We had soup, salad, entree, and dessert.
>
> We had cold, spicy cucumber soup; a green tossed salad; roast beef with Yorkshire pudding; and ice cream for dessert.

Note that the first clause has a comma in it. Ideas that contain commas are best divided by semicolons.

COLONS are a kind of equals sign, used to separate an idea from an explanation that follows immediately. For example:

> It was a great trip: a week in London, two weeks driving around the Cotswolds, and a week in Paris.

EXCLAMATION POINTS should be used sparingly. They're appropriate only if you're quoting sentences that contain them or if you're saying something startling.

> And then he said, "Get out, before I throw you out!"
>
> Mom, I've won the lottery!

DASHES indicate pauses in a more arresting form than commas or semicolons.

Even if I had the chance—and I have been offered a job—I wouldn't leave you now.

QUOTATION MARKS pose a confusing question. Does a punctuation mark at the end of quoted material go inside the final quotation mark or outside it? The answer depends on what country you're in and which punctuation mark it is.

In the United States, a comma or a period is shown inside the quotation marks; a semicolon or a colon is shown outside. You can remember this by a trick: "If it's alone (, .) it stays inside, but if it has a friend (; :) it goes outside."

Irving Berlin wrote "God Bless America," among other things. He also wrote "White Christmas."

The title of the article was "No"; this doesn't tell us about the subject.

In Great Britain final punctuation marks always go outside the quotation marks.

However, if what you are quoting is a question or an exclamation, the question mark or exclamation mark is placed inside. If you are quoting something and questioning it or are surprised at it, place it outside. Hence,

"I've lost 20 pounds already!" she cried.

Did she say "I've lost 20 pounds already"?

Citations

Citations of references are now often given as endnotes instead of being put at the bottom of the page on which the reference number appears. Here are some examples of proper form.

Endnotes are listed immediately after the end of the text.

When citing a from a book:

1. June True, <u>Finding Out</u>, 2nd ed. (Belmont, Calif.: Wadsworth, 1989), pp. 344–362.

When citing from an article:

2. R. L. Goldstein and J. T. Albert, ''The Status of Black Studies Programs on American Campuses, 1970–71,'' <u>Journal of Behavioral and Social Sciences</u> 20 (1): 12.

In the text the reference numbers come immediately after the end of the idea or quote. The citations are listed on the endnote page in numerical order.

Bibliographic notes are listed in the **bibliography**, always in alphabetical order by first author's surname.

When citing a book:

```
True, June. Finding Out, 2nd ed. Belmont, Calif.: Wadsworth,
    1989.
```

When citing an article:

```
Goldstein, R. L., and J. T. Albert, ''The Status of Black
    Studies Programs on American Campuses, 1970—71,''
    Journal of Behavioral and Social Sciences 20(1): 1—16.
```

If you are referring to an author more than once, it is enough to cite the author's surname and the page number.

```
True, p. 325.
```

If you are citing more than one work by that person or work by someone of the same name, however, you need to use the title, too.

```
True, Finding Out, p. 325.
```

Once you have had to return to the library to look up the details you forgot to note down, you will be convinced that this rule is most important:

Take all notes on each citation, in the correct form, when you first encounter it in the library.

Illustrations

Some of the illustrations you might use are:

charts
data distribution
diagrams
graphs
maps
tables not in text

Any or all of these are fine as long as they meet the essential requirement of clarity. They must make the message clearer.

Typing Instructions

Unless you have been told to do it differently, margins should be one inch on all sides, the page number one inch down and one inch in from the right-hand side, then double-space before starting to type text. Don't forget to paginate. (Always make it easy for the reader.) Start two inches down for the beginning of a section, the table of contents, or the bibliography. Type on one side of the paper and double-space the lines. You must underline words if you want them to be considered to be in italics. Do this for book or journal titles. Titles of articles are always in quotation marks. Don't forget to put your name on the front of your paper, along with the name of the instructor, the name of the course, and the date submitted. All these things usually go under the paper's title and somewhat toward the right. If the paper is a team effort, list the authors alphabetically by surname, but with first names first, thus:

```
Abigail Adams
Henry Clay
Harriet Tubman
George Washington
```

Finishing Up   When your paper is all done, proofread it to make sure it's all right. If you have time and can get someone to read it again, do it.

Good luck with this paper and all future papers!

Proposal Writing

Chapter 4 lists eight points that anyone hoping for grant money should cover in the grant proposal. The grant applicant should establish that:

1. the question is worth asking.
2. the proposed staff has the proper **credentials**, or degrees and diplomas, and is capable of doing the research.
3. the methods and time schedule are feasible.
4. no one will be hurt by the project.
5. no important political group will be offended.
6. the budget is realistic.
7. the project is appropriate for the agency considering it.
8. the results will be usable by somebody.

None of these can be safely left out; all must be carefully considered. A proposal is written from the granting agency's point of view, which may not coincide exactly with yours. However, the agency is the decision maker because its review committee's decision is crucial to your funding. Let's look at each of these points and consider what might be an agency's bases for accepting or rejecting your application.

The Question is Worth Asking

Granting bodies have become increasingly concerned about this issue in recent years, partly because public and private budgets have been greatly reduced. Another reason is the publicity that has been given to what some public figures consider to be "trivial" research. Scrutinizing public spending can hardly be criticized, but some studies have been ridiculed unfairly. A study of the mating habits of sowbugs might sound silly to some, and be a prime candidate for criticism; but it could yield important results to agriculture.

If you want the committee to see your project's serious intent and its scientific character, phrase the study description and title very carefully. Avoid stuffiness and academic jargon, but don't sound flippant. Consider the following alternatives:

1. "A quasi-familial gerontological socioenvironment in a diurnal institutional setting"
2. "A geriatric day-care center in a state hospital"
3. "Mom and Pop go to nursery school"

The first title is tedious to read and, were the whole application written in the same vein, would diminish the project's chances of being funded. It appears to be meaningless jargon intended to hide an insubstantial idea.

The third title would be worse because it doesn't sound serious. Spending public money *is* serious, and humor is out of place.

The second example is the title of a successful National Institute of Mental Health Hospital Improvement Program grant application.

Another influence on whether your question is seen as worth asking is what issues are in the public consciousness. Some years race relations get a lot of attention; other years the vital issue may be juvenile delinquency, drugs, pollution, or energy. Areas of human interest fluctuate in popularity.

There's more interest in old age now than in the 1950s because the average age of our population rises as "baby boomers" get older. Born in 1945, the first cohort of the "baby boom" has reached middle age. Also, as health practices improve, more people become old, generating more interest in this category.

Since what is on the public stage can cause the committee members of granting institutions to see relevance or miss it in your proposal, you ignore it at your peril. You shouldn't pick a topic just because it is "in," but you can look for and explain the ways in which your topic fits society's present concerns.

After you have clearly explained what you are proposing to do and why it is important to pursue this question, you address the second issue, the staff of the project.

The Proposed Staff Has the Proper Credentials and Is Capable of Doing the Research

You prepare a list of all positions to be filled, from director to the lowest-paid workers. You list only the titles for the nonprofessionals ("driver," "typist," "attendant," and so forth), but you must provide details about the people who will fill professional positions.

Academic researchers are usually expected to hold graduate degrees and/or to have published in the field of the project's topic. Relevant service in some institution or program is well regarded. Each professional candidate submits a brief résumé, listing degrees, titles, and experience. Writing this is not a task for the modest. One's accomplishments should be trumpeted, and every shred of evidence should be scraped up to show that one is not only qualified but ideal for the position. People reading the proposal don't usually know the candidates and must rely on what they read. They judge the suitability of the staff choices by résumés. (Applicants don't always get to appear before the committee.)

If you convince the committee that you are qualified and experienced enough to do the job, they will be reassured that you will use their money wisely. This is important. More projects ask for help than they can accommodate. You are selling and they are buying. They look for the "best buys."

The agency's application form asks you to outline your time schedule and methods.

The Methods and Time Schedule Are Feasible

It's a good idea to find out how much detail is wanted. Granting institutions have representatives who are available to answer questions. Application instructions should be read carefully also. Your presentation should be clear and in plain language. The committee members may not be completely ignorant of the topic, but they're usually not professionals in your field and usually not conversant with its jargon and techniques.

You want to provide ample information to show exactly what it is you propose to do, what method you will use, and how long it will take. Write a description and ask someone not in your field to read it. If it doesn't make sense to that person, rewrite it until it does.

It helps to describe the proposed methods and to cite prior research that has successfully used them. Maybe you are going to take somebody's method and modify it. The committee needs to know that you're not just thrashing about in the dark but know about previous research and are building on it. The requirements of the scientific method include relevance and contribution to the body of knowledge. Reassure the granting committee that you're fulfilling these.

Don't drop names. Reference to another's work should be succinct; assume, however, that at least one reader has never heard of it and provide a brief explanation. All references require a complete citation, which can be included in an alphabetized list at the end of the proposal and indicated in the text by the use of superscripts or reference in parentheses: (Brown, 1919).

Time limits are usually imposed on grants. Be realistic in estimating how long each phase of your project will take. The grant committee expects you to meet your deadlines. Failure to do so damages future credibility. The committee members want results for their money, and they want them when you promised them. Part of your basis for choosing an agency to which you apply is their established granting periods. These time limits determine when you can start drawing money and when you have to stop. (See the worksheets at the end of this appendix for some methodological and estimating ideas.)

No public or private institution can afford bad publicity, public outcry, or political retaliation. This means you have to consider points 4 and 5 very carefully, because the institution will.

No One Will Be Hurt by the Project

There are humane reasons for not wanting to hurt anyone, and there are practical reasons. Governments want to stay in office; foundations want public support. If they fund research that hurts the subjects, they will suffer, too.

Government grants require a supervising committee to safeguard the rights and welfare of human beings involved in research. You specify where and how this committee will be set up in the institution or agency sheltering your project. (Many institutions have permanent committees for this.) The supervising committee reviews your project and must approve it before you can start. Specify how your subjects will be recruited, informed, and treated. Reassure the committee that you've considered any possibility of an unpleasant aftermath, and say how you intend to avoid it.

No Important Political Group Will Be Offended

A subcultural or racial project, or a project on any political minority should be discussed beforehand with knowledgeable and prominent representatives of that group. They'll tell you if your project contains some inadvertent offense to them and if what you're doing has any kind of political implications. They can suggest possible benefits to "their people," as well as possible improvements in your method.

After consulting appropriate people, reveal this to the grant committee, showing that you are being responsible. If similar work has been done without unfavorable repercussions, you can mention it. You can have a staff consultant from the subject group serving on the project.

You have to apply for a grant months before you would actually begin the project, so you must remember the inflation rate and the other cautions outlined in Chapter 4.

The Budget is Realistic

Be careful not to ask for unnecessary items and extravagant sums, but be sure to ask for enough money to avoid the possibility of running out of it before you are finished.

Make a list of necessary personnel and purchases, carefully estimating and justifying each item. You supply a detailed accounting of hourly rates, overhead costs, fringe benefits, rentals, supplies, and fees. You also report expenditures during the course of the project. An expense can be justified by citing specific instances of recent similar expenditures.

The preparation of a budget should be thorough, not casual. It requires lots of checking and "homework." You can't afford to make mistakes. The committee must know that you can do the job with the money you request and that you won't waste it.

Let's look at ways of estimating financial needs for a project and then examine funding sources.

It is important to be inclusive. You can delete items later. Take the outline, line by line, and note all implied expense. It's handy to have a separate notebook page for each category so that expenses are automatically grouped when you are finished.

Facilities and Equipment   Facilities are the room(s) you need for headquarters, data processing, testing, training, or writing. Equipment includes things you need to work with in the headquarters or out in the field. An office needs furniture, office machines, telephones, light, heat, supplies, and cleaning. Your project might require a van, cameras, tape recorders, transcribers, one-way mirrors, testing devices, sound-proof cubicles or jungle gyms. The space and part or all of the equipment may already be rentable at the project site. Sometimes the institution with which you are working (school, agency, clinic, hospital, or business) provides space and equipment at no extra cost; but that institution is usually entitled to a payment for **overhead** expense. Overhead is a percentage of your budget. For example, if you need $75,000 and if the overhead required is 25 percent of the total budget, you have to ask for $100,000, so you'll have $75,000 left. The institution processes purchases and staff paychecks and "manages" your budget. They need to be reimbursed for the cost of the services, facilities, and equipment they provide.

Personnel   Personnel costs are salaries and wages, including consulting fees and fringe benefits, which are a percentage of the salaries and wages paid. To estimate this cost, you need to know the number of people and their compensation as well as their estimated working period. You have to find out the current rates for each type of employee and remember that inflation may increase the amount by the time the project is in full swing. It is often necessary to hire people to begin working before they can go out to gather data in order to allow for a training period. The personnel department of your institution can help with these estimates.

Data Collection   This category is considered separately from facilities and equipment because it involves designing and is not just a matter of buying something to use. The pieces of paper on which you record data are called data collection instruments, or simply **instruments**, and they vary from a single sheet of paper with a tally list or checklist, to fifty-page questionnaires. You can buy standard tests and **scales** (a questionnaire with questions in a specific order and special scoring), but you must buy as many as you need. Such tests are copyrighted, so you may not buy one copy and reproduce it.

When you design instruments yourself, you need to reproduce them. This process is not cheap. There's a per-page charge for supplying reproducible copy and a per-hundred charge for reproducing it. If you're mailing questionnaires, postage is a big item. You might have to arrange for collating, stapling, folding, envelope preparation and stuffing, and questionnaire numbering. Some questionnaires have answer sheets, and sometimes you need special pencils to mark on them so that the computer may read them. If you need artwork or charts and you have no staff artist, you must buy it by the piece, line, or square inch, as one does with advertising copy.

Subjects Subjects are the people you intend to study. If they are answering anything, they are also called respondents. You have to locate them. The process of rounding up subjects is called **casefinding**. This can mean buying mailing lists and spending hours on the phone making appointments. It can include travel: room and board, mileage, fares, and entertaining. If you send people away from the office to do fieldwork, you have to pay their bills while they are there. This can add up. Think about mileage costs. The writer recalls a week when she drove 999 miles to and from interviews. Mileage was 5¢ per mile then. It is 20¢ per mile at this writing. That week's mileage for *one* worker would now cost $199.80! Finding subjects and getting to them may involve paying them, maybe for the time they lost from work while serving as subjects.

Analysis Everything it takes to transform your data into summaries of statistics is included here. Completed questionnaires must be prepared for processing in whatever form you have planned. If you use computer analysis, data must be **coded**, or transformed into numbers that are keyed to explanations in a register called a **code book**. Then the data have to be entered into a terminal so that the computer can record them for storage and retrieval. The computer also has to be programmed to get the information in the form you desire. The time the computer takes to do this and to perform any of its computations is billed by the hour. After the computer produces your output, someone has to interpret it and incorporate this information into a report. All these expenses are included in the budget.

Publication The scientific method includes publication; the sharing of your research outcome with the scientific community. Publication expense includes costs similar to those incurred in preparing data collection instruments. The report has to be typed and reproduced. Depending on the sponsorship, or source of funds for the project, you have to submit several typed copies to an institution or agency, or you may have to submit a single copy to a journal or publisher; at other times a larger number of printed copies or one reproducible copy is required. If you have to mail anything, remember to allow for postage; if you are not sure of getting it published, you may have to send it out again and again. In some academic disciplines journals charge per page for publishing articles that they deem worthy of publication. (See pp. 443–444 for a worksheet to estimate costs, and Figure C.1.)

FIGURE C.1   **Estimating the costs of a research project**

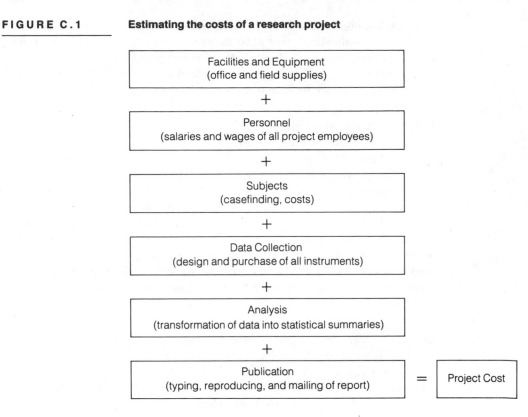

At this point you might think about how much cheaper it would be to use available data. Costs for many of the items could be reduced or eliminated altogether. For example, you could work alone. Facilities are public, and equipment is minimal. There is no overhead. If your grant application is denied, using available data is a possibility.

Part of choosing a granting agency lies in their mandate. You wouldn't go to the National Institute of Health with a grant request for saving the whooping crane. You must show the agency to whom you apply why your project is appropriate for them.

The Project Is Appropriate for the Agency Considering It

Many publications announce available grants. The institution or agency you work for may have a **grants officer**, who will help you decide which granting body is appropriate for your application. This decision is based partly on the amount of money you need and partly on the topic, since granting bodies limit their awards in both respects.

Now you do some homework. Read the agency's published material on the kinds of grant they distribute. Read their official mandate, and check into the grants they have already awarded. If your project is a type they haven't supported before, a creative approach might be to persuade them that this is the direction they ought to be taking to keep in step with the times, to fulfill their obligation to their public, or to meet the spirit in which their agency was founded.

Remember that you are dealing with intelligent people who are usually educated and will recognize condescension instantly. Don't take the position of the superior professor lecturing to the ignorant masses. Say only what you really mean and can support if challenged, and maintain the highest respect for your audience. You are convinced of the project's value or you wouldn't be proposing it. All you are really doing is finding an effective way to present something in which you believe.

The last point has to do with practical application.

The Results Will Be Usable by Somebody

It's harder to justify funding for "pure" research than for "applied" research. Pure research refers to inquiries for the satisfaction of scientific curiosity. Although this kind of inquiry is legitimate and even laudable, funds are scarce and human needs and problems great. Research resulting in progress toward meeting needs and addressing problems is usually favored. You will be wise to consider how the outcome of your project can benefit us all and bring this out carefully in the proposal.

The discussion of potential benefit should say when, where, and to whom the findings might be useful and describe how they may be exploited, specifying the problems to be solved or conditions eased. For example, what clinical purpose could your findings serve? What crucial piece of information could it provide for what endeavor? Consider the efficiency and economy of the improvement, and don't forget the "quality of life" benefits.

In summary, remember that committees who review applications for possible funding have to justify their choices to someone. Make it easy for them to justify choosing yours. Give them a clear, honest, comprehensive description of your proposed work, including all your valid selling points. Don't pad it or ramble, but make it easy to read and understand. The committee will appreciate it, and your chance of receiving an award will be increased.

Some Methodological and Estimating Ideas

Choosing Methods   The methods you use will be chosen from the possible range permitted by the topic and the subjects. You can't interview infants, mail questionnaires to illiterates, observe deviance, or experiment on people without their collusion. If you want people to answer questions, interviews provide better access to people; permit depth and clarification; and allow you to include context in your analysis. Questionnaires are cheaper, easier, and less likely to embarrass people.

Once you've chosen a questioning device, you choose a mode of administration. Will you interview in person or by phone? Will you administer questionnaires singly or in groups, or mail them? One solution is to use a variety of data collection methods. The Census Bureau uses this tactic. They send questionnaires to everyone, but some are longer than others, and some people are visited by an interviewer. Of course, you can use an interview with a questionnaire as part of it.

Estimating Time   Suppose you intend to watch schoolchildren at play to record their playmate choices for 15 minutes at a time—before school, during recess, and while they wait for their bus. You intend to show a film during the afternoon to one group of children (the experimental variable). You want to see if the film affects the playmate choices of the experimental group. You have got the necessary permissions, the technical equipment, and the film. Here's a possible schedule for each day:

8:00 A.M.	Arrive at office, pack gear
8:15	Leave office for school
8:30	Arrive at school (assuming short distance)
8:45–9:00	Observation I
9:00–9:30	Pack gear, back to office
9:30–11:00	Miscellaneous clerical, phone calls
11:00–11:15	Back to school
11:30–11:45	Observation II
12:00	Write notes on observation II (Notes on observation I were done at the office)
12:30–1:00 P.M.	Lunch
1:00–2:30	Set up film, show film, pack up
2:45–3:00	Observation III
3:00–3:30	Pack gear, back to office
3:30–5:00	Clerical, phone, notes

You can see this schedule is rigorous. Though it covers 9 hours, you have collected and recorded only 45 minutes worth of data (three observation periods). You'd be tired at the end of this day. If the school is at a greater distance, you'll probably stay there all day and do your office work (except for the observation notes) on another day. If you're lucky, the school will provide a quiet place for writing and waiting. If not, you may be waiting in your car, a supply closet, or a nearby luncheonette.

Theoretically, you can observe a different school every day and do five each week. A sample of 100 schools could be done in twenty weeks this way. It is highly unlikely that you could accomplish this because schools are closed on many days and not open *to you* on others. Schools observe holidays, convention weeks, special assemblies, and tests. You'd do very well to complete your observations in six months.

With one assistant, you might get your 100-school sample covered in two-thirds of the time. Why not in half? Because you and the assistant will spend time coordinating your work, comparing notes, standardizing your procedures, and scheduling conferences.

Data collection is tiring. Conducting a depth interview of about 2 hours is as much as you should plan for one day. You spend the balance of that day writing up the interview and taking care of other clerical matters, such as setting up further appointments. Brief interviews and questionnaires can be handled in greater quantity, but remember to allow for time between them. Whether you go to the respondents or they come to you, your project may be delayed by traffic, misunderstood directions, floods, fires, snowstorms, and strikes. Appointments may be broken and rescheduled several times.

Here's a list of things for which the time needed should be estimated:

project establishment; staffing

planning; organization and scheduling

data collection

data processing

analysis

report writing

To get a good time estimate, forecast as carefully as you can how long you will need for each item, multiply each by the number of times you intend to do it, and add about 30 percent of the subtotal.

Worksheet C.1   *Estimating time*

Instructions: Begin by listing the pieces of data you need and the activities you have to carry out to get them. Your guesses will be "rough" because you lack experience. Record the time in the appropriate unit: days, weeks, or months. Add the columns and transform all data into months. For this purpose a week is 5 days and 4 weeks equal one month. A "day" is about 6 hours, not counting lunch.

1. Pieces of data needed:

2. Activities necessary to get data:

3. Time schedule estimate:

    a. Establishing the project staff,
headquarters, equipment, clearances   ____   ____   ____

        Planning, instrument design, testing
instruments   ____   ____   ____

    b. Data collection (use additional sheets if
needed):

Item	No.	Time For Each	Days	Weeks	Months
____	___	____	___	___	___
____	___	____	___	___	___
____	___	____	___	___	___
____	___	____	___	___	___

(Multiply item by time and carry to "time needed" columns. Don't forget travel, meals, breaks, and "lost" time.)

    c. Data processing:
        Summaries   ____   ____   ____
        Coding   ____   ____   ____
        Analysis and preparation of report   ____   ____   ____
        Totals   ____   ____   ====

4. Time summary:
    a. Number of months estimated   ____
    b. Add 30% of item 4a   ____
    c. Total time estimated   ====

Item 4c is the time you should estimate for your project.

Worksheet C.2 *Estimating money*

Instructions: Now complete the following budget for the same project. (Use additional sheets if needed.)

		Salary	No.	Twelve-month Period
1.	Personnel			
	a. Title:	$_____	× ____	$_____
	b. Title:	$_____	× ____	$_____
	c. Title:	$_____	× ____	$_____
	Subtotal for personnel			$_____

		Price	No.	
2.	Equipment and Supplies			
	a. Item:	$_____	× ____	$_____
	b. Item:	$_____	× ____	$_____
	c. Item:	$_____	× ____	$_____
	d. Item:	$_____	× ____	$_____
	Subtotal for equipment and supplies			$_____

3. Travel

    a. Fares $_____

    b. Mileage $.20 per mile   No. miles____ × .20   _____

    c. Hotel, meals, miscellaneous   _____

    Subtotal for travel $_____

4. Miscellaneous

    a.   Telephone service $_____per month $_____

    b.   Rent $_____per month   _____

    c.   _____   _____

    d.   _____   _____

        Subtotal for miscellaneous $_____

5. Overhead (find out what your institution requires) _____%.

6. Inflation hedge is 10%.

Totals

Now you can estimate your final budget.

			Totals
1. Personnel	$_____	plus 10%_____	$_____
2. Equipment/supplies	$_____	plus 10%_____	$_____
3. Travel	$_____	plus 10%_____	$_____
4. Miscellaneous	$_____	plus 10%_____	$_____
Subtotal			_____
5. Overhead (see accompanying overhead chart)			_____
Grand Total			_____

(*Note:* Leftover money returns to the grantor.)

OVERHEAD CHART

If overhead is: 10%, add 1/9 of subtotal
                 15%, add 3/17 of subtotal
                 20%, add 1/4 of subtotal
                 25%, add 1/3 of subtotal
                 30%, add 1/2 of subtotal
                 40%, add 2/3 of subtotal
                 50%, double subtotal

Worksheet C.3 *Adjusting the ideal to the real*

Instructions: Using worksheets C.1 and C.2, imagine that you have been told you have a good chance of getting a grant, however, the grant will be limited to 75 percent (three-fourths) of what you requested. Modify your plans in order to complete the project *without sacrificing validity*. Be realistic. Don't rely on donations of time or money.

1. Amount originally requested: _____

2. Three-fourths of that amount: _____

3. Subtract item 2 from item 1 to get new figure: _____

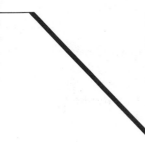

APPENDIX D

Using Research Skills for Profit

BY EMILY G. ALBERT,
Consultant

Introduction

Research methods and techniques developed in academic settings are often adapted for use in commercial market research firms. The $2 billion U.S. market research industry, comprising approximately 150 major firms, affords an opportunity for students with social research skills to use them in the study of commercial markets.[1] Research is also done in sales, marketing, and product planning departments within American corporations, as well as in nonprofit organizations. Market research, like other social research, studies human behavior; but market research is specifically concerned with people as consumers. Here, their behavior is important only as it affects the way they purchase goods and services. Human behavior is as complex in the purchasing of goods and services as it is in other areas, and the industry that studies purchasing behavior has developed techniques to break that complexity down into manageable parts.

Questions concerning consumer behavior are asked of market research firms. Who is buying our product? How much and how often do they buy? Who is buying our competitor's product? Why do they buy a particular brand? How satisfied are they? What is the highest price we can charge them? Many data collection approaches are used to answer these questions, ranging from in-person interviews, focus groups, and phone and mail surveys to electronic scanning devices used on UPC symbols in supermarkets.

Industry Profile

The market research industry has been growing at about 13 percent a year.[2] Its primary customers are the American and foreign businesses who market products or services in the United States. The market research business is highly responsive to the customer needs, and several recent growing trends in these needs have encouraged corresponding growth in the market research industry. American firms are greatly concerned about foreign competition. Competing with goods more cheaply manufactured overseas, they are showing renewed interest in ways of differentiating American products in the market, so that a higher price tag will be justified. They hope to accomplish this by emphasizing quality and service, concepts important to the consumer. Survey research is designed to define consumer needs and preferences so business can provide better service and create an image based on what consumers say they want.

Foreign customers are important to the health of the U.S. market research industry, providing about 27 percent of overall revenue.[3] They use market research to determine if and when a new product manufactured overseas should be introduced into both existing and new American markets.

Another important trend in U.S. and foreign industry that fuels market research business is the interest in market segmentation. Many companies want to identify market segments (specific groups of people with the same needs), so they can advertise and distribute their products effectively. Market segments may be based on residence by geographic region, income, age, or interest in specific activities. Properly segmenting the markets they serve saves companies advertising expense.

Market Research Methods

Research methods used range from simple surveys and questionnaires to complex statistical analyses. Many of the guidelines and techniques in the methodology of social research presented in this book are directly translatable into the market research field. There is a hazard, however, when research is done for paying customers. They often have pre-set notions of what the research findings should be or have a political interest in slanting the findings. Take, for example, the case of a vice-president of marketing who is set on acquiring another firm to expand into a new product area in order to improve sales in her department. She is concerned about her job, because sales of the traditional product line have been steadily dropping over the past few quarters. She may call in a market research firm to do a study she hopes will confirm her positive view of the potential market for the proposed product so she can sell the idea to the board of directors.

These situations can easily exert pressure on a market researcher to provide the *desired* result at the expense of an *objective* analysis of the situation, because customers may be lost if their assessments of situations are contradicted. Ground rules and ethical standards in market research have evolved to avoid this type of pressure, which could severely damage the reputation and usefulness of the industry as a whole. Not only that, but a research firm can be sued if a business takes an unprofitable action on the strength of an overly optimistic market research report.[4] Unfortunately, statistics generated from market research studies are often cited in industry articles and conferences out of context in order to influence decisions. There is little a market research firm can do except to avoid any misrepresentation of data in its own work.

Types of Research Firms and Job Opportunities

Three major types of firms are dedicated to market research. These are opinion pollsters, industry watchers, and consultant firms.

Opinion pollsters are firms that seek demographic information and use short questionnaires to collect data from the public. They most often use telephone calls but also question people in public places such as malls or downtown areas. They rarely perform sophisticated data analysis but report results such as frequency of response to a question and relative popularity of political candidates. They typically employ an operating staff of canvassers at low pay. College degrees are usually not required. Students are typically encouraged to apply for summer and evening work. Managers in these firms generally do have bachelor's degrees and above. Their responsibilities range from managing the interviewer shifts and designing questionnaires to managing the processing and analysis of the data, and client relations.

Industry watchers are firms specializing in tracking and reporting on industries and markets within those industries. They sell both data and analysis of simple and complex markets. Simple markets would include those for a basic product, such as toothpaste, while complex markets include complete areas—data communications, for example. Industry watchers are widely quoted in government and business publications. Many of the Wall Street investment firms, which have done industry watching for years in order to assess the attractiveness of company stock for their clients, have begun selling their analyses on products and markets in direct competition with the market research firms. They provide their reports first to their clients as "insider" information, and after the securities buying/selling is done, they send the information to a database vendor for public access and sale.

Industry watchers employ a full range of research methods, and generally hire bright people with bachelor's and master's degrees to conduct the research and write up the analyses. Analysts specialize in specific markets and companies and maintain close contact with people within their target areas. Managers in industry-watching companies include people (many at the doctoral level) who specialize in a particular area, such as quantitative or qualitative research methods or statistical analysis. There is usually a senior research director as well. Most of these firms offer custom research as well as market analyses, and many offer educational seminars and conferences. They are headquartered in the United States, but many have offices throughout the world so they can offer information on international markets.

Marketing consultancies are firms that offer custom market research to clients in addition to other services related to the sales and marketing and product planning areas. They are usually connected in some way to general management consulting firms, dedicated to helping corporate clients solve complex business problems. Some consultancies are specialists in particular market areas, such as computers and telecommunications. Marketing consultancies generally hire top business school graduates and technical specialists, but they often have research analysts with four-year degrees and summer interns who are working on graduate degrees. Starting salaries are high in this field. Clients for these firms are usually very large corporations.

Notes

1. Council of American Survey Research Organizations, cited in "Special Report: Research Business Review," *Advertising Age* May 11, 1987, pp. S1, S2.
2. *Ibid.*
3. *Ibid.*
4. Council of American Survey Research Organizations, cited in "Beecham vs. Saatchi," *Advertising Age*, July 13, 1987, pp. 1, 86.

Using Computers

A computer combines the functions of a typewriter, a calculator, and a filing system. It does the typing, erasing, and rearranging of written work just as we used to do by hand, as well as some things too skilled for most of us. It files and retrieves information much more quickly than the old systems and will print out selected information from its files. Although working with a computer can be time-consuming, it processes work and presents you with beautifully executed jobs at high speed. It compares with the automatic washer in this respect. You might spend a lot of time using it, but you do a lot more laundry for the time spent, with a lot less work.

Uses and Types of Computers

Many offices now have computers and expect employees to use them for writing reports, keeping records, planning projects, and accounting. There are more sophisticated uses, such as computer-aided design (CAD) and policy making, and less sophisticated uses, such as playing games and running simple simulations, but typical ways computers are used in offices are writing, filing, and computation.

Some offices also use telecommunication, which is talking through a computer to a computer elsewhere. People send inquiries and get information from data banks, which are large computer files. The machine has to have a device called a **modem**. The name comes from the words *modulate* and *demodulate*, which are the technical processes the device employs.

What you can do is limited by the type of computer you have, the model of printer you have, and whether you own the software to do a specific job. Software is copyrighted, and it is a federal offense to copy it unless you have a *license* to do so. Schools and large companies might pay the vendor of the software for permission to make copies for students or employees. The ordinary consumer just buys one copy of the software and makes a working copy of it, putting the original away for safekeeping.

The software has its hardware requirements printed on its package. On one of my **PCs** (personal computers), a Kaypro 4, I can run (use) any program written for the CP/M machine, with a 64K **kilobyte** limit, and it has a modem built in.[5] These specifications are the operating system of the computer (CP/M) and the amount of memory, or work space, it has (64K). [*Note:* A kilobyte, or K, is 1024 bytes, or units of computer memory. A megabyte, or M, is 1000K. A typed page occupies about 2K.] A 64K machine allows you to work with about 30 pages at a time. Another machine I have is a little Radio Shack portable (Model 100), with 32K. I use it for notes and schedules. It has all its programs permanently installed in its memory, and it has a built-in modem, too. It can run on batteries or plugged into a wall socket.

The 64K machine has two **disk drives** with slots in which to insert floppy disks, either with programs on them (software) or blanks, ready to have my material recorded on them. Generally I put a program in one disk drive and a file disk in the other to hold what I am going to write. Broadly speaking, what I do is use the 64K memory to work on a chapter, then save it to the file disk, clear the machine's memory, and work on another chapter. The work space, or memory, is like a desk on which you work. You use it over and over.

When you see references to larger amounts of memory, it means only that the work space is bigger. My third computer, Turbo Kaypro, has 768K; I can run sociology simulations on that machine that won't go on the others because the simulations require too much work space. You can get personal computers with large amounts of work space, called **megabytes**. They use a component called a **hard disk**. No matter how many megabytes the salesman is trying to sell to you, it still means "a bigger desk to work on." I have dozens of disks on file with many K (kilobytes) of material on them, all produced on my trusty 64K machine. A machine with a hard disk can store all that on the hard disk and still have plenty of work space. In other words, a hard disk combines work space with filing space. The advantage to it is quick access to everything and no floppy disks to handle. The disadvantages are that if the hard disk goes bad, or "crashes," you lose everything on it; and you need a complicated directory to find your files. My floppy disks are labeled and I store them in labeled boxes. You make second copies (**backups**) of floppy disks in case of accident and you have to back up a hard disk, too. Backing up a hard disk requires the purchase of some additional equipment and tapes to back it up on.

My Turbo Kaypro is a DOS (disk operating system) machine. That means it uses the IBM-compatible operating system and can run any DOS program up to its memory limit. It has a **microchip** in it that allows it to run CP/M programs, too. Its screen is amber, not green like the other Kaypro's or gray, like the Radio Shack portable. One of my daughters has a Macintosh, which has still another operating system. I can't run the programs she uses and she can't run mine. The various computer brands and models are like any other appliance: a wide choice of styles and features exists. There is no shortcut. If you want to buy one, you have to do your homework.

A **mainframe** computer has a huge amount of filing and work space and is connected to many terminals and one or more printing stations. It is a **time-sharing** system. That means that a number of people can work at terminals simultaneously. The machine allots a specific amount of work space to each. There are also smaller installations of personal computers that share the same software storage and the user can **download** a software program for use at the PC or terminal as needed. This means that the machine copies the program into the individual machine's memory for the user. When the user quits, using a specified "signoff" procedure, the software copy is erased and the PC awaits the next user's pleasure. Some terminals can **emulate**, or pretend to be, PCs. A software program called IRMA will transform a terminal into a PC and back again to a terminal for you.

At our school, Trenton State College, in New Jersey, we have a wide variety of equipment installed in a number of labs as well as individual offices. Students generally use the PCs for writing papers and doing computer programming or accounting homework, since the software needed is available to them. I send my sociology students to the PC labs to run simulations, too.

Why You Might Use a Computer

Word Processing   The advantage of a computer over a typewriter is the ease with which you can correct mistakes and edit your work, rearranging as much as you want to *before* you print it out. You have to learn the commands specific to the software package you are using. For example, I am using one called Perfect Writer to produce this manuscript. On all machines a movable light called a **cursor** indicates where you are and where the next character you type will appear. If I want to delete a word I have typed, I move the cursor to the space directly before it, hold down the ESC (escape) key and hit the D. The word disappears. I can retrieve the last thing I deleted by holding down the CTRL (control) key and hitting the Y. Each software program has its own command system. The program comes on a disk or disks and you get an instruction book with that and sometimes a command card with often-used commands on it for quick reference.

Once I have written something and I'm satisfied with it I can give the command to save it on my floppy disk. In this case, I will hold down CTRL and hit XS. After that I can give a brief series of commands and the machine will send the material to the printer. I will already have turned the printer on (very important) and inserted the paper. Since I use continuous feed paper, I can go have a cup of tea while it prints out my work. If I'm in a lab at school my work will be printed as soon as its turn comes. The system puts newly ordered work into a queue and does it "first come, first served."

Possibilities   There are programs to check your spelling and some to check your grammar. You can order your copy single-spaced, double-spaced, bold-faced, or underlined, and with some machines, in different type faces. The programs get fancier and fancier as the movement called "desktop publishing" develops. Some computers, such as Apple's Macintosh, will let you produce flyers with pictures as well as text, reports with charts in them, and so forth.

Filing   Computer filing systems are great because once you have the information entered, you can print out lists of things in a number of different sortings. For example, putting my name and address list on a disk using my Kaypro 4 and a program called Perfect Filer allows me to record key words on each person's record so that I can then use a specific key word to ask the program to format a list of only certain people. It would be little trouble for me to get lists of:

>   colleagues
>
>   Christmas card recipients
>
>   relatives
>
>   teammates
>
>   social friends

I can have them sorted by surname, city, state, or zip code, and they will be alphabetically arranged within those categories. I can print names only, names and addresses, names and phone numbers, etc. I have to learn how to set up the system. I have used the filer to sort words and produce an alphabetically ordered glossary for a 600-page manuscript. I taught a student how to use a DOS filer called PC-File III and he worked out a system, making a record for each of his parents' horses, recording their breeding, feeding, veterinary care, and daily schedule. His post-graduation plan is to work in the family horse breeding business. His computer system allows him to print out lists with specific data about all the horses in his file, lists of horses scheduled for vet visits "this month," and many other useful retrievals.

Accounting   Small businesses can put all their records on computer disks and use the machine to keep track of sales, purchases, accounts receivable and payable, inventory and payroll. Bookkeeping of all types is feasible using one of the many accounting programs available. **Spreadsheets** are like ledger pages, columns stretching across the page with a wide one at the left for the description. The advantage of the computer is that it does the arithmetic work very quickly. If you have asked the computer to total a long column and then you change one of the amounts, the computer automatically changes the total. You can also add, subtract, multiply, or divide all the figures at once. Say you wanted to decrease a whole budget by 10 percent. You can command the program to do that, using a formula, and it will change every figure instantly. I use a bookkeeping system called Quick Check Plus on my Kaypro

4 and I have it print out monthly statements so I can see exactly why I haven't any money left over. Accounting students use a more sophisticated program called Lotus 1-2-3 to do their assignments.

Programming   I mentioned programming homework. Students who take courses in one of the programming languages (**BASIC, COBOL, PASCAL**, etc.) learn to write the sets of instructions that tell the computer what to do. These sets of instructions must be precisely written and can be very lengthy. A set of instructions written by somebody else is what you are buying when you buy a software program. You are paying for the (often considerable) time it took to write the program, the book of instructions for using it, the disk(s) it is on, and the packaging. Sometimes the purchase includes **support**, or the privilege of calling the vendor for help when you have a problem using the program. Taking one course in BASIC and learning to write very simple programs will give you an appreciation of programmers' work.

Ready-to-use software doesn't require knowledge of programming, and software itself gets easier to use as time goes on and improvements are made. It also does more things on personal computers than was possible only a short time ago. The next two uses required a mainframe when I began to learn how to use computers, but there are PCs now that can be programmed to provide tables and graphs and to perform statistical tests.

Constructing Tables and Graphs   All kinds of tables and graphs are possible on the computer, both standard types and those of your own invention. Once your data have been keyed into the computer, you can ask the machine, via SAS, SPSS^x, MINITAB, or whatever you are using, to construct and print out frequency distributions, cross-tabulations, histograms, scattergrams, simple graphs, pie charts, and many others. Each package has its own selection from which you choose, referring to the appropriate handbook to determine the correct command. One limitation is that you have to be hooked up to a printer that is capable of printing the graph or table you want.

Some printers are more versatile than others (and more expensive). I have, for example, a Dynax 15, which is a daisywheel printer. It makes the characters by rapidly rotating a wheel with all the characters on it and striking the paper through the printer ribbon, similar to the action of the typing ball on an IBM Selectric typewriter. If I want a different typeface, I have to buy another daisywheel. My printer is great for text but it doesn't do graphics. Other printers have a system called **dot matrix**, which uses dots to form the characters and can make a wider variety of them, as well as various other forms and outlines. Dot matrix printers are faster and can do graphics. The most versatile are the laser printers, which are expensive.

Manipulation of Data and Computation of Statistical Tests   I have not tried using a PC for these jobs, but I have processed data using MINITAB, SPSS^x, and SAS in the past year. Once the data is keyed in, and that *can* be a long and tedious operation, the data manipulations you can do are truly marvelous. You can get frequencies and the measures of central tendency and dispersion for your variables. You can select variables and have them combined into new ones:

> take age of husband and age of wife, and make a new variable:
> difference in age between spouses

subdivide your cases by any variable's category:

> print out cases by categories for the variable marital status to get a list of single, married, separated, divorced, and widowed people

reorder your cases by ID number or alphabetically in an instant, and add, subtract, multiply or divide scores for each case, producing new variables.

In addition to data manipulation, you can perform many statistical tests, depending on the package, *without doing any of the work yourself*. If you want to get real appreciation for this benefit, calculate some by hand. One or two examples should do it.

The modem makes it possible to communicate with other computer installations. Before we had a powerful enough mainframe at school and the packages to use, we had to call the New Jersey Educational Computer Network (NJECN), where we had an account, and use their facilities. We learned how to ask the computer to do this, how to sign on, how to identify ourselves so that the bill would go to the right place, and how to sign off. In between the ID and the signoff, we ran our data, and the NJECN computer sent the results to our printer at the school. Now our installation permits doing the work "at home."

Telecommunication Using telecommunications, you can call (access) a commercial service such as the one called "The Source." A pilot I know calls "The Source," via his PC, for up-to-the-minute flight information. You can get everything from movie reviews to stock market quotes. There are other commercial, governmental, and academic services providing general and specialized information. You can join one of many groups called **bulletin boards** to send and receive messages, just as if you were talking on the phone, except that what you send and what you receive is not audible, but visible on your monitor. Some charge and some don't, but the phone company charges for the time on line.

Searching Data Banks Our library has a computer search service. I can get a printout of bibliographic references on almost any topic to get me started on my review of the literature for it. I have to consult the librarian in charge of this, and we decide together what **key words** we will feed into the computer so that it can look for references containing them. We also decide which data banks we will use. Using them costs money, so you can't just look at everything. I would probably be searching Sociological Abstracts for references on topics I am pursuing, for example. There are already a large number of data banks, some general and some specific, and there are indexes to them in the library. If I wanted to, I could arrange to search a data bank from my PCs at home, too.

Computers do many more things than I have mentioned above, from regulating the heat in a building to simulating the movement of planets and stars. Will you use one in any of the ways I have mentioned? There are some predictable times when you might find it worth your while.

When You Might Use a Computer

Writing an assignment on a computer gives you an advantage because all mistakes can be corrected and all changes made *before* the work is printed out. Even if the printing installation available to you uses cheap paper and doesn't change the printer ribbon often enough, producing light copy, you can produce a "finished" copy from which it will be easy to type a fair copy on good paper. You can then change anything, such as page numbers, to the style requested by the instructor. The work of composing is much easier because making changes doesn't mean retyping or a messy paper.

You may be in charge of an organization's records. Putting the information in a computer file will make your work a breeze from then on, because the records are so easy to update and the computer will print out many types of report for you. You can even write a form letter and the computer will produce one for each person in a designated category of the file, with the individual's name and address on it. It will type name and address labels, too. A spreadsheet program will keep track of the group's finances and will produce the monthly or quarterly treasurer's report you need.

As you go through school you will no doubt encounter an assignment to do research. If the appropriate data bank is available, a search for relevant literature is much easier to do when you begin with a computer search. The items the computer turns up will lead you to others that are not in a data bank. It's a good start. Many homework assignments either direct you to use a computer or are best done on one. The machine you will use depends on the nature of the assignment and the facilities available. There are, however, certain things you should always bear in mind, before you go to the lab, while you are there, and after you have finished using it.

Before You Go to the Lab

Facilities Take the trouble to find out where *all* computer facilities are on campus which are open to your use. List them, and note, for each one:

> the hours and days it is open
> who the person in charge is
> the lab phone number

what kind of machines there are
  how many of each kind

whether you can print out your work

what kinds of ID number(s) you need to use the machines
  how to get such numbers.

whether they have operating system instructions for you

whether they have instructions for you for the package you want to use
  how to get those two handouts (get them as soon as you can)

Materials   It is pointless to go to the computer lab unless you have your work organized. Check to make sure that you have your assignment, any reference books you need (such as simulation instruction manuals), your data file or code sheets, your codebook, your manuscript outline, or whatever. Before you leave, envision yourself sitting down at the machine ready to work. Do you need a floppy disk? Pens and pencils? A note pad? Paper clips? Rubber bands? Tissues? Change for a phone call or the hallway snack machine? I have been called upon to supply all of these items for forgetful students at one time or another. Provide for your predictable needs.

Goals   Know what you want to accomplish before you leave for the lab. Know how much time you have, so you can get ready to sign off and leave without rushing. Know when the lab's busiest times are and avoid them. Don't wait until the last minute to do an assignment, only to discover the machines all in use. Make a list of your objectives for each trip. If you are using a mainframe package to manipulate data or perform statistical computations, use the handout or package handbook to write out the instructions you will use NOW. If you think everything out carefully, you will use the computer to greatest advantage and not waste time at the lab.

By all means, read the handouts in advance, slowly. Take them with you. If the school offers a course in using the machines, take it. These courses are brief, but invaluable.

When You Get to the Lab

Assistant   If this is your first visit, look up the person in charge and say so. The assistant will help you if you ask. Your first visit might well be limited to learning how to turn the computer on and off and trying some of the procedures described in the system handout. The assistant might very well have a tutorial or starter program and will show you how to run it. I have found these assistants uniformly helpful. (Yes, I'm a faculty member, but I don't always identify myself.)

Handouts   Accept whatever handouts are offered by your instructor or at the lab. They are really helpful. I save mine in a folder and often find it necessary to use them to refresh my memory. You can't remember everything about every machine, package, program, or printer. Packages are revised often and instructions change, so it's wise to get current advice.

Up and Running   Typical sequence:

Sit down.

Turn on computer if not already on (some labs leave them on all day).

Call up system, using your ID, if necessary.

If running data, make the file, enter the data, and save it every ten lines.

Call up the package and enter the commands you have prepared.

Run the program and have it printed out.

Sign off.

Go get your printout.

If you are just using a PC for an assignment, you download the program you want, follow the instructions, write your material or whatever, save it, and print it out. It's a streamlined version of the sequence given above because you don't use your own list of commands (program).

When You Return from the Lab

Remember that the computer is a tool, not a thinker. When you produce printout, you need to look it over. If it's a manuscript, proofread it. As noted above, you may have to retype it. If it's a report, check each line and consider carefully what the results mean.

If you used a computer to manipulate data and do statistical tests, your job is just beginning. Now you have to study the output and decide what it signifies for your investigation. You have to consider the levels of measurement and what the percentages of responses mean. Also consider what effect your coding categories may have had on the pattern of responses and how to interpret them. Remember, numbers aren't everything. Think of the social significance of your results.

Glossary

accessible approachable

accidental sample a sample composed of whoever was available

accretion accumulation; something piling up as the result of some activity

administered questionnaire a list of questions whose answers are filled in by the respondent in the presence of the researcher

affective emotional

aggregate sum up (data); organize and tabulate

alienation helplessness in the face of social conditions

alpha the region of rejection of the null hypothesis (located at the tails of the normal curve of error)

analysis careful examination of a whole and of its parts, including the relationships among them

analysis of variance statistical comparison of sample variances to measure their dispersion and see if they represent different distributions

announced observation an observation preceded by telling the subject(s) that you are going to do it

anomie lack of group regulation; lack of clear norms

anonymity the state of having no name acknowledged

ANOVA acronym for analysis of variance

appendix section added to a book or report that contains details to supplement the text (correct, but seldom used plural: appendices)

area sample a multistage sample, beginning with a random selection of geographical areas

arithmetic mean average

array   numbers in a line; ordered by size; a rectangular arrangement of quantities in rows and columns

associated   varying simultaneously (no causation implied)

available data   information already collected, not necessarily for the same reasons you have for wanting it, but organized in some way for analysis

average   score that results when all scores are summed and the total is divided by the number of scores

average deviation   average distance from a measure of central tendency

back matter   reference material at the end of a report

backup   a duplicate computer record, on either disk or tape

ballooning the sample   taking an additional random sample and discarding all subjects from it except those belonging to a category that was insufficiently numerous in the original random sample

bar graph   graph with bars, usually vertical, proportionate in length to an amount of something illustrated

BASIC   a computer command language

benchmark   a point of known measurement, to serve as a reference point for measuring other things

bias   distortion

biased   influenced; not objective; twisted

bibliography   list of works consulted by the author

bivariate   involving two variables

bivariate analysis   an examination of the relationship of two variables

Bogardus Social Distance Scale   composite measure to determine how close subjects are willing to get to specified groups

brevity   shortness of duration

bulletin board   a computer communication system that can be called; through which one receives and sends messages

byte   a unit of computer memory (holds one character)

captive group   people in institutions who are not free to leave or to refuse to serve as subjects

casefinding   rounding up subjects (may involve persuasion)

categorically based groups   groups or classes of people who have some characteristic in common

categorize   sort into distinct and mutually exclusive subgroups

category   a classification based on a characteristic deemed important by the members of a social system; a variable classification

causality   relationship between the stimulus that produces an effect and the effect itself

cell space in a table where a frequency or percentage is written

circular argument statement in which the premise and the conclusion can change places without changing the argument

circumlocution speaking in a roundabout way; hinting

circumstantial evidence data that would lead you to believe something happened, but which are not conclusive proof of it

citations footnotes or endnotes (literally, quotations)

clarity clearness; ease with which something can be understood

classification systematic grouping into categories

closed-end question question that presents a choice of prepared answers

closure tendency for something incomplete to be perceived as complete when the missing part(s) is supplied by the observer's mind

cluster sample multistage sample consisting of random selection of groups as the first stage, possibly subgroups as successive stages

COBOL a computer command language

code system of numbers assigned to the categories of variables

code book book listing the codes and their meanings

coded transformed into numbers for computer entry

cohort people sharing the year of a significant event such as birth, marriage, or graduation

cohort study study using a sample of people who share the year of a significant event

collapse to combine adjacent categories

composite measure scale, index; a summary of scores on individual items

composite score score computed from individual question scores

computer output wide tape with printed results of computer operations (the printer is an accessory to a computer)

concept idea

conditional association relationship between two variables when controlled for a third (or more)

confidence interval that portion of the normal curve in which we think our sample falls (estimated by computation)

confidentiality secret-keeping

conflict theory social system analysis focusing on conflict

content analysis careful examination of communications to detect and record patterns

contingency question question that depends on the answer to a previous question

contingency table   bivariate or multivariate table

control   a person or item to whom nothing is done, to use for comparison with a person or item to whom something *has* been done

control for   to divide a variable into categories and examine the relationship between the independent and dependent variables for each category

control group   group, not manipulated in any way, used to provide a standard against which the experimental group is measured

controlling   examining a variable's categories to see what proportions of each category's members fall into the categories of a second variable

control variable   variable that is assumed to have an effect on the relationship between an independent and a dependent variable and that is, therefore, controlled for

correlation   tendency for two things to vary simultaneously: rising together, falling together, or rising and falling in opposition to one another

credential   diploma, degree, certificate, or other evidence that a researcher is trained

cross-sectional research   research project with one sample and one data collection period

cross-tabulation   bivariate or multivariate table; the relationships it represents

culture shock   intense dismay at behavior markedly different from one's own standards

cursor   a flashing light on a computer screen to mark where the next typed character will appear

data   information, especially that collected for research analysis

data bank   a computer file of information, usually large, intended for reference

data card   same as computer card; long, narrow card with holes punched in it corresponding to number-labels that represent data in a code book; rarely used nowadays

data collection period   time between the first and last dates upon which data were collected

data matrix   an array of data rows and columns

deductive logic   reasoning from theory to the empirical world

degree of freedom   the number of cross-tabulated frequencies in a table that are free to vary when the marginals are known

demand characteristics   things about the data collection process that lead the subjects to think the researcher is expecting a particular response

demographic   pertaining to the study of populations (births, deaths, migration, illness)

dense sample   sample composed of a majority of a population

density   crowdedness; compactness

dependent variable   variable assumed to vary in response to an independent variable

descriptive research   research organized to provide a complete account of something so that it may be classified

descriptive statistics   mathematical statements that describe the dimensions and patterns of a sample or population

deviation   distance of a score from a specified measure of central tendency

differentiation   the increasing specialization of parts

direct mail questionnaire   a set of questions designed to be mailed to respondents, filled out, and returned

direct methods of research   ways in which data are collected while the subjects are aware of the researcher's presence, whether or not they know that research is being done

direct presentation   asking a question point-blank

disk drive   slotted receptacle for computer disks that makes the information on them available to the work space for use and editing

disproportionate stratified random sample   stratified random sample in which the subgroups do not appear in the same proportions as they do in the population from which the sample was drawn

documentation   instructions for using computer hardware or software

dominant   having the power to control others

dot matrix   a printing system that forms characters by printing many small dots

double-barreled question   two questions phrased as one

download   to copy a computer file from one computer to another or to a terminal

dummy tables   tables with blank cells

dynamic   changing; in motion

dysfunction   a drawback to the smooth working of a system

echo   probe that repeats part or all of the most recent answer

elaboration   the adding of variables to a bivariate analysis

empirical   derived from observation, experience

empirical verification   observing the real world to see if a theory holds

emulate   duplicate the functions of

entry strategy   tactic for gaining entrance to a group

equation   mathematical statement (formula) of equality between two statistical expressions

equilibrium   a balanced state

erosion   a wearing away (indicating that something has been used or taken)

ethical safeguards   rules designed to prevent bad conduct

ethics   principles of good conduct

ethnomethodological   research that employs a wide variety of techniques and that concentrates on values and norms

evaluation   an examination and judgment

evaluation research   research done to assess the worth of a program

exotic   unfamiliar; strange

experiment   test made to see if a hypothesis holds true; controlled test of two or more groups that are measured before and after some are exposed to a treatment

experimental group   group introduced to the experimental variable

experimental mortality   loss of cases from an experimental or control group, for any reason

experimental variable   treatment in an experiment; independent variable in an experiment

explanatory research   research organized to answer a question

exploratory research   research organized to become familiar with something

extension   probe that asks for more information to expand the most recent answer

external validity   agreement between what is true of the research subjects (sample) and what is true of the population from which they were drawn

feasible   capable of being done

field   branch of knowledge or discipline; set of columns assigned to one variable

file   a named portion of material on a computer disk or tape

forced-choice   paired comparisons; closed-end questions supplying two answers, one of which must be selected

formula   a mathematical statement

FORTRAN   a computer command language

fourfold table   cross-tabulation of two variables with two categories each, resulting in four cells for frequencies

frequency count   number of times something happens and is recorded

"front" matter   information that a person or group wants outsiders to see as representative of them

front matter   material in the front of a book before the main text: title page, table of contents, and preface

function   use; feature that contributes to the smooth working of a system

functionalism   social theory focusing on systemic operation; assuming that conflict is disruptive, subject to compensatory correction by the system, as it operates automatically

generalizability   applicability to a wider group than was actually studied

glossary   list of words with their definitions

grant   an award of money to do a specific project

grants officer   staff member in an institution or agency who helps people prepare grant applications and do related tasks

guided group interaction   early groupwork technique developed at Highfields, New Jersey

Guttman scale   composite measure that arranges items so that you need know only one to know the pattern of a respondent's score

hard copy   copy printed out on paper

hard disk   a permanently installed data disk

hash marks   //// (crude symbols used to tally something)

Hawthorne Effect   tendency of people to respond positively to being singled out for study

heterogeneity   variety in a group

histogram   bar graph in which the bar widths correspond to the variable's interval width (interval or ratio data only)

history   whatever is happening outside an experiment

hold constant   to examine a variable one category at a time, letting another characteristic vary as it will (see **control for**)

homeostasis   physiological equilibrium

homogeneity   uniformity in a group

hypothesis   testable assertion about the relationship between two variables

identify   to incorporate someone or something into one's own personality so that the object is cherished and defended as zealously as one's very self; to place; to label

illogical thinking   pursuit of ideas without subjecting them to the rules of reason

incident   mental hospital term meaning a disruptive event that is usually written in the daily record

independent variable   variable that is assumed to cause change in the dependent variable

index   composite measure that represents a trait by summarizing several scores; list of words with page references

indicator   data that are accepted as evidence of the presence or absence of something

indirect methods of research   ways in which data are collected without the researcher being present at the time the behavior takes place

inductive logic   reasoning from the empirical world to construct a theory

inferential statistics   mathematical facts used to generalize beyond a sample

informant   member of a group who is willing to serve as the researcher's source of information about the group, introducing the researcher to the others, interpreting language and actions, and revealing the past

in-group   group that has strong identification as a group of insiders and rejects all others from participation in and knowledge about group secrets

in-language   variation of standard speech that assigns new meanings to words meant to be understood only by in-group members

institutional group   formal organization such as a club, school, or union

instrumentation   wear and tear on instruments and observers

instruments·   forms on which to record data

intangible reward   abstract benefits

interaction   behavior that takes someone else into account

interaction of selection bias and experimental variable   process that occurs when existing sample distortion is intensified by an experiment

internal validity   agreement between what the data indicate is true and what is actually true

intersubjectivity   agreement of two or more research project results

interval data   data that can be sorted, ranked, and spaced equally

intervening variable   another name for control variable

interview schedule   list of questions for the interviewer to ask

interviewer effect   changes in subjects' behavior because they are taking the interviewer into account (does not have to be an actual interview)

inverse correlation, or negative correlation   two things varying in opposite directions simultaneously

isolate   person depicted in a sociogram whose symbol has no interaction arrows coming to or going away from it

judgmental sample   sample selected according to the researcher's evaluation of each subject's suitability

key words   descriptors entered into a computer, which the machine will use to search a data bank

kilobyte (K)   1024 bytes

labeling theory   an analysis of the way language is used to attach meaning to a person

leading the witness   asking a question in a way that indicates the answer desired

level of measurement   degree to which the researcher can manipulate the data

liaison   means of communication

Likert scale   composite measure indicating strength of opinion

logic   reasoning in which the conclusion follows from the premise

longitudinal study   research project with more than one data collection period and possibly more than one sample, taken at different times with the object of measuring change (trend, cohort, or panel)

macrosociology   the study of society as a system

mailed questionnaire   questionnaire sent to a sample of people by mail, accompanied by a request that it be filled out and returned

mainframe   central computer capable of serving many terminals and sending files to other computers and to printers

mandate   orders; assignment

manual recording of data   recording by hand

marginals   totals of rows and of columns in a table

matching   selecting two groups of individuals who are similar in one or more characteristics, forming two parallel groups

maturation   any change caused by the passing of time

mean   average

mean square   average squared deviation (variance)

measure of association   way to estimate the strength of relationships between variables

measure of central tendency   way to determine the grouping of scores in a sample

measure of dispersion   way to determine the distribution of scores in a sample

measuring   reducing data to numbers that indicate strength or frequency of occurrence

mechanical recording of data   recording by machine

mechanical solidarity   commitment of group members who work together at similar tasks

median   middle point in an array

megabyte (M)   1000 kilobytes

microchip   a small piece of silicon holding a computer's electronic system

microsociology   the study of interaction within a system

mode   most frequent score

modem   a connection between the computer and the telephone

monograph   a treatise on a particular subject

multidisciplinary approach   researchers from more than one scholarly field working together on a project

multifaceted research   data collected in more than one way for the same project

multiple correlation   correlation of more than two variables simultaneously

multiple-treatment interference   cumulative effect of testing

multistage sample   sample chosen from progressively smaller groups in several steps

multivariate   pertaining to three or more variables

multivariate analysis   an examination of the relationship of more than two variables

multivariate measure of association   way of estimating the relationships between more than two variables

N, n   number of cases

natural experiment   analysis of spontaneous events that can be regarded as satisfying the conditions for an experiment

natural setting   place where people ordinarily live their daily life

negative correlation, or inverse correlation   two things varying in opposite directions simultaneously

nominal data   data that can only be sorted

nonparticipant observation   observation made while the researcher remains uninvolved in the ongoing activity of the subjects

nonrandom sample   sample that cannot claim to be random and therefore cannot be generalized

normal curve of error   pattern of random scores when plotted on a histogram; popularly known as the normal curve

null hypothesis   prediction that observed events are random

objectivity   freedom from bias, including emotion and speculation

occupational groups   groups of people belonging to the same or closely related occupations

open-end question   question that does not suggest any choice of answers

operational definition   definition to work with for the duration of the study

operationalization   working out definitions and ways to collect data

ordinal data   data that can be sorted and ranked

organic solidarity   commitment of interdependent group members working at different tasks

output   the result of computer operation, usually in hard copy, but it technically includes output to a screen as well

overgeneralization   applying something more widely than is justified

overhead   operating expenses assigned to your project by the institution in which you work (rent, janitorial services, electricity, and so on)

package   prepared set of instructions for a computer, usually recorded on a disk or tape

paired comparisons   same as **forced-choice**

pairing   counting similar and dissimilar pairs in two rank orders

panel study   longitudinal study using the same sample for each data collection

parameter   mathematical fact about a population; a dimension

partial correlation   association of two variables in a multiple analysis

participant observation   observation made by a researcher who joins in the activity being observed

PASCAL   a computer programming language

PC   personal computer

pilot study   trial run of a project to test procedures and instruments

plagiarism   using someone else's words, ideas, or illustrations without giving them credit

population   group of people or things in the same category

population pyramid   double bar graph, indicating the number of people in each cohort in a population, by sex

positive correlation   two things varying in the same direction at the same time

posttest   data collection after the experimental variable has been introduced to the experimental group

posttest-only control group design   experimental design that eliminates pretesting

premature closure of inquiry   making a decision based on too little data

premise   piece of evidence being cited to support a conclusion

pretest   the first measurement in an experiment; a trial administration of a question, an interview, or a questionnaire

primary   personal, intimate

privileged communication   any communication that can be kept secret in the face of a court order

probability   likelihood of something happening by chance

probability average   mode

probe   utterance intended to stimulate an expansion or clarification of an answer just given

prompting   reminding

proportionate stratified random sample   stratified random sample in which the subgroups appear in the same proportions as they do in the sample's population

proposal   application made to a potential sponsor that describes and explains your project and argues for its worth

purposive sample   sample selected according to the researcher's evaluation of each subject's suitability (same as **judgmental sample**)

qualitative   concerned with qualities

qualitative data   information about things that cannot be measured (e.g., feelings, values, standards)

quantitative   concerned with amounts

quantitative data   information about things that can be measured exactly and objectively

quasi-experiment   experiment characterized by lack of control over subjects

quota sample   judgmental or purposive sample proportioned by group membership

randomization   drawing two or more samples from the random sample already drawn from the population

random sample   sample in which every unit has an equal chance to be chosen

range   distance between the extremes of an array

ranked data   data ordered from least to most or vice versa

rate   number per thousand in a period of time (usually one year)

ratio data   data that can be sorted, ranked, equally spaced, and arithmetically manipulated

reactive effect of arrangements   effect the setting has on the subjects

reactive effect of testing   effect the testing process has on the subjects

recall lapse   progressive forgetting

reference group   group that provides our standards

region of rejection, or alpha   area under the normal curve that is regarded as having so little probability that one rejects the null hypothesis if the sample falls within it

reification   misplaced concreteness

relevance   quality of being appropriate to the matter at hand

reliability certainty with which you could collect data again and again in the same way and get the same result

replicate to repeat a study in exactly the same way

research studying something thoroughly and by using the rules of the scientific method in order to discover, classify, or detect

research design plan for a research project

reviewing the literature examining prior writings on a subject in order to sum up what has already been said and done on a topic

role expected behavior for someone occupying a particular status

role limitations restrictions on behavior because of the role assigned to a particular status

sample part of something that is regarded as typical of the whole; subjects from whom data are actually collected

sample statistic mathematical fact about a sample

saturation sample whole population

scale list of questions or statements, the answers to which will be scored

scalogram Guttman scale

scientific method way to conduct research that specifies objectivity, honesty, thoroughness, and service

scientific research research that observes the rules of the scientific method

sculpting having group members arranged in a tableau in a pattern meaningful to one of them

secondary impersonal; businesslike

selection bias distorting the subsamples' comparability

selection-maturation interaction maturation effect on only part of the sample

selective perception seeing what one wishes or expects to see and screening out the rest

selective recall selective perception applied to the past

semistructured interview interview for which the researcher is provided with the research question and a flexible interview schedule

serendipity making accidental discoveries

signposts brief directions telling respondents which question or page to turn to next in a questionnaire

skew to distort the distribution

snowball sample sample of a network obtained by having each subject suggest others

social change any modification in the culture or organization of a society

social Darwinism   the attitude that survival of the fittest applies to people in social systems

social dynamics   movement and change in a society's culture or organization

social fact   anything existing in a society that exerts pressure on the people to conform to it

social significance   implications for the good of the social system; the social importance of something

social stability   persistence of a cultural or normative pattern

social statics   order and stability in a society

socializer   one who trains someone else for membership in a group

sociogram   map of interaction, with symbols representing people or locations and arrows representing movement, communication, or choice

sociology   the study of society

sociology of knowledge   the study of the social origins of ideas

Solomon four-group design   R. L. Solomon's modification of classical experimental design whereby two groups that have not been pretested are added

split-ballot technique   using two different forms of a questionnaire so that the responses to one may be compared to the responses to the other

sponsor   person or organization contributing the money for a research project

spontaneous response   unprompted answer

spreadsheet   a computer facsimile of a ledger page

SPSS^x   a computer command language

SPSSG   a computer command language

square   a number multiplied by itself

standard deviation   measure of dispersion showing how far one must proceed away from the mean to include a specific area of the normal curve of error

standard error   standard deviation of a distribution of samples

star   person depicted in a sociogram whose symbol has the most arrows directed to it

statistical regression   tendency for extreme scores to change in the direction of the middle

statistical significance   likelihood that something could have resulted by chance

statistical test   test for typicality of the numbers of something

statistics   a language of formulae; a system of number statements; field of study concerned with such formulae and number statements

status set   all the statuses one person occupies at any given time

stimulus   another word for **experimental variable**

stratified random sample   sample chosen randomly from two or more distinct subgroups

structured   according to plan; organized

structured interview   an interview composed of preworded questions

structured observation   observation organized into categories in advance

subcultural groups   groups that practice variations of the dominant way of life in a society

subject   person or thing studied

subjective   letting your own point of view get in between you and the facts

subordinate   under the control of another person or of a group

support   a question-answering service provided by the publisher or manufacturer of computer software or hardware

symbolic interactionism   the analysis of the establishment of social definitions

synthesis   a drawing together of related items to form a coherent whole

systematic sample   sample selected from a list, at fixed intervals, the first selection having been made randomly

tails   ends of the normal curve of error

tally sheet   checklist

tangible rewards   concrete rewards, something measurable

terminal   accessory to a large computer that ties in to its capabilities

territoriality   tendency to shift one's physical position until one is comfortable with the distance from others

testing   (in an experiment) the effect of the tests on the subjects' behavior; (questions) trying questions out to see if they are understandable to the respondents

testing for significance   using inferential statistical tests to check the probability of a result

test statistic   score that presents the result of a statistical test (see list of test statistics at the end of Chapter 10)

text   body of a report

theoretical definition   commonly accepted meaning

Thurstone scale   composite measure that indicates strength of opinion

time-sharing   a computer system which many people use, paying for it by an hourly rate, charged only for actual time used

Total Fertility Rate   a measure of family size; the family size that would be produced if each birth cohort of women maintained for their entire breeding life the birthrate they showed in the year examined

trace   visible mark; residue

transcript   manuscript typed from a record or tape (written records included)

trend study   longitudinal study that uses the same population to sample successively

t-**test**   statistical test for the difference between sample means

Type I error   rejecting the null hypothesis when it is really true, that is, assuming statistical significance mistakenly

Type II error   accepting the null hypothesis when it is really false, that is, assuming absence of statistical significance mistakenly

typology   list of types

univariate   pertaining to one variable

univariate analysis   an examination of the distribution of a variable

unobtrusive groups   samples of evidence, or of available data

unobtrusive measures   ways of collecting data without coming face-to-face with the subjects; using unobtrusive groups

unstructured   lacking organization; unplanned

unstructured interview   an interview for which the researcher has the research question and general outline only

values   opinions about what is good and what is bad

variable   something that can vary

variance   range of differences; the average squared deviation

verbatim   word for word

verification   checking to see if something is correct

vignette   a little story

vital statistics   literally "life numbers," that is, birth and death rates, marriages, divorces; for communities, the aggregation of these rates

warm-up question   question asked to prepare the respondent for a subsequent question containing the indicator

z-**score**   a test statistic to express the number of standard deviations a particular sample is from the population mean

zero-order association   bivariate relationship when not controlling for a third variable

Bibliography

Abrams, R. H.
    1943   "Residential Propinquity as a Factor in Marriage Selection." *American Sociological Review* 8:288–94.

Adams, Henry
    1928   *The Education of Henry Adams.* New York: Book League of America.

Albert, June True
    1960   "Limitations on the Free Exercise of Religion in the United States." Unpublished.
    1966   "Religion and the Reaction to Chronic Illness: Juvenile Diabetes Mellitus." Unpublished M.A. thesis, Rutgers University.
    1972   "The Sexual Basis of White Resistance to Racial Integration." Unpublished Ph.D. dissertation, Rutgers University.

Albert, June A., and Edward Wellin
    1963   *Literature Review and Bibliography on Social Aspects of Dentistry.* Mimeographed. Trenton: State of New Jersey Department of Health.

Ariès, Philippe
    1962   *Centuries of Childhood: A Social History of Family Life,* translated by Robert Baldick. New York: Knopf.

Asch, Solomon
    1952   *Social Psychology.* Englewood Cliffs, N.J.: Prentice-Hall.

Audubon, John James
    1937   *Birds of America* New York: Macmillan.

Babbie, Earl R.
    1979   *The Practice of Social Research,* 2nd ed. Belmont, Calif.: Wadsworth.

Bart, Pauline
    1971   "Depression in Middle-aged Women," in *Women in Sexist Society,* edited by Vivian Gornick and Barbara K. Moran. New York: Basic Books.

Bart, Pauline, and Linda Frankel
    1980   *The Student Sociologist's Handbook,* 3rd ed. Morristown, N.J.: General Learning Press.

Berscheid, E., R. S. Baron, M. Dermer, and M. Libman
1973 "Anticipating Informed Consent: An Empirical Approach." *American Psychologist* 28:913–25.

Bettelheim, Bruno
1969 *The Children of the Dream.* London: Macmillan.

Beyer, William H., Ed.
1968 *Handbook of Tables for Probability and Statistics*, 2nd ed. Cleveland: Chemical Rubber Company.

Birdwhistell, Ray
1970 "There Are Smiles. . . ," in *Kinesics and Contexts: Essays on Body Motion Communication.* Philadelphia: University of Pennsylvania Press, pp. 29–39.

Black, James A., and Dean J. Champion
1976 *Methods and Issues in Social Research.* New York: Wiley.

Bogardus, E. S.
1933 "A Social Distance Scale." *Sociology and Social Research* 17:265–71.

Borgatta, Edgar F., and George W. Bohrnstedt
1981 "Some Limitations on Generalizability from Social Psychological Experiments," in *Readings in Social Research*, edited by Theodore C. Wagenaar. Belmont, Calif.: Wadsworth.

Bouchard, Thomas J., Jr.
1981 "Unobtrusive Measures: An Inventory of Uses," in *Readings for Social Research*, edited by Theodore C. Wagenaar. Belmont, Calif.: Wadsworth.

Bowen, Elenore Smith
1964 *Return to Laughter.* New York: Doubleday.

Brandt, Richard M.
1972 *Studying Behavior in Natural Settings.* New York: Holt, Rinehart, & Winston.

Bryan, James H., and Mary A. Test
1967 "Models and Helping: Naturalistic Studies in Aiding Behavior." *Journal of Personality and Social Psychology* 6 (4):400–407.

Campbell, Donald T., and Julian C. Stanley
1963 *Experimental and Quasi-experimental Designs for Research.* Skokie, Ill.: Rand McNally.

Cantril, Hadley
1940 *The Invasion from Mars.* Princeton, N.J.: Princeton University Press.

Coleman, James S.
1957 *Community Conflict.* New York: Free Press.

Collins, Robert A.
1980 "Estimating the Benefits of Individual Retirement Accounts: A Simulation Approach." *Journal of Consumer Affairs* 14(1):124–41.

Copi, Irving M.
1953 *Introduction to Logic.* New York: Macmillan.

Coser, Lewis
1971 *Masters of Sociological Thought.* New York: Harcourt, Brace, Jovanovich.

Council of American Survey Research Organizations
1987 Cited in "Special Report: Research Business Review." *Advertising Age* May 11, pp. S1, S2.

1987   "Beecham vs. Saatchi." *Advertising Age*, July 13, pp. 1, 86.

Dillman, Don A.
   1978   *Mail and Telephone Surveys: The Total Design Method.* New York: Wiley.
Dillman, Don A., Jean Gorton Gallegas, and James H. Frey
   1976   "Reducing Refusal Rates for Telephone Interviews." *Public Opinion Quarterly* 40:66–78.
Durkheim, Emile
   (1897)   *Suicide*, translated by John A. Spalding and George Simpson.
   1951   New York: Free Press.

Edwards, A. L., and F. P. Kirkpatrick
   1948   "A Technique for Construction of Attitude Scales." *Journal of Applied Psychology* 32:374–84.
Ellison, Ralph
   1952   *The Invisible Man.* New York: Random House.

Fashing, Joseph, and Ted Goertzel
   1981   "The Myth of the Normal Curve: A Theoretical Critique and Examination of Its Role in Teaching and Research." *Humanity and Society* 5(1):18–23.
Feinbloom, Deborah
   1976   *Transvestites and Transsexualism.* New York: Delacorte Press.
Festinger, Leon, Henry W. Riecken, and Stanley Schachter
   1956   *When Prophecy Fails.* Minneapolis: University of Minnesota Press.
Festinger, Leon, Stanley Schachter, and Kurt Back
   1950   *Social Pressures in Informal Groups.* Stanford, Calif.: Stanford University Press.
Fox, Renée
   1959   *Experiment Perilous.* New York: Free Press.
Francese, Peter K.
   1979   "The 1980 Census: The Counting of America." *Population Bulletin* 34(4): whole issue.
Frey, David P., and G. J. Frey
   1978   "Science and the Single Case in Counseling Research." *Personnel and Guidance Journal* 56(5):263–268.

Gerard, Harold B., Roland A. Wilhelmy, and Edward S. Conolley
   1969   "Conformity and Group Size," in *Social Psychology: Readings and Perspective*, edited by Edgar F. Borgatta. Skokie, Ill.: Rand McNally.
Goffman, Erving
   1959   *The Presentation of Self in Everyday Life.* New York: Doubleday.
Goldstein, Rhoda Lois, and June True Albert
   1974   "The Status of Black Studies Programs on American Campuses, 1970–71." *Journal of Behavioral and Social Sciences* 20(1):1–16.
Graham, Harvey
   1951   *Eternal Eve: The History of Gynaecology and Obstetrics.* New York: Doubleday.
Guttman, L.
   1944   "A Basis for Scaling Quantitative Data." *American Sociological Review* 9:139–50.

Hall, E. T.
  1959   *The Silent Language*. New York: Doubleday.
Heap, Norman Arlen
  1959   "A Vocabulary of Tobacco Growing in Fayette County, Kentucky." Unpublished M.A. thesis, Louisiana State University.
  1966   "A Burley Tobacco Word List from Lexington, Kentucky." *Publication of the American Dialect Society* 45:1–27.
Hedderson, John
  1987   *SPSS^x Made Simple*. Belmont, Calif.: Wadsworth.
Henley, Nancy M.
  1979   "Tactual Politics: Touch," in *Social Interaction*, edited by Howard Robboy, Sidney L. Greenblatt, and Candace Clark. New York: St. Martin's Press.
Henshel, Richard
  1980   "The Purposes of Laboratory Experimentation and the Virtues of Deliberate Artificiality." *Journal of Experimental Social Psychology* 16:466–78.
Henslin, James M.
  1979   "What Makes for Trust?" in *Social Interaction*, edited by Howard Robboy, Sidney L. Greenblatt, and Candace Clark. New York: St. Martin's Press.
Hibbert, Christopher
  1987   *The English: A Social History 1066–1945*. New York: Norton
Higgins, Paul C.
  1980   *Outsiders in a Hearing World*. Beverly Hills, Calif.: Sage.
Hodge, Robert W., Paul M. Siegel, and Peter H. Rossi
  1964   "Occupational Prestige in the United States: 1925–1963." *American Journal of Sociology* 70:286–302.
Hoffman, Joan Eakin
  1980   "Problems of Access in the Study of Social Elites and Boards of Directors," in *Fieldwork Experience: Qualitative Approaches to Social Research*, edited by William B. Shaffir, Robert A. Stebbins, and Allan Turowetz. New York: St. Martin's Press.
Hollander, Anne
  1978   *Seeing Through Clothes*. New York: Viking Press.
Hooper, E., L. Comstock, J. M. Goodwin, and J. S. Goodwin
  1981   "Patient Characteristics That Influence Physician Behaviors." *Clinical Research* 19(1):38A.
Hoover, Kenneth
  1980   *The Elements of Social Scientific Thinking*, 2nd ed. New York: St. Martin's Press.
Humphreys, Laud
  1970   *The Tearoom Trade: Impersonal Sex in Public Places*. Chicago: Aldine.
Hutchinson, E. P.
  1967   *The Population Debate*. Boston: Houghton Mifflin.

Jahn, Janheinz
  1962   *Through African Doors*. Translated by Oliver Coburn. New York: Grove Press.
Jones, James H.
  1981   *Bad Blood: The Tuskegee Syphilis Experiment*. New York: Free Press.

Karp, David A.
1980 "Observing Behavior in Public Places: Problems and Strategies," in *Fieldwork Experience: Qualitative Approaches to Social Research*, edited by William B. Shaffir, Robert A. Stebbins, and Allan Turowetz. New York: St. Martin's Press.

Kennedy, R.
1943 "Premarital Residential Propinquity." *American Journal of Sociology* 48:580–84.

Kirkham, George
1976 *Signal Zero*. Philadelphia: Lippincott.

Klemesrud, Judy
1981 "Voice of Authority Still Male." *New York Times*, 2 February, p. A16.

Labaw, Patricia
1980 *Advanced Questionnaire Design*. Cambridge: Abt Books.

Labovitz, Sanford, and Robert Hagedorn
1981 *Introduction to Social Research*, 3rd ed. New York: McGraw-Hill.

Lagrow, Steven J., and Jane E. Prochnow-Lagrow
1983 "Consistent Methodological Errors Observed in Single-Case Studies: Suggested Guidelines." *Journal of Visual Impairment and Blindness* 77(10):481–88.

Lamberg-Karlovsky, C. C., and Martha Lamberg-Karlovsky
1973 "An Early City in Iran," in *Cities, Their Origin, Growth and Human Impact*, edited by Kingsley Davis. New York: Freeman.

Lewis, Karen Gail
1980 "Children of Lesbians, Their Point of View." *Social Work* 25(3):198–203.

Liebow, Elliot
1967 *Talley's Corner*. Boston: Little, Brown.

Likert, Rensis
1932 "A Technique for the Measurement of Attitudes." *Archives of Psychology* 140, p. 52.

Luckenbill, David F.
1981 "Criminal Homicide as a Situated Transaction," in *Readings for Social Research*, edited by Theodore C. Wagenaar. Belmont, Calif.: Wadsworth.

Malec, Michael A.
1977 *Essential Statistics for Social Research*. Philadelphia: Lippincott.

McCall, Michal
1980 "Who and Where Are the Artists?" In *Fieldwork Experience: Qualitative Approaches to Social Research*, edited by William B. Shaffir, Robert A. Stebbins, and Allan Turowetz. New York: St. Martin's Press.

Mead, G. H.
1962 *Mind, Self and Society*, edited by Charles W. Morris. Chicago: University of Chicago Press.

Merton, Robert
1941 "Intermarriage and the Social Structure." *Psychiatry* 4:363–74.

Middleman, Louis I.
1981 *In Short: A Concise Guide to Good Writing*. New York: St. Martin's Press.

Miller, Delbert C.
1977 *Handbook of Research Design and Social Measurement*, 3rd ed. New York: McKay.

Mills, C. Wright
1959 *The Sociological Imagination*. New York: Oxford University Press.

Molzen, Celeste
1977 "Analysis of Female Role Assignments in Television Advertisements." Unpublished, Trenton State College.

Moreno, Jacob L.
1934 *Who Shall Survive?* New York: Beacon House.

Moynihan, Daniel
1965 *The Negro Family: The Case for National Action*. Washington, D.C.: Office of Planning and Research, United States Department of Labor.

Myrdal, Gunnar
1944 *An American Dilemma*. New York: Harper & Row.

Newman, Evelyn S., and Susan R. Sherman
1979 "Community Integration of the Elderly in Foster Family Care." *Journal of Gerontological Social Work* 1(3):175–86.

Orne, Martin T.
1962 "On the Social Psychology of the Psychological Experiment: With Particular Reference to Demand Characteristics and Their Implications." *American Psychologist* 17:776–83.

Parry, H. J., and H. M. Crossley
1950 "Validity of Responses to Survey Questions." *Public Opinion Quarterly* 14:61–80.

Parsons, Talcott, with Robert F. Bales, James Olds, Morris Zelditch, and Philip E. Slater
1955 *Family, Socialization and Interaction Process*. New York: Free Press.

Population Reference Bureau, Inc.
1981 *Population Reference Bureau, 1981 World Population Data Sheet*. Washington, D.C.

Reynolds, Larry
1966 "A Note on the Perpetuation of a 'Scientific' Fiction." *Sociometry* 29: 85–88.

Richardson, Stephen A., Barbara Snell Dohrenwend, and David Klein
1965 *Interviewing: Its Forms and Functions*. New York: Basic Books.

Riley, Matilda White, and Anne Foner
1968 *Aging and Society: An Inventory of Research Findings*, Vol. 1. New York: Russell Sage.

Roethlisberger, F. J., and W. J. Dickson
1939 *Management and the Worker*. Cambridge: Harvard University Press.

Rosenthal, Robert, and Lenore F. Jacobson
1968 "Teacher Expectations for the Disadvantaged." *Scientific American* 218:19–23.

Roth, Julius
   1975   "Hired Hand Research," in *Fist Fights in the Kitchen: Manners and Methods in Social Research*, edited by George H. Lewis. Santa Monica, Calif.: Goodyear.
Runcie, John
   1980   *Experiencing Social Research*, rev. ed. Homewood, Ill.: Dorsey.

Sawyer, H. G.
   1961   "The Meaning of Numbers." Speech before the American Association of Advertising Agencies. Cited in *Unobtrusive Measures: Nonreactive Research in the Social Sciences*, edited by Eugene J. Webb, Donald T. Campbell, Richard D. Schwartz, and Lee Sechrest. Skokie, Ill.: Rand McNally, 1966, p. 41.
Selltiz, Claire, Lawrence S. Wrightsman, and Stuart W. Cook
   1981   *Selltiz, Wrightsman, and Cook's Research Methods in Social Relations*, revised by Louise H. Kidder. New York: Holt, Rinehart, & Winston.
Sherif, C., M. Sherif, and R. E. Nebergall
   1965   *Attitude and Attitude Change: The Social Judgment–Involvement Approach*. Philadelphia: Saunders.
Simpson, George
   1969   *Auguste Comte: Sire of Sociology*. New York: Crowell.
Soldo, Beth J.
   1980   "America's Elderly in the 1980s." *Population Bulletin* 35 no. 4, November.
Solomon, R. L.
   1949   "An Extension of Control Group Design." *Psychological Bulletin* 46: 137–50.
Som, Ranjan Kumar
   1973   *Recall Lapse in Demographic Inquiries*. New York: Asia Publishing House.
Sorokin, Pitirim
   1956   *Fads and Foibles in Modern Sociology*. Chicago: Regnery.
Spinrad, William
   1979   "When Integration Works," in *Interracial Bonds*, edited by Rhoda G. Blumberg and Wendell James Roye. New York: General Hall.
Stember, Charles H.
   1961   *Education and Attitude Change*. New York: Institute of Human Relations Press.
   1976   *Sexual Racism*. New York: Elsevier.
Stevens, S. S.
   1946   "On the Theory of Scales of Measurement." *Science* 103:677–80.
   1951   "Mathematics Measurement and Psychophysics," in *Handbook of Experimental Psychology*, edited by S. S. Stevens. New York: Wiley.
Sudnow, David
   1967   *Passing On: The Social Organization of Dying*. Englewood Cliffs, N.J.: Prentice-Hall.
Swazey, Judith P., and Renée C. Fox
   1979   "The Clinical Moratorium," in *Essays in Medical Sociology*, edited by Renée C. Fox. New York: Wiley.

Thompson, Hunter
    1966   *Hell's Angels.* New York: Random House.
Thurber, James
    1945   "University Days," in *The Thurber Carnival.* New York: Harper & Row.
Thurstone, L. L.
    1931   "The Measurement of Social Attitudes." *Journal of Abnormal and Social Psychology* 26:249–69.
Toseland, Ronald W., James Decker, and Jim Bliesner
    1979   "A Community Outreach Program for Socially Isolated Older Persons." *Journal of Gerontological Social Work* 1(3):221–24.
True, June A.
    1979   "Miss Anne and the Black Brother," in *Interracial Bonds*, edited by Rhoda G. Blumberg and Wendell James Roye. New York: General Hall.
Truzzi, Marcello
    1968   "The Decline of the American Circus: The Shrinkage of an Institution," in *Sociology and Everyday Life*, edited by Marcello Truzzi. Englewood Cliffs, N.J.: Prentice-Hall.
Turabian, Kate
    1967   *A Manual for Writers*, 3rd rev. ed. Chicago: University of Chicago Press.

van de Walle, Etienne, and John Knodel
    1980   "Europe's Fertility Transition: New Evidence and Lessons for Today's Developing World." *Population Bulletin* 34(6):whole issue.
Van Hasselt, Vincent B., and Michael Hersen
    1981   "Applications of Single-Case Designs to Research with Visually Impaired Individuals." *Journal of Visual Impairment and Blindness* 75(9):359–62.
Vidich, Arthur, and Joseph Bensman
    1968   *Small Town in Mass Society: Class, Power and Religion in a Rural Community*, rev. ed. Princeton, N.J.: Princeton University Press.

Wagenaar, Theodore C.
    1981   "Some Guidelines for Reading and Assessing Research Reports in the Social Sciences," in *Readings for Social Research*, edited by Theodore C. Wagenaar. Belmont, Calif.: Wadsworth.
Wang, Chamont W. H.
    1987   "On the Scientific and Non-Scientific Practices of Statistical Inferences." Unpublished, Trenton State College.
Warwick, Donald P.
    1981   "Social Scientists Ought to Stop Lying," in *Readings for Social Research*, edited by Theodore C. Wagenaar. Belmont, Calif.: Wadsworth.
Webb, Eugene J., Donald J. Campbell, Richard D. Schwartz, and Lee Sechrest
    1966   *Unobtrusive Measures: Nonreactive Research in the Social Sciences.* Skokie, Ill.: Rand McNally.
Weeks, H. Ashley
    1963   *Youthful Offenders at Highfields.* Ann Arbor: University of Michigan Press.
Weiss, Robert S.
    1968   *Statistics in Social Research.* New York: Wiley.

West, W. Gordon
    1980   "Access to Adolescent Deviants and Deviance," in *Fieldwork Experience: Qualitative Approaches to Social Research*, edited by William B. Shaffir, Robert A. Stebbins, and Allan Turowetz. New York: St. Martin's Press.

Whyte, William Foote
    1955   *Street Corner Society: The Social Structure of an Italian Slum*, 2nd ed. Chicago: University of Chicago Press.

Wilson, Suanna J.
    1978   *Confidentiality in Social Work*. New York: Free Press.

Women on Words and Images
    1972   *Dick and Jane as Victims: Sex Stereotyping in Children's Readers*. Princeton, N.J.: National Organization for Women.

Zelditch, Morris, Jr.
    1969   "Can You Really Study an Army in the Laboratory?" In *A Sociological Reader on Complex Organizations*, rev. ed., edited by Amitai Etzioni. New York: Holt, Rinehart, & Winston.

Zelditch, Morris, and Philip E. Slater
    1955   *Family, Socialization and Interaction Process*. New York: Free Press.

Index